The Office of Peter
and the
Structure of the Church

Hans Urs von Balthasar

The Office of Peter and the Structure of the Church

Translated by Andrée Emery

Ignatius Press   San Francisco

Title of the German original:
Der antirömische Affekt
© 1974 Verlag Herder KG, Freiburg im Breisgau

Cover by Victoria Hoke Lane

With ecclesiastical approval
© 1986 Ignatius Press, San Francisco
All rights reserved
ISBN 0-89870-020-5
Library of Congress catalogue number 86-80787
Printed in the United States of America

Contents

I
The Circle Closes

II
The *Mysterium* of the Church

III
Living the Miracle

Introduction

Why write this book? The intention is to show that there is a deep-seated anti-Roman attitude within the Catholic Church—for the moment we are not concerned with what is outside her—and that this attitude has not only sociological and historical grounds but also a theological basis and that it has to be overcome again and again by the community of the Church. Nothing is farther from us than "papolatry". We shall take seriously and appraise realistically the misgivings about the Church's leadership, from the very beginning, through developments in the course of history, down to the present.

We are aware that in the twentieth century we have been blessed with several selfless popes who were sincerely devoted to the cause of Christ, and we shall resist being influenced by this fact. We shall not dissociate, as if by magic, the events of this century from the, at times, shady history of the papacy. Though we do not deny the past, we remember Montalembert's admonition: "To judge the past, we would need to have lived it; to condemn it, we would need not to be indebted to it for anything."[1] And we recall Möhler's wise remark about the antipapal sects of the twelfth century who dreamed of a spiritual and holy Church: "They dared to accuse the indomitable Church, which had endured many storms and upheavals, with having failed in her mission. Had these creations of fantasy and selfishness— and we cannot but recognize them as such while not denying what-

---

[1] "Pour juger le passé il aurait fallu le vivre; pour le condamner il faudrait ne rien lui devoir." *Discours à Malines* (1863).

ever good was in them—had they borne the burden that weighed on the Catholic Church, they would have vanished in a trice into the void from which they emerged."[2]

In this introduction we shall attempt first to substantiate theologically the truth of these statements. Then we will look at the disputed reality of the Church, and lastly—keeping in touch with theological reality—we will outline a proposal which will be developed in the second and third parts of this book.

1. The Postulate: "The Word Became Flesh"

In this axiom St. John captures the essence of God's definitive revelation, as it is described in detail in all the Gospels. The Word, the Greek *logos*, Hebrew "wisdom", eternally with God, was also the divine principle by which God created all things, the light by which he has illuminated all things for all time.

The Word is God's artistry, creating and ordering in sovereign freedom; omnipotent, not bound by anything except his own plan and will; not limited by the darkness of finiteness nor by the sin that cannot apprehend, obstruct or arrest this all-pervading light. To comprehend a thing, a truth, to understand it—Latin *perstare* —means to have intellectual command of it and to be able to contain it in comprehensible categories. A dawning comprehension of the unfathomable, divine transcendence is already shown in the law of the Old Testament, which was intended to point to the indwelling *mysterium* of divine light and divine truth. But it is allowed to harden into a quasi-magical formula for discernment and action, through which, in the end, "darkness" actually manages to obscure the inpouring light. The Old Law thus becomes contradictory and tragic.

Something new and unheard-of happens when the Word—of himself,

---

[2] *Symbolik*, par. 37.

from the God "with whom" he is—becomes flesh. Flesh is the existential man whose presence and manifestation is his individual body. True, the "man of flesh" is infused with a soul that issues from God's breath and sets him apart from animals and plants. Still, according to Scripture man remains—together with his fellow creatures—"flesh".

Flesh means being born; it means growing, finding nourishment, being able to procreate; and it means dying. Flesh means being part of a chain of ancestors; through it the individual is mysteriously identified and determined. This is why two Gospels begin with the family tree of Jesus. No carnal being initiates itself. All are born into a community that has existed before them and that possesses a tradition that molds them.

The tradition into which Jesus, the Word-made-flesh, was born is the Old Testament. Hence the law: *factus ex muliere* and *factus sub lege* belong together (Gal 4:4). For the Jews of Jesus' time, the Spirit of God was present where the law of Moses—the expression of God's covenant with Israel—was being kept. In the episode of the Presentation, Luke emphatically repeats five times, "the law of the Lord", "the law of Moses" (Lk 2:22–39). Everything is to be fulfilled according to this law. And in the midst of the event, the Holy Spirit (three times) inspires Simeon. It is in obedience to the law that the flesh of Jesus is circumcised, the flesh of Mary is "cleansed" and the New Covenant takes over from the Old—in the child who will become a sign of contradiction "for the fall and rising of many" and in the mother whose heart "shall be pierced by a sword".

"Flesh" means further that human potentialities are determined by a complicated and specific biological structure of which the thinking and acting individual is for the most part not conscious. The ordinary acts of seeing and hearing demand nearly inconceivable, not yet fully understood physical and psychological prerequisites which are always imperiled. They can malfunction: there are the blind, the lame, the deaf and people stricken with all kinds of illness. There are also prisoners, the oppressed, the destitute, the persecuted and those who

11

are impeded by the narrow limits of bodily reality. For the sake of all these Jesus comes to us in the flesh (Is 61:1–9; 58:6; Lk 4:18).

Flesh is delivered to flesh defenseless. It can be left lying at the gate as was Lazarus; it can be imprisoned and beheaded like John the Baptist. It can become a "plaything" of Christian, Jewish and pagan factions, as the rejected Jesus was in his Passion. ("They did to him whatever they pleased" [Mk 9:13].) Though these factions may hate each other, they are united in their game: the man must go. "His own people received him not" (Jn 1:11). He must die "outside the camp" (Heb 13:12). Flesh cannot withdraw. It can be slapped, spit upon, scourged, crowned with thorns, nailed to two beams and mocked unto death.

The relatedness of the individual to the community is an accomplished fact in the flesh. The individual is born into ethnic and human history and is initiated into it by others. The complexity of his own organs and limbs (of which some can be missing from the outset or can be severed later) reminds him that he, too, is merely a member of a body, the *polis,* the people, mankind—and, moreover, a member that can be dispensed with easily. Just as his bones and his muscles cannot choose where they will be but have their particular place in his body, aligned and meshed with the other parts in this manner and no other, so to be able to function meaningfully, the individual must find his particular place in the social body. His physical and political function there is specific. It is given to him. He must perform his function, fulfill his role.

To be socially effective, the Word-made-flesh cannot escape from the hard reality of this individual and social determinism. The enfleshment of the Word is not something that can be revoked. "Handle me and see; for a spirit has not flesh and bones as you see that I have" (Lk 24:39). And neither can the organism that is called his Church avoid being flesh. She is the Body of Christ (Eph 1:22–33)—and this is the precise meaning of "flesh" (1 Cor 6:13–20), a body that has "members" (Rom 12:4–5). Only insofar as the individual fits into the place assigned to him by Christ (Eph 4:11) and functions according to the laws of the entire body does this body mature; only thus does the individual come "to mature manhood, to the measure of the stature of the fullness of Christ" (Eph 4:13). "We are to grow up in every way into him who is the head, into Christ, from whom the whole body, joined and knit together by every joint with which it is supplied, when each part is working properly, makes bodily growth and upbuilds itself in love" (Eph 4:15–16).

What an image! Not that of a community of free individuals who choose to join forces together in a social contract, each for his own benefit, but rather of a community decreed and determined from above, that nevertheless reaches its "fullness", its "maturity" and "unity" only through the cooperation of all the intimately interrelated members.

But where, in all this, is the loudly proclaimed "freedom of the Christian"? Why not first ask what constitutes the freedom of Christ? Christ's freedom consists fundamentally in the Word becoming flesh. The *logos* was not "cast into" the determinism of the flesh but stepped into it freely, willingly and unconstrainedly. His whole existence in the flesh flows from this act of his own free will. This, however, is an act of the divine free will of him who is "with God", who is "sent" by God into the flesh and who freely fulfills this intention of God. "Sacrifices and offerings thou hast not desired, but a body hast thou prepared for me; then I said, 'Lo, I have come to do thy will, O God', as it is written of me in the roll of the book" (Ps 40:7–9; Heb 10:5–7).

Determinism is transformed to its very depths by this prior free will. Secondly, however, this means that the flesh is completely exposed, as a result of free choice, to its fellow members. Here the mentality of the "world" will show itself; it cannot endure such a freely willed initiative by God, which it feels to be an attack on the totally enclosed "stability" of cosmic laws. Therefore it pours resentment and hatred on the one who, supported only by God, is delivered defenseless to the world.

The Church, which is the Body of Christ, will be in exactly the same position. Those who are of this body have been "born" before the world existed, "not of blood, nor of the will of the flesh, nor of the will of man, but of God" (Jn 1:13). And because of this they find themselves, with Jesus, exposed: "Blessed are you when men revile you and persecute you and utter all kinds of evil against you falsely on my account" (Mt 5:11). "If they persecuted me, they will persecute you" (Jn 15:20). This is the structure of our Christian freedom: coming together with Jesus from beyond the "world" (because with the Son we are children of God), closely bound to him in the determinisms of the flesh, delivered defenseless to the opposition of a world that cannot tolerate such freedom yet sees it demonstrated precisely in this opposition and—in the unfathomable mystery of Christ and the Church—receives this freedom as a gift from the one who bears the opposition vicariously.

But has not Christ freed us from the law (Gal 5:1)? "So, brethren, we are not children of the slave but of the free woman" (Gal 4:31), of "Jerusalem above" (Gal 4:26). Yes, we are made free of the imposed, heteronomous law that had continually led us to attempt to capture God and his free light in the nets of our wisdom and expertise. Paul refers to this when he says that we are "freed from the law of sin and death", or more simply, "freed from sin" (Rom 8:2; 6:3; 6:22). But we are freed by the Word-made-flesh. This is "the perfect law, the law of liberty" (Jas 1:25),[3] which means that, anchored all the more deeply in the flesh, we are not merely "hearers of the word" (in the form of law) but "doers of it" (James 1:22–25). It is thus that we come to be "Church", living by Christ's freedom, which springs from obedience to the Father and ends exposed on the Cross.

[3] H. Schlier, "Das vollkommene Gesetz der Freiheit", in *Die Zeit der Kirche* (Herder 1956), 193–206.

2. *The Fact: Anti-Rome*

Looking from this point of view at the anti-Roman attitude in the Church, we cannot but suspect that it has something to do with the Church being flesh and with the close interdependence of her members. The Church as a whole is not pure spirit nor angelic idea, and neither are her leaders. This would not be appropriate for the Church of the Incarnation. The members clash hard with each other; and they get weary in their activity. As well as taking pleasure in his active role, man can also feel constrained by the limits of his ability to express himself, bored by its staleness and pained by the work it entails. But there is more: the human body is moved by a spiritual principle immanent in it. The system, "man", has a certain autonomy and integrity. The body of the Church is guided by a "head" who is above her and is "supernatural" in relation to her. The function of the Church's leadership, particularly that of the papacy, is unceasingly to focus attention on this transcendence and even to represent it. To the extent that the body sees itself in immanent, i.e., sociological, terms, it is uncomfortable with this transcendence. In this sense Corinth was made uncomfortable by the "phenomenon" of Paul, and it remonstrated loudly. It sought the reason for its anti-Pauline attitude in the personal character and behavior of the apostle, in his seemingly autocratic actions—his opposition to the original Jerusalem community—and this was not softened by Paul's lengthy self-defenses. *Qui s'excuse, s'accuse.*

The person of Paul disappears, but the office of Peter remains, as does that of the apostles, the bishops. The anti-Pauline feeling lives on as an anti-Petrine attitude. It is with this that we are concerned, and therefore we shall strictly limit our investigation and omit a great many related, pertinent problems. We shall not become involved with the theology of the papacy or even with the theology of the Church. Nor shall we discuss Catholic collegiality and whether or not the origin of the bishops' authority derives from the college of apostles, nor the relationship of the "Twelve" — and consequently the structure of the hierarchical offices in the Church — to the "priesthood of the People of God". There is a wealth of material and information available on all these questions. Our inquiry is directed solely to the strangely irrational phenomenon of the anti-Roman attitude among Catholics; the same attitude outside the Catholic community is of only marginal interest to us here.

We find Luther's legacy, *"Hoc unum me mortuo servate: odium in pontificem Romanum"*,[4] less disturbing than the habitual parting words of an English priest acquaintance: "Goodbye, keep away from Rome." As a result of his studies in Church history he may have come to believe that there was more reason for an anti-Petrine attitude than the people of Corinth had for a resistance to Paul. But Vatican II proclaimed the ideal of the Church's existence and self-understanding as a balance between collegiality and papal supremacy and, even more importantly, as a balance between the responsibility of the People of God and that of their leaders. Therefore the good cleric could at least have asked himself whether his negative attitude toward the leadership did not increase the latter's isolation, thus putting needless obstacles in the way of the desired integration.

It is commonly said, "You cannot trust Rome", meaning that Rome will always be the same: she wants to rule, and she misuses the supreme authority given her for service to impose legalistic obedience on the people. Hence her adherents regress with her from evangelical freedom to the alienating religion of the law, the Old Covenant. *Newman*, in his early, still Anglican work, *The Prophetic*

[4] "Preserve this one thing when I am dead: hatred of the Roman pontiff." H. Preuss, *Martin Luther, der Prophet* (Gütersloh 1933), 173. I am indebted for this quotation to Fr. Yves Congar who, a few days before I finished the present work, most graciously lent me his paper on *Le Complexe antiromain*. He concentrates nearly exclusively on this attitude in the Middle Ages and in the sects which dissociated themselves from the Catholic Church. This is exactly the topic that we have excluded from our study.

Office of the Church, strongly expresses this distrust. Let us listen to him:

> Roman teaching by its profession of Infallibility, lowers the standard and quality of Gospel obedience as well as impairs its mysterious and sacred character; and this in various ways. When religion is reduced in all its parts to a system, there is hazard of something earthly being made the chief object of our contemplation instead of our Maker. Now Rome classifies our duties and their rewards, the things to believe, the things to do, the modes of pleasing God, the penalties and the remedies of sin, with such exactness, that an individual knows (so to speak) just where he is upon his journey heavenward, how far he has got, how much he has to pass; and his duties become a matter of calculation. It provides us with a sort of graduated scale of devotion and obedience, and, so far, tends to engross our thoughts with the details of a mere system, to a comparative forgetfulness of its professed Author. But it is evident that the purest religious services are those which are done, not by constraint, but voluntarily, as a free offering to Almighty God. There are certain duties which are indispensable in all Christians, but their limits are left undefined, as if to try our faith and love. For instance, what portion of our worldly substance we should devote to charitable uses, or in what way we are to fast, or how we are to dress, or whether we should remain single, or what revenge we should take upon our sins, or what amusements are allowable or how far we may go into society; these and similar questions are left open by Inspiration. . . . A command from authority to a certain point acts as a protection to our modesty, though beyond this it would but act as a burden. . . . This is the true Christian liberty, not the prerogative of obeying God, or not, as we please, but the opportunity of obeying Him more strictly without formal commandment. In this way, too, not only is our love tried, but the delicacy and generous simplicity of our obedience consulted also. Christ loves an open-hearted service, done without our contemplating or measuring what we do, from the fullness of affection and reverence, while the mind is fixed on its Great Object without thought of itself. Now express commands lead us to reflect

17

upon and estimate our advances towards perfection, whereas true faith will mainly contemplate its deficiencies, not its poor attainments, whatever they be. It does not like to realize to itself what it does; it throws off the thought of it; it is carried on and reaches forward towards perfection, not counting the steps it has ascended, but keeping the end steadily in its eye, knowing only that it is advancing, and glorying in each sacrifice or service which it is allowed to offer, as it occurs, not remembering it afterwards. But in the Roman system there would seem to be little room for this unconscious devotion. Each deed has its price, every quarter of the land of promise is laid down and described. Roads are carefully marked out, and such as would attain to perfection are constrained to move in certain lines, as if there were a science of gaining heaven. Thus the Saints are cut off from the Christian multitude by certain fixed duties, not rising out of it by the continuous growth and flowing forth of services which in their substance pertain to all men. And Christian holiness, in consequence, loses its freshness, vigor, and comeliness, being frozen (as it were) into certain attitudes, which are not graceful except when they are unstudied.[5]

Does not the young Newman here sum up all the objections of the anti-Roman attitude against the "system" which stands like the Great Wall of China, hard, impenetrable and rationalistic, between the soul and God, between the believer and the living Christ of the gospel? And even if the Christian could find, as in a code or hieroglyph, the original, living meaning of God's communication, the Roman form has a gratuitously alienating effect. The mediation offered is superfluous. It invites contradiction.

As this turned out, Newman learned better when he became acquainted with the Catholic saints and the Fathers of the undivided Church. He found, not alienation, but a blessed intimacy with fellow

[5] John Henry Cardinal Newman, "Lectures on the Prophetical Office of the Church", in *Via Media of the Anglican Church* (New York: Longmans, Green & Co., 1901), 102–5.

believers and with God, guarded in faith and in love by the unity-creating energies of the Church. The Church's minimal demands on the lukewarm and mediocre are all open-ended and are meant to stimulate free spontaneity. And while a demand of the gospel professed only in books can—and frequently does—leave us mired in sloth, what comes to us from the living authority of the Church challenges us unremittingly. Even if it does not affect us in practice, just knowing that, in the midst of what is happening now in the world, there is such a living, guiding and goading center stops us from being indifferent. And if we listen to her, she gives us a sublime, buoyant certainty that we are not straying from the right path and are not subject to the risks and dangers that threaten lonely seekers.

But can we trust an authority that has failed so often, failed so humanly? Which has also failed frequently in those universal instructions which, though not in the "infallible" category in the narrower theological sense, were influential in shaping history? The decision is not a matter of opinion because the Gospels speak of Peter and his office in clear language. In his exposed position, placed there by Jesus himself, he is subject to temptation in a special way. "The gates of hell will not prevail against it" does not mean that the Church and the office of Peter will not be attacked from all sides but rather that it will be the magnetic pole that attracts the darkest powers of world history: "Simon, Simon, behold, Satan demanded to have you, that he might sift you like wheat" (Lk 22:31). How insistent is this twice-repeated name! But the tempter and the tempted are brought even closer together—even to the point of exchanging roles: "He rebuked Peter and said, 'Get behind me, Satan! For you are not on the side of God but of men'" (Mk 8:33).

Infallibility, according to Vatican I, is not a personal trait of the empirical Church or of her representatives, but—in the words of Reinhold Schneider—it is the rock that juts out from temptation's foaming turmoil and, by the merciful act of God, saves the Church from foundering. Scandal reaches the Church not only from the outside but also from the inside. "Structure", which, because of its impersonality, seems immune to scandal, can become the prime seat of infection. Only discernment of spirits can help here, received in answer to fervent prayer, such as the saints have offered for themselves and for us all. It is not the structure, not the form, not the skeleton of the body or of the community that is dead and needs to be surgically removed; it is the spirit enlivening the body that is good or bad.

One should note with what *hardness* Jesus forms Peter to make him the "rock" and to enable him to support his brothers. No censure, no humiliation is spared him. He must learn that the love of Christ is uncompromising at the very core of his "meek and lowly" heart. Peter not only has to learn this: he has to teach it to those entrusted to him. He is forbidden to be merely meek and lowly without also—in the name of his Master—representing the inexorable love of God, whose demand for "more" might seem to the lukewarm person to be a "law" externally imposed, but in reality it is built into him. The saints knew how to distinguish between the representation of this "more" and the weakness of the representative. But a further step is needed: one has to distinguish what in the harshness of the demand is the all-too-human element—the packaging—and the core to which obedience in faith and love is owed. Those who are not saints prefer to distinguish between the "sinful structure", against which revolt is permitted or even commanded, and the substance which, they presume, can be directly derived from the Gospels, bypassing any ecclesiastical structure. Here, however, they are already part of the ideological process that aims to disincarnate the existential Church as the flesh and body of Christ by splitting the "for me now", subjectively valid *logos* from the "superfluous" structure, the *sarx,* which must be discarded. Yet, what the New Testament calls *pneuma* does not blow exclusively in a *logos* stripped from its *sarx.* It is for this reason that we must question—from the standpoint of the New Testament—the discrediting of ecclesiastical structures or the intention radically and fundamentally to "change" them. The New Testament shows us a Church which, in a hard shell—hardened through suffering—shelters the tender and sweet fruit of the Spirit exhaled on the Cross. *De forti egressa est dulcedo.*

As we refer back to the New Testament to find an explanation of the anti-Roman attitude that has persisted throughout history to the present day, we come to our third point, a recommendation.

3. Integration

Pascal says in his *Pensées:* "If one contemplates the Church as unity, then the pope who is her head is also the whole. If one perceives her as plurality, then the pope is only a part. From time to time the Fathers of the Church thought of the Church in one way or the other . . . but they emphasized both; they excluded neither. A plurality that cannot be integrated into unity is chaos; unity unrelated to plurality is tyranny." (And he adds: "Only in France can it be said that the council is over the pope.")[6]

In this book we, too, will concern ourselves with unity and plurality, but we want to take a new approach. We do not claim to give practical directives in Church affairs, and because of this some readers may lose interest. Our main aim is to argue *theologically,* and adhering as closely as possible to the gospel of Jesus Christ, that the role of the office of Peter — even as defined at Vatican I! — is both indispensable and, at the same time, relative. The anti-Roman animosity rests, today more than ever, on a narrow view of those fundamental doctrines laid down in the New Testament which should be self-evident to Catholic eyes. More profound thinking will reveal the office of Peter as *one* of several indispensable elements in the ecclesiastical structure, thus freeing it from the pyramid-like isolation to which it consented, partly involuntarily, by permitting itself to be modeled on the pattern of Imperial Rome and, partly voluntarily, in reaction to the encroachments of medieval emperors.

[6] *Pensées* (ed. Chevalier), 809.

The tension between primacy and collegiality seems to me insufficient to describe the force-fields that bear upon the Church. Translating these into categories of "monarchy" and "democracy" is even less satisfactory. Much deeper, more fundamental tensions are in play, and only by perceiving these—if Christian theology would deign to do so—can the atmosphere be rid of poison.

To be truly of service, our thinking should delve into the theological depth of ecclesial reality. It is not sufficient to survey the papacy in general, from a cultural-philosophical or sociological point of view. Nor can attempts to explain the reigning pope with a dose of depth-psychology clarify the situation and repair the damage done. Such personal "disclosures" can be sensational, but they are basically injudicious even if they are written in praise of the pope, as were the conversations of Jean Guitton with Paul VI,[7] in which the author admits that he put much into the mouth of the Pope which the latter had not said. Such publications may claim to provide informative criticism, as the book by the two authors who call themselves Hieronymus.[8] Or they can attempt to shed light on the tragedy of the papacy by applying a professional stethoscope to the souls of three recent popes, from the ivory tower of a world-historical viewpoint (as did Reinhard Raffalt).[9] Or, finally, as Fritz Leist did in *The Prisoner*

[7] *Gespräche mit Paul VI* (Fischerbücherei 966, 1969). Much more serious and with more content is the well-balanced book by David A. Seeber, *Paul, Papst im Widerstreit. Dokumente und Analysen* (Herder 1971). Seeber attempts to develop a psychology of the Pope which does justice to his complicated personality. On the other hand, in view of the incredible complexity of the situation, one would like to ask the author whether in the instances where he expresses a prudent reserve—after allowing for all circumstances—he would have had the courage to make different decisions. Is it at all possible in a world such as ours to expect an individual, whoever he may be, to find a solution that suits everyone and that he can put into practice all by himself?

[8] *Vatikan intern* (Stuttgart: Deutsche Verlagsanstalt, 1973).

[9] (Munich/Zurich: Piper-Verlag, 1973.)

of the Vatican,[10] they can stir up past historical trash to muddy the presently clear waters. We name these authors only to state emphatically that we will not do what they have done. What we want to do is to revive a theological understanding of the constellation given in the New Testament in which every pope—including the present one—has his ordained place; he can only represent this constellation together with the whole Church and can only fulfill his role in obedience to Christ.

There will probably be complaints that we are hiding behind abstractions to avoid hard and dramatic personal problems. But the set of tensions with which we intend to deal—and which have existed from the very beginning—seems to us much more dramatic than the small, passing and unavoidable tensions between personalities, their abilities and competencies. We ourselves are inserted together, inexorably, in the real "Body" of Christ. We can no more shrug off coresponsibility than we can distance ourselves from the Catholic Church's past as something alien that does not concern us. How could we renounce solidarity with the "structure" of the Church, as does, for example, Regina Bohne, when in reference to the Day of Judgment, she has the temerity to say: "This day . . . must be feared more by the structure . . . much more *than by us,* the 'flock'."[11] We will not deny the uncomfortable past during which, no doubt, the papal power and rule were not always understood in the light of evangelical service. But who among the Church's present critics can be certain that his criticism is made purely for the sake of the gospel, of bringing about the unity which Christ desired?

That in the New Testament the concept of *exousia* means both supremacy and service, or rather supreme power given for service, does not need to be repeated *ad nauseam.* Ultimately every citizen, from the President down to the most insignificant civil servant,

[10] *Der Gefangene des Vatikans* (Munich: Kosel-Verlag, 1971).

[11] *Das katholische System, Kritische Texte* 11 *(Benziger* 1972*),* 46.

understands that giving effective service to the community requires not only professional competence but also officially assigned and socially accepted authority. And why cannot Catholics really understand St. Paul's distinction between "bodily weapons" that he rejects and "spiritual weapons" that he certainly is empowered to use against every stronghold of pride that raises itself against the truth of God (2 Cor 10:4–6)? The *exousia* that Jesus entrusts to the Twelve on choosing them can be expressed in Latin only as *potestas,* in English, as "fullness of authority". It is the means by which they are empowered effectively to help the People of God whom they are to "judge" (Mt 19:28; Lk 22:30). Is this incomprehensible? It seems so, at least to some, since, according to Frau Bohne, Jesus wanted a "church of free brotherhood", "anarchical", "free from any authority. . . . "[12]

Since the network of tensions in the Church is visible—as was the man Jesus—she has naturally a sociological and psychological exterior which should not be underestimated, because we cannot (adequately) separate the visible from the invisible Church. Nevertheless, the Church is first of all a *mysterium* (as Jesus is God's only begotten Son first of all and not as an afterthought), and as this *mysterium* she is Christ's Body and his Bride. And only by being this *mysterium* does she become the People of God, a socio-psychological reality. Therefore the tensions which we will describe all point to that *mysterium;* they are its necessary expression, not shortcomings on the part of the Church that need to be corrected by "changing the structure". The mystery of God cannot be manipulated. The visible contours of the Church's structure might perhaps be somewhat modified, provided we do so while obediently contemplating the mystery underlying the system, but only to bring out in bold relief the form that, from the very beginning, has been a stumbling block. We could even put it like this: our aim should be to remove the unreal stumbling blocks so that the Church's *real stumbling block* can become more evident to the

[12] Ibid., 9.

whole world. Insofar as the Church is the fullness of Christ that has been given to us, we are not the Church: the Church precedes us; we have been raised in baptism in her and through her. We can no more discuss and control the Church as if we were "above" her than we can control God. We *receive* the word and the sacraments. We cannot change, increase or decrease them. In the same way we also receive the fundamental constellation of Christ which we shall come to in the second part of this book. This constellation precedes us, and we cannot make it more or less than what it is; we cannot manipulate it.

But we hope to accomplish one thing: to reintegrate what has been isolated from the wholeness of this constellation—and what in such isolation may seem abstract, unreal, even grotesque—into the mystery of the whole. The reconciliation of primacy and collegiality, announced by Vatican II, is one aspect of this integration. It has other aspects, too, which up to now have not been given sufficient attention, perhaps because they are more difficult to express in concepts and proportions that can be grasped immediately.

Let us set aside for the moment the much-talked-about tension between office and charism, because it cannot be adequately resolved. "Office" in the New Testament clearly has a charismatic aspect. But who has taken the trouble to look at great personal sanctity (the charism that is unique and a gift but which has to be genuinely accepted and lived) in its theological tension with the principle of ecclesiastical office? Who has looked at it, not polemically, but constructively, so as to integrate it into the total theology of the Catholic Church? If we think that this is impossible, we must at least admit that the current theology comprehends only partial aspects of the *mysterium* of the Church. Only a person who has grasped this can try—nonpolemically, impartially—to show how the tension-filled facets of Christ's *one* truth mirror each other: the truth of an objective teaching and the corresponding objective leadership; the truth of a personal, unique call, the truth of a genuinely intuitive theology (which in some aspects might be ahead of and not always in conformity with the Church's theological stock-in-trade); the truth of a simple faith that trusts, in darkness, not wishing to know any other truth than that of God's guiding. . . . All this cannot be looked upon as unconnected and unrelated, as a tired "pluralism" maintains. We should rejoice over the richness of the Church's perspectives and be challenged by it to see in three or more dimensions what is usually presented rather flatly.

It is precisely in this multi-dimensional reality, which is much richer than our textbook wisdom ever dreamed of, that the essential form is safeguarded from sinking into a purely external, and therefore "changeable" or even dispensable, "structure". Spiritual Platonism or sterile structuralism cannot comprehend the living form of the Church. Indeed, the struggle against external structures is the last stage in the process of an illness diagnosed correctly by Madeleine Delbrêl: "A world which once was made Christian seems to be emptying itself out from within: first it gets rid of God, then of the Son of God, then that which he mediates of divinity to his Church, and frequently it is the façade which is last to collapse."[13]

[13] *La Joie de croire* (Seuil 1967), 29.

I

The Circle Closes

The Phenomenon

1. *Peasant Rebellion*

The anti-Roman attitude is as old as the Roman empire and also as the claim to primacy by the Bishop of Rome. That it has increased is no wonder: this has been the common attitude of the churches that forsook communion with Rome. But that this spiritual position should still be considered appropriate within the Catholic community even after Vatican II—where the "People of God" were given priority and the pope, freed from his isolation, returned to the collegiality of the bishops—is, to say the least, an alarming phenomenon.

To use, for once, the nonsensical division of humanity into a "left" and a "right", we can say that the "left" is closed to the monarchic, aristocratic, bureaucratic and any other "cratic" claims of the central "apparatus", while the "right" is split: there is a small segment in which "papolatry" still prevails, but the majority is plagued by a growing fear that the Pope might be captured by the "progressives", if he himself is not a "leftist" who, at the expense of the "silent Church", spins questionable diplomatic threads to Moscow and Peking. [Paul VI is meant. The original text was published in 1974—Ed.]

Of course, there is—and always has been among Catholics—a healthy popular sentiment that is faithful to Rome without being blind to the faults and human failings of the curia and even of the pope. Ordinary common sense is able to handle this as a matter of course and without embarrassment. But this sentiment (sound, from the Catholic point of view) is steadily undermined by the mass media,

29

the press and the numerous publications which demonstrate their Christian "adulthood" by an arrogant and even venomous superiority toward all that comes from Rome, happens in Rome or goes to Rome.

Whatever comes from Rome is measured by current criteria of theological or sociological research and is declared a priori to be behind the times. This reaction finds two expressions: the subject matter is treated ironically, and, having been filtered through a critical sieve, it is presented in small doses; or it is simply treated with complete silence. Catholics who are aware of the sarcastic, disparaging, large-scale onslaught against the Church, and primarily against Rome, are not necessarily equally alert to the more harmful, insidious methods employed by their own camp. They are not sufficiently heedful of the frequent shifts of emphasis by which some unimportant matter is made to appear an event of the greatest significance or a test case, while the truly important is sold short and the truth is misrepresented and conveyed in a distorted form.

Any authority that acts without giving detailed reasons is labeled "repressive", while the theological or sociological arguments opposing it are given free rein and can conduct a literally interminable delaying operation. People will not see that after Vatican II the primary task is the practical integration of the "People of God" and the responsible leadership established by Christ, and also that within this leadership primacy and collegiality can coexist. (We shall avoid the term "hierarchy", which is of late vintage and is moreover no longer understood in its original meaning.)

However, this process of integration takes much patience on the part of all involved; it demands cooperation and heartfelt likemindedness. One can and should see Vatican I as the final word after centuries of equivocation, ending the debate and making room for a new, more interesting, more fruitful discussion, namely, concerning *communio* in the Church, the dialogue in Christian love between those who have been misleadingly called the "bottom" and the "top". The ancient Church simply referred to the relationship of the apostle and his community. Such a relationship might seem difficult today because we are not used to it. Perhaps also because it demands more active participation in the process of integration not only from Rome but also from the provinces, whose contribution must be something far more than a "critique of ideology" or "creative disobedience".

We want to state this right at the beginning, once for all: nothing could be more injurious to real *communio* than the thoughtless or even malicious equating of the "authority" Christ gave his chosen disciples—a gift of divine love for his Church—with the manner of despotic control exercised by the great power conglomerates in world history, from the empires of Assyria, Alexander and Rome to fascist and communist totalitarianisms. Such a misrepresentation masks a resistance to the Church's authority to govern, which is derived from the gospel (where *exousia* is correctly translated as *potestas*) and is rightly called the power of jurisdiction in practice and theory in the life of the Church as well as in canon law. What else could be meant when the power to bind and loose are granted to Peter and later to the other eleven? And how could a shepherd, if he is not provided with authority, lead a flock and defend it against "savage wolves" attacking from without and, "from among you", men who will distort the truth and lead astray any who follow them (Acts 20:29–30)? The shepherd and his office are the dominant symbols of the gift of authority, as even those who perpetually polemicize against "sacerdotalism" in Church leadership acknowledge.

When Fritz Leist—about whom we shall say more later—on principle and in the name of the gospel rejects the Bishop of Rome's juridical authority and instead favors the Orthodox "honorary primacy", he forgets that this title is foreign to the Gospels; it derives from an imperial and diplomatic frame of reference. By his radical rejection of Vatican I (hence, also, of Vatican II) and his simultaneous claim to remain a Catholic, Leist finds himself—just like his prime source, Döllinger—between two stools, on the floor.

Obviously, anyone who knows Church history will admit that the spiritual (and also truly juridical) evangelical authority was often combined with the exercise of secular power. We recognize this today, we deplore it, and we repudiate it for the future. However un-Christian or sinful these combinations may have been (often, but not always), it is just as unevangelical and a cause of scandal when people suspect a priori every decree of Church leadership to be a disguised or open lust for power or, in any case, a misuse of the *exousia* entrusted to it. Interestingly, this suspicion is characteristic of the same people who, while continuously accusing the Church of encroaching on the secular sphere, proclaim that today the main task of the Church (and not only of involved individuals) is to change the structures of society through revolutionary coercion!

People who experienced rigid fascist and nazi principles of obedience and their consequences in their own countries are perhaps more inclined to label any form of obedience "immaturity" or "cowardice". They see their contribution as being to "democratize" the Church. Yet, anyone familiar with the gospel must realize that the ground plan of the community that Jesus founded cannot be described as either monarchy, oligarchy, aristocracy or democracy.

Countries with strong national church traditions and those that strive for this kind of system of government for their church will as a matter of course interpret the integration sought by Vatican II in terms of a distancing of the national episcopate from Rome. Citing the Gallican idea of *réception,* they filter all instructions coming from Rome, and those demanding too much are set aside or are combined with what seems more "fitting" to the national culture. Catholics in countries that have a non-Catholic majority pride themselves on a one-sided, unreciprocated "magnanimity" in ecumenical outreach, thinking to show their spiritual breadth by themselves giving up the medieval "prejudices" demolished four hundred years earlier by the Reformation churches. Thus, at little cost, they manage to produce a leveled-down Catholicism and also a deliberate distancing from the antiquated Roman center.

Western countries that are influenced by communist propaganda and expect all salvation to come from a "change of structures" (meaning "sinful structures", as one often reads) like to imply that capitalism was spawned by the medieval papacy and to present the "hierarchy" as a superstructure foreign to Christ and in practice invented by Paul. They glorify the saints in the history of the Church as "avowed nonconformists" and "potential dissidents", and apply Jesus' accusations against the pharisaic hypocrites to the Roman curia and the bishops who are subservient to it. They also deny that the faithful have obligations to ancient, totally out-of-date dogmatic statements: "It must be said of the Roman Church system that it has found itself in radical opposition to the commandments of God and of Jesus Christ and still does so today. . . . Has the Roman Church structure none of Christ's compassion?"[1]

Countries which, not long ago, fell under the influence of imported rationalistic, supranatural theologies, according to which the contingent form of the Church seemed to be sanctioned *in toto* from heaven, now—as the supernatural halo has faded under the influence of modern pragmatism and cybernetics—see everything in the Church as "restructurable" according to the categories of modern society, particularly the sacral-feudal behavior of the official hierarchy. They see no reason why the office of Peter should not be changed into a rational presidency with a limited term of office.

Of course, this disposes of obedience in the Church—as understood by the Gospels and by Paul—as allegedly feudalistic and hence outmoded. The priest—and preeminently the pope—"cannot represent a hierarchical institution, the decision-making processes of which are modeled unmistakably on an absolutistic pattern, and at the same time live up to individual and social expectations of truly participatory decision-making and the defense of the individual against the

---

[1] Regina Bohne, "Das katholische System", *Kritische Texte* 11 (Zurich: Benziger, 1972): 66, 80.

interests of the institution".[2] From this point of view, the program of the Council—to unite primacy and collegiality, general obedience and personal freedom—seems to involve a blatant contradiction.

We could truly speak of contradiction if the alternatives of determining truth in the Church were, on the one hand, to question the *sensus fidelium,* followed by an authoritative decision of the Church leadership, and, on the other, to take a poll to find the truth by majority vote. The "hierarchical-feudal system" then would collapse as "anachronistic" and "dysfunctional",[3] and "the place of the ruling hierarchical authority would be taken by the authority of the expert".[4] Obedience is rendered to a "superior" only insofar as he is able to show his competence, and the extent and degree of this competence is determined by the one who is to obey: the pastor's by the parish community, the pope's by the community of the faithful. A particular consequence of this would be the downgrading of the mystery of faith to the level of rational-theological comprehensibility, on which level the differences in theological opinion would be negotiated between the so-called "ecclesiastical teaching office" and the theological profession.

If Rome were to approach a dilemma formulated in this way and failed to rule in favor of the view set forth by the modern "freedom" ideology, she would be attacked as a matter of course as being "in principle blind to all that is new",[5] showing "blindness and rigidity in leadership",[6] "immobility" and outdated "authoritarian behavior"[7] and

[2] *Reform und Anerkennung kirchlicher Ämter, ein Memorandum der Arbeitsgemeinschaft ökumenischer Universitätsinstitute* (Munich: Verlag Kaiser; Mainz: Matthias Grünewald, 1973), 75.

[3] Ibid., 79, 80.

[4] Ibid., 82.

[5] Ibid., 64.

[6] Ibid., 174.

[7] Ibid., 15.

opposition to "legitimate demands for democratization"[8]. Disappointed and embittered, people would conclude that "papal, and consequently episcopal, centralism is increasing rather than decreasing", strengthening the impression that "the institutional Church with her structure and laws lags far behind the demands of today's consciousness of freedom".[9]

Most of these accusations—insofar as they do not attack personal weaknesses but attempt fundamentally to criticize the Church's structure—are incurably *romantic*. They lose sight of the real experience of two thousand years of Church history and hold on to the two extremes: on the one hand, a gospel—seen in the rosy light of Renan—of "powerlessness" and the "blessedness of the poor and oppressed"; on the other hand, a Marxist critique of society which, by "changing the structures" (a new mythical-magical spell), hopes to establish that evangelical paradise.

Ferdinand Guimet has demonstrated correctly that the exponents of this naiveté, who like to adorn themselves with the gifts of the Holy Spirit, are actually archaeologists: by undertaking exegetical excavations they endeavor to find a prepentecostal Christianity where the later structural details are as yet indistinct. One need only read Fritz Leist's interpretation of the Petrine texts to stumble in every sentence over words such as "alleged", "probable" and "perhaps". They want to establish a "coincidence" with the Christ-"event"— without the Holy Spirit's mediation in the Church—at a point in time when the disciples were still steeped in Judaic spirituality and were still to some extent captives of a totally un-Christian political theology. These theologians, according to Guimet, "made a slow start in grasping the real meaning of faith and are so hopelessly late that they can only exhaust themselves in their vain attempt to catch up with it".[10] Findings of archaeology, obtained by disregarding history or rejecting

[8] Ibid., 22.
[9] Ibid., 45.
[10] Fernand Guimet, *Existence et éternité* (Paris: Aubier, 1973), 50–51.

35

its burden, cannot bring tidings of salvation to the present. Even less so because these advocates, captives in the hothouse of modern ideologies, not only distance themselves from the Church's past, but they throw stones at her, feeling frustrated by her power which continues to reach effectively into the present. In contrast to the great theologians of the last generation who were subjected to pressure by the Holy Office and bore it silently, today, though such pressures have ceased, they whine like children at the dentist's even before their teeth are touched. They swear to "mount the barricades" if their Christian and human freedom should be limited in the least.

While we do not fail to recognize some legitimate points in Fritz Leist's invectives against the "prisoner of the Vatican"[11]—i.e., the wish to banish the taboos associated with a popular "papolatry" which is still operative—they are false and offensive in three ways: 1. the already-mentioned equating of jurisdictional primacy[12] with a worldly claim to sovereignty; 2. basing this claim on the mythical-magical roots of the pagan *Roma aeterna*[13] and claiming that the concept of a royal "savior"[14] was derived from the fertility myths of Egypt, citing the fact that the popes everywhere erected the phallic obelisks of the Pharaohs—in short, he attacks the unbridled elevation of the pope's sacredness, his endowment with *mana*,[15] the sacralization of his entire surroundings, especially his "court",[16] the transformation of the Vati-

---

[11] Fritz Leist, *Der Gefangene des Vatikans: Strukturen päpstlicher Herrschaft* (Munich: Kösel-Verlag, 1971).

[12] For "honorary primacy", see ibid., 300f.

[13] Ibid., 86.

[14] Ibid., 106ff.

[15] Ibid., 66, 69, 127.

[16] Ibid., 24ff. ("The papal court, the structure and the attitude of the curia— these are the greatest obstacles to an ecumenical meeting without reservation with Rome", 30). The papal "court" is psychologically interpreted as "a rampart around an institution that feels threatened because the Lord is far off . . . a protecting power because of the deep, unresolved anxiety at being abandoned on the earth", 40.

can State into a "hierocratic monarchy",[17] making a pseudo-Christ of the pope (who mistakenly believes that he is a mediator,[18] even a "universal father");[19] and finally, 3. categorically calling for the withdrawal of the statements of Vatican I as unbiblical, thus enabling a basis to be found for collegiality within the Church (which otherwise would remain a "squared circle",[20] a "vicious circle"[21]) as well as for an ecumenical outreach.

Then there is the poor theologian, laboring in "fear" of the (long since abolished) Index and of the (still benignly watchful) Congregation for the doctrine of the Faith, formerly the Inquisition. One is amazed how courageously these theologians are able to mask their secret fears! The indisputable good will of Paul VI remained powerless as long as he himself was a "prisoner under the dominance of the curia and of the Roman ideology",[22] "imprisoned by these pictures of saints and of the Fathers",[23] imprisoned "in the structures of a feudal law, a sacral kingship".[24] All he could do, therefore, was to think solipsistically,[25] holding monologues with himself.[26] Leist does not miss sounding the Germanic note: "This system has its Romance origin written on its brow and will never be able to penetrate the Germanic countries."[27]

Let us reply to Leist, in jest, by concluding our preliminary over-

[17] Ibid., 46.
[18] Ibid., 53ff.
[19] Ibid., 59ff., 70ff.
[20] Ibid., 316.
[21] Ibid., 320.
[22] Ibid., 318.
[23] Ibid., 79.
[24] Ibid., 316.
[25] Ibid., 281ff.
[26] Ibid., 139.
[27] Ibid., 328. In the end, Leist reveals that it was not his task "to show how the office of Peter—or more correctly(?) how the service of Peter—should look today" (351). This holds for most faultfinders: they do not know how to make realistic application.

view of the scope of the anti-Roman attitude with a quotation from another German:

We Europeans find ourselves confronted with an immense world of ruins; some things still tower aloft while other objects stand moldering and dismal, but most things are already lying on the ground, picturesque enough. Where were there ever finer ruins? This city of decay is the Church. We see the religious organization of Christianity shaken to its deepest foundations: belief in God is overthrown; faith in the Christian ascetic ideal is now fighting its last battle. But the strangest thing is that those who exerted themselves most to retain and preserve Christianity are the very ones who did most to destroy it—the Germans. It seems that the Germans do not understand the essence of a church. Are they not spiritual enough? In any case the structure of the Church rests on a *southern* freedom and liberality of spirit and equally on a southern distrust of nature, man and spirit. It rests on a knowledge and experience of man that is entirely different from that found in the north. The Lutheran Reformation, in all its length and breadth, was the indignation of the simple against something "complicated"; to speak cautiously, it was a coarse, honest misunderstanding. Today we can see plainly that, with regard to all the cardinal power issues, Luther was fatally limited, superficial and imprudent. He fumbled, he tore things up, he handed over the holy books to everyone—which meant that they got into the hands of the philologists, that is, the destroyers of any belief based on books. He demolished the concept of "church" by repudiating faith in the inspiration of the councils; for the concept of "church" can only remain vigorous as long as it is presupposed that the inspiring Spirit which had founded the Church still lives in her, still builds her, still continues to build its own dwelling-house. He gave back sexual intercourse to the priest: but three-quarters of the reverence of which the people are capable (and particularly the women of the people) rests on the belief that a man who is exceptional in this regard will also be exceptional in other matters. It is precisely here that the popular belief in something superhuman in man, in the miraculous, in the saving God in man, has its most subtle and

38

suggestive advocate. Having given the priest a wife, he had to *take from him* auricular confession. Psychologically this was appropriate, but thereby he practically did away with the Christian priest himself, whose profoundest utility has ever consisted in his being a sacred ear, a silent well, a grave for secrets. "Every man his own priest"—such expressions and their peasant cunning concealed, in Luther, the profound hatred of the "superior man" and the rule of the "superior man" as conceived by the Church. Luther destroyed an ideal which he did not know how to attain, while seeming to combat the degeneration thereof. It was he, who could not be a monk, who repudiated the rule of *homines religiosi;* he consequently brought about within the ecclesiastical social order precisely what he so impatiently fought against in the civil order, namely, a "peasant revolt". He knew not what he did.[28]

2. *Provincialization*

Let us leave, for a moment, the anti-Roman accusations and look briefly at the results they have achieved. We shall disregard the romantics with their demands for demythologization and aspirations to evangelical freedom and allow the realists to speak, those who drew doubtlessly legitimate inferences from the ideas of Vatican II and from the accompanying decentralization of many faculties and powers of authority which had accumulated in Rome. We shall not waste words here on the positive side of this sharing of power, such as the upgrading and stimulation of regional responsibilities. This is obvious. But when we look at the overall picture, we cannot help being alarmed at the strong negative voices—loudest among them, that of Cardinal Suenens—demanding the dismantling of curial centralism.

[28] Friedrich Nietzsche, *Die Fröhliche Wissenschaft,* 358. Anyone can verify what sentences and figures of speech I have omitted without ellipses. He could also profitably read the entire essay.

To begin with we should note that besides the individual episcopates, the Council particularly emphasized and recommended regional and national bishops' conferences. Thus, those faculties of the central Roman curia and newly established jurisdictions that have been shifted to an individual diocese will appear in a twofold form: there will be not only a diocesan commission or coordinating body but also an interdiocesan one, or—as in France—the bishops' conference will set up a permanent office with several departments. This results in a disproportionate multiplication of ecclesial bureaucracy—a curia multiplied by the number of dioceses, multiplied by the number of bishops' conferences. The "Church militant" has become, according to one wisecrack, the "photocopying Church". Moreover, in the synods of some countries, where the right of the kingly-priestly people to participate in ecclesial decision-making is provided for, the flood of paper grows to legendary proportions and cannot be coped with by any normal working person. This also places an exorbitant demand on the time of both the bishops and the synod participants, and there is an increased danger that committees and synods will now be subject to manipulation (the word is unavoidable here) in many ways. The same could also hold for bishops' conferences, especially when the overburdened individual members must leave important tasks, the formulation of far-reaching decisions, the drafting of religious textbooks or liturgical texts, etc., to the commissions, the composition of which cannot be planned as carefully as that of the Roman curia, where a candidate for an important position or for membership on a particular commission can be drawn from a pool of international experts. One cannot blame individual bishops when they identify only partially with directives and statements that are issued under constant pressure from the standing bureaus of bishops' conferences—as actually happens in some regions; nor can they be blamed when the hoped-for pluralism is achieved more on a national than a diocesan level. The time may not be far off when some of the bishops will be grateful that they can call upon the pope as a

40

defender of freedom against a more or less anonymous bureaucratic machine.

This simple observation is sufficient, for our purposes, to establish the usefulness of the Roman curia, particularly as hard-working an organization as the present one. Like all governmental bodies composed of people, it will always give some cause for criticism, but no one can accuse the present curia of the gross abuses of earlier times. Some red tape was already eliminated by Paul VI, but perhaps there is still a call for further curtailment. One suspects that, first of all, it is the appendages of clerical bureaucracy—ranks, orders, titles—as well as the image of the pope as it is projected by the curia to the Christian and non-Christian public that need voluntary or involuntary pruning. Perhaps there will come a time for an end to the large-scale deployment both of finance and of personnel.

However, we should ask ourselves in this transitional period— when Catholics are behaving like adolescents playing "adult", though they are anything but—if it was not prudence on the pope's part (rather than lust for power) that caused him to maintain such a well-functioning apparatus, despite friction, with the help of much excellent collaboration.[29] In order that an eye may look kindly, a mouth may smile, a hand reach out, to make these indivisibly simple, human, universally understood gestures possible, what an inexpressibly complicated network of muscles, nerves, blood vessels is presupposed! People are not pure spirits; not even the one who *ex officio* must fulfill an irreplaceable task: like the saints, his whole existence is to be a sign, but the charism and prerogative of the saints (or of some of them) was not put into his cradle at birth!

But let us return to the experiment that brought proliferation of the apparatus on diocesan and interdiocesan levels. Ecumenical councils have had a lively history. At some, people were bribed; at others, they

[29] This is not the place to investigate the finances of the Vatican. We refer the interested reader to Corrado Pallenberg, *Vatican Finances* (London: Owen, 1971).

were beaten up; at others, shots were fired. Political pressures of all kinds were the order of the day. Nevertheless — *Dei providentia et hominum confusione* — some gains were made for Christianity. On the other hand, the immense expenditures in time, health, money and materials on the part of national synods have not yet been justified. In all the bustle, one thing stands out: as never before, the Church is preoccupied with herself, and, in particular, the clergy are preoccupied with themselves. They struggle for identity (which is a clinical problem), they practice individual and collective "navel-gazing", and the greater the confusion of voices, the less a national church knows who she really is. The talk is of orthopraxy and changes in "structure" in Brazil, but with their empty agendas the speakers are midgets in comparison to the great laymen of the *Kulturkampf.* Some might even look with secret envy at the much-maligned curia, where there is less talk and more effective action.

Is this a preparatory phase of Christian democracy? Or is it something like Coué's self-help therapy by clerics and laymen who are anxious about their identity? One is inclined to suspect that the great movements and reforms of the Church, in the present and the future, will not be initiated by such panels and boards but by saints, the ever-unique and solitary ones who, struck by God's lightning, ignite a blaze all around them. This process is totally different from skillful organization. Saints have no time to worry about their identity.

Perhaps we should find out how a people "produces" a saint: by prayer and penance, by ardent faith passed on from a mother to a chosen son . . . , by a desire to be one within the Church, a desire that suddenly becomes reality in a living, effective, flesh-and-blood unity.

But the saint is always characterized by a passion for catholicity. He knows that he himself is an individually insignificant member; he might have this or that position, but he is always a member of the living *whole* by which and for which he lives. Hence, a saint would never accept the tired, resigned or stubbornly defiant particularization of today's "theological pluralism". *Pluralism* in its strict sense — opinions within the Catholic Church which from a human point of

42

view cannot be harmonized—is provincialism and as such a denial of catholicity. More precisely, it denies the reality of the principle of unity of the *Catholica,* from which all members, with their particular mandates and perspectives, are nourished. Today, a self-respecting theology should aspire to realign the disjointed components of Christian truth, bringing together those that seem opposed or irrelevant in practice or in theory. It should be insightful enough to rise above unfruitful dialectics and quiet down all the clamor that declares that the principles are irreconcilable (e.g., primacy versus collegiality).

Of course, this will entail a fundamental decision: whether to relativize and break up the concrete unity of the *Catholica* into an abstract unity of *humanitas*—as the consistently pluralistic theologians feel compelled to do today—or to hold fast to the real unity of the *Catholica* even when she has to open herself without limitations, for example, to ecumenism with its myriad problems and, even further, to all religious and atheistic mankind, without disavowing the law of her origin, the ground of her being, that molded her in the form in which she lives and develops. This openness that, today more than ever, is indispensable to the credibility of the *Catholica* presupposes a secure knowledge of her own, distinct identity; as a woman can open herself and give herself to a man only if her actions are feminine, not masculine or feminist.

And to take a look at the final mystery: in the triune God, distinctiveness and limitlessness are not contradictory. The Divine Persons, because they are God, do not limit one another in defining one another.

He who closes his mind to this background mystery is doomed to a merely sociological understanding of the Church's structure and hence will find contradictions and incompatibilities, while the Christian who lives within this *mysterium* happily experiences these tensions as livable and fruitful. Perhaps the most fruitful of all is the one that is dismissed by some as "squaring the circle". An obvious example is that Catholics accept true, unlimited obedience as being compatible with real responsibility for oneself, as so many saints in religious orders—not to speak of the authentic Jesuits—have exemplified. To the non-Catholic this is totally incomprehensible. This seeming contradiction ultimately can only be resolved in contemplation of the Trinity. Casual Catholics often point to the saints but only to raise the issue of their conflicts with, and suffering at the hand of, authority; their strident tone is totally at variance with the attitude of the saints, who would refuse to allow anyone to take a stand on their behalf against the Church. Of course, the trinitarian mystery of obedience, entrusted to men, is always threatened because the same obedience in faith to the Divine Word is demanded from both the one who commands and the one who obeys. But which of the gifts that God has given to men is not endangered or cannot be used contrary to divine intention?

The unfolding of the *christological mysterium* in the Church also demands an almost unimaginable plurality of thought, which is something quite different from a disintegrating pluralism. Paul already makes it clear that the Christian who follows the Lord is crucified to the world, dying daily, but also—and not less truly—lives with the risen Lord, yes, with the One taken up to heaven. The situation in the world and in the Church—providence—will allow him to experience both of these states without falling into the pits of false humility or triumphalism. Again, seen from the outside, this seems impossible.

Finally, the Catholic holds that *Holy Scripture* as a whole is *inspired* and, with all its variegated coloring, belongs to the Church. While its many dimensions have been greatly expanded by modern exegesis, it remains essentially a *unity* that is not above or parallel to the unity of the Church but is inseparably related to it. It is the archetypal dialogue, addressed by Christ—as the Word of the Father—in the Holy Spirit to the Church, which responds in faith. Objective exegesis, i.e., one that bears in mind this origin of Scripture, is able to go on unhampered, almost infinitely, discovering aspects and uncovering layers that show the growth of ecclesial faith to full maturity. However, exegesis fails to maintain objectivity the moment it isolates single factors within this growth, playing them off against the integrated whole. (For example, some purely hypothetical community structures in Pauline Corinth are set against the fully developed Church structures of postapostolic times, described by the Bible and verified by contemporary or subsequent witnesses, such as Clement of Rome, Ignatius, et al.) Within the faith of the Church, plurality of thought need not be feared. Doctrinaire pluralism, the results of research outside the Church, is not as alarming as the attitude of scholars (or any other Christians) who stand with one foot in the faith of the Church and the other in a self-fabricated religion or in an unecclesial neutrality, pursuing an existential pluralism that borders on the schizophrenic.

If a person seriously and systematically denies the possibility that the faithful could live by the trinitarian, christological and pneumatological mysteries and, despite this negation, lays claim to being a good Catholic—perhaps even better than the pope—his error must be exposed to the faithful by the pastoral office, just as such errors were exposed by the apostles, without fear of offending against charity, in their actions and writings in the service of faith.[30] It is self-evident that this service is not to be exercised by fire or sword or without regard for human rights (as was objected—and not without cause—against some of the preconciliar processes of the Holy Office). This is not the place to investigate how far this ideal has been integrated into all areas. Nevertheless, to deny—under the pretext of freedom of research and the modern pluralism of ideas—any competence to the authority of the Church in judging where the limits of Catholic faith are being

---

[30] A few texts in the New Testament that indicate these boundaries are Mt 18:15–17; Rom 14:1, 16:17; 1 Cor 5:5, 5:9; 2 Thess 3:14–15, 3:6; 1 Tim 1:20, Titus 3:10–11; Heb 10:24–25; 1 Jn 2:19–20; Jude 22–23; Rev 22:15, etc.

transgressed means questioning that the origin of the Church's authority is part of the mystery of revelation.

The world seems to become more united, or rather, more standardized in eternals, as a result of technology. At the same time it also becomes more provincialized, because the whole has grown to such an inconceivable size that it makes exploration by the serious seeker nearly impossible. Therefore he is inclined to limit himself to a narrow specialty: education in the humanities is replaced by specialized training even in early education. Countries yield to the tendency to fragment into their component groups; and no one can reach an overview of the results and methods of the "exact" sciences (while the so-called "inexact" arts and humanities ape "scientific" methods). Conferences of specialists multiply, striving for a unified approach, while of course really great minds who, like Leibniz, can encompass the basic dimensions of all human knowledge are increasingly rare. Hence, philosophy loses its nerve; hence, theology is specialized and provincialized.

General dogmatic theology is attempted only exceptionally and as "teamwork"; and then it means *tot capita quot sensus.* It is replaced partly by popular tracts and partly by an unmanageable flood of specialized research in exegesis, Church history and canon law: specific areas of a previously united dogmatics. The lack of a convincing overview encourages people to take refuge in the allegedly "closer-to-life", practical subjects: religious education, religious group dynamics, critical sociology of religion and of the Church, liberation and third-world theologies. Theological contacts across national boundaries are rapidly weakening. In Germany, no one knows what theology is being produced in Poland, in spite of its great quantity. Except for one or two theologies of revolution, hardly anyone knows what significant French, Spanish, Italian—not to mention African, American or Australian—works have appeared.

Furthermore, does not the voice of God sound loud and clear enough from the distress of the world to get a hearing and prompt

46

obedience? Must we listen to the seemingly superfluous and irritating duplication of this voice coming from Rome, which never concentrates on the most urgent issues but often enough insists on adherence to secondary or incomprehensible directives. In the midst of this busy, praxis-centered splintering, the Roman monolith, representing an utopian unity, appears untimely, unrealistic, pretentious, dilettante; its statements ring with false rhetoric, diplomatically veiled—in short, they are unbelievable. It is the ideal butt for the sarcasm of a "critical Catholicism". Anything that comes from Rome—even if it is issued by a panel or board that met in Rome only by chance and in which no Roman participated (as, for example, in the International Theological Commission)—is brushed aside as irrelevant and "passé". Perhaps this is why the "Club of Rome" has received such a small hearing despite its apocalyptic warnings.[31]

3. *Being a Pope Today*

The two "Hieronymi", who do not spare their sarcasm against the curia, give a rather benevolent psychological evaluation of Paul VI,[32] though they dwell perhaps too long on the fact that he once compared himself with the Spanish antihero. (Prior to his journey to Asia and Australia he asked, not without humor, with whom people would compare him: "David versus Goliath? Others may say Don Quixote.") Nor do they accept the nickname "Hamlet" given to him when he was still Archbishop of Milan by Roncalli, then in Venice. Reinhard Raffalt, however, who attacks Paul VI's whole line of policy

---

[31] See Johannes Gross, "Die Welt wird Provinz", in *Frankfurter Allgemeine Zeitung* [August 3, 1973]; Alvin Toffler, *Future Shock* (New York: Random House, 1971), 231–85.

[32] Hieronymus, *Vatikan intern* (Stuttgart: Deutsche Verlagsanstalt, 1973), 227–81.

("Where is the Vatican heading?"),[33] persistently rides this particular horse: "Hamlet on the Chair of Peter" is the title of a long chapter. At the same time, it is not clear what the point of resemblance is; it could hardly be because Paul VI did not act—he acted far too purposefully for Raffalt, but unfortunately in a "left" direction that went against the Raffalt's grain—and hardly because he made some "errors of thought"[34] in his policies, because this is exactly what Hamlet did not do. Perhaps it is simply that both were deep, undertook complex and symbolic deeds (the "play within the play") and also that external circumstances forced them to change their tactics. But the comparison limps because Hamlet again and again had to delay decisive action, while Paul VI always acted purposefully and consistently. Thus the parallel is unfortunate. Had it merely consisted in "Thinking . . . our state to be disjoint and out of frame" and in Hamlet and Paul complaining "That ever I was born to set it [the world] right!", then comparison could be made with many tragic heroes and many a tragic pope, such as Gregory the Great, who was certainly no Hamlet.

[33] Reinhard Raffalt, *Wohin steuert der Vatikan?* (Munich and Zurich: Piper Verlag, 1973). From the numerous reactions to Raffalt's book we call attention to Joseph Schmitz van Vorst, "Wohin die Ostpolitik Pauls VI. steuert", *Frankfurter Allgemeine Zeitung* December 22, 1973), which sets unification with the Orthodox as the goal; N. Benckiser, "Gott aussparen?", *Frankfurter Allegemeine Zeitung* (January 2, 1974), cautiously agrees; Ad. Holl, "Verwirrt vom Vatikan", *Welt am Sonntag* (November 18, 1973): the diagnosis is correct, but what would Raffalt himself do? Hansjakob Stehle, "Wenn einer rot sieht", *Die Zeit* (December 17, 1973), writes that Raffalt draws "a caricature of what the Vatican's Ostpolitik is. . . . (She) is not and never has been oriented toward ideological coexistence . . . but favors a sober and practical *modus vivendi* for the faithful in countries with atheistic governments"; Walter Dirks, "Römisches Allzurömisches", *Die Welt* (January 3, 1974): "It is as if the Church began with Constantine" (there is hardly any mention of the gospel); Max von Brück, "Vom Mut, unmodern zu sein", *Süddeutsche Zeitung* (December 1 and 2, 1973): "Raffalt's approach is too crude"; G. W., "Wohin steuert der Vatikan?", *Rheinische Merkur* (November 30, 1973): "it is one-sided . . . Constantinian".

[34] Raffalt, *Wohin steuert der Vatikan?* 140, 218f., 225, etc.

The paradox in Raffalt's thinking, in exact contrast to that of people like Hernegger or Leist, is that he is in love with the redemptive symbiosis of the ancient and the papal Rome and that the rupture of this by Vatican II—and even more by the clearly pursued policies of Paul VI—compels him to adopt a scathing, though dignified, antipapal attitude. He becomes one of the most qualified speakers of the Church's right wing, of those traditionalists who were already greatly upset by Leo XIII's openmindedness toward "socialism". As a result he too, basically faithful to Rome, falls like they do between two stools.[35] Even in his *Das Ende des römischen Prinzips*[36] (which we shall discuss later on), Raffalt has described the abandonment of the pagan Roman foundation (*Sancta Maria Sopra Minerva*), of *aequitas* and *pietas* as cosmic piety, as the sense of balance between heaven and earth, of what is right (*jus*), as being responsible for the destruction of Peter's primacy. His little boat, having weighed anchor, has become prey to the waves.

However, the Pope cannot be made responsible for this state of modern civilization. And if he, according to Raffalt, acts in an "inconsistent"[37] and "dialectic" (not necessarily schizophrenic)[38] manner, one might simply ask the author what course he would have taken in the same situation.

If we were to sum up Raffalt's attitude and the position he rejects, we might say that he wants "harmony",[39] something immanent in ancient Rome which became transcendent in Christianity, relating the believer to eternal life through the glorification of the emperor, Christ. One of Raffalt's accusations is that the papacy, by turning

[35] Ibid., 8.

[36] Reinhard Raffalt, *Das Ende des römischen Prinzips,* Münchner Akademie-Schriften 52 (Munich: Kösel-Verlag, 1970).

[37] Ibid., 240.

[38] Ibid., 247.

[39] Ibid., 75.

toward socialism, "comforts uncounted millions of *today*'s poor and oppressed with the idea of salvation *tomorrow*" and deprives them of the "other-worldly consolation" that alone might help them endure their present misery.[40]

This "harmony" is incompatible with the "tensions" that, according to Raffalt, are unbearable and derive from the Council's, and subsequently Paul VI's, attempt to achieve "too many things all at once", to reconcile by force things that are in practice irreconcilable. That the community of "bishops, together with the pope, are successors of the apostles" and that the "supreme government of the Church is the business of the bishops together with the pope" (in Raffalt's none-too-exact formulation) "indicate an annihilating defeat of the conservatives and an imminent danger for the Holy See".[41] Moreover, "fraternity had to be practiced without limiting the papacy; this inconsistency lay at the root of the future tragedy[!] of Paul VI's entire pontificate".[42] The latter steers "a wavering course between the desire for fraternity and the right to demand obedience".[43]

We can readily agree with Raffalt that, measured by the precepts of the art of secular government, there exists a "contradiction" here; also that when Paul VI, in good Leonine tradition, made the daring statement before the World Council of Churches in Geneva: "I am Peter", the WCC "heard it without comprehension".[44] What Raffalt says of the Jesuits is more revealing: "Mature individuality and at the same time total submission according to the principle of obedience— this was the absurd[!] tension in which the members of the Ignatian

---

[40] Ibid., 254. In the Zagorsk conferences on June 15, 1973 (the grand finale of Raffalt's book), "the sense of the transcendental in the Christian faith was relegated to second place", 286.

[41] Raffalt, *Das Ende,* 40–41.

[42] Ibid., 41.

[43] Ibid., 14.

[44] Ibid., 49.

company lived."[45] To him, the Jesuit principle is "absurd" because he looks at it only from a psychological-sociological point of view and not within the logic of the christological mystery. But are personalities like Francis Xavier or Peter Canisius really absurd or schizophrenic? And from the same perspective, is it really absurd when the Council, followed by Paul VI, strives to integrate fraternity with obedience to the final authority of the pope? Is this really not feasible according to the New Testament? Is it unattainable for men of faith? Is "consultation" truly incompatible with "authority", "service" with "power"?[46] Without a doubt, *more* is demanded from Christians than from those living in a simpler system, be it absolutism or liberalism. But should not this "more" be expected of Christians, considering the christological and trinitarian mystery of the gospel?

Raffalt adduces much disturbing material, from which he draws apocalyptic inferences: the "roots" of tradition have been "sawn off", and hence nothing can bloom any more.[47] Through the "internationalization of the curia" a "permanent senate of bishops" is made possible;[48] by limiting the age of voting cardinals, this office has been functionalized, and, as a result, the very principle of hierarchy is attacked.[49] It becomes "democratized",[50] and the most extreme theories of Balducci are no longer utopian.[51] The new blueprint for the order of the conclave disrupts the establishment of the cardinalate (with its ties to the see of the Bishop of Rome) and also "changes the papacy". "The Bishop of the Universal Church chosen by his fellow bishops

[45] Ibid., 233.
[46] Ibid., 37.
[47] Ibid., 97.
[48] Ibid., 40.
[49] Ibid., 113.
[50] Ibid., 259ff.
[51] Ibid., 71ff.

does not necessarily 'have to' be Bishop of Rome as well."[52] Papal succession must be reinterpreted to open the way for "a kind of Church presidency".[53]

I make just two comments: The Christian people are the "true Israel", but they are not, as it were, the people "of the flesh" under the Old Covenant, bound to a land and a "holy city". Rome is not the successor of Jerusalem. In essence she is not holier than the rest of the world redeemed by Christ. Neither is Christianity built on graves, not even on the graves of the apostles,[54] but on the fact of Jesus' Resurrection, a sign of which was the empty grave.

Secondly, the cardinalate as a continuation of the suburban offices of Rome has been, at least in part, a fiction for a long time. Nevertheless, it can be retained legitimately even with further internationalization and even in an altered form. In whatever manner the electoral college is established, its purpose definitely remains to elect the successor to

[52] Ibid., 271. We are faced here with a question of theological importance. Thinking in terms of the New Testament, could the ties of Peter's office to Rome be identical with or even similar to the tie of Israel to the "Holy Land" and the Temple of Jerusalem in the Old Testament? After Jesus' Resurrection, is it possible to speak of an area or a city that is holier than any other? From then on is not every country both holy and profane? We do not intend to question the (theologically inevitable) fact that the succession of Peter's primacy has been exercised by the Bishop of Rome; this is indisputable. But must Rome necessarily be the seat of the pope? It might indicate a relapse into Old Testament ways of thinking to suppose that the "exile" of a pope to Avignon or Savona or Gaeta is comparable to Israel's exile to Babylon or to the diaspora.

[53] Ibid., 273.

[54] Obviously, establishing a patriarchal seat because the grave of an apostle is there is not less questionable than the Roman claim, which seems more substantial in that both princes of the apostles were in Rome and most probably were martyred there. Moreover, the same problem holds for any of the patriarchal seats as it does for the Roman seat (mentioned earlier in footnote 52). It is conceivable that the geographical tie to the oldest patriarchal seats might become impossible at some time in the future, and, if succession is valued, the seat would have to be transferred to some other location.

Peter, who, up till now, has always been the Bishop of Rome. (Resignation is possible, as the case of Pope St. Celestine V shows, to whose grave in Fumone Paul VI made a pilgrimage.) Christianity is the religion of the last times. It awaits eagerly, not apathetically, the return of the Lord: "Maranatha", "Come, Lord Jesus". How then could we cling to an earthly city or to feudal traditions!

But Raffalt has a much more serious grievance. It is the socio-political course of the new papacy, which began with Leo XIII. Since his *Quadragesimo anno* and John XXIII's *Pacem in terris,* it has become more deeply involved in a dialogue with socialism and even with the doctrine of the Third Rome. In place of the emperor of the "Second Rome", Byzantium, and in place of the tsar, the actual head of the Russian Orthodox Church (with her hundred million members) is a Soviet "Minister of Church Affairs", whereas only one percent of the faithful owed allegiance to the Patriarch Athenagoras.

In his youth, Montini was already an enthusiastic antifascist. As a student, together with friends, he founded the polemical paper *La Fionda (The Battle Front).* Later he became chaplain of the antifascist Catholic student organization FUCI, which was abolished as a result of the concordat with Mussolini.[55] Montini, then in the Secretariate of State, was necessarily involved in collaboration on this concordat.

When he was elected in a two-day conclave as the successor of John XXIII and the leader of the ongoing Council, the cardinals knew that they had elected a progressive pope.[56] The view that unfolded before Paul VI's eyes was, in accordance with his view of catholicity, strictly universal. Within a smaller radius, he took the ecumenical movement for granted, but even what was central to this, his journey to Jerusalem, aimed at far broader horizons. The address he gave there echoed the famous thought of Louis Massignon: Abraham was the point of

---

[55] See Hieronymus, *Vatikan intern,* 230ff. The statement of Raffalt that Montini had no experience in pastoral practice is contradicted here.

[56] Raffalt, *Das Ende,* 23.

convergence of the three great monotheistic religions, Judaism, Christianity and Islam. Pope Paul was consistent in advising against a one-sided relationship with the new state of Israel and stressed continued consideration of the Arab world.[57]

But this openness would not have been complete without involving Moscow and Peking, with whom the Holy See untiringly sought rapport. At times when these superpowers were in conflict, competing for supremacy, the Holy See found itself in a quandary as to which side to take,[58] and not because Moscow held sway over the fate of the Orthodox Christians and Peking over a preconciliar Catholic Church (now separated from Rome) of three million(?), but because communism, as such, with its similarly "catholic" (i.e., total) claim is a worthy and even a necessary dialogue-partner with Rome.

Because of these seemingly utopian relationships, Paul VI had to distance himself from the radically anti-Soviet attitude of some individuals and groups in the Eastern world. Raffalt's strongest reproach echoes the bitter complaints of Cardinal Slipyi, the deceased Archbishop-Primate of the Ukraine, that the Holy See let down entire churches in the East that remained faithful to Rome. There were painful situations with Hungary, Czechoslovakia, Lithuania, Russia, China, Taiwan. . . . It also ignored the protest writings of Solzhenitsyn, while registering hardly noteworthy diplomatic successes which bound the "Goliaths" with whom "David" was negotiating to scarcely anything at all. Would a show of good will touch them, or was Paul VI perhaps—as he himself said—Don Quixote, and thus a danger to all of Christendom?

Raffalt does not fail to point out another of Paul VI's hoped-for dialogue-partners, the United Nations,[59] whose goal was the same as

[57] Ibid., 156, 184, 191, 195f., 201ff. About the political background of the meeting with the head of the Copts, see 214f.

[58] Ibid., 177, cf. 160.

[59] Ibid., 6of., 111f.

his, world peace, and which, even in its form, strives toward a catholicity of mankind. Of the UN, Paul VI said, "You are the bridge between peoples. . . . We are tempted to say that your character to some extent mirrors in the secular world what our own Catholic Church wants to be in the spiritual order: one and universal." "What he meant", continues Raffalt, "was to make the Church a mirror image of the United Nations. . . . In the end, the Church had to reform herself into a flexible, universally useful world organization, whose bid for cooperation the United Nations could no longer refuse",[60] and so Raffalt is back to the idea of "functionalizing the hierarchy". So much for Raffalt.

At this point I add a comment. It is not intended to canonize the ideas of any pope: possibilities are limited by the bounds of earthly contingencies, and—measured by the universality of the reign of Christ—all such ideas are questionable, whether they come from a Leo I or a Gregory I, Hildebrand or Innocent III, or from one of the popes of the final years of the Church-State. But just as a pope cannot and must not govern without realistic political prudence, neither can he govern without the firm foundation of that faith which conquers the world (1 Jn 5:4). Measured in terms of pure *Realpolitik,* this faith will always seem utopian, "foolish" (1 Cor 1:18, 21, 25, 27), quixotic. Is not "Don Quixote", together with Dostoyevsky's "Idiot"—beyond all that is time-bound in the symbol—the most powerful symbol of Christ in world literature? And when in the end these two fail, was not Jesus similarly a failure? Was success ever a measure of Christian life? Moreover, who knows? The network of coordinates that Paul VI tried to establish may yet prove valid at some future time.

Pope Paul is mockingly criticized for being a master of symbolic gestures (each journey's destination being a well-calculated chess-move to impress the masses), whose symbolism remains merely aesthetic and ineffective. They appear sentimental and without effect in

[60] Ibid., 111–12.

today's sober, technological world. This criticism is unjust because it is good that for once the highest expression of the Church, which from the world's point of view is impotent, is not Vatican politics but a personal communication in generally understandable images. It is a mistake, therefore, to expect an overly objectified, extremely cool expression of the Church's attitude from such an exponent. Being a Christian is hard. The Christian cannot copy Christ because he is unique, but he should nevertheless follow him. This will give him confidence to live the paradox of being a child as well as a mature adult, "remaining humble, while knowing that he is one who is sent",[61] and, yes, of being both father and brother.[62] Though Raffalt called these paradoxes "absurd", they are reported in all the biographies of the saints as accomplished facts and are represented to the ordinary Christian as worth striving for, with God's grace.

Naturally the true Christian—and particularly this Pope—is a puzzle to the psychoanalyst. As we have said, the key to understanding is buried deeply in the mystery of the Trinity and the Incarnation. Paul VI can always be criticized from both sides. His Credo gives the impression of being traditionalist. Some may smile at his romantic "father" idea: how can anyone feel that he is "the father of the whole family of mankind"? "Even when children do not know their father, nevertheless that is what he is. The knowledge of his fatherhood enables him to focus on each individual, making each person a whole world, even at a single encounter, or even if that person is an infant. The consciousness of being a father is the essence of being a pope."[63]

[61] Ibid., 18.

[62] Ibid., 14, 40.

[63] Ibid., 24. Other important texts are to be found in Jean Guitton, *Dialogues avec Paul VI* [The pope speaks] (Paris: Fayard, 1967). Some quotes from this are presented with malicious comments by Fritz Leist, *Der Gefangene des Vatikans*, 70–82. New positive insights into the nature of human and Christian fatherhood are conveyed by the work of Marcel Légaut (see below).

The complement is his Marian piety and his understanding of the motherhood of the Church; from both of these stems his emphasis on celibacy, his understanding of obedience in the Church and perhaps also his generosity which, for example, permits a totally dissident church like that of China to continue without expelling her from the father's house.

Otherwise, Pope Paul's policies appear progressive but unromantic: he can deal with human suffering, disappointment and loss in a seemingly detached way. It is alleged that a "mirror image of the UN" is his concept of the Church. The comparison is not poorly chosen, except that it does not take into consideration the *mysterium*-character of the *Catholica,* which is bound to be reflected wherever there are attempts to represent the universality of mankind, beyond all ethnic differences and without destroying them.

This by no means implies that Paul VI wanted to make a spiritual UN out of the Church—his distancing of the *Catholica* from the ecumenical World Council of Churches speaks clearly enough of that—but rather that the special interests of both catholicities, each in its sphere, are of great concern to each other. Actually, the pastoral constitution *Gaudium et spes, luctus et angor* says much the same.

Lastly, in Jerusalem Paul VI spoke about the "traitor Peter" and made a public confession of Christendom's sins, and particularly of the sins of the papacy. He is well aware of the burden of the past weighing on the Church. On the other hand, he cannot simply disavow that horizon of Catholicity that the popes (e.g., from Gregory VII to Boniface VIII) mapped out in a historically conditioned and unique way and permit it to shrink into petty provincialism. He sublimated the *suprema potestas* of the great medievals into the idea of a purely spiritual "loving fatherhood". That is why he dared to woo the love of his children even though without much return (to Raffalt's great displeasure; he finds this positively embarrassing).[64]

As we have said, it is not our intention to present the personal ideas of Paul VI as infallible; we merely want to clarify them somewhat. This cannot be done by psychological soul-searching but only by integrating them into the theological framework. We leave it an open question whether these ideas fit perfectly into the theological system

---

[64] To repeat: the intention of this book is not to discuss the present politics of the Vatican, even less to justify its actual projects. In regard to these, see the comprehensive work of W. A. Purdy, *The Church on the Move: The Characters and Policies of Pius XII and John XXIII* (New York: John Day Co., 1966); also see Peter Nichols, *The Politics of the Vatican* (London: Pall Mall Press, 1968). Nevertheless, a short reflection about these politics, particularly in regard to the Eastern bloc, should be added here. The thinking of Paul VI cannot simply be described as strongly Petrine; he thinks also in a Pauline, missionary and universalistic way. ("Perhaps in Montini's manner of relating the Petrine and Pauline principles we may discover the very key to his pontificate": David A. Seeber, *Paul, Papst im Widerstreit* (Freiburg im Breisgau: Herder, 1971), 40–41. Moreover, as mentioned before, Paul VI's thinking is also Marian; but we may ask whether this Marian thinking did not receive a strong impetus from Fatima, where, allegedly, in a private revelation, the "conversion of Russia" was foretold. If this were so, then the Marian aspect (as we understand it) is quite limited, in a manner that brings it into serious and perhaps insupportable conflict with the (Pauline?) diplomacy that is one of the pope's functions. Is it at all possible to place "politics" in the service of "mysticism"—two categories which for Péguy imply irreconcilable attitudes? Concretely: can someone at the same time claim universal "mystical fatherhood" when, in the name of political wisdom, having in mind the eventual well-being of future generations, he must close his ears to the cries and bloody tears of oppressed Catholic people and their tortured priests, who thus see themselves orphaned, compelled to seek refuge in God alone and in the "Church of the saints"? Perhaps this is simply the contemporary tragedy of the Petrine office (about which Reinhold Schneider knew so much), again showing its interior limitations and the obvious necessity of taking its proper place in the christological constellation, as we shall show it. Without challenging the fatherly character of the Catholic office (following Paul, cf. 1 Cor 4:5 and Gal 4:19), this must ultimately humble itself before the powerful command of the Lord: "And call no man father on earth, for you have one Father, who is in heaven" (Mt 23:9).

of coordinates that will be developed in the second and third parts of this book, or whether, perhaps—though in a very spiritual manner—they evince a claim for totality that goes beyond what is assigned to the office of the Shepherd. We do not presume to give a positive or negative answer to this question. The history of this recent papacy is not yet closed; the last word has not been said.

This brief reply to Raffalt's charges is only incidentally included here, by way of anticipation of what follows. The subject of this first part is the phenomenon of the (present) anti-Roman attitude within the Catholic Church. It has grown more intense and is at least as strong as it was in the last century, but there is something new in that the attack is being launched simultaneously from both the progressive and the conservative sides. Never before has the circle closed as it has today. We shall consider the strange unity manifested in this refusal, and in evaluating it we shall arrive at our own thesis.

The Refusal

1. *The Way Back*

The history of the Church appears to have reached a cul-de-sac with Vatican I at the latest. Such a display of naked authority by the pope—an authority neither influenced nor shielded nor protected by a liberal surrounding—seemed intolerable in a period that increasingly thought of itself as mankind's "age of freedom". Moreover, the method by which this authority has been customarily manifested (essentially unchanged since the Middle Ages) in addition to the events associated with Modernism, the triumph of Thomism, the persecution of the so-called *nouvelle théologie* even after Vatican I—possibly as a consequence of that Council—all these things form a relentless crescendo. Some day it will finally become unbearable to listen to, and people will cry, "Enough! Stop it!"

What is so odd is not only that this finale cannot be pinpointed historically but that there were always people who gave voice to such a cry, so it is obviously not related to its intensity but to the thing itself, the reality of the papacy. Others will not grasp what is happening in any case, particularly if their perspective is that of the comparative history of religions. We must disregard here any psychological extenuating circumstances for those who find the claims of the papacy intolerable, no matter how grave these grievances may be from a human or a Christian point of view, since they concern the *how* of the Christian exercise of authority. About this much could be said, and it would not be easy to arrive at a consensus, because *how* the divine or

God-given authority is expressed — as seen in the Bible — can appear in extreme instances hard, ruthless, exorbitantly demanding and even cruel. This important question, namely, how God himself gave orders to the patriarchs, to Moses, the judges, the kings and the prophets, cannot be dealt with here. Neither can we discuss in detail how the prophets and John the Baptist rendered judgments in God's name, nor how Jesus, the Suffering Servant, is ruthlessly commanded and himself commands ruthlessly; nor can we examine the incisive and incontrovertible sharpness with which Paul gives his directives nor the finality with which even John pronounces a Yes or No, a "left" and a "right".

Everyone knows how Jesus dealt with Peter, and if by chance this is taken simply as a pedagogical method of dealing with a sinner who has to do a lot of quick relearning, we would do well to remember how Jesus spoke to his Mother, who was not a sinner. It is as if the heedless disobedience of Adam and Eve could be balanced only by a similarly heedless demand of obedience. Confronted by it, a man may cry out or fall silent, he may cringe or writhe like Elijah (who could go no further) or Jeremiah (who refused to go) or like Jesus on the Mount of Olives before he succeeded in giving a Yes to God's command; he does this, not in strength, but in extreme weakness, as in a dying breath; he utters this Yes with the apex of his soul, while everything in him cries No. . . .

One could contend that this kind of commanding and obeying is limited to the realm of the Bible; where it occurs later it takes place directly between God and the soul, without mediation by human authority. In an extreme instance, a man might give an unconditional command in the name of God but only on the basis of a personal authority accepted by the disciple who has entrusted himself freely to his master, as in the tradition of the *pater pneumatikos* in the Eastern Church (from the Desert Fathers, through the Byzantine monks to the *startsy*). Here there is a personal relationship, well founded in human nature; the one who obeys can review, judge, ratify or renounce this relationship. Hence, his judgment is definitely part of his obedience. For example, he is free to seek a *pater pneumatikos* until he finds one who is congenial. Thus he is obeying his own judgment, at least partly, even when something difficult or unexpected is commanded.

However, the authority given by Christ to Peter among the Twelve exceeds this type of relationship, first of all because it is not personal but social and universal, affecting the entire flock. Once in a while the shepherd might leave the flock temporarily to go in person after a lost sheep bleating in the dark. But "abandoning the flock" is not within the shepherd's normal assignment. Therefore, Peter has the final responsibility for the Church he tends, and the individual obeys not only as a private individual but also as a more-or-less anonymous member of the flock. Moreover, the shepherd's task also entails "binding and loosing", "opening and closing", objective functions that do not depend on the particular human or Christian qualities of the one who holds the key.

To speak in terms of Church history, this is the decisive step beyond Donatism that Augustine dared to take. As desirable as it would be that the holder of supreme Church authority be a spirit-filled saint, it is neither Peter nor Judas who baptizes but Christ. This holds not only for sacramental acts but also, within the office given to Peter, for jurisdiction, as "binding and loosing" and "the keys" clearly symbolize. The flock follows simply because Peter commands or goes ahead: "Simon Peter said to them, 'I am going fishing'. They said to him, 'We will go with you'" (Jn 21:3).

Naturally there are difficulties here because in Scripture commands are for the most part delivered personally, and that is how it should be; but there are some naked commands too. Not only does God himself command what seems nonsensical or inhuman (Hos 1:2–10; Ezek 4:1–17; 5:1–17; 12:1–6; 24:15–17), but men give commands in God's name without any other credentials than his mandate (Amos 7:14–17). Most prophets' commissions are of this kind. Anyhow, what identification does the one personally chosen have? Is commanding in resonant tones of conviction or being clothed in goatskin and eating locusts a mark of accreditation?

In the person of Peter—as the head of the Twelve, in whom their real authority receives its final cogency—real biblical authority is to be addressed to the faithful of all times, including those living today. This seems surprising, unlikely and shocking, particularly to our contemporaries, since "with the death of the last apostle" the period of biblical revelation is considered "closed". It is an intrusion into the realm of personal freedom; it manifests a relapse from the status of being God's children to the constraints of being servants (—but what about the "Suffering Servant"!—), as Newman, when still an Anglican, complained of Romanism. And the New Testament Christian is a born Donatist: he immediately calls for personal credentials from anyone who comes with demands that are not absolutely self-evident. How great a triumph it is, then, to be able to point to the scandal-filled history of the papacy, which seems to nullify a priori any demand that it might make today.

Should not the papacy do penance for a thousand years or two before daring to present any new demands in the name of Christ? A few indistinctly murmured words of apology are not enough. Christendom has the right to perceive at least a glimmer of Christ's personal authority in the individual who issues demands in his name. Did not Christendom have to cover its eyes for centuries to avoid seeing who was in command and what was going on in the Holy City, whence came, instead of holy directives, anathemas, interdicts (often for purely secular gain) and shocking oppression?

A secularized Rome that continues to exercise spiritual authority in a worldly manner—using legitimate "spiritual weapons" together with forbidden weapons of the "flesh" (2 Cor 10:4) and trying to justify these by more and more novel falsifications (including the theory of the "two swords")—elicits reactions ranging from serious concern as to how the "head" might be reformed to popular indignation or the simple refusal of obedience, often in the name of the gospel.

63

Church history is filled with manifold variations on this theme, inevitably ending in the call, "Enough of Rome!", so much so that it becomes a genuine *theologumenon*. But in the midst of all the uproar the echo of another word is heard: "We do not want this man to reign over us" (Lk 19:14). "This man"—for we know the Scriptures and how our God manifests himself—identifies himself with God: "Who do you claim to be?" (Jn 8:53).

We do not intend to present the historical details of this uproar; it would entail covering every century and all phases of the Catholic Church's history. What interests us is the curious unanimity of quite diverse movements: they all seem to agree in this one thing. What could be more disparate, for example, than the spirit of Jansenism and that of the Enlightenment? Yet they joined forces in Febronianism, and also at the Council of Pistoia, on the grounds of their joint No to Rome. The voices sound in such confusion that it is hard to distinguish them: the most diverse protests and counterproposals cannot be entirely separated. (The classification that we here suggest is merely tentative.)

The *leitmotif* throughout is that of setting limits within which the Roman authority may be legitimately, or at least tolerably, exercised. Beyond this point, in conscience, one must say No.

Such protests began already at the time of the early popes. Until Victor, says Artemon (about 250), the papacy was intact. But from Zephyrinus on, he says, this changed.[1] The Montanists, together with Tertullian, but also Hippolytus (and to a certain extent Cyprian), think according to this same pattern. The anti-Roman attitude likes to look traditionalist.[2] People always maintain that things were different in earlier times. The art is to pinpoint the time and place of the change. Marcion does not shrink from putting this right in the middle

[1] Anonymous author cited by Eusebius, *Ecclesiastical History,* 5:28, 3.

[2] See Gustave Bardy, *La Théologie de l'Église, de saint Irénée au concile de Nićee* (Paris: Cerf, 1947), chap. 1.

of the New Testament. He follows Paul, but only the pure, unadulterated Paul. Marcion believes that only he knows how to rescue this Paul from the accretions.

a. A Pope, but Not This One

In most instances, complaints do not begin with charges against the pope's person but against his retinue: it is the cardinals, the curia who are all at fault. Ever since the curia was established as a large administrative body, complaints have not ceased. They began in the Middle Ages: freed from imperial power in the struggle over investitures, the Church became subject to a much harsher slavery under the Roman curia. In the middle of the twelfth century all spiritual and secular literature was up in arms: theologians, historians, poets "in general do not attack the power nor the rights of the pope but aim a torrent of sharp words and bitter complaints . . . at the corruption of the clergy by the curia, at the simony of a 'spiritual' court in which each stroke of a pen, each document, is weighed in gold and where benefices, dispensations, permissions, absolutions, indulgences and privileges are bought like goods from a merchant".[3]

Döllinger, who writes these lines, continues with the frightening predictions and threats of St. Hildegard and St. Brigid against the Roman abuses and later quotes from St. Catherine's appeal to Gregory XI the statement that she smelled the stink of infernal depravity in the Roman curia. The Pope responded that she had only been there a few days. She replied: "I am bound to say that I smelled the stink of the

---

[3] Ignatz Döllinger, *Das Papsttum,* a revision by J. Friedrich, 1892, *Janus, Der Papst und das Konzil,* 105. On the development of the curia, see: C. Bauer, "Die Epochen der Papstfinanz", in *Historische Zeitschrift* 138 (1928): 457–503; K. Jordan, "Die Entstehung der römischen Kurie", in *Zeitschrift der Savignystiftung für Rechtsgesch. Kan.* pt. 28 (1939): 97–152.

sins which flourish in the papal court while I was still at home in my own town more sharply than those who daily commit them."[4]

The reform Councils of Constance and Basel had the reform of the curia primarily in mind, but even in the first weeks of Martin V's reign (he was elected after the settlement of the Great Schism) the abuses reappeared. Most of the zealous popes tried to reform the curia, but none succeeded to the extent he had hoped for. The curia is even larger today, and unless the central administration of the Church is to be abolished, it remains an indispensable department that, today, cannot be accused of the abuses common in the Middle Ages. However, it cannot claim, as a whole, the charism of holiness or infallibility. It is part of the *ecclesia mixta,* and only the naive would expect it to be the model of a "pure church". Lamennais was an innocent of that kind. In 1832 he said that the pope was all right, but his entourage was insufferable; shortly after that he came to the conclusion that one could not pry the pope loose from his surroundings. Hence he began to distinguish between Gregory XVI the man (who could be seduced by Metternich) and Pope Gregory (who was infallible). Since this did not work out, he simply denounced the entire Roman claim as unjustified.[5] Of course, this had already been the Enlightenment's point of view,

---

[4] Ibid., 179.

[5] "The Pope is pious and well-intentioned; but being a stranger to the world he is not fully aware of the state of the Church and the state of the world and the state of society. Immobilized by the secrecy that surrounds him with darkness, he weeps and prays." To the Countess de Senfft, February 10, 1832, in *Correspondence générale,* ed. Louis le Guillou, vol. 5 (Paris: A. Colin, 1974): 87. Cf. Louis le Guillou, *L'Évolution de la pensée religieuse de Félicité de Lamennais* (Paris: A. Colin, 1966), 157, cf. 178–79. Under the pretext that the pope has authority over the spiritual but not over the temporal, Lamennais leaves the priesthood to devote himself to politics: here the pope can no longer tell him what to do. In the same letter we read: "Twenty years more of this situation, and Catholicism will be dead. God will save it through the people: what do I care about the rest? My politics is the triumph of Christ; my legitimacy is the law; my homeland is the human race which he has ransomed by his blood."

and Tyrrell, later, in *The Church and the Future* (1903), said hardly anything different.

"The papacy but not this pope" is a further step. Beginning with Gerson, Gallicanism attempted this step (with the best of intentions, theologically) by trying to differentiate between the *sedes,* which is incorruptible, and the *sedens,* who is not. This approach was mistaken and impracticable from the outset, as de Maistre pointed out.[6] Gasser, in his final address at Vatican I, emphasized that infallibility is not a prerogative of an *abstract* papacy but of the pope actually reigning.[7] Bossuet, despite his sincere identification with the Church, forever wavered in his position regarding the papacy, measuring with "two measures and two weights"[8] and taking shelter under similarly useless distinctions which simultaneously pledge obedience and refuse it. Moreover, there is the whole Gallican issue of *acceptation* (*"toujours des énigmes!"* remarks de Maistre),[9] which plays on the ambiguity of being "in one accord" with the spirit of the Church *communio,* on the one

---

[6] Joseph de Maistre, *Du pape* [The pope], *Oeuvres complètes,* vol. 2 (Lyons: Vitte et Perrussel, 1884): 82, 85, 87.

[7] J. P. Torrell, "L'Infaillibilité pontificale est-elle un privilège 'personnel'?", *Révue des sciences philosophiques et théologiques* (1961), 229–45. A particularly outstanding example of anticurialism is that of the Servite, Paolo Sarpi (1552–1623), the influential counselor of the Republic of Venice in its struggle against the pope and the curia. He ignored his summons to Rome and the excommunication that followed his nonappearance just as the Serenissima [the Republic of Venice] did the interdict imposed on it. An unsuccessful attempt to murder him, allegedly engineered by the Vatican, only enhanced his fame. His intended funeral became a triumphal procession. Correspondence between him and Bellarmine about the authority of the papacy and the curia shows him unyielding. Nevertheless, he is determined to remain a Catholic so as to help undermine the papal and curial system. He certainly sympathized with Protestantism, not as a dogmatic system, but as a means of reforming the Catholic Church, which the advocates of Conciliarism as well as many humanists had sought.

[8] A. G. Martimort, *Le Gallicanisme de Bossuet* (Paris: Cerf, 1953), 588ff.

[9] De Maistre, *Du pape,* 142.

hand, and simply obeying the directives of superiors on the other. Y. Congar has written on what is justified and what is not in this approach.[10] The reservations of Gallicanism do not at first touch the *communio.* Rather, they wish to qualify every papal decision, be it by an appeal to a council or by a stipulation that the directives must be accepted by the whole Church (bishops and flock) to be valid.

Another kind of stipulation is applied by the Jansenists, who support papal authority as long as it does not clash with a higher forum, e.g., the authority of St. Augustine, the authentic interpreter of the Pauline doctrine of justification. There were endless quarrels over the bull *Unigenitus,* about its range, its interpretation and about the earlier distinctions made by the Jansenists between the *quaestio facti* and *juris.* (The Pope condemned the statements of Baius or Jansenius, but did he condemn them in the sense in which the authors meant them? This, it was thought, would have gone beyond his competence.) All these were attempts to avoid an unappealable final decision by the existing papal authority. Surely conscience is the final authority of an individual's moral behavior, but when a community within the Catholic Church refers to a dictate of its collective conscience against a final papal decision, it has already lost the sense of the Church *communio.* (Some present integralist groups should take note of this.) We have already noted that the right wing could actually unite with the left wing—as Jansenism did with the Enlightenment of the Emperor Joseph II—in the same anti-Roman front.

Affirming the papacy while simultaneously disavowing the pope is nowhere more notable than in the *Church of Utrecht,*[11] which issued from the Jansenist upheaval. The Dutch clerics, educated in Paris and Louvain, were taught mostly Augustinian theology. Many Jansenists

[10] Yves Congar, "Reception as an Ecclesial Reality", in *Concilium,* vol. 77, ed. Alberigo Weiler (New York: Herder and Herder, 1972), 43–68.

[11] For a short and clear overview, see V. Conzemius, *Katholizismus ohne Rom* (Zurich: Benziger, 1969), 45–55.

fled to Holland because they could not in conscience agree with the sentencing of Jansenius. Codde, the Archbishop of Utrecht who was accused in Rome of Jansenism, refused—backed by Quesnel—to sign the anti-Jansenist declaration of Alexander VII and was suspended. Thereupon the Chapter of Utrecht took the matter into its own hands and elected a bishop, who was consecrated by Dominicus Varlet (a missionary bishop sympathetic to Jansenism) but was not, of course, recognized by Rome.

Nevertheless, Utrecht did not want to break away from Rome. In 1763 a provincial council was held and in its declarations said: "The Lord assigned primacy to St. Peter over the other apostles. The Bishop of Rome, as a worthy successor, exercises primacy by divine right over the other bishops. This primacy is not merely a matter of honor but also a primacy of supreme authority." To the pope is "entrusted the care of the whole Church". The schismatic character of the Eastern Church, separated from Rome, was emphasized. This was meant as a serious attempt to reestablish relations with Rome but was frustrated by intrigues, and Clement XIII declared the Council of Utrecht invalid.

After Vatican I, the first Old Catholic bishop to be consecrated in Utrecht was J. H. Reinkens in 1873, and the local church was incorporated into the wider context of the Old Catholic Church. In 1889 the other Western churches that were separated from Rome joined the "Union of Utrecht". The old Church of Utrecht remained the most conservative among them.

The separation of the Church of Utrecht happened at a time when the central leadership of the Church was already ecclesiologically established but its "infallibility" not yet defined. Forming the Old Catholic Church expressed a conscious No to Vatican I, and therefore its theological position is rather distinct, leading to a view which we shall discuss further in the next section. It desires to find a balance between fully accepting the primacy instituted by Christ and denying the legitimacy of its more recent developments. Döllinger, who gave

69

the impetus to the founding of the Old Catholic Church but never joined it, placed (in 1896, his middle years) the limit of the papacy's normal development in the ninth century: "After that ... a more artificial than natural, and a more pathological than healthy, development from the primacy to the papacy took place, a change rather than a development, that caused the break-up of the previously unified Church into three hostile, separate church bodies."[12] With this, the model of the "branch theory", or the so-called ecclesiological "classicism", was formulated.[13]

b. A Papacy As It Was Before

Whenever the ideal model of the Church is projected into the past, usually into the times of unbroken unity, any likelihood of giving perfect obedience to a contemporary authority vanishes because the episcopacy will beware of claiming for itself the authority model for which Rome is being censured. This is what happened in the Eastern Church, in Anglicanism and in Old Catholicism. Calvin's personal manner of church leadership found no followers. But this did not seem necessary because in the "classical" period the great ecumenical councils that determined the norms of orthodoxy were called together

[12] Döllinger, *Das Papsttum,* preface, xiii.

[13] At this point one could trace a long history of concrete resistance to papal directives (within the context of a fundamental obedience), including those directives that are obviously doubtful because they rest on purely worldly claims. One would then encounter the famous *"filialiter et oboedienter non oboedio, contradico et rebello"* of Robert Grosseteste, who was a zealous advocate of papal authority but in that particular case did not find that there was the requisite basis for all papal mandates, namely, conformity with "the doctrine of the apostles and of Our Lord Jesus Christ" (Letter 128, ed. H. R. Luard, Roll Series [1861], 436–37); and finally one would arrive at the insulting letter of Bishop Firmilian of Caesarea to Pope Stephen, in which the Pope is called "insolent", "arrogant", "mischievous" and "childish"; his opinion about the baptism of heretics is thought of as absurd and the Pope obviously crazy. (Text in Bardy, *La théologie de l'Église,* 205–6.)

by the emperor and not by the pope. Sanction from Rome was valued as a sign of final acceptance, a seal of unity, rather than an indispensable condition of the decision's validity. With great oversimplification, with Friedrich Heiler, one could draw a contrast between this and later periods: "Old ecclesial autonomy versus papal centralism".[14] Still, Heiler recognizes the evangelical foundation of a "primacy with authoritative leadership",[15] but this was to be an honorary authority, an office of teaching, supervision and leadership, and not a "real universal, jurisdictional primacy". This latter began to develop in the confusion resulting from the mass migration of peoples. The whole subsequent central legal system can be legitimized only as *jure humano.* Some of it is a development from the classical period, and some of it is distortion. Heiler hopes with Joachim of Fiore that it is still possible to have a "total change in the papal institution" that will yield a *papa angelicus.* And one does not necessarily have to disagree with Heiler when he measures the pope's way of exercising authority against the paradox of Jesus Christ—authority in humility—as long as it is clear that humility is not the same as renouncing authority (as, for example, when Celestine V shrank from the burden of responsibility).

We do not have to enter here into discussion of the various forms of ecclesiological classicism. It is sufficient to know that according to this point of view it is not a person but a general consensus—citing the first five councils in which, allegedly, all that is essential was formulated—that determines the canon of orthodoxy and the basis for all future decisions. The *Eastern Church,* which never explicitly acknowledged Rome's jurisdictional primacy, merely completed a long overdue step of separation when Photius rejected, not the Roman primacy as such, but Rome's claim to be the highest Church authority, with the power

---

[14] Friedrich Heiler, *Altkirchliche Autonomie und päpstliches Zentralismus.* This book is pt. 1, vol. 2 of *Die katholische Kirche des Ostens und Westens* (Munich: Reinhardt, 1941).

[15] Ibid., 374.

to interfere in disciplinary and legal concerns of other patriarchates,[16] instead of a court of appeal or arbitrator who is called upon only occasionally.

If one looks at this difference, which in itself is small, and disregards the accumulated hostile emotions, one could well imagine that an ecumenical dialogue could take place. But for us this is not the determining factor. We are concerned here with the loss of the highest forum, the one that effectively embodies christological obedience.

Such a forum is lacking in *Anglicanism* too, and all of Newman's struggles are related to this absence. The theologians of the Caroline era, primarily John Pearson, accepted the consensus of the Fathers of the first councils as the only valid authority for the Anglican Church. This, for them, was the authentic exegesis of the revelation recorded in Scripture, because the Church at that time was still united both in faith and in love. Bishop George Bull developed this doctrine, which was the starting point for the young Newman. The impossibility of employing criteria of epochs far in the past in the formulation of present decisions makes this ecclesiology seem romantic and encourages low-church, congregationalist and, eventually, "latitudinarian" (liberal) movements.

Seen in the light of day, the theology of the *slavophiles,* led by Chomjakov, seems no less romantic. They emphasize unity of faith and thought (*sobornost*) as the criterion, when in fact dissension prevails between the national churches, and patriarchs are without effective authority. (Soloviev's criticism is appropriate here.)

Protestant attempts to draw a line of demarcation between legitimate and corrupt Church leadership is of no greater assistance. Sohm's distinction between a charismatic-sacramental and a juridical leadership,

---

[16] Endre von Ivánka, *Rhomäerreich und Gottesvolk* (Freiburg im Breisgau: Verlag Karl Alber, 1968), 80. For more exact details see François Dvornik, *Le Schisme de Photius, histoire et légende* (Paris: Cerf, 1968). On the present situation, see Afanassieff, et al., *La Primauté de Pierre dans l'Église orthodoxe* (Zurich: EVZ–Verlag, 1961).

which latter supposedly won the upper hand in the second millennium, is untenable. The primacy of Rome (attested by Irenaeus and implied by Ignatius of Antioch) and the particular office of the bishop (so clearly spoken of by Ignatius and by Pope Clement) provoked a bitter struggle, suggesting that the period of "early Catholicism" existed only in the first century. The Pastoral Letters are already affected by this struggle, as well as large parts of the Pauline corpus. One has to manipulate the text so arbitrarily to find a "canon within the canon" that even the most diminished classicism destroys itself, and one is left with Bultmann's dualism, which cannot be put into practice in terms of any concrete, contemporary church: the obedience of faith may be due to God (somewhat as in Islam), but it has no deep connection with the Jesus-event, and even less with ecclesial office. Just as in Orthodoxy and Anglicanism the point of reference was projected into the past and is comprehensible there only as a social consensus, so in the radical developments of Protestantism the demand for obedience can be made only by God; by the Holy Spirit who inspires the Church but is never incarnated in any institution.

It would be simplistic and unjust to close this "destructive" overview of Church history without recognizing the longing of many Catholics to find the—if not lost, then long-neglected—model of primitive Church unity in the centralized system of the last century. In the eighteenth century the expression *ultramontanism* came into being, first as an insult, then, adopted by Lamennais' circle, as an antinationalist slogan. Soon again, however, noticeably in the German *Kulturkampf,* it regained its original, disparaging meaning. In the overheated, nearly hysterical atmosphere of the years before and after Vatican I, a sober position regarding the question of a Catholic's obligations toward the pope was rarely, if at all, possible.[17]

Some German Catholics felt the danger of basing theology, not to

---

[17] Cf. K. Buchheim, *Ultramontanismus und Demokratie. Der Weg der deutschen Katholiken im 19. Jahrhundert* (Munich: n.p., 1963).

mention a mode of life, exclusively on the last council. They were by no means Modernists but included such diverse individuals as the "liberal Catholic" Albert Erhard and the antipolitical "religious Catholic" Franz Xaver Kraus. Even though the latter was labeled as having an "anti-Roman complex" or paranoia, just as much as some "Modernists" (and with more reason), and though his judgments are one-sided or simply false (for example, with regard to Leo XIII), it is still worth listening to his attempt to define ultramontanism:

> 1. Ultramontane is he who puts the concept of the Church above that of religion. 2. Ultramontane is he who confuses the pope with the Church. 3. Ultramontane is he who believes that the kingdom of God is of this world and that—as the medieval curialists maintained—the power of the keys given to Peter includes secular jurisdiction over princes and nations. 4. Ultramontane is he who thinks that religious conviction can be coerced by world power or can be destroyed by it. 5. Ultramontane is he who is always ready to sacrifice a clear command of his own conscience to an edict of a foreign authority.[18]

Who would not heartily agree with each of these points, particularly when the word "foreign" (authority) is used in its fullest sense? Newman thought and spoke no differently, and neither did Guardini, who liked to quote Kraus. Today "ultramontanism" in the sense defined above is found only in small splinter groups. Vatican II basically fulfilled the demands and longings for the center to be integrated into the periphery, fusing together the top and the bottom. Nevertheless, until this integration has become fully alive and expressed in practice, until it becomes second nature, the road may still be a long one.

---

[18] F. X. Kraus, *Tagebücher,* ed. H. Schiel (Cologne: Bachem, 1957), xviii. Cf. H. Raab, "Zur Geschichte und Bedeutung des Schlagwortes 'ultramontan' im 18. und 19. Jahrhundert", *Historisches Jahrbuch der Görres-Gesellschaft* 81 (1962): 159–73.

c. Peter, but No Pope

The third kind of refusal stems from an interpretation of the New Testament that holds that the full authority of apostleship is historically unique; it is the founding charism, whereas the presbyters and bishops appointed by the apostles are far below them in rank and authority. The focus has radically shifted from the authority of the successors of the apostles—the bishops, and among them, at the center, Peter's successor—to the apostles who were invested with full authority by Christ. This is a common thesis of Protestantism that can be presented with manifold nuances. One may even doubt the authorization of the Twelve by Jesus or—in radically eschatological schools of thought—interpret the establishment of this group by Jesus only in view of the anticipated apocalyptic coming of the kingdom and therefore with no intention of establishing succession.[19] On this view it was Luke's reinterpretation of the present as being "the middle of time" rather than "the end of time" that actually brought about a continuation of the Church structure as well as its theological problems.[20] One might share Oscar Cullmann's opinion that "he who proceeds without prejudice, on the basis of exegesis . . . cannot seriously conclude that Jesus here (in the scene in Matthew's Gospel where he hands over the keys to Peter) had successors of Peter in mind." Moreover, "in the entire New Testament, the apostolic function is always unique, christologically possible only at the beginning of the building of the edifice."[21] For Cullmann, the Catholic inference of succession appears to be a misunderstanding of the fundamental posi-

---

[19] Overbeck, Loisy, A. Schweitzer and his school.

[20] Hans Conzelmann, *Die Mitte der Zeit* [The theology of St. Luke], 5th ed., (Tübingen: J. C. B. Mohr, 1964). "Eschatology as an imminent hope belonging to the present cannot by its very nature be handed down by tradition", 89.

[21] Oscar Cullmann, *Petrus. Jünger–Apostel–Martyrer* [Peter: disciple–apostle–martyr], 2d. ed. (Zurich: Zwingliverlag, 1952), 238f., 240.

tion of all New Testament thought. "In opposition to Hellenism, it is characteristic of the thinking of Jesus, as of all biblical thinking, that the continuous has its roots in events that are unique."[22] That, of course, is true, but not in such a one-sided way that (as Hegel says), when we look back to an ever more remote historical past, its actual significance becomes more and more lost; and it certainly does not mean that the living person, capable of making decisions, is replaced by the writings (considered to be fully authoritative equivalents) left behind by the founding generation. This substitution of *sola scriptura* for living authority was an expression of the vehement opposition to the actual situation of papal authority in the Middle Ages. This tendency was already present in the poverty movements and, in a more moderate form, in the Catholic reform movements that held up the idea of the *vita apostolica* to the lifestyle of the decadent contemporary clergy. This thesis is a secondary derivative of the ongoing polemics. To restrict the Lord's words to Peter, cited by Luke, "And when you have turned again, strengthen your brethren" (Lk 22:32), to the situation of the apostles immediately after the Resurrection seems highly artificial.[23]

Already Thomas Aquinas felt prompted to refute the idea of a purely personal transmission of authority by pointing out that Jesus' Church had to endure until the end of time and therefore had to be endowed by him with a structure and not merely with a foundation.[24] Aquinas wrote this to refute Joachim of Fiore and all the extreme spiritualists who considered any structure for the hoped-for spiritual Church—apart from the monastic structure—inappropriate.

[22] Ibid., 243.

[23] "Obviously, the words refer only to Peter personally" (Döllinger, *Das Papsttum*, 14). It is quite possible that Pope Agatho was the first to claim them for the primacy. Also, as is well known, it was not until the third century that the popes interpreted Matthew 16:18 as applying to the primacy. So much the better: papal primacy is thus seen to have existed and grown organically without theological reliance on scriptural proof-texts.

[24] *Summa contra Gentiles*, 4, 76.

Jean-Jacques von Allmen, meditating upon Luke 22, notes that Jesus spoke to Peter "in the context of the Eucharist". In other words, "in the context of what Jesus wanted to remain until his return". Allmen saw that the consequence of this insight was that the unity of the individual churches is to be understood on the model of the unity of the apostles, and, hence, the concept of the Roman primacy appears to be "well founded". Perhaps, continues Allmen, "the apprehension that all of us Reformed theologians sense when we realize that we cannot circumvent the problem of apostolic succession comes from our own conscious or unconscious feeling that if there is an apostolic succession, then there is without doubt a specific Petrine succession within this succession."[25]

Thus, for all those who adhere to a real (sacramental) succession — Orthodox, Anglicans, Old Catholics — the primacy of Peter remains a goad against which they are always trying to kick. The attempt to soften it into an "honorary primacy" is totally alien within the context of a Church that knows no other honor than that of the "last place", of service rendered without thanks. This interpretation derives from the ideology of the Byzantine Empire. (We have already mentioned that Photius himself saw in the Roman "preeminence" a legal right that should be exercised when requested and should never be a spontaneous reaction.) If there is any primacy, it is modeled on Peter's primacy within the college of the apostles; even if there were shown to be twelve patriarchal sees in apostolic succession, it would not

[25] See Jean-Jacques von Allmen, *Irenikon* (1970), quoted by Henri de Lubac in *Les Églises particulières* (Paris: Aubier-Montaigne, 1971), 106–7. An important point has to be added: the moment of the *parousia* is near for Jesus in a meaning unique to him; this meaning was expressed in the consciousness of the disciples, not identically but analogically, in the awareness of a future that had already been determined. Cf. my essay, *Zuerst Gottes Reich, Zwei Skizzen zur biblischen Naherwartung* (Benziger, 1966). If we take this literally, Jesus' announcement of the nearness (which we understand analogically) must seem a contradiction to his establishment of an apostolic succession.

77

change anything. The only real question is the *manner* in which the primacy of jurisdiction is exercised in actual Christian practice. The Eastern Church may be critical of this, but she should not forget that Pope Clement's exhortation—issued with truly ecclesial *agape* at the time of his intervention at Corinth—was far more than a gentle reminder of one of Christ's commandments: the function of government demands authority, even in Christian love, and this presupposes obedience.

There is no middle position here. Radical Protestantism well understood this, both when it rejected the papal claim as "anti-Christian" and when it joined forces with those who demanded "freedom from Rome". In a narrower sense, this was a movement in answer to the *Kulturkampf,* which was sustained primarily by the Evangelical Alliance and the *Gustav-Adolf-Verein.* In Austria and Southern Germany considerable effort and money were expended to induce Catholics to desert Rome,[26] which produced only modest results. Later its place was taken by a nazi, anti-Roman propaganda (from Chamberlain to Rosenberg and Ludendorff).

For our purposes it is important to point out that the radical, theologically founded negation of the Roman claim to leadership, as it must necessarily arise in Protestantism, is not essentially different from the polemics of those churches that agree with Rome in most theological principles but are all the more stubborn regarding specific points of disagreement. Neither do these polemics differ much from those found in Catholic circles which, while they recognize to a certain extent the supremacy of Rome, bristle all the more against the manner in which authority is exercised by the successors of Peter. The office of Peter seems to hold the same kind of negative fascination for all of them.

---

[26] Bibliography in *Lexikon für Theologie und Kirche,* 2d ed., vol. 6 (Algermissen); cf. "Evangelischer Bund", in *Die Religion in Geschichte und Gegenwart,* 3d ed., 2:789ff.

2. *The Unity of Negation*

In fact, what else remains common to the churches separated from Rome and dispersed in all directions but the rejection of the center's rightly or wrongly assumed claims of God-given authority, claims that keep the No of the dissidents alive and embittered? *Pascal* said: "The pope is the number one. Who else is universally known? Who else is acknowledged by all, able to influence the whole body because through him runs the main artery that nourishes it? How easy it was to let this degenerate into tyranny! That is why Jesus Christ laid down this precept: *Vos autem non sic.*"[27] Lamennais, utterly exasperated by this Roman claim, retorted: "I will subscribe to everything; not only to what is asked of me now but to whatever may be asked, even the declaration that the pope is God, the great God of heaven and earth, who alone is to be adored!"[28]

The abandoned center can never be a matter of indifference, something left aside; rather, if one wants to remain a Christian, it is the stumbling block that hinders one from being a Christian—it is the Antichrist. Luther was certainly not the first (—more like the last—) to ascribe this role to the pope; the Greeks did it long before him, as well as the Albigensians in the Middle Ages, not to mention Frederick II and those distant pupils of Joachim who unjustly claimed to base themselves on his teachings. Then there was the letter from Lucifer to the Pope in Avignon, which circulated in 1351, addressed to "his Vicar on earth", in which the Prince of Darkness thanks him and all his cardinals and prelates for what they had contributed to the struggle against Christ. This animosity was carried to the limit by the so-called Anonymous of York (ca. 1100) who contrasted the pure Church of Christ with that of Rome, which is the devil's church, and called for obedience to the former and resistance to the latter.

[27] Blaise Pascal, *Pensées,* ed. Jacques Chevalier (Paris: J. Gabalda, 1925–1927), no. 810.

[28] Lamennais to Montalembert, January 1, 1834.

What interests us here is not the immense number of anti-Roman protests[29] but rather their common focus which unifies the dissent. This has often been emphasized by Catholic apologists and theologians, most strongly by *de Maistre* and Soloviev. "It is a basic fact", writes the former, "that every non-Catholic church is 'protestant'. It is futile to distinguish between schismatic and heretical churches. I know well what is meant, but ultimately the distinction is merely verbal, and every Christian who rejects *communio* with the Holy Father is a Protestant or soon will be: he is a person who protests—silently or loudly—and always will be."[30] What links all of them together is a common hatred of the unifying principle: "This hatred is the sole but all-embracing bond that links all the separated churches."[31] Among themselves they are tolerant: "Did we ever find that Protestants bother to write books against Greek, Nestorian, Syrian, etc., churches, even though they hold dogmas that Protestants abhor? They avoid this. Rather, they defend these churches, they flatter them, they are ready to agree with them, because they see any opponent of the Holy See as an ally."[32] "The Russian Church recognizes, as we do, the Real Presence, the need for confession and priestly absolution, the same

[29] Joseph Benziger, "Invectiva in Romam, Romkritik im Mittelalter vom 9. bis zum 12. Jahrhundert" (Diss., Munich, *Historische Studien,* vol. 404, 1968). H. Preuss, *Die Vorstellungen vom Antichrist im späteren Mittelalter und in der konfessionellen Polemik* (Leipzig: n.p., 1906). G. Blochwitz, "Die antirömischen deutschen Flugschriften der frühen Reformationszeit", in *Archiv für Reformationsgeschichte* 27 (1936).

[30] De Maistre, *Du pape,* 445. It is needless to say that if we refer to this, in its own way magnificent, monolithic book (which, however, was not at all valued by Pius VII), our project has nothing in common with its fundamental thesis: absolute secular and spiritual monarchy.

[31] Ibid., 448. Joseph Bernhart says this about "the dogmatic struggles of the fourth and fifth centuries": "Fundamentally, no matter how much the parties desired to advance the cause of Christ, it was a question of life or death for the new religion. What the diverse camps had in common was opposition to Rome." *Der Vatikan als Weltmacht* (Munich: List, 1949), 51.

[32] Ibid., introduction, xxxvi.

number of sacraments, the intercession of the saints, veneration of images, etc. Protestantism, in contrast, rejects these dogmas and customs and even abhors them. But if it encounters any of these in a church separated from Rome, it takes no offence at them. The cult of images particularly, which was so solemnly condemned as idolatry, loses all its poison. . . . Russia is separated from the Holy See: that is sufficient for it to be seen as a brother, a fellow Protestant."[33]

Although none of these churches that call themselves by various names dared to strike the word *catholic* — which is the proper name of the Roman Church[34] — from the Creed, what units them "catholically" is their No to Rome: "All enemies of Rome are friends."[35] De Maistre also remarks that the atheistic Enlightenment directed the whole force of its attack against the Roman Church. Soloviev, who is far less suspect of fanaticism than the controversial Count, says practically the same. He notes that the three decisive differences between the Eastern and the Latin Church "have no positive element": the Spirit does *not* proceed from the Son, Mary was *not* immaculate from the instant of her conception, the pope has *no* claim to juridical primacy. "The pseudo-orthodoxy of our theological school consists of polemic negations." "Your entire 'orthodoxy' and your 'Russian concept' are merely a nationalistic protest against the universal authority of the pope."[36]

And since every church, by separation from Rome, wishes to

[33] Ibid., 448.

[34] Ibid., 472–73; cf. 467f.

[35] De Maistre, *Du pape,* 531–32. De Maistre introduces interesting Protestant testimonies, e.g., one from Pufendorf: "The invalidation of papal authority has brought into the world the seeds of unending discord. Since there was no longer a highest authority to put an end to the controversies that arose on all sides, the Protestants wrangled with each other, with their own hands tearing out their entrails." Quoted from p. 64 of *De Monarchia Pontificis Romani* (Frankfurt am Main: n.p., 1688).

[36] Vladimir Soloviev, *Russland und die universale Kirche* [Russia and the Universal Church], vol. 2, *Sämtliche Werke* (1954): 201–2.

accomplish a "reform" in the direction of Christian origins and Christian authenticity, Rome is left to appear as the one who fell away from this origin and who hinders a return to this original unity. (The "Roman innovations" gave Newman trouble longest of all.) The churches that seceded appropriated the idea of unity in love, the nonjuridical unanimity of hearts (*sobornost*), and Rome was left only with the dried-out, ghostlike, abstract skeleton, the "institution" stripped of all living flesh.

The pretended indifference towards this "rightly abandoned" entity in fact hides a perpetual obsession with it. All fingers point to the empty space. In this sense—and only in this sense—can it be said: "The primacy of the pope is the principal dogma without which Christianity cannot continue to exist; all churches that reject this dogma, the consequences of which they attempt to conceal from themselves, are also unconsciously united by it."[37]

3. Unity as an Abstraction

The negation created a purely formal unity, but this unity, deriving from negation—within every non-Catholic church as well as between them—remains *abstract* in content, because the most concrete factor of unity has been eliminated.

Thomas Aquinas proved the necessity of this actual unity in several ways: from the necessity that in controversies concerning the faith the final decision be made by a presiding authority; from the appropriateness that the unique Bridegroom of the Church be represented in person throughout time; from the innumerable scriptural statements referring to the office of Peter that, as primacy, must be transferable in succession.[38]

[37] De Maistre, *Du pape,* 476.
[38] *Summa contra Gentiles,* 4, 76.

82

Wherein then lies the unity of the Church, the unity of the different churches, if this focal point is removed? Döllinger, in his early writings, cites a Protestant theologian: "It is untrue and confusing to speak of unity when this is merely sought after, existing only as a concept, and when nothing can be presented that shows the alleged unity numerically."[39] Möhler says in his *Die Einheit in der Kirche:* "To call the external manifestation of internal unity the 'empirical concept' of the Church, which must be replaced by the 'ideal', means to put an *abstraction,* an empty concept, death, in the place of *life.*"[40]

In what, we may further ask, could such an ideal consist if it were not at the same time the concretely manifested reality of unity? That is why the Anglican Newman complained that the (then) existing unity of the English church was *abstract;* in truth one should speak about "churches".[41] And to quote Soloviev again: "If the Russian and Greek churches cannot express their solidarity by actions in life" (which, according to Soloviev, they cannot do because they are national churches for whom a universal council would be impossible),

[39] Ignatz Döllinger, *Die Kirche und die Kirchen* (Munich: n.p., 1861). The author cited is Lechler, *Lehre vom heiligen Amte* (1857), 139.

[40] Johann Adam Möhler, *Die Einheit in der Kirche,* ed. J. R. Geiselmann (Olten and Cologne: Hegner, 1956), 213f.

[41] John Henry Cardinal Newman, *The Via Media of the Anglican Church,* vol. 1, (London: Longmans Green and Co., 1891): 201, note 9: "There is no one *visible* Church. Church is an abstract word, signifying *one body.* Anglicans, like Independents should talk of the Churches." Cf. de Maistre, *Du pape,* 450f: "Where the bond of unity has been broken, there is no common tribunal anymore, and hence neither is there an unchangeable standard of faith. Everything is reduced to the judgment of the individual and of the civil authority." Likewise de Bonald: "In the proper sense of the word, there is no Church anymore among Protestants, if the word 'Church' is understood as a *communio* of Christians united by one faith, the same religious principles and the same means of sanctification; they are simply groups of people among whom the more cultured and better educated have ceased to have any link to Luther, Calvin, etc." *Demonstration philosophique* (*Werke,* 1840), 229., note 1.

"then their 'unity in faith' is merely an *abstract* formula that accomplishes nothing and has no binding power."[42]

We have already seen how retracing the past to find a binding, unifying canon leads to a "canon within the canon", and how this fragments even the last possible principle of unity, the New Testament and the Gospels, and how "under the burning wind of science", of exegesis, all concepts of Church unity except one melt away.[43] Scripture alone—without tradition and the teaching of the Church, whose authority is supported by Scripture—is incapable (contrary to the common assertion on the part of Protestants) of prevailing against "historico-critical" exegesis, which has grown practically into a monopoly.

Möhler, in his *Symbolik,* has written a few strongly worded pages (which are as valid today as they were then) about the nearly schizophrenic dichotomy between Protestant church piety and Protestant exegesis: "Without doubt, if the Church were a historical or antiquarian society, if she had no self-concept, no knowledge of her origin, of her essence and her mission", then she would have to search with the exegetes for her selfhood in Scripture. "She would be like someone who, by researching documents he himself has written, tries to discover whether he really exists!"[44]

And since throughout the centuries every commentator (not only scholars but the ordinary religious person) reads a new meaning from the literal text of the Bible, the principle of *sola scriptura* necessarily leads in one of two directions: on the one hand, everyone must be ready to conform his personal faith to the newest interpretation. But, "whoever then says, 'this is my faith', has no faith at all. Faith, unity of faith, universality of faith, are all one and the same."[45] On the other

[42] Soloviev, *Russland and die universale Kirche,* 228.

[43] De Maistre, *Du pape,* 452, 455.

[44] Johann Adam Möhler, *Symbolik,* ed. J. R. Geiselmann, vol. 1 (Cologne and Olten: Hegner, 1958), 422, 438.

[45] Ibid., 423.

hand, he must agree that canonical Scripture can be subjected to contradictory interpretations. Therefore, "Holy Scripture, because it accommodates all meanings, has none of its own", and the Catholic Church "was foolish to assume a meaning in it, a single, particular meaning."[46]

Thus, "Holy Scripture, when *abstracted* from tradition and the Church"[47]—which existed before Scripture and determined its canon, and which possesses an original understanding of its total meaning— could not subsequently bring forth the Church by and from itself. As Möhler aptly said "concerning the relationship of ecclesial exegesis to erudite scientific exegesis of Holy Scripture",[48] it is not by exegesis that the Church gains an overall grasp of the revelation that she "heard from the mouth of Christ and from the apostles" and which "by the power of the divine Spirit is indelibly imprinted in her consciousness, or, as Irenaeus says, 'in her heart'. If the Church had to obtain her dogmas through scientific research, she would become enmeshed in the most absurd contradictions and would annihilate herself. Since the Church herself would have to conduct this research, her presence would have to be presupposed, yet at the same time she would have to be regarded as nonexistent, still waiting to attain her own being . . . through divine truth."

The a priori of the Church's understanding is axiomatic for the Catholic researcher. He cannot simultaneously be a believer and a "neutral" investigator: "An individual cannot at the same time believe in a particular teaching and not believe in it."[49] And if someone refuses the premise of the Church's faith as being distorting lenses, how will he manage to read Scripture without such glasses in the allegedly *abstract objectivity* of "pure historical science"? "You will always need

[46] Ibid., 432.
[47] Ibid., 424.
[48] Title of section 42, ibid., 436.
[49] Ibid., 437–39.

to use eyeglasses, but take care that it is not just any glass-grinder who makes them and puts them on your nose."[50] (The objection that Möhler oversimplified the antithesis—because he did not discuss the Protestant confessional documents—is perhaps correct but not relevant. What authority do these writings have? Where did they get their authority and who enforces it?)[51]

At the beginning of this century, *Blondel* and *Loisy* exchanged a few letters in which Blondel tried to convince the proponent of abstract historical objectivity that he could never jump from there into the *mysterium* of Christ's self-awareness, through which the faith of the Church came to be. These are tragic letters: they were too late. Loisy's decision against faith had already been made, secretly; its concealment was merely tactical. But Blondel shows him that he has the same schizophrenia between the historical Jesus and the Christ of faith that we know from Bultmann; the same historical relativism in theology[52] that excludes from consideration the mediating a priori knowledge which the Church possesses.

Twenty years later *Erik Peterson* and *Adolf von Harnack* (against whom Loisy's first work—criticized by Blondel—was directed) agreed, in an exchange of letters, that since it was impossible to return with Karl Barth to the principle of Scripture, one had to question whether the Church would still exist, and, if so, in what way?

Peterson: "The Church ceases to be a 'public' entity if she relinquishes a dogmatic standpoint." Harnack: "Protestantism has to concede that

[50] Ibid., 427.

[51] Cf. Geiselmann's explanations in the appendix, vol. 2 (1960), 626ff.

[52] René Marlé, *Au coeur de la crise moderniste. Le dossier inédit d'une controverse* (Paris: Aubier, 1950), 87: "... our faith, still medieval in form, will lose its externals ... the pious fiction of a classical theology is only a construct, destined to disappear to make way for other constructions (because material means are always needed) to protect the spirit of the eternal gospel." This is Blondel's summary of Loisy's much deeper thought. He himself demands "prolegomena to any future exegesis" (90). *Complete Correspondence*, 70–113.

neither can it desire nor can it be a church like the Catholic Church, since it rejects all formal authority." Peterson: Then, all that remains are unofficial assemblies. The theological faculties would have to be abolished; history of dogma in any case. . . . Harnack agrees: "A dogma without infallibility has no meaning." "I do not know what will become of the Evangelical churches. But as you rightly surmise, I can only *welcome* a development that leads further to autonomy and to a pure community of conviction after the manner (I am not afraid to say this) of Quakerism or Congregationalism. I am not particularly worried about how we will stand up to and appear in comparison to Catholicism, Americanism or Russia, and so forth. I have no doubt that we will find a way and suitable forms, without *ecclesial* absolutism."[53] Instead of Harnack's carefree attitude, we now have the World Council of Churches' profound anxiety; we shall have more to say about this.

According to *Heinrich Schlier,* who followed the solitary road traveled by Newman and Peterson, "precisely this movement, not only in its theoretical basis but also in its actual course, shows that it is not open and unprejudiced toward the essence of the unifying unity and avoids its claim to totality—its only alternative then being to square the circle."[54]

Schlier, in his calmly resolute *Kurze Rechenschaft,* saw through the hopeless abstractness of the Protestant principle, which never really entered, with the Incarnation of the *logos,* into the "historical substance of the world", never identified with God's real, definitive decision for the world that goes so far "that the provisional (the world), in its wholly concrete temporality, contains within it things that are ultimate". That is why Church and tradition already appear

<hr />

[53] Adolf von Harnack to Erik Peterson, *Theologische Traktate* (Munich: Kösel-Verlag, 1931), 292–322.

[54] Heinrich Schlier, "Kurze Rechenschaft", *Bekenntnis zur katholischen Kirche,* ed. Karl Hard (Würzburg: Echter, 1955), 169–92; quotation, 192.

in the New Testament; that is why "faith is defined in concrete statements", that is why there is office and authority, celibacy and monasticism. "The situation of the individual, unbiased exegete, opening the Bible as if for the first time, is an illusion and an *abstraction.*" Exegesis only makes sense within the one Church,[55] the ministry of which Schlier (perhaps better than any other German theologian) has explained in terms of its origins.[56] Such a Church cannot be a "branch" of a historical unity which no longer exists; it has to exist throughout history as the "earthly-heavenly *actualization* of the world-embracing, loving will of God".

However, conversions, particularly notable ones, have become less frequent today. As a consequence of the ecumenical movement and an alleged "new understanding of the Church", even the Catholic clergy counsel against it: the convert would be deserting his own church in order to take his place among the *beati possidentes;* more important than the personal event of discovering is the striving together, the "convergence" toward a unity that already seems to be in sight. An increasing openness of Rome toward the World Council of Churches and joint "Conversations"—the results of which are highly publicized—give the impression that the Roman Church is finally ready to renounce her "splendid isolation" and her claim to sole validity and is willing to

---

[55] See Heinrich Schlier, "Die Einheit der Kirche", in *Hochland* 44 (1952): 289–300. This is a programmatic article not included in his collection of essays. An equally programmatic article, relevant to the idea of "accountability", is "Das bleibend Katholische. Ein Versuch über das Prinzip das Katholischen", in *Das Ende der Zeit* (Freiburg im Breisgau: Verlag Herder, 1971), 297, 320.

[56] Cf. Schlier's contribution in *Schreiben der deutschen Bischöfe über das priesterliche Amt* (1969) [Letter of the German bishops on the priestly office] and other relevant studies: "Grundelemente des priesterlichen Dienstes im Neuen Testament", in *Theologie und Philosophie* 44 (1969): 161–80; "Der priesterliche Dienst", pt. 1: "Ursprung und Frühgeschichte", in *Quaestiones disputatae* 46 (1970), 81–114. Newly revised as "Neutestamentliche Grundelemente des Priesteramtes", *Catholica* 27 (1973): 209–33.

take her place in an all-embracing Christian union of all confessions that are pledged (in one way or another) to the gospel of Christ, a unity that is supposed to transcend her. We shall now have to ask what kind of unity this might be.

Forms of Abstract Unity

If, in the following, three forms of abstract unity are set forth, they are but variations on the same theme, namely, a *sociologically* defined unity that is inevitably all that remains of a no-longer-understood or rejected theological and practical unity of the *Catholica* as the Body of Christ (derived from his Eucharist) and as the People of God (by virtue of the election and authorization of the Twelve).

Here, this sociological unity might be directly attributed to an overemphasis on "structure" in the Catholic Church, as Robert Spaemann and Alexander Dru have impressively proven in, respectively, *Der Ursprung der Soziologie aus dem Geist der Restauration; Studien über L. G. A. de Bonald* (Munich 1959) and *Erneuerung und Reaktion; die Restauration in Frankreich* 1800–1830 *(Munich* 1967*), respectively.*

When a Church structure is artificially erected, a religious "form" or "structure" can come into being that has little to do with true spiritual forces of faith but might perhaps be rationalized positively as a folk tradition. For example, Napoleon needed a Church structure as part of his empire—just as he needed a legislative and educational system and road building—and Consalvi, Pius VII's secretary, was not disinclined to provide him with one; to it, de Bonald and de Maistre contributed an ideology rooted in the principles of social tradition and of the *ancien régime,* and highly placed gentlemen were ready to buy bishoprics for high sums. Saint-Simon, and also Comte and much later Maurras (who came to know de Bonald through both the former), were able to take their starting point from here. However, this "folk tradition"—because of its connections with antirestoration and anti-Christian movements—could also be exposed negatively as a mere "façade", an ideology with no living roots, either in the people or in a convincing philosophy, which de Bonald thought he could do without. It is according to this sociological model that, for a century and a half, Marxism has understood not merely restorative Catholicism but any kind of Catholicism and thereby attempted to disregard its claim to uniqueness.

The reaction to such formalism can fall into the opposite extreme by seeking unity beyond—higher or lower than—the form willed by Jesus Christ. The ways of doing this are practically innumerable, and they mix and mingle in newer and newer combinations. Formalism can show itself as clericalism, as when Napoleon wanted "good priests", but priests who were also Gallicans, distanced from Rome; such clericalism could equally well be taken over from Rome or played against her, but in any case it was a charge to be leveled at Rome. The extreme opposite of this model is quintessentially anti-Roman because it destroys the unity which is the point of reference for the hierarchy. It can be pneumatic, from early Montanism through Messalianism to the Spirituals and Fraticelli of the Middle Ages, to the Rosicrucians and all kinds of proponents of a third, eternal gospel, to the contemporary Pentecostal movement which cuts right across the denominations. Or it can be a more or less enthusiastic Christian humanism that dreams of an all-embracing Christian religion: from the heavenly Council of Nicolas of Cusa through the Enlightenment and the Christian lodges, represented in large numbers at the Congress of Vienna (which is why Christian princes resented the Pope's ban on freemasonry),[1] to the Catholicism of Lamennais, a religion of universal human truth, first with the pope as the head, then without him. It can also take the form of a many-faceted "Modernism" that strives to salvage what is enduring in evolution from the domain of "structure"

[1] J. Schmidlin, *Papstgeschichte der neueren Zeit,* vol. 1 (Munich: Verlag Josef Kösel and Friedrich Pustet, 1933): 140.

and place it (cf. Tyrrell, von Hügel, Sabatier) in the sphere of religious needs, mystical experience or neoplatonic contact with the formless and form-transcending Divine. At present there are numerous offshoots of this basic tendency, which, whether their approach is more "spiritual", more rational or more mystical, locate the unity of the true Church (if the word may still be employed) far away from the papacy or from any authority whatsoever. It is not astonishing that all these currents apply either Marxist or structuralist ideological critiques to the Petrine Church leadership and to all that goes with it and, particularly today, present a mixture of pneumaticism and criticism in an artificial combination of contradictions.

A Catholicism that is based upon this kind of spiritual tradition will ultimately be inclined—even though inwardly poorly prepared—to enter into ecumenical dialogue as a self-assured partner, because it sees itself as bringing unity to the confessions—a unity expressing itself in the more or less loose "unions" or agreements, a unity it already possesses as its own. It will assume, *bona fide,* that ecumenism's emphasis should be increasingly on that which is common to all confessions: it will assume that the disquieting, excessive and irreducible claims of Catholicism, above all, the papacy, should be relegated to the periphery for the time being. After all other things have been taken care of, these annoying obstructions may be disposed of in one way or another. Hence, ecumenism becomes a movement toward an abstract unity (though its adherents think it to be quite concrete), because the concrete focus created in the Petrine office is either totally ignored or put at the end of the agenda.

This approach seems all the more legitimate and urgent because "Christendom" (though the word now means something totally different from what it meant in the Middle Ages)[2] surely owes the world—on account of all the religious wars and reciprocal charges of

---

[2] Bernard Landry, *L'Idée de chrétienté chez les scolastiques du XIIIe siècle* (Paris: Presses Universitaires de France, 1929).

heresy—a proof of internal reconciliation and a unified front against unbelief, proof, too, of an inner unity. (This unity of mind is the second category of abstract unity. But, insofar as it also involves unions, concordats, negotiations of all kinds, it also relates to our first category of abstract unity.) And thus the ecumenical attitude in the *Catholica* becomes a powerful motive force for advancing the first two attempts at abstract unity—the first of which is explicitly sociological, the second still sociological though it is initially more psychological—giving them a preponderance over the concrete principle which, since it is untimely, must retire into the background for the present, if not forever.

These matters are of such pressing importance that we must look at them more closely, though we can do it only briefly by commenting on a few examples.

1. *The Quicksand of Language*

At the time of the Bourbon Restoration, the Church could most tellingly be described as "institution". With her nature as *communio* virtually disregarded, the Church of Christ was seen only from the side of her human activity, as part of the state or on the model of a state, or in intrinsic unity with a state (Byzantium, Moscow, Anglicanism). But it should not be forgotten that at that same time there existed an equally powerful romantic countermovement.

Our century has moved away from the spirit of the Restoration (except for integralist circles), but two men emerge who, though not at all alike, reflect something of that period: Charles Maurras and *Reinhold Schneider*. The first, an atheist, saw the Church only as the exterior form of a mediterranean culture that should be preserved at all costs. (Such preoccupation with a corpse need not detain us here.) Schneider must be taken considerably more seriously, particularly the Schneider of the Escorial (and of Potsdam) but also of "Winter in

Vienna". For him, "form", the Catholic form, is the result of the excessive demands, the violence which flow from absolute service rendered to the noble hearts of kings. For Schneider, this tragic coercion that created the magnificent form has nothing to do with legitimacy. "The secret of the phenomenon is not in the blood (of kings); it is rather in the challenge itself." In this lies the real nobility of kings. Where much is demanded, much will be achieved. There is only one precondition: "that this demand be wholly understood and put into practice as a mode of life".[3] Precisely by being an anvil, a king becomes the hammer; by being acted upon, he becomes an agent; by being shaped, the mold.[4]

There can be no doubt that Schneider's world view is (as his last phase shows) inclined toward tragedy. "Thus, existence appears as a terrible self-contradiction: laws are laid down for living that contradict life itself—and still, those who comply with these laws are bathed in a radiance that gives life its value. Everything is sacrifice, even life itself."[5] Thus Schneider finds himself in a twilight between the real Christian *mysterium* that quite certainly underlies the external form of the Church (and he has looked deeply into the hearts of popes to get a glimpse of it) and a metaphysics of life that stems from Schopenhauer, Nietzsche and Simmel, and that hardens the mystery of the Cross, of everlasting love, into an impersonal law of life. Here he becomes vulnerable; his thinking keeps circling round the legitimacy of sovereign power. All form is the shell of defenseless life; all form is blood that is shed. Peter "rules" only by virtue of his own crucifixion.

But Schneider remains the exception in the new Catholic era, and

---

[3] Reinhold Schneider, *Die Hohenzollern. Tragik und Königtum* (Cologne and Olten: Hegner, 1963), 10–11.

[4] See my book, *Reinhold Schneider, sein Weg und sein Werk* (Cologne and Olten: Hegner, 1953), 46.

[5] Reinhold Schneider, *Corneilles Ethos* (Frankfurt: Insel Verlag, 1939), 26f.

therefore he is not understood when he tries to express ideas that are Catholic. Only his non-Catholic, tragic, pessimistic side ("Winter in Vienna") is emphasized, in a distorted fashion, and he is canonized as the "mystic of the night".

Generally, however, something totally different emerges, namely, Marxist criticism, in league with Freudian and Nietzschean criticism, of the Catholic form, a form which is not an artificial political restoration but a straightforward manifestation of life. This criticism has created a vocabulary which, disseminated by the press and the mass media, has been accepted uncritically even by Catholics. They talk in foreign tongues, they look at themselves with alien eyes and, because they are told this incessantly, consider themselves "alienated". Yet what they think they have to learn from outside, they have long possessed within. They have forgotten it because they believe what they are told, that the unity of the Church is not the concrete unity of the Body of Christ, each member of which is anointed and "once for all fully informed" (Jude 5), but merely an abstract sociological unity.

Thus they learn from Marx the priority of *orthopraxy* over ortho-doxy, as if the faith of Christianity did not consist in the affirma-tion and acceptance of God's action for the world, an acceptance that is meant to become a decisive act of self-offering to God and to men.

If the primacy of God's action is surrendered, so is faith, and all that is left is the self-creation of man — Marx's theory.[6] In the same trend of thought, truth is equated with *authenticity* (particularly in France) as the newly discovered virtue of the Christian. Anything axiomatic falls under the "suspicion of ideology". (It was Rudolf Hernegger who first introduced this term into the realm of Catholic faith and

[6] This attitude was already condemned by Leo XIII under another name, "Ameri-canism": Denziger-Schönmetzer, *Enchiridion Symbolorum* (Barcelona: Herder, 1967), 3344.

theology.)[7] Suspicion is expressed by appending the suffix "-ism". Once understood, the suffix can be dropped because it now adheres invisibly to the word: hence, authority, as an ideology, becomes *authoritarianism,* paternity *paternalism,* tradition *traditionalism,* and the one who reacts becomes *reactionary.* This can create serious repercussions when fundamental terms of biblical revelation are involved, the critical undermining of which threatens to invalidate their content. The God of Jesus Christ is essentially "Father", both "my Father and your Father" (Jn 20:17), "from whom every family in heaven and earth takes its name" (Eph 3:15). This includes even Paul's fatherhood in relation to the community as his "children" (1 Cor 4:14–15).

If we were to accept the sociological statement that we are living today in a "fatherless society" (Mitscherlich), or the even more extravagant hypothesis that culture began with "patricide" (Freud), the concepts of Christian and ecclesial fatherhood would become not merely questionable but unintelligible, so much so that retaining them would be equivalent to an antisocial, ideological "paternalism". Thus the Christian idea would be sabotaged at all levels: from the Trinity to Christology and ecclesiology and well into the practical relationship of the faithful to priests and spiritual leaders. (A priest today is commonly addressed as *Père* in France and as "Father" in England.)

"Authority" is unmasked as a socially detrimental ideology in pejorative words borrowed from sociology. It is *repression,* that is, an impermissible and presumptuous limitation of freedom that can elicit only *frustration* in the violated subject, making him a client for psychotherapy. A very specific and rather superficial sociological notion of freedom underlies this view, which no longer has anything in common with the Christian concept of freedom which is won only

[7] Rudolf Hernegger, *Ideologie und Glaube, eine christliche Ideologiekritik,* 3 vols. Vol.1: *Volkskirche oder Kirche der Gläubigen* (Nüremberg: Verlag Glock und Lutz, 1959); *Macht ohne Auftrag* (Olten and Freiburg im Breisgau: Walter, 1963).

by conquest of self and is learned through ecclesial discipline (Gal 5:1–26).

Much could be said about the necessity of exercising ecclesial authority in the spirit of Christian fatherhood and even motherhood. But the claim that all authority is modeled on state coercion is certainly mistaken, both from the human and from the Christian point of view.

The mystery of the *communio sanctorum* that does justice both to the worth of the individual person in his direct relationship to God and to the interdependence of all believers—because each one is indispensable to the "completeness of the members", the "full stature of Christ"—cannot be rendered in purely sociological categories. This direct relationship of the individual to God—which, from the Christian point of view is what gives the individual his worth for the community—is made to appear as a *private* matter (while there is nothing private in the Body of Christ). The interdependence of all appears here as ecclesial *democracy,* a totally inadequate category when applied to the Church. This would imply that the sovereign power (*kratos*) lies in the people of the Church (*demos*). Yet the Church is governed solely by Christ in the name of the triune God. He delegated the spiritual authority to govern to the Twelve and to their successors (Mk 3:14) but in such a way that everyone has some share in it, e.g., in the forgiving of each others' sins (Mk 6:12, etc.).

If one wanted to describe the Church's structure, at all costs, in sociological terms, one would have to describe it, with Lord Acton, negatively: nothing resembles the political concept of monarchy less than papal authority. Neither can one speak of an aristocratic element, since the essence of aristocracy is possession of inherited personal privilege. Least of all can one describe the Church as a democracy, because in such a system all authority is held by the sum total of individuals.[8] Having said this, one could go on to state positively that

---

[8] Lord Acton, *Rambler IV,* cited by Ulrich Noack, *Katholizität und Geistesfreiheit* (Frankfurt am Main: n.p., 1962), 325–26.

the Church participates analogically in all three forms, and even in ancient times[9] this kind of constitution was considered the best possible.

Mired in the quicksand of non-Christian terminology, criticism of the Church finds itself necessarily limited and even in contradiction with itself. Having branded the living organism of the Church—which can only be understood on the basis of the grace of Christ—an ossified *organization,* an *institution,* an *establishment,* it comes face to face with the decisive questions: what shall be done with this *institution* in the rehabilitation of the Church? Is it a question of "changing the structure", as one of the slogans demands, for example by replacing the allegedly monarchical structure with a supposedly democratic or parliamentary one? But then we would again have a "structure", a new form of "establishment". (This word is on every tongue today, but its original meaning—the agreement between the King of England and the Anglican Church—is known only to a few.)[10] And this, to be able to function, would probably need a more cumbersome bureaucratic apparatus than the Roman curia. (Consider the mountains of paper produced by the present national and diocesan synods.)

According to another slogan, the existence of any institution implies "manipulation" of the masses whom it holds in its clutches. Should therefore all structures be abolished with a view to creating an amorphous "brotherhood"? The sectarian character of this idea, which, according to Joseph Ratzinger's apt remark, at least allows for the

[9] Plato, *The Laws* 691–692 (applied to Sparta), Polybius, Cicero. In regard to the problem of democracy in the Church, cf. Joseph Ratzinger and Hans Maier, *Demokratie in der Kirche. Möglichkeiten, Grenzen, Gefahren* (Limburg: Lahn-Verlag, 1970), as well as Hans Maier's foundational work *Revolution und Kirche. Zur Frühgeschichte der christlichen Demokratie,* 3d ed. (Munich: n.p., 1973).

[10] Joseph de Maistre, *Du pape* [The pope], 516, in *Oeuvres complètes* (Lyons: Vitte et Perrussel, 1864–1886). Concerning the Anglican church constitution he says: "This is a circumscribed and local institution diametrically opposed to universality, the exclusive sign of the truth."

concept of God's fatherhood, is amply documented by Church history.[11] Thus, perhaps, the Church could avoid becoming a *ghetto* — something people are much afraid of, whatever the word means; whether it refers to the scandal that the Church has an identity *at all,* a structure that differentiates her from the world, or that she does not sufficiently practice "openness to the world" — which is only possible on the basis of such a particular structure. The fact that diverse groups use the same slogans, always pejoratively, while they totally disagree about what is to be done with the reality referred to, shows the abysmal lack of thought in this allegedly critical Catholicism.

However, might we not discover a positive, central concern in this ideological criticism, namely, a concern for the universality of the Church and her mission for mankind? And since mankind is a tangible sociological entity, the Church's mandated duty to it should also be comprehensible sociologically, as having a potentially progressive character of unity. We have spoken of a language that alienates: might it not indicate a genuine concern?

2. Under the Spell of Humanitarian Mysticism

If one looks for the origin of this concern for the Church's mission to all men, it will be found — hidden but definitely there — in the thought of Abbot *Joachim of Fiore,* [12] who was highly praised and commended by seven successive popes. The basic idea of his trinitarian historical schema is quite clear: Old Covenant (Father) and New Covenant (Son) relate to each other as might be expected: from these two

[11] Ibid., 24, note 9.

[12] For this short reference to Joachim of Fiore, we follow the thorough, well-documented study by Henri de Lubac, *Exégèse médiévale,* vol. 3 (Paris: Aubier, 1961): 437–538, rather than Ernst Benz's *Ecclesia spiritualis* (Stuttgart: W. Kohlhammer, 1934).

99

emerges a third historical age, that of the Spirit, embryonic in the clerical Church of the Son but emerging in the era of spiritual men, the monks, the contemplatives. (The era of the Father, the Old Covenant, was considered to be that of the laity and the married.)

The transition from the second to the third age (*tertius status*) is held to be that from Peter to John.[13] Then is revealed the *evangelium aeternum,* which is "spiritual and not so circumscribed that it can be contained in a large book".[14] The introductory teaching of Christ is transcended (*relicto praeceptorum Christi inchoationis sermone*)[15] into perfection and—this is important for us—into *freedom.*[16]

For Joachim this did not mean a reform of the Church by a return to origins but rather transcending these origins into a more advanced future. Therefore, according to him, the Petrine Church structure will be left behind, not because it was not the original government of the Church—a modern idea, which would have been inconceivable to Joachim—but because the element of fear inherent in this authority will be superseded by the freedom of love.[17] "Thus will Peter now be girded and led where he does not wish to go and will speedily end his course."[18]

Yet, any anti-Roman sentiment was far from Joachim, though he was often accused of this. Nor, as can be seen, did he want to proceed from "Church" to "humanity" but rather to progress from obligation

---

[13] Joachim of Fiore, *Liber introd.* 19 (fol. 17–19), *Expositio in Apocalypsim,* pt. 4, C. 14 (fol. 170, 1), *Tractatus super quattuor evangelia,* ed. Ernesto Buonaiuti (Rome: Istitùto Storico Italiano, 1930), 275.

[14] Joachim of Fiore, *Super 4 Evang.,* 275.

[15] Joachim of Fiore, *Expositio in Apoc.,* prol. (fol. 1, 4).

[16] Ibid., (fol. 175, 3–4); *Vita S. Benedicti,* c. 15.

[17] De Lubac, *Exégèse médiévale,* 3:462ff.

[18] Joachim of Fiore, *Liber figurarum,* ed. Leone Tondelli (Turin: n.p., 1940). This statement in particular suggests to de Lubac that the book may have been written by a student.

to freedom[19] and from Christ to the Spirit.[20] Nonetheless this was sufficient to move the investigating commission of Angani to say, "This teaching leads ultimately to the abolition of the clergy, in other words, of the Roman Church and of obedience to her."[21] This is objectively correct. It is the result of substituting for the traditional ecclesial concept of Catholicity and authority a new, implicitly socio-logical concept that will appear conclusively later in the idealistic metaphysical system, in which the progress of the Spirit is the exposition of the Trinity (Schelling, Hegel). The subject (S) gains an over-view of the (trinitarian) Absolute, fixing the christological and ecclesiological authority (A) at a specific point and thus relativizing it.

Once the identity between "Christendom" and "mankind" was superseded, Joachim's stepping beyond the Petrine Church led, by an inner logic, to a new equivalence of "Catholic universality" and "mankind". One can trace the route of this idea from early Protestantism (Sebastian Franck) to the English, French and German Enlightenment and their catechisms. More important for us is that it continues unbroken from the Enlightenment to the "progressive" Catholic universalism of the Romantics, who wanted to expand the totality which is present in the Church in germ, as it were, to embrace all mankind.

---

[19] Fear and servitude represent the Old Testament, filial service the New Testament and freedom the third era. The first one corresponds to old age, the second to mid-life and the third one to childhood. Joachim of Fiore, *Concordia,* bk. 5, c. 84(fol. 112, 2).

[20] The era of childhood is placed in the arms of the "aging Roman Pope" as was the child Jesus in the arms of Simeon. "Cum talis puer manifestatus fuerit in Ecclesia Dei, qui sit utique contemplativus, justus, sapiens, spiritalis et qui ita possit succedere episcoporum ordini . . . quomodo Regi David successit Salomon, quomodo Petri principi apostolorum Johannes evangelista, quin potius quomodo ipse Christus Johanni baptistae." Joachim of Fiore, *Tract. super 4 Evang.,* 87.

[21] H. Denifle and F. Ehrle, *Archiv für Literatur und Kirchengeschichte des Mittelalters,* 7 vols. (Freiburg im Breisgau: n.p., 1885–1900), 1:102, 120.

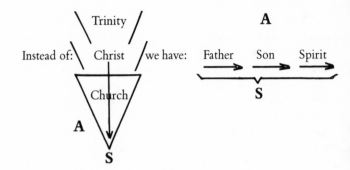

(See Novalis' *Christendom or Europe,* or Friedrich Schlegel, but also Drey's historico-theological systems.) This is precisely where *Félicité de Lamennais* comes in, whose final No to the papacy (between 1832 and 1834) was perhaps the most tragic event of nineteenth-century Church history.[22] The logic of the about-face from papal triumphalism[23] (from the 1816 *Essai sur l'indifférence* to the periodical *L'Avenie* in 1830) to complete repudiation of Rome is quite simple if one know Lamennais' point of departure: "Christianity since Jesus Christ, a natural development of the intelligence, is universal reason manifested

[22] If not otherwise noted, the reference is to Lamennais, *Oeuvres complètes* (1836–1837). The most important study about his development, including numerous unpublished letters and documents, is Louis le Guillou, *L'Évolution de la pensée réligieuse de F. de Lamennais* (Thesis, Paris, 1966).

[23] Lamennais, *Oeuvres complètes,* 2:lxviii. Louis Bouyer, *La Décomposition du catholicisme* [The decomposition of Catholicism] (Paris: Aubier, 1968) presents this turnabout clearly (8off.), demonstrating his thesis that integralism and progressivism are merely two sides of the same thing.

by the witness of the Church."[24] There is only *one* universal (catholic) truth, and (according to the traditional thesis of de Bonald) this has been given to the human race by God at the beginning. This truth has the authority of God,[25] but since mankind has a tendency to particularize, *this* universal divine authority also has to be represented by Christ's Church in the face of egoism's resistance. It is this truth that corresponds to the "social consciousness" (*sens commun*) of mankind (later Lamennais will say "of the people"), and therefore when the papacy deviates from his idea and stands in the way of progress toward freedom (the "eternal gospel" of Joachim)—as when it condemns *L'Avenir* and Lamennais' ideas—it can be simply disregarded. With equal justification he could say that "obedience is the very essence of Christianity"[26] and could even suggest swearing eternal

[24] Like de Maistre, to whom he owes much (cf. the book review, 8:101ff., and the essay "Le Pape" in *Avenie* (1830), 10:206ff. In chapter 6 of *De la religion* he adopts de Maistre's basic principle ("the more pope, the more sovereignty; the more sovereignty, the more unity; the more unity, the more authority; the more authority, the more faith", Letter, February 8, 1810) thus: 1. No pope, no Church. 2. No Church, no Christianity. 3. No Christianity, no religion (at least for all the people who were Christians) and, consequently, no society (8:107–47). In an unpublished letter to de Bonald, Lamennais assures the latter of his complete agreement, especially in regard to the original revelation in which "faith is the foundation of reason" that accepts and agrees with the revelations of the Absolute Reason. He speaks of "the infallibility of human reason" (Le Guillou, 39). Thus the voice of history becomes the echo of personal faith. De Maistre did not think any differently: "There is no dogma in the Catholic Church . . . which does not have its roots in the ultimate depths of human nature and consequently in some universal opinion, more or less muddled but nevertheless common in principle to all peoples of all times." De Maistre, *Du pape,* 132.

[25] "What, in fact, is the authority which all ought to obey? Is it power? That would be absurd. Is it the authority of one man or several? No, but universal reason manifested by testimony or by the word" 2:lxvii.

[26] Lamennais, *Entretiens sur la vie spirituelle,* quoted by le Guillou, in *L'évolution,* 100, note 13.

allegiance to the pope as the leader of mankind.[27] Christianity could be celebrated as the emergence of humanity from servitude to freedom, because we are today advanced enough "to discover in Christian dogma the universal laws of creation and, as it were, to loose them from it".[28] Lamennais, a poor theologian, was no worse in this point than most theologians of the Enlightenment and Romantic periods: he never could distinguish between nature and grace. In this he had precursors on whom he built: Huet, who attempted to derive the wisdom and religions of all nations from biblical revelation,[29] and even more Bergier, who recognized only one progressive revelation throughout human history and put forward the opinion that "the unbeliever who accepts the dogmas of universal religion and seeks the truth sincerely has the same faith as Christians. It is not faith that he lacks, only more accurate instruction. He will be saved in and by Christianity, and in this most universal sense there really is no salvation outside the Church."[30] To Lamennais, who had adopted these theories, obedience to the pope or to one's own reason are two aspects of the same thing.

Everything personal in Lamennais' encounter with the papacy was painful. On a pilgrimage to Rome, Montalembert, Lacordaire and Lamennais were all ruthlessly and senselessly humiliated. Lamennais could not find there his exalted ideal of the pope: "Rome, Rome, where are you? What has happened to your voice that gave courage and woke the slumbering? Today all they will say is 'Give in'. Pray, pray for the Church! Surely she will not perish! But why must we remind ourselves of this so often and so bitterly?"[31]

After his break with Rome, Lamennais was utterly broken. He was "old, poor, burnt up with fatigue and sorrow, without followers,

[27] Lamennais endorses the papal demands without reservation in December 1833.
[28] Lamennais, *Oeuvres complètes,* 10:342.
[29] Le Guillou, *L'Évolution,* 26.
[30] Ibid., 31.
[31] To the Countess de Senfft, October 2, 1828.

without any support but God and his conscience".[32] But the real tragedy was clearly that Lamennais was dominated by the concept of catholicity that *he* could understand, that he (like Joachim) could grasp. This was to him the real Church, while the clerical, curial Church was left aside like some distorted by-product, ripe for dissolution.[33]

Thus the trend was set well past the end of the century, practically to Péguy:[34] progressivism versus clerical integralism. But one must always remember that both derived from Romantic monism. The consequences were unforseeable, and this was illuminated as by a lightning-flash in the disappointed Saint-Beuve's last article about Lamennais: "Let me tell you that there is nothing worse than to awaken faith in the souls of others and then suddenly to take to your heels and leave them stranded. . . . How many souls do I know whom you have taken with you in your pilgrim's pack, and when you laid it down, they were left by the wayside. Public opinion, the voices of flatterers, new people who feel attracted by great talent will, no doubt, comfort you and help you to forget. But even if my cry should sound like an accusation, I shall denounce your forgetfulness."[35]

We cannot but glance briefly at a second tragedy that stands out from the multitude of tragedies in the period of Modernism.[36] Here the

[32] To Benoit d'Azy, May 12, 1834.

[33] Lamennais, *Affaires de Rome: des maux de l'Église et de la société.*

[34] The reconciliation is still questionable here, if one considers Péguy's last turnabout in *Note conjointe,* and its opposition of "flexible morality" to (the casuistic Roman) "rigid morality". The true reconciliation occurs in Bernanos' priestly figures, designed in sharp contrast to Henri Brémond, this ex-Jesuit friend of Tyrrell, particularly his false "flexibility".

[35] Quoted from Alexander Dru, *Erneuerung und Reaktion. Die Restauration in Frankreich 1800–1830 (Munich: Kösel-Verlag, 1967),* 134.

[36] Besides Tyrrell's real tragedy, we should mention those of Laberthonnière and Blondel. Loisy turned his back on faith much earlier, and Brémond had an ambivalent attitude toward it. (It was Tyrrell who persuaded him to remain a priest.) The problems of Loisy and Brémond were wholly personal.

deep, loving faith of a convert to Catholicism was ultimately led to a church of the future without Rome. *George Tyrrell,*[37] the temperamental, emotionally unstable Dubliner, given to outbursts of hate, was a Jesuit and a nearly fanatical Thomist who became acquainted with Loisy and with German philosophy through the fateful Baron von Hügel. As a result of his successes, he acquired a very high opinion of himself. Even in a "people's church"—if it is not to be a mere "mass assembly" but a true *consensus fidelium*—it is only the few, he felt, that are the leaven.[38] And if Catholicism is to survive at all, the only hope lies in a little group of truly spiritual people, who are at present "a weak and oppressed minority"[39]—perhaps even including some who had been excommunicated. (But was not Jesus, too, excommunicated by the Jews?)[40] They might survive the "rapidly dying Church"[41] and lead her to true, open catholicity. That is why, like Döllinger, the suspended and excommunicated Tyrrell, despite offers from Anglicans and others, had no thought of leaving the Catholic Church. "Why should the Modernist leave his Church?"[42] It would be wrong "to leave a service-able house simply because the chimneys smoke". Soon, outside in the

[37] Bibliography: Michael Loome in *The Heythrop Journal* (July 1969): 280–314. In *Through Scylla and Charybdis, or the Old Theology and the New* (London: Longmans Green and Co., 1907), Tyrrell put together his most representative articles for the German translation, *Zwischen Scylla und Charybdis oder die alte und die neue Theologie* (Jena: Diederichs, 1909). From his numerous writings we draw attention to the last one, the collection that appeared posthumously, *Christianity at the Crossroads* (London: Longmans Green, and Co., 1909). See also the carefully edited correspondence between Tyrrell and Brémond, with a short, well-balanced introduction by Maurice Nédoncelle, *Études Brémondiennes* 3 (Paris: Aubier, 1971).

[38] Tyrrell, *Christianity at the Crossroads,* 318.

[39] Tyrrell, *Through Scylla and Charybdis,* 19, "a feeble and oppressed minority"; cf. 62: "Then in following this minority . . . we are following a surer than average reading of the social mind."

[40] Tyrrell, *Christianity at the Crossroads,* 227.

[41] Ibid., 280.

[42] Ibid., 281.

cold, "forgetful of smoky flues, we would wish we were back".[43] Tyrrell tells the Indian tale about the man who could live neither with nor without his insufferable wife.

Actually, Tyrrell's problem is totally different from that of Lamennais. While the latter wanted the existing hierarchical Church to transcend herself into the "abstract" unity of a church of mankind in which authority is founded on the reasonableness of the original revelation, the christocentric Tyrrell holds fast to the Church as founded by Christ as well as to her Catholic integrity and her Mystical Body. But, as so often happens, here too the decisive role is played by the historical milieu of ideas and philosophies: Romantic monism changed by the end of the century to life-philosophy (*Lebensphilosophie*),[44] most clearly expressed in Bergson's categories of experiential intuition (genuine awareness of the reality of life) and mechanistic conceptual reflection (what was necessary but lacking in the former). Sertillanges tried to harmonize this system with Thomism, but a whole generation used it as a direct expression of their (Christian) piety. Applied to the Church, her proper mode appears to be the intuitive, quasi-mystical, direct grasp of the truth of revelation. Her improper mode is the reflex, rationalizing but always deficient analysis of the mystery into concepts and statements and, as ("infallible") theology, the attempt to "organize" the Mystical Body of Christ, the "institution" and hierarchical authority.

It should be noted that Tyrrell's philosophical evaluations and his constant criticism of the rational and institutional is not influenced by Marxist criticism; it is others who combine it with the latter. The

[43] Tyrrell, *Through Scylla and Charybdis,* 83f.
[44] We say "changed" because the dualistic philosophy of life is already latent in German idealism and was even in some instances explicit, for example in the late works of Fichte and in Schopenhauer, from whom Nietzsche took it. We have attempted to describe this sequence in our *Apokalypse der deutschen Seele* (1937–1939) as a transition from the Prometheus principle to the Dionysius principle.

107

antithesis between religious intuition (*lex orandi*) and rational reflection upon it (*lex credendi*) occupies Tyrrell's entire thought so much that there is no room for a second system of categories, that of the psycho-social philosophy of religion. Even though he refers to this repeatedly,[45] and it threatens to deflect him in the direction of considering religious experience in all world religions to be the same, a "universal spirit"[46] (in the sense of Lamennais), he does not carry it through in the end. In such a view, Christ would appear merely as the "reformer" of the "divinely natural"[47] "religion of humanity",[48] of the universal river of tradition.[49] Authority would belong to the "collective understanding, collective will and collective feeling of the community", to which the individual intellect must submit.[50] But this model of religious philosophy and religious history remains marginal for Tyrrell. He employs it merely apologetically in his magnificent last essay *Christianity and Religion,* in which all great religions claim catholicity (i.e., complete explanation of life and the satisfaction of religious needs). He rejects as sterile the idea—originating in the Enlightenment and Rousseau—of a rationally constructed universal or natural religion.[51] Such a synthesis cannot be obtained by leveling differences and rounding off sharp edges. Science might attempt this kind of synthesis of concepts, but religion cannot.[52] Tyrrell courageously con-

[45] Tyrrell, *Through Scylla and Charybdis,* cf. 175, 277f.

[46] Ibid., 230.

[47] Ibid., 76.

[48] Ibid., 24, 36, 45.

[49] Ibid., 208; cf. *Christianity at the Crossroads,* 252. "There has not been and cannot be a new religion, any more than a new language. Each is a bifurcation of some branch that is itself a bifurcation; and all can trace their origin to a common stem that has grown out of a root idea—the idea of religion." This is understood in the sense of Christian Romanticism (Herder, Hamann) and of Catholic Romanticism (Drey, F. Schlegel) and ultimately in the sense of the Church Fathers' Logos doctrine.

[50] Tyrrell, *Through Scylla and Charybdis,* 58, cf. 38.

[51] Tyrrell, *Christianity at the Crossroads,* 231–44.

[52] Ibid., 250.

cedes that the Catholicism of the Roman Church wins in the competition of world religions.

Thus, all depends on how the polarity of the life-philosophies is interpreted. This is the real issue. In particular, the catholicity of Catholicism requires that all human faculties of both body and soul be taken into account.[53] Neither of the poles can be dispensed with. However, in all attempts to describe this polarity, the difference in levels is invariable. Only intuition, the inmost depth that experiences the touching of the Divine, is religious in its origin; Christianly speaking, it is the "passive" acceptance of revelation. Similarly invariable, though arrived at in diverse ways, is the gap between the spheres of revelation and of reflex theology.

Above all, Tyrrell ties reflection and *language* together so that both stand in contrast to wordless, ineffable revelation. In this he differs from Heinrich Schlier, who resolutely defends the point of view that the Word of God, having become flesh, has by this act of revelation adopted human language. This is diametrically opposed to Tyrrell's frequently adduced differentiation between a permanent and only slightly variable folk religion, to which "dogma" belongs, and a highly reflex theology, which in its individual expressions follows the ideological mainstream of the times (and thus also vanishes with it) and which moreover needs continuous, unbiased, critical self-reflection. On the one hand, the latter is a corrective,[54] but, on the other hand, it remains a purely skeletal,[55] external form.[56] Its concepts have only sym-

---

[53] See the frequently reprinted article from *The Month,* said by Tyrrell to be programmatic, on "The Unity of Catholic Belief", that appears as "Lex Orandi, Lex Credendi", in *Through Scylla and Charybdis,* 100–124, and see also numerous later attempts to refine the problem, several of which were resolved in the same book. Catholicism has to take into consideration all aspects of the human condition, including the bodily-sensual as well as habit-formation, etc. Cf. ibid., 24–98.

[54] Tyrrell, *Through Scylla and Charybdis,* 96, cf. 11f.

[55] Ibid., 205.

[56] Ibid., 11, 75.

bolic, and hence variable, values.[57] As a rationalization of what is religious, it kills the prophetic spirit in the Church.[58] Its "statements" cannot presume infallibility, as theology as such cannot claim divine authority.[59] Strong biblical anthropomorphisms about God are for the most part preferable to theological abstractions. The important thing is to disentangle the "two spheres".[60] "Development" in Newman's sense of the word only attaches to the second sphere.[61]

It is at this point that Tyrrell's increasingly intense anti-Roman attitude has its beginning, with the discovery that the papacy is "the great lie" and the "headquarters of the devil".[62] This is preceded by a progressively deepening alienation from the Society of Jesus, from its founder[63] and from its superiors, whom he finds "rigid" and "repressive".[64] The members who are in any way successful are those "who do not let themselves be crushed". "On the whole, I do not find SPN (St. Ignatius) particularly attractive."[65] After Tyrrell left the Society of Jesus and was excommunicated, his tone became rather pamphleteering.

But this is only one side of the polarity, emphasizing the chasm, the subordinate character of the second pole, its distance from the center, its continuous need to be criticized. The other side is given equal emphasis: the poles are inseparable. (No panic! There is no intention of throwing overboard both theology and the institution.)[66] "A revela-

[57] Ibid., 218, 231f.

[58] Ibid., 212f.

[59] Ibid., 209.

[60] Ibid., 13f., 228f.

[61] Ibid., 200.

[62] Letter 86 to Brémond, *Correspondence,* 237f.

[63] Tyrrell, who commented warmly on the *Exercises,* sees in Ignatius mainly the "mystic" (Letter 3) and "the art of adaptation", "malleability" (Letter 4) and "flexibility" (Letter 6).

[64] Letter 6, ibid., 54.

[65] Letter 8, ibid., 60.

[66] Tyrrell, *Through Scylla and Charybdis,* 325.

tion that lacks the counterpoise of theology, that speaks a dead language . . . and a theology that lacks the counterpoise of revelation and takes no account of the continual, progressive self-manifestation of God in the religious life of humanity . . . both of these are equally fruitless." But neither pole is permitted to hamper the free development of the other: "This is what happens whenever revelation asserts itself to be a divinely ratified theology and offers its prophetic enigmas as scientific truth, or when theology would force revelation to follow the directions, methods and pace of theological development, thus equivalently putting fetters on that religious experience which is its own subject matter and cutting off its own source of nourishment."[67]

This mutual dependency (N.B., on the basis of the wordlessness of revelation!) actually confirms theology and with it the institution: revelation is in need of interpretation not only as free charismatic prophecy but also as dogma, as sacrament (which presupposes a priesthood), as irreducible authority, in short, as institution.

Trying to do justice to both sides of Tyrrell's polarity, one finds his system of thinking not unlike that of Plotinus. Above everything there is the ineffable and wordless "One", which is externalized as the "All" (*Catholica*); below it there is the *nous,* the "reflecting" spirit that can be received from the One in the ecstasy of intuition but essentially remains eternally restless, a reflection that can never overtake its subject. This tendency toward Plotinus' way of thinking is more important in Tyrrell than his potential but always latent inclination to sociological (abstract) catholicity. Both will appear in the future and also in combination. Finally, because the "One" on which all depends remains ineffable, truth can be manifested only in the existential attitude of "truthfulness", which Tyrrell, with other Modernists, long before Hans Küng, glorifies as one of the chief Catholic virtues, in

[67] Ibid., 291.

contrast to Roman officialdom's craftiness and secretiveness.[68] It is regrettable that, with his own manipulations and dishonesty in the politics of his Order and of the Church, he so little lived up to his ideal.

Instead of concerning ourselves with the purely sociological changes that are presently at work in the Church but remain theologically irrelevant, let us describe a third example who deals with the abstract (and hence sociological) unity of the Church in a serious theological framework: the model of *Marcel Légaut,* who consistently tries to connect the trends of the period between the two wars with what is going on today in the postconciliar epoch.[69] Légaut was first a professor of mathematics in Rennes, where he became known as a charismatic leader of the spiritual groups that were a kind of French parallel to the German Youth Movement (Guardini, Burg Rothenfels). During the war and afterward he became a taciturn mountain farmer and astonished the world in 1970–71 with a systematic program for a contemporary understanding of the Church and for a thoroughgoing reform. Lapidary axioms are set forth; for example, "the degradation of faith [*foi*] into mere beliefs [*croyances*] accelerated with the spread of Christianity".[70] Or, "Religions of authority are doomed to disappear."[71]

[68] A few texts: *Through Scylla and Charybdis,* ix, 81, 223f., 225f; *Christianity at the Crossroads,* 248, 243. Cf. also the misuse of the principle of infallibility in *External Religion: Its Use and Abuse,* 4th ed., (n.p., 1960), 128f.

[69] Principal works: *Prières d'un croyant* [Meditations of a believer] (Paris: Grasset, 1935); *La Communanté humaine* (Paris: Aubier, 1938); *Travail de la foi* (Paris: Seuil, 1962); first part of main work, *L'Homme à la recherche de son humanité* (Paris: Aubier, 1971); second part of main work, *Introduction à l'intelligence du passé et de l'avenir du christianisme* (Paris: Aubier, 1971); both in German by Herder, 1972–1973; M. Légaut and François Varillon, *Débat sur la foi,* arranged by the Centre Catholique des Intellectuels Français (Paris: Desclée de Brouwer, 1972); "Pour entrevoir l'Eglise de demain", in *Lumen vitae* (French ed. March 1972): 9–40.

[70] Légaut, *Introduction,* 73.

[71] Ibid., 220.

Such axioms are from time to time balanced by things such as: "The coexistence of a religion of authority and a religion of personal vocation is characteristic of Christianity. The contradiction implied by this coexistence ultimately lies at the core of Jesus' life."[72] One gathers from this that the unity of the Church is understood by Légaut both abstractly (sociologically) and concretely (christologically). How could this be?

The point of departure is twofold. One is an exact scientific approach that endeavors to differentiate clearly between the conceptually known and the *mysterium* toward which faith continually strives and which the "theologians and doctors" mistakenly try to conventionalize with rationalistic formulas.[73] It is no accident that here the young Légaut is connected by some threads to Modernism. (He continues Tyrrell's line of thought.) He draws upon Teilhard, but most of all he is imbued with the Bergsonian system of categories: the same reality of "life" (Légaut calls it "existence") can be found in the tension of an ascending movement (striving for unique, concrete selfhood) and the relaxation of a descending movement (sinking back into a general, abstract surrender). Both movements, in their "paradoxical simultaneity", are inherent in the "universal, endless struggle" of human existence.[74] To understand this transposed use of the Bergsonian system, another point, already mentioned, has to be added: the relationship between the charismatic personality of the leader and the disciple (described by Légaut always in categories of spiritual fatherhood and sonship). The disciple is initiated into the "distinctness" of his selfhood and into the absolute solitude where the initiating father must leave him to himself. If he

[72] Ibid., 240, 242.

[73] Légaut and Varillon, *Débat,* 17.

[74] Légaut, *Introduction,* 240; cf. *L'Homme à la recherche,* 114: "These two movements are unceasingly intertwined, struggling against each other without one ever succeeding in definitely overcoming the other."

fails in this ascending movement to spiritual selfhood, the disciple slips back into the "alienation" of the "material" collective: he becomes a sociological statistic, part of a herd, conventional, legalistic, outwardly authoritarian, traditional, supplanting "faith" (*foi*) by a multitude of "beliefs" (*croyances*). He replaces active "remembering" (*souvenir*) with the "automatism of memory",[75] (again following Bergson).

It would be enlightening to establish the relationship of these elements of the system to two concepts used by Karl Rahner, the "transcendental" and the "categorial", even though Rahner's concepts derive from Idealism, while those of Légaut come from "life-philosophy". But the distance from Fichte to Bergson is not great. In both instances what has form — the definitely shaped, dogmatic, impersonally authoritarian — is assigned to the sphere of the categorial or extrinsic. However, both emphasize that life always needs both these spheres (that was also, of course, Tyrrell's ultimate conclusion), thus avoiding a direct relativization and devaluation of the Church as organization, institution, Magisterium, guardian of tradition, and so forth.

But Légaut is not concerned with contrasting the two spiritual spheres. He sees one and the same life in the struggle between its tendency of "upward and onward" and its tendency to "regress and relax". To remain alive and vital, the "greatness of man" needs this interior "struggle between the necessary and the impossible", this "fundamental opposition" between two factors that are "necessarily complementary but actually incompatible".[76]

Even in purely anthropological terms man needs society, which created him but also claims him entirely and thus becomes "the grave

[75] Légaut, *Introduction,* 27, note.

[76] Ibid., 220; cf. *Travail,* 145: The original vision of the Spirit hovering over the waters: two elements, one heavy, massive, a prey to determinism, subject to inertia; the other impalpable, light, airy, living and free.

114

of the individual".[77] Society forever remains the person's "testing-ground" by its "pressures" that can border on "nearly legitimate cruelty".[78] This is to keep the individual alert in his unending search for selfhood (*recherche* is a basic concept). No insipid synthesis here—between being "alive" and having "form", between communion and the institution of the Church—such as Yves Congar spent his whole life proposing.[79] "Such coexistence is rarely peaceful. For the authority that heads the institution, it is always disquieting, and it is always painful for those who hear and follow the call to *communio.* . . . What counts for me is the open confrontation [*affrontement*] between the two."[80]

The twofold movement of human existence is anthropological before it is Christian. For Légaut, this anthropological step toward selfhood[81] is accompanied by a constant anxiety caused by the question that man himself cannot answer, "Who am I?"[82] This becomes articulated in the questions of love, fatherhood and death, which inevitably replace fundamental theology. The person who, in his "seeking" and "struggling"[83] for selfhood and self-awareness,[84] does not reach this open-ended question in perfect "truthfulness" (*sincérité, authenticité, intégrité, lucidité, fidélité, honnêteté, droiture, rectitude,* etc.), can find no way to Christ, to his interiority, but is left in the vestibule of the authoritarian, doctrinaire Church, where his attitude remains that of conventional "practice", in ecclesial *"aliénation"*.[85] For once man reaches maturity and tries to find the meaning of his existence, he is inevitably placed before a choice: either he understands himself as part of the

[77] Légaut, *Travail,* 96.
[78] Ibid., 146, 150.
[79] Ibid., 23; *Débat,* 35–36.
[80] Légaut and Varillon, *Débat,* 35–36.
[81] Légaut, *Travail,* 37.
[82] Ibid., 49–50.
[83] Ibid., 20, 47; *Introduction,* 15, 29, 71, etc.
[84] Légaut, *Travail,* 66.
[85] Légaut, *L'Homme à la recherche,* 114.

all-embracing cosmic unity (thus giving up his individuality), or he affirms his uniqueness, "having faith in himself",[86] and from this perspective discovers the value of things.[87] It is because of the starkness of this either/or that everything is judged mercilessly as "ideology" that cannot be justified by the "I-self" or the search for this "I".[88] This also includes everything in Christian revelation that seem unassimilable by the individual and his "authenticity".

Légaut is very contemporary at this point: the issue is "authentic" faith versus its decadent ecclesiastical forms. Thus he recommends complete identification with the true faith of the first disciples and of those Christians who can be called such in the full sense of the word, but only partial identification with what in the Church is mere *croyance* (belief) and therefore "ideology". As in Tyrrell and in Modernism, any reality in the Church that the individual cannot accept directly through the *méthode d'immanence* is "objectivistic" and belongs to the sphere of "habit", which is unavoidable but must be continually challenged and contested.

Légaut, though he is neither theologian nor exegete, plunges here into biblical origins. The position of the Christian in the Church is the continuation of Jesus' position in the midst of Israel, his people. Jesus does not even attempt to deal first with the leaders, who represent law and tradition,[89] but turns from the outset to the poor and powerless, who, ever since the Old Covenant, have possessed a human openness toward his program of "beatitudes". His disciples, caught up in the messianic ideology, from which they never fully free themselves and to which they later of necessity return, do break through in their highest moments to true faith in his unfathomable personality that transcends all their expectations. But

[86] Ibid., 11–31.
[87] Ibid., 117–23.
[88] Ibid., 125–44.
[89] Légaut, *Travail,* 135.

already in the composition of the Gospels, in the apostolic catechesis as in the reports of the Easter event, "faith" and "belief", genuine kerygma and ideological garb, are mingled, so much so that we—the present generation in particular, because of modern exegetical procedures—must continually grope our way through the "ambiguities"[90] of the "letter". We have to find our way within the sociologically determined narrow range of the documents and their equally limited, thousands-of-years-old, traditional interpretations to a meeting of our own seeking self with the self of Jesus, who alone can give fulfillment.

Jesus' own "subversive", "independent" attitude toward official Judaism, his "trenchant, judgmental and even provocative" attitude,[91] also permits the Christian to confront "eternal Judaism",[92] "Judaism of all times"[93] in the Church. We too may experience the memorable encounter of Jesus with Caiaphas, the "crucial confrontation of two authorities": that of Caiaphas, "legal, centuries old, based on an impressive tradition, aware of the loving and vengeful presence of a faithful and jealous God",[94] and that of Christ.

Légaut was accused of Marcionism, even of Manichaeism,[95] but this impression is only created (albeit necessarily) by the ontology that uniformly underlies all historical events. Légaut emphasizes positive elements in the New Covenant, such as God's call in Christ (*religion d'appel*), more than in the Old Covenant, which is generally and rather exaggeratedly understood as a pure *religion d'autorité*.[96] While the Church must necessarily maintain her sociological-authoritative basis, the individual remains just as free as he was in the Old Covenant to

[90] Légaut, *Introduction,* 25. The word and its synonyms recur frequently.
[91] Légaut, *Travail,* 133, 135.
[92] Ibid., 137.
[93] Ibid., 139.
[94] Ibid., 134.
[95] Légaut and Varillon, *Débat,* 33, 61.
[96] Ibid., 63. He himself admits it.

follow God's call in all sincerity, even outside the realm of the Bible,[97] or to misinterpret it in the direction of mere "practice". Even Jesus' life could be misunderstood (because of his miracles) as messianic in the Judaic sense: how much more so the doctrinal character of ecclesial pronouncements,[98] the ideology of the Church's *Credo*,[99] the presence of masses of Christians who are such merely by habit or social conformity, the Church as "establishment"[100] and her cheap adaptation to the surrounding paganism without effecting profound change,[101] the continuous summons to "holy obedience"[102] as a poor substitute for personal faithfulness to Christ,[103] the "paternalistic" admonitions of a clergy[104] no longer aware of the secret of true personal fatherhood.[105] All this subverts Christians to adhere to a Christianity that, today more than ever, has lost the right to exist. For Légaut, the typical example is the legalization of the "evangelical counsels", which replace the Christian's personal faithfulness and dedication to Jesus by being institutionalized into a juridically defined "canonical state", with its "optional superfaith".[106]

In 1933, Légaut dedicated his *Prières d'un croyant* to *Mater Ecclesia*, introducing them with a dialogue with the Church: "Mother, you have not disappointed me; praised be the One who sent you to men to extend his presence among them. Thanks to you I have believed and

---

[97] Légaut, *Introduction*, 45; *Travail*, 149. This is an important element in a potential theology of mission, to provide nations who missed the preparation that the Old Testament provides with a religious anthropology that somehow, by a similar experience of *"carence d'être"* (*L'Homme à la recherche*, 26), leads them to look for the fulfillment which salvation brings.

[98] Légaut, *Introduction*, 35, 60.

[99] Ibid., 62, 77, 158.

[100] Ibid., 29.

[101] Ibid., 72, 275.

[102] Ibid., 36.

[103] Légaut, *L'Homme à la recherche*, 113.

[104] Légaut, *Travail*, 27.

[105] Ibid., 147.

[106] Légaut, *Introduction*, 238, more fully: 339; also *Travail*, 147f.

have seen!" In 1970 such expressions would hardly have been possible. All that is now valid is the encounter of an entirely isolated man[107] in his failure (*échec*)[108] with the absolutely unique Christ, in the exclusive confrontation of the *général* and the *universel*[109]. Meanwhile, all else in the Church is ambiguous to him: as "call", it is wholesome, as legalistic "authority", baneful.

At the same time one must remember that for Légaut this ambiguity cannot be overcome because it is the structure of all that is worldly and hence justifies the authenticity of his struggle. But even though the *contradiction* in the Church between what is christological and what is sociological is intrinsic,[110] this does not mean that the present form of the distribution of hierarchical authorities must be retained nor, above all, that objectivistic paternalism is the legitimate mode of exercising authority.

In his plan for a future Church, Légaut sees—one might say, with the naiveté of a Rousseau—a qualitative change in authority: whenever possible, only personal authority should be recognized as valid (that is, pneumatic competence)[111] as in the case of Jesus, who had authentic authority only in virtue of the power of his radiant personality. In any case, the present age cannot accept or understand any authority other than that of a call:[112] and reaction against legalistic authority is a sign of life.[113] Today it is up to the members of the Church to radiate personal authority.[114] An "extreme decentralization" must take place[115]

---

[107] Légaut, *Introduction,* 43, note: "Man, in his fundamental reality, is solitary, even if he is not aware of his isolation." The resemblance to Ionesco is striking.

[108] A key word (*Travail,* 82–102) as in Jaspers.

[109] Légaut, *Travail,* 22, 155ff; *Introduction,* 34.

[110] Légaut, *Introduction,* 240.

[111] Ibid., 235.

[112] Ibid., 209ff.

[113] Ibid., 223.

[114] Légaut, "Pour entrevoir l'Église", 16.

[115] Ibid., 21.

so that the individual bishop can once more become truly the spiritual father who leads his own and raises them in Christian responsibility.

In the course of time, the pope's power became unduly amplified, and his interventions were unnecessarily multiplied. From now on, the pope should be permitted to act merely in a subsidiary capacity. But also the dioceses (which need to be increased in number) must be disentangled from the proliferation of their innumerable committees, whose activities are spiritually sterile.[116] If greater value were placed on the pneumatic element, there would be new vocations and also the *right kind* of candidates for the priesthood. The religious order that would answer the present needs of the Church has not yet made its appearance. The identity of the Church depends on a faith that is new in each new age, a faith like that of the disciples when they first recognized the Lord, with all the difficulty of those first moments which pierced through their traditional expectations.

In Légaut's radical criticism of all that is purely sociological in the Church, it should not be overlooked that his essential point lies in his fundamental anthropology: love, and primarily fatherhood, which he describes with great warmth and depth, is in direct contrast to the idea of a fatherless society and patricide as the origin of the community of brothers. In this, the Christian roots of Légaut, the peasant and youth-movement member, remain intact. But are these sufficient to ensure healthy development? It is doubtful. Life-philosophy has a fundamental and pretheological distrust of form and structure (which it regards as merely frozen life, whereas in reality, of course, all life has organic form). Furthermore, the youth movement had a fundamental distrust of any authority except pneumatic authority (which, if followed through, would lead to Donatism). Without questioning Légaut's personal integrity, it must be said that all this only serves to bring him back to the mindset of Modernism. He is unable to get beyond it.

The almost complete dismissal of the papacy is only a typical

[116] Ibid., 39. The small cell as the only true Church today: *Introduction,* 28, 378ff.

consequence: for Légaut, the real unity of the Church is solely in the inexpressible and even invisible "authenticity" of private faith in its relationship to Christ. Many such solitary believers can in fact form an "authentic" cell of the Church, but their visibility is something accidental, fortuitous. Everything that is visible—hierarchically administered sacraments, official preaching, the hierarchy itself—belongs per se in the sphere of sociology and becomes suspect of being ideology.

Thus, behind Légaut's idea of the Church lurks the spectre of Plotinus. It is more alive today than ever before, because it is, in effect, that religiosity which holds the essentially real and ultimate to be ineffable and beyond concepts. Hence, it negates the Word of God who became flesh. One meets this Plotinism everywhere in Catholic thought today, among outstanding thinkers such as Stanislas Breton (*Foi et raison logique* [Seuil, 1971]) or the Victorinus scholar, Pierre Hadot (*Plotin ou la simplicité du regard* [2d ed., 1973]). In Légaut this Plotinism was the legacy of a generation that was influenced by the young Augustine, the young Newman and Kierkegaard, who desired to make "God and myself" the focus of religion. But they forgot how much the Church became for Augustine and Newman an objective, essentially unambiguous medium of communication, despite all the criticism that both of them never ceased to apply to her empirical form. A Plotinian-Buddhist solipsism vis-à-vis God degrades the Church—despite all Légaut's protests—to exactly that nonintrinsic, and hence *abstract,* unity that would in fact separate her from the concrete uniqueness of Jesus Christ.

3. Carried Away by Ecumenism

From the foregoing it becomes obvious that the ecumenical endeavor's necessary, theologically unavoidable concern to unite the Christian confessions gives rise to an equally necessary and unavoidable obstacle:

the negative unity of non-Catholic denominations, which is nowhere more evident, the consensus nowhere more solid, than in the rejection of the Roman claim. Quite obviously, then, this embarrassing topic must be shifted to the end, and in the meantime topics must be addressed where unity—real or apparent, whole or partial—already exists. These themes then, as a matter of course, are not only given priority in time but also in importance. Is it not infinitely more important to agree on the nature of God's loving self-revelation in Christ, on the redemption of the world, on the divine Sonship of Christ, on faith, love and hope—yes, even on the Church as the People of God and, eventually, on the ecclesiastical ministry—than on this most thorny point, the Petrine office and the privileges attached to it by the Catholic Church?

Who would not be glad to have a presentation of Catholic doctrine such as that given in the Dutch Catechism, that seems to make the faith of the Church more accessible to non-Catholics?[117] Who would not welcome the unprecedented announcement of the *Neues Glaubensbuch [New Catechism]*,[118] setting forth the "common faith of the Church"? Out of its five component sections, this book devotes four to the faith shared; only one section speaks about "questions that are still open between the churches", and they are presented so irenically that paths to mutual understanding seem to open up everywhere.

The first-mentioned book deals rather comprehensively with the "priesthood of the People of God" and follows this with thirteen chapters on the office of the bishop but finds a single chapter sufficient for "Unity through Peter's Successor". The two subsequent

[117] *Glaubensverkündigung für Erwachsene* [A new catechism: Catholic faith for adults], German edition of the Dutch Catechism (Nijmegen and Utrecht, with imprimatur of Cardinal Alfrink, 1968).

[118] *Neues Glaubensbuch. Der Gemeinsame Glaube,* ed. J. Feiner and L. Vischer, 6th ed. (Zurich: Herder and Theologischer Verlag, 1973).

chapters return in conclusion to the priesthood of the people as a whole. The Petrine theme is reduced to a negligible detail.

In the second work it is not surprising to see this theme (which, incidentally, is best treated by Karl Lehmann) deferred to the last possible moment.[119] This suggests that the preceding major theological questions have already attained an unambivalent meaning, or at least are close to attaining it. This is unaffected by the problems still open, namely the papacy and Mariology, the relation between the written word and tradition, grace and works and the number of the sacraments. Practical ways of resolving these latter are suggested. Therefore, the troublesome article about the pope can be relegated to the periphery, all the more so since, from Vatican II on, communion between the Roman Catholic and Orthodox Churches is permitted, even though the latter does not accept Rome's primacy of jurisdiction.

Hence, a draft resolution of a Swiss synod seems quite right to say that "Primacy and infallibility of the pope belong *therefore* to those doctrines of faith, the formal nonapproval of which does not exclude a mutual community in the sacraments. . . . What, however, is necessary, is an agreement on the *central* content of the faith."[120] The memorandum of the Working Party of the Ecumenical University Institutes of Germany, entitled *Reform und Anerkennung der kirchlichen Ämter* (*Reform and recognition of ecclesial ministries*),[121] condenses the question under consideration to one parenthetical remark (in no. 5): "Formal recognition of ecclesiastical offices (can) now take place. . . . Remaining differences in the structure of ministries would then no longer divide and separate the churches. Thus, apart from the as yet unclarified question of the papacy's universal office of leadership, both confessions are given the significant opportunity of working together to develop the

[119] Ibid., 631–43.

[120] Proposal of the Fifth Interdiocesan Fact-finding Commission, pt. 2, no. 4, 5, 4, in *Schweizerische Kirchenzeitung,* 31–32 (1973).

[121] Munich: Verlag Kaiser and Mainz: Matthias Grünewald, 1973.

future form and structure of ecclesiastical ministries. . . . "[122] In this, as in innumerable other ecumenical papers, such as the important statements of the *Groupe des Dombes,*[123] people are quick to speak about "*the* Church" as if this great body about which Catholics and Protestants speak were univocally the same, and hence, as if the Eucharist, concerning which they produce joint statements, were the same for both. The question of who has the last word on the content of this concept is either bracketed out or it is tacitly assumed that, in fact, it is the jointly deliberating group of theologians themselves. As is frequently said in ecumenical discussions, they feel that the convictions they share outweigh the remaining disagreements. On the basis of this, they presume to represent the *desired* unity on the subject under discussion as a *unanimity* already attained.

The papers of the *Groupe des Dombes,* printed in Taizé, speak somewhat more cautiously than the above-mentioned memorandum. They are aware of the unresolved problem of the meaning of the apostolic succession. Nevertheless they propose intercommunion between Catholics and Protestants on the basis of "shared eucharistic faith",[124] unanimity which is attained by disregarding (or replacing?) the ultimate instance which can determine whether there is unanimity or not. We are not concerned here with the difficult question of intercommunion. This merely furnishes an occasion to point out the almost inevitable pattern of ecumenical dialogues, whereby the papacy, the very epitome of the question of ministry, is put to the end of the discussion; a blind eye is turned to the one office that can finally

[122] Ibid., 6. The parenthesis in the sentence, as placed, makes the meaning unclear. Does it mean that the confessions *have* the chance jointly to determine the structure of the office if they *disregard* the unresolved question? Or: *would they have* the chance if this particular question were resolved?

[123] *Vers une même foi eucharistique? Accord entre catholiques et protestants* (Les Presses de Taizé, 1972). *Pour une réconciliation des ministères. Eléments d'accord entre catholiques et protestants* (Les Presses de Taizé, 1978).

[124] *Vers une même foi,* 17–28.

banish the abstractness of all other agreements and is able to give them their proper ecclesiological concreteness.

It should once more be emphasized that we do not intend to detract from the urgency of ecumenical dialogue; nor do we reject this typical sequence of theological negotiations out of hand. It seems to be a psychological necessity, theologically defensible so long as what is presently relegated to the periphery is not treated as a trifle, a thing of no importance. This cannot happen, of course, in the dialogue with Orthodoxy, because the other dogmatic difficulties are largely only excuses for delaying the discussion of the painful point. Here, however, this point assumes the character of a *differentia specifica*, affecting the whole *genus* under discussion, particularly when the attempt is made to minimize it by putting the pope in the "last place", where he—like Paul and the rest of the apostles—nevertheless becomes a focus for the eyes of "the world, angels and men" (1 Cor 4:9).

Having said this, there is no need to speak of Catholic attempts (e.g., in the *Bensberger Kreis*) to build the Church upon some kind of minimal consensus of basic communities, who on principle want to have nothing to do with Rome, nor probably with any other institutional structure. These "open communities", which are urged to join in "working parties" and to unite in an "open church", can only end up in complete chaos. All they have in common—for a time—is sociological criticism (which always needs an object) and pneumatic enthusiasm. Neither of these has anything in common with the Christian, not to say the Catholic, life of faith.

A Catholic can turn and twist as much as he likes; he cannot go back before Vatican I, which was solemnly confirmed by Vatican II (*Lumen gentium* 22). As always, definitions effect an integration into a larger, all-embracing whole. And this whole has been available for a long time: it is the indefectibility of the believing Church, of which the indefectibility of the Petrine office is only a particular aspect, theologically undergirding and confirming the reality of the unifying

Holy Spirit. One may say that Vatican I has locked a door here so skillfully that no one can open it again without bringing down the whole edifice, the entire Catholic structure. It is dishonest to play with the idea of opening this door. But it is also futile frantically to avoid the biblical word "authority" (*exousia*), substituting "service" for it, because all biblical authority exists solely for service. Indeed, the People of God benefit from a service only when "authority" is effectively present: for authentic proclamation, for government, for administering the sacraments. To drive a wedge between authority and service is also dishonest. Today, more than ever, it is absolutely necessary for the Church to have a tribunal that guarantees unity in the interpretation of revelation, because the earlier, naive integrity of biblical texts has been unsettled by exegesis, and exegesis splinters in all directions. Real authority—the authority of the whole hierarchy, i.e., the bishops with the pope in their midst—is needed to show not only a practical but also an objectively guaranteed right way through the confusion of opinions and hypotheses. Neither biblical texts nor the sixteenth-century creeds (nor those of later times) can substitute for this authority.

The reluctance of the pope to subordinate the Catholic Church to (even a loose) abstract unity of a World Council of Churches is not only understandable but inevitable, because no misunderstanding can be permitted here. But real ecumenical dialogue does not depend on such a subordination, and even less so when the unity it envisages is a loose one and in the future. The *Catholica* will also have to resist the temptation to confuse her empirical character of being a "part", in the realm of the purely human, with her theological character. In other words, she should not see her potential "complementarity" to other denominations or cultures as a theological lack, to be remedied by convergence in a synthesis of all Christian denominations. Not even the many (and at times dreadful) mistakes that the Church, composed of sinners and led by fallible humans, has committed throughout history, and for which she must apologize and make tangible atonement, can keep her from believing that the infallibility promised her (and no other infallibility!) is irrevocably guaranteed.

How can this be without the Church becoming the laughingstock of the world, which unceasingly holds up to her the list of her sins? In other words, how can the office of Peter, without negating itself, come down from the top of the pyramid where it is usually pictured, and where, for too long, it has seen itself? How can it so integrate itself with the total life of the Church that it can be the guarantor of concrete unity in the concrete center of the Church? This the following chapters will attempt to show.

II

The *Mysterium* of the Church

The Real Christ in His Constellation

The foregoing chapters have described the escalation of the anti-Roman attitude to the point where Rome became reduced to an abstract socio-ecumenical principle. This was accomplished by isolating the "Roman principle" from the larger unity in which it is embedded and for which it is intended. It can function and be rightly understood only when integrated into this larger unity.

In what, then, is the Roman principle embedded? Two answers must be at once rejected as inadequate. If we suppose that it is thus embedded only in the universal Church, the conclusion readily follows that "authority is given by God to the (whole) Church, to be transmitted by her to the shepherds who are her servants for the good of souls", which "is to be understood in the sense that the authority of the ecclesial office and ecclesial leadership is transferred by the community of the faithful to the shepherds".[1] The universal Church appears here as a final forum, whose relation with the redemptive event of Christ is no longer perceptible. If one tries, like Lamennais, an even more comprehensive positioning of the Roman principle in the entirety of God's revelation in human history — where the papacy becomes nothing more than a current representation of the God-given natural law of authority — the outlines of biblical salvation history, as well as of Christ's Church, become blurred and general, and (quite clearly in

---

[1] This statement of the Council of Pistoia was condemned by Pius VI as "heretical". Denzinger-Schönmetzer, *Enchiridion Symbolorum* (Barcelona: Herder, 1967), 2602, cf. 2603.

the case of Lamennais) human social consciousness takes precedence over papal authority. The papacy again appears, as in the previous interpretation, only as representative of a universal forum.

Both of these attempts miss the obvious point in the history of Christian origins that the office of Peter derives from his real relationship with Jesus Christ, a relationship which, in the genesis of the Church, remains sharply defined and distinct. But in the debates on the question of ministry, this sharpness of definition is usually dealt with as if the office could be treated in isolation. While this may be practical as a method, it has devastating theological consequences: in the *mysterium* of the Church—which has to be interpreted by the *mysterium* of Christ—no element makes sense if it is isolated from the whole.

Such isolation of the Roman primacy has nevertheless been attempted to some extent even within the Catholic Church. This too could only lead to an abstraction (though of another kind) expressed in the dichotomy (which is hard to analyze but recognizable everywhere) between the image of the Church as *societas perfecta* and that of the Mystical Body; between an official clerical theology and a more or less private "spirituality" (to which perhaps the veneration of Mary and of the saints belongs).

We must attempt to reunite, as in their origin, the elements that have become dissociated. Only in a stable integration can the primacy's function be understood in its vital meaning. In the *mysterium* of the Church no individual member can be successfully isolated from the whole living organism. Anatomical dissection can only be performed on dead bodies. Everything is interrelated with everything, which however does not mean that the function of a particular member—of the eye, the tongue, the kidney—cannot be very precisely defined *within* the whole and recognized as indispensable. This "law" is already evinced in the central figure of Jesus Christ, who cannot be detached either from his trinitarian or from his salvation-historical ecclesial context.

132

1. Christ as the Concretization of the Triune God

Jesus Christ is not a "principle" or a "program" but a man of flesh and blood, born in Galilee, pierced by a Roman lance on the Cross and seen by his disciples resurrected, bearing the marks of his wounds. Nevertheless, not one document in the New Testament—neither the letters of Paul nor the synoptic Gospels, let alone the Johannine writings—explains the existence of this Jesus of Nazareth otherwise than as the fulfillment of the promises of God, whom he calls his Father. And at the same time these explanations either presuppose or recount the beginning of the gift of God's Spirit to believers. From then on, the law is not above them but in their hearts, and hence they are not slaves any more but have become freemen and children. Jesus does not merely announce a true doctrine as prophets or wisdom teachers did. In his very existence he is Truth revealed by God. His birth is already truth: the Word of God becomes "flesh" and dwells among mankind; and his death, his descent to hell and his Resurrection are equally truth. These are not mere materially expressed symbols of God's attitude toward the world; they *are* his very attitude, which is no mere feeling but purpose, action and commitment.

If, according to Catholic teaching, the sacraments "contain and confer the grace they visibly signify",[2] then Jesus Christ—in his Incarnation, in his hidden and public life, in his death on the Cross and in his Resurrection—is the primordial sacrament. The giver is God (the Father), and the saving grace bestowed through this sacrament is God's Holy Spirit.

Through Jesus of Nazareth, the real man of flesh and blood, God himself becomes definitively concrete. By the uniqueness of Jesus' existence and his transcendent destiny in the Resurrection, we not only learn to know who and what God is but, in our own existence, we become partakers of him: we receive his Spirit who alone can

[2] Ibid., 1606.

fathom the depth of the Godhead. He does not merely perform before us the drama of his eternal love, he makes us participants in that drama. According to Paul, his love is poured into our hearts by his Spirit, and John says that no one can assert that he knows God who does not himself possess this love and live it. In the flesh-and-blood reality of Jesus, God's reality does not merely become concrete to the point where love can clearly distinguish the trinitarian "outline" of God in its uniqueness: "Thus is he, and he alone!" There is more: we are carried away and permitted to "experience" the inmost content of God's form through the participation of faith: "If you abide in my word," says Jesus, "you will know the truth, and the truth will make you free" (Jn 8:31–32).

The truth about Jesus therefore—according to his own testimony—cannot be comprehended except in that mysterious "abiding" in the word, where "abiding" is both receptive faith and decisive action, and the "word" is Jesus' self-expression as well as his being-uttered by the Father and declared by the Spirit. This is the objective fact that is both historical and more than historical, in that the reality of the true God shines mysteriously through the real man Jesus. The true God who manifests himself here is thus the forever-supreme, all-encompassing Father who speaks the incarnate Word. He is the Creator of the cosmos, the source of all being and the bestower of all grace (Eph 1:1–10). The Spirit who interprets this Word in world history—that is, the Father's uttering and the Son's being-uttered—is the one who reveals the eschatological fulfillment toward which all human striving and endeavor are directed. It is the figure of the real Jesus that spans the widest possible distance between Alpha and Omega. He encompasses both, and as the world is created in him and all judgment is given him, he himself *is* both.[3] And within the immensity of this scope he exemplifies in his historical existence what God in his relation to Israel

[3] Cf. Hans Urs von Balthasar, "Die drei Gestalten der Hoffnung", in *Die Wahrheit ist symphonisch* (Einsiedeln: Johannesverlag, 1972), 147ff.

(and hiddenly in his relation to mankind as a whole) has intended and done. Only against the background of what (since Jesus' coming) is called the "Old Covenant"—but which might be more precisely termed the "temporal covenant", with the implicit promise that it will become "eternal" (Heb 13:20; cf. Is 55:3; 61:8; Jer 32:40; 50:5; Ezek 16:60; 37:26)—is that Covenant ratified which gives us eternal salvation through Jesus' repudiation, rejection and abandonment by God. Everything, Israel's most extreme tribulations—from Lamentations to Job and the Suffering Servant—becomes actual in Jesus: he *is* the summation of God's relations in history with his world.

That in Jesus Christ the triune God becomes concretely manifest explains both aspects of Jesus' conduct, his stepping forth and his drawing back: he comes forth with the full authority of the triune God whose concrete expression he is. He does not merely refer to God (as the Baptist pointed to Jesus); he *is* in "power" (Jn 5:27; 10:18; 17:2) the incarnate sovereignty of this God. But in stepping forward he does not draw attention to himself but manifests the Father: "Why do you ask me about what is good? One there is who is good" (Mt 19:17); "No one is good but God alone" (Lk 18:19). And exactly in this self-transcending reference to the "Father who is greater" (Jn 14:28), in this deferring to the Father, he proves himself not merely humanly humble but divinely authentic, as the one who "has come in the Father's name" (Jn 5:43), who as the Son of God does not seek his own honor and will "but the will of him who sent me" (Jn 6:38). He is not, as God, "your Master and Lord" and, as man, the one who humbles himself to wash the feet of his disciples (Jn 13:14): as God, he is the Lord who humbles himself and, as man, in the shame and ignominy of his Passion, he is surrounded by the majesty of God. Everything in the Church stems from, and is understood in, the mystery of the distance between the unique Master and "you (who) are all brethren" (Mt 23:8).

2. The Christological Constellation

All men are interrelated in a human constellation. One sole human being would be a contradiction in terms, inconceivable even in the abstract, because to be human means to be with others. The God-man Jesus Christ is no exception: as God *as well as man* he exists only in his relation to the Father in the unity of the divine Holy Spirit.

Because of this, Jesus' relation to others cannot be limited solely to his human nature: he stands as an indivisible whole within a constellation of his fellow men. This constellation is an inner determinant; it has relevance for his divine humanity. It is essential, not accidental, to his being and acting. He cannot be detached from his constitutive human group, though this fact in no way infringes upon his sovereign position. If one attempts to detach Jesus and the doctrine about him (Christology) from this constitutive group, his figure—even when kept in the trinitarian context—becomes hopelessly *abstract.* Clearly this holds not only for Protestant Christology but implicity also for Catholic Christology, insofar as the persons essentially associated with Christ are assigned to separate theological treatises, if a place is found for them at all in dogmatics.

Let us first name the most important persons on the horizon of the New Testament who belong to this constellation. The choice is not easy because beyond this selection there are other individuals with significant theological positions and assignments who deserve to be taken into consideration, such as Joseph, Jesus' foster father, Mary Magdalen, the witness to the Resurrection, the "friends" of Jesus, Martha and Mary, and also the Jews who were sympathetic to him— Simon, Nicodemus, Joseph of Arimathea—and, in particular, Judas Iscariot, whom Jesus chose, fully knowing that he would reach the goal set before him through Judas' betrayal.

Besides the Baptist, other major representatives of the Old Testament appear in person: Moses and Elijah are present at the Transfiguration of Jesus. They also play a role in Jesus' discussions with the Jews and certainly an important one in the understanding of his mission.

But close to Jesus and theologically more significant are the *Baptist,* his *Mother* and the *Twelve* (with *Peter* on the one side and *John* on the other) and finally the one "born out of time", *Paul.* (James, the brother of the Lord, will be mentioned later in another context.) At least these, if no others, belong to the constellation of Jesus and are therefore integral to Christology. Hence it is misleading when Catholic dogmatics has little to say about the theological positions of the Baptist, the Beloved Disciple and the "Apostle", when it makes Mariology a distinct, isolated treatise and deals with the Twelve, headed by Peter, only within the doctrine of the Church. (Earlier, the discussion centered almost exclusively on Peter.) True, it is not possible to talk about everything at the same time; division into treatises is a necessary expedient. But such division should be made only after the primary relationships have been shown, in that very constellation which gives the major figures mentioned above their significance. This also holds for Jesus himself. His relationship to each of these persons is in accord with the Father's plan of salvation history. These relationships are personal and not purely "objective" (such a thing does not exist in this realm.) Their intimacy is understandable to us in a preliminary way, of course, only on a human level. But we can appreciate it more deeply by meditating on the indications given in Scripture. This is not the place to develop the point, as our topic is limited to Jesus' relationship with Peter (naturally, in the immediate context of the "Twelve"). But it is axiomatic that while this relationship is a definite and distinct one, it can in no way be treated in isolation.

The chronological sequence is by no means unimportant theologically. At the beginning, at the center of the event of the Incarnation stands Mary, the perfect handmaid, who consents to become physically and spiritually the mother of her Son as well as of his work. This maternal relationship changes to some extent with Jesus' maturing to an independent adult person, but it can never cease to exist.

137

Even the election of the Twelve, with Peter at the head, cannot be wholly independent of this primary, all-embracing relationship. The Mother has her place in it.

But between these two events lies the mysterious, humanly obscure yet theologically deeply significant relationship between the *Baptist* and Jesus. The Gospels and the Acts of the Apostles touch on it only in snatches, hard to reconcile fully. But all agree in giving the Baptist a decisive importance in the historical placement of Jesus' mission. John's eschatological preaching and his penitential baptizing are undoubtedly historical, as is Jesus' baptism by him. It is clear that the Baptist points to the One who comes after him, even if he has no foreknowledge and later becomes unsure whether Jesus is the "one who is to come".

It is certain that Jesus' mission superseded John's and that some of John's disciples went over to Jesus; also that Jesus drew attention to the extraordinary figure of the Baptist and his role in closing the "Old Covenant". It is probable that for a while Jesus was among the Baptist's group of disciples and that his own mission ripened there, humanly speaking, to its final maturity. The intimate personal relationship of the two is inaccessible to us. We can see only the objective relationship between the Old Testament in its self-transcendence, personified by the Baptist, and the dawn of the "kingdom of God" that draws near with Jesus. However, within the objectivity of missions there are also subjective human relationships between those commissioned. In this instance they are—as shown in their objective, respectful references to each other—of an unimaginable tenderness. They are the two pivotal links that, forged together, make the chain of God's historical plan of salvation unbreakable. This emboldened John—the disciple who most likely went over to Jesus at the bidding of the Baptist (Jn 1:35–39)—to place on the lips of the latter the spontaneous phrase, "the friend of the bridegroom" (Jn 3:29), a distinction that none of the Twelve would have dared to claim. They were addressed by Jesus as "friends" only in the hour of the Eucharist (Jn 15:14–15).

138

Therefore it is theologically correct that medieval representations of the Last Judgment show the two great intercessors before the Divine Judge to be, not Mary and Peter, but Mary and the Baptist. The latter embodies the fullness of the "Old Covenant", the initial phase of the Father's salvific action, and, through the meshing of their missions as well as their personal intimacy, he is closest to Jesus after the Mother, Mary. Just as Mary, the opening phase of the New Covenant, at the visit of Jesus' family (Mk 3:31–35), is relegated, together with the "brothers", to the Old Covenant which is now being abrogated, John who stands at the threshold of the New Covenant (Mt 11:11) is lifted over the threshold into the New as "Elijah who is to come", as "more than a prophet", as "the greatest born of woman" (Mt 11:9, 11, 14) whose "arrest" (Mk 1:14) signals Jesus' entry upon his own self-oblation. In the work that Jesus is inaugurating, such a man cannot be left behind and forgotten. He becomes part of it as the one who is the earthly initiator of Jesus' mission. His feast—until lately preceded by a vigil—is celebrated a few days before that of Peter and Paul. But in the theology of the Church he is forgotten.

The choosing of the Twelve comes later. According to Mark it is one of the first acts of Jesus' public life, primarily looking toward the future: a symbolic, solemn founding of the New Israel, yet aware of the past which the Baptist personifies. The twelve tribes, long ago dispersed and existing only fictionally,[4] are given a genuine renascence.

In the (pre-)Lucan version, the bestowing of dominion in the kingdom is not merely a promise concerning the final Judgment: "As my Father appointed a kingdom for me, so do I appoint for you that you may eat and drink at my table in my kingdom and sit on thrones judging the twelve tribes of Israel" (Lk 22:29–30). "In Luke, the legal fact of dominion is already established in a single act by Jesus, imply-

---

[4] Thus in the *Testament of the Twelve Patriarchs,* a much-read Jewish document of the first century B.C., with Christian interpolations.

ing that, if this is to remain a reality, it has to be a juridical transfer"; in other words, it is a "real dominion, to be exercised in the future with authority already promised in the present". Moreover, Jesus' reference to the supreme fullness of authority that he has received from his Father gives "at the same time the juridical origin of the exercise of the delegated full authority".[5] In Luke's account the present and future delegation of full juridical authority is bound up with the themes of the eucharistic meal, the betrayal, service as a criterion of rank and with Jesus' special prayer for Peter. The consequence of this was therefore correctly understood: this juridical function is valid for the entire life of the Church, and the "thrones" or "seats" mean those occupied by the apostles and their successors.[6]

[5] Heinz Schürmann, "Jesu Abschiedsrede, Lk 22:21–38", pt. 3, *Neutestamentliche Abhandlungen*, 20, 5 (Münster: Aschendorff, 1957): 41–43.

[6] Clement of Rome, *Letter to the Corinthians*, 44, 2–3, in *Ancient Christian Writers*, vol. 1 (New York: Newman Press, 1946): 10–11. Clement is concerned with the investiture of successors. Tertullian, in *On Prescription against Heretics*, in *The Ante-Nicene Fathers*, vol. 3 (New York: Charles Scribner's Sons, 1918), 260, specifies: " . . . run over the apostolic churches, in which the very thrones of the apostles are still preeminent in their places, in which their own authentic writings are read, uttering the voice and representing [*repraesentantes*] the face of each of them." In the fourth century it was common to designate various churches, particularly in Rome, as "apostolic seats" (Basil to Ambrose, letter 197, 1: "The Lord himself transferred you from the judges of the earth to the chair of the apostles"), *The Fathers of the Church*, vol. 28 (Washington, D.C.: The Catholic University of America Press, 1955), 42. Pacianus of Barcelona states that the bishops, as "possessors of the apostolic seats" (Migne, PL 13, 1057bc) may also be called apostles. For Jerome (letter 15, 1), Rome is "the seat [*cathedra*] of the apostle Peter". Even the thrones mentioned in Revelation 20 as serving as seats of judgment are understood, beginning with Augustine, to refer to the successors of the apostles who exercise their function as judges within the Church: "'And I saw seats and them that sat upon them, and judgment was given.' It is not to be supposed that this refers to the Last Judgment but to the seats of the rulers themselves by whom the Church is governed" (*The City of God*, 20, 9). Numerous texts that repeat this point of view are mentioned in an unpublished study by J. M. Garrigues and M. J. Guillou, "Le Statut eschatologique et le caractère ontologique de la succession apostolique".

Jesus' awareness of his kingship that he possessed already here on earth[7] is expressed in this "bequest" of the kingdom entrusted to him by God. And what at the end seems like an act of "bequeathing" has its beginning in the sovereign call of those he "desired", the Twelve whom "he appointed to be with him" (Mk 3:14), whom he formed and "sent out to preach" and endowed with "authority" (v. 15).

One look at the Master will suffice to make us understand that, for him, "power of authority", the awareness of his sublime mission, is naturally and intimately linked to the humility of "service". He is even ready to give his life without question and as a matter of course for those he serves (cf. Mk 10:42-45; Lk 22:25-30; Jn 13:13-17). In forming the Twelve to be the core of a wider circle of disciples, Jesus assiduously seeks to make them comprehend him in his essential *being* — not only by teachings in which he proclaims himself and deeds that can and are to be imitated — just as it is the primary vocation of the Twelve "that they abide in him". They are to share his mind, his mandate, his authority, his zeal and dedication and, finally, in the upper room his flesh and blood and, in his farewell address, his trinitarian love: all this hangs together. Hence, being sent to preach (Mk 3:14; 6:12) and having the authority to act (e.g., "drive out demons", Mk 3:15; 6:7, 13, and "cure the sick", 6:13; cf. also Mt 10:1; Lk 9:1-2, 6) are one and the same. Plenary authority can refer to proclaiming the word as well as to the power of acting, because in Jesus, the incarnate and acting Word, both are one. He describes his mandate in the prophetic words of Isaiah (Is 61:1-2; 58:6; cf. Lk 4:18-21) as a bringing of glad tidings to the poor, the imprisoned, the blind, the oppressed, as well as an actual liberation of them. The two together are the *evangelisasthai,* the announcement of the "good tidings" and of the "year of the Lord's grace". And when Mark, at the beginning of his Gospel (1:1, 14), then Paul and then the Acts of the

[7] Schürmann, "Jesu Abschiedsrede", 44, note 159.

Apostles speak of the "gospel" and of service to it (Rom 1:9), these are always to be understood as one whole, indivisible unity.

Within this community of the Twelve with Jesus—in life, mission and authority—*Peter* and *John* stand out. Peter is mentioned in all four Gospels in texts that cannot be disregarded, so much so that when someone insists on the "pure gospel" he must, like it or not, swallow the fishhook of these texts. We shall return to these later. In the meantime just two points: first, Peter's singular participation in Jesus' authority and responsibility obliges him also to participate specially in Jesus' spirit of service and his readiness to suffer (Mt 16:23–25; Jn 13:6–10, 36; 21:18–19). Secondly, in the Gospel of the Beloved Disciple—which describes the accomplishment of John's special mission and the Lord's love for him and his love for the Lord—the primacy of Peter is put right at the beginning (Jn 1:42, cf. Mk 3:16). The whole culminates in a subtly composed, symbolic doctrine of the Church (Jn 20:1–10; 21:1–25) in which the task of "office" (Peter) and the task of "love" (John) become so intertwined that it is Peter from whom "greater love" is demanded (Jn 21:15), and it passes to him from John. Thus the greater love passes from John to Peter, but, according to the sovereign will of the Lord of the Church, John "remains" with Peter (in whom office and love have become one). Peter's perplexed question of how to reckon with this is dismissed with the repeated command to follow: "If it is my will that he remain until I come, what is that to you? Follow me!" (Jn 21:22).

More than ever it is made obvious here that in the *mysterium* of the Church the parts are clearly articulated and yet inseparable from each other. Peter needs the Johannine love to give the Lord the answer worthy of his office, and he also receives this love. Hence, from now on, Johannine love has its place in Peter, but missions given by Jesus do not cease. In the unfathomable mystery of Jesus' good pleasure, John retains his own mission, distinct from that of Peter. One can say neither that love turns into office (i.e., that office has the sole claim to

love) nor that office and love are two structurally separate and opposing elements. (Of course, we are not, and do not wish to appear, in
agreement with the false Donatist doctrine that an official act performed without love, in the state of serious sin, is invalid.) Rather, we
are made unmistakably aware that the structure emerging from the
constellation around Jesus can in no way be reckoned or dealt with
according to "structuralist" patterns, not only because this constellation always has a personal dimension[8] but because the person around
whom the relationships crystallize is unique (because divine) and
therefore does not come under any general law. What Johannine
love is cannot be approached from a purely anthropological point of
view. It is Jesus' unique divine-human love within the Church. Neither can the Petrine office be accounted for entirely in sociological
terms. It is participation in Christ's divine-human authority in the
Church.

The bursting of all comprehensible models in the constellation
around Jesus can become most perplexing to human reason. Take the
seeming contradiction introduced by the call of *Paul* to an apostolate
that ranks with that of the Twelve. He has to fight hard for it, all the
more so because his vision of the Risen One, which makes him and his
mission coequal with the first witnesses, is of a totally different kind.[9]
Paul is and remains supernumerary, because with the election of
Matthias his place has already been filled. And yet he is legitimate,
even among the "super-apostles", "even though I am nothing" (2 Cor
12:11). He is indeed "nothing", for the heavenly Jerusalem remains
built upon twelve foundation stones, and no provision is made for a
thirteenth gate (Rev 21:14). And yet the lion's share falls to him in his
apostolate and his theological grasp of the *mysterium* of Christ; he is

---

[8] Similar to the structuralist texture in *Pensée sauvage* by Claude Lévi-Strauss
(Paris: Plon, 1962).

[9] Ernst Käsemann, "Die Legitimität des Apostels", in *Zeitschrift Für Neutestamentliche
Wissenschaft* 41 (1942).

associated with Luke and Mark; his exploits make up the largest part of the Acts of the Apostles.

Paul represents the "Passion of Christ" to the communities and for them, so he himself becomes a "type" as he models himself on the "type" of Christ. Not only does this introduce an unprecedented existential intervention—prelude to the great missioning of saints in Church history—but also an unheard-of clarification of what will be called office and authority in the Church. Again, the two sides are inseparable from each other. Paulinism is not only what Luther extracted as "doctrine" from the Letters to the Romans and Galatians but also that other part which deals with Church government in the Letters to the Corinthians, which sounds more authoritarian than any successor of Peter would have dared to be. (How mild the Letters of Clement sound by comparison!) This, naturally, is of more than merely antiquarian interest for the later Church: so *this* was the way the charismatic Church of Corinth was really ruled with the assistance of the Holy Spirit! But authority in the Church, the precise anatomy of which Paul has made plain, theologically as well as pastorally, for all ages of the Church on the basis of his own experience, is just as distinctively marked by the unique Christ-event as was the earlier Peter-John "structure": it is an authority that proceeds in harmony with the community and—using all the resources of charity, with a heartfelt and ministerial love and a trusting reference to the immanence of Christ's Spirit in the faithful (2 Cor 13:5)—strives to create *communio*. It threatens with a regrettable but legitimate "naked" authority only in the extreme instance when the apostle does not find in the community the proper loving obedience required by faith (2 Cor 12:20–21).

Just as Peter builds on John and John is within (and beside) Peter, the Petrine aspect perhaps appears nowhere more clearly than in Paul. Conversely, Pauline influence is unmistakable in Peter's letters,[10] which

---

[10] K. H. Schelkle, *Die Petrusbriefe, der Judasbrief* (Freiburg im Breisgau: Herder, 1961), 5ff; cf. the entries under "Paulusbriefe" in the index.

are evidently intended to transmit wholly Petrine tradition. Again, we see two striking figures (who do not in the least blur each other and who have distinct theological and ecclesiological valences) in *perichoresis*, nor could it be otherwise among the members of the "living Body of Christ".

Still, not every member communicates in the same way with the other. Within the manifest structure (which we stress is not definable in terms of tight distinctions) there are delicate lines of relation, most clearly drawn and represented by Luke and John. Luke portrays a family relationship between Mary and the Baptist, and, as Paul's companion, he circumspectly builds a bridge between the latter and the Gospel tradition. Luke and John both bring to light deep, hidden mariological dimensions. In the episode at the foot of the Cross, told only by John, he who in the beginning of the Acts of the Apostles is always shown together with Peter becomes "son" and guardian of the Mother. Thus he is shifted into a discrete but totally indispensable central position (mediating between Peter and Mary, between the official, masculine Church and the feminine Church) which alone can give these two dimensions of the Church's *mysterium* their place and proportion. Only where these concrete proportions are seen, understood and meditated upon in the light of faith, can one speak to advantage about the office of Peter in the Church. Moreover, this cannot be isolated from its most intimate connection with and within the *collegium* of the Twelve, each of whom was explicitly called by name.

3. *Peter in the Structure*

a. Not in Isolation

From the outset it becomes obvious that the communion of the *Catholica* cannot be characterized exclusively by the Petrine principle and thereby placed in opposition to other Christian communions and communities. We are not concerned here with investigating to what extent the papacy's self-image in the course of Church history may have contributed to such a biased characterization. Suffice it to say that this view must be rejected. Of course, Peter is an essential element in the above-described system. He is not in the least vague or undefined, but his figure is justifiable only within the structure. Once this is recognized, any attempt to play off against each other a "Petrine" (Catholic), a "Pauline" (Protestant) and a "Johannine" Church (the last standing either for the Eastern Church or for a synthetic church of the future) is doomed to failure.

Though the idea has a long history,[11] it is primarily *Schelling* who, in two of his final lectures on the philosophy of revelation, developed it with an undeniably anti-Catholic barb, because he had to defend himself against suspicion of having Catholic sympathies.[12] Typical of this approach is that Peter, Paul and John are not seen concretely as real symbols [*Realsymbole*] but are presented as abstract principles supposedly tending in opposite directions. The reasoning goes like this: "The obvious intention of Christ was that all[!] authority *be vested* in Peter and derive from *him*. But the extraordinary call of Paul, who received his apostolic office directly from the Lord, and so

[11] The history of this idea could be traced as far back as Joachim of Fiore (to whom Schelling refers) and his followers: Schwenckfeld, Sebastian Franck, Lessing, Herder, Quinet—indeed as far back as Tertullian. But it is also sustained by the tensions between primacy and collegiality, obedience and freedom, visibility and invisibility of the Church, etc., that cannot be eliminated from any balanced ecclesiology. Schleiermacher, Marheineke, Drey and the Russian religious philosophers and theosophists were influenced by Schelling. On the subject, see J. R. Geiselmann, *Einführung in Möhlers Symbolik* (Darmstadt: Wissenschaftliche Buchgesellschaft, 1958); also his *Johann Adam Möhler. Die Einheit in der Kirche und die Wiedervereinigung der Konfessionen* (Vienna: F. Beck, 1940).

[12] Friedrich Wilhelm Joseph von Schelling, *Sämmtliche Werke,* vol. 2, sec. 4 (Stuttgart: J. G. Cotta, 1856–1861), 324, note.

was declared to be independent of Peter[!], conflicts with this. Paul's resoluteness in disclaiming all dependence on Peter shows clearly that he was aware that he himself was free and an authority independent[!] of Peter."[13] The "conflict" postulated here is entirely contrary to history. It trivializes the "right hand of fellowship" given in Jerusalem (Gal 2:9), plays two "authorities" against each other and passes over Paul's real authority over the communities so as to make him an abstract principle of the (reformed) "freedom from" the "strict legalism" that Peter embodies and with which "everything has to start". This is again unhistorical since the Petrine principle, conceived as "strict legalism", by no means characterizes the beginning of the Church's history.

But Schelling has something else in mind. In contrast to the visible Church, provided with a ministry, he advocates "the truly *universal* church [if church be here the right word], which can only be built in the Spirit and can only survive where Christianity is perfectly understood and is fused with universal science and its new discoveries".[14] In other words, this would be a church of humanity in which faith is sublimated by knowledge and in relation to which "Protestantism . . . can only be a transition", an antithesis. "However, this church is still in the future." It will be Johannine, "at last a truly universal church".[15] Moreover, it is utopian: a church "of that second, new Jerusalem" that John saw descending from heaven, "in which the Gentile world and Judaism both find their place, existing in its own right, without restrictions, without external authority of any kind, since everyone comes to it voluntarily." It is "at last a truly *public* religion . . . as a religion of the human race possessing at the same time the most exalted science." And Schelling, who is deeply convinced of the irreversibility of the Reformation, adds: "In no other way can

[13] Ibid., 314.
[14] Ibid., 321.
[15] Ibid., 327.

Christianity suit Germany. After the Reformation, we can call Christianity ours only in this way or not at all."[16] It is unclear how the Petrine principle could fit into this synthesis except as an *obsolete* past, to which Peter as founder is consigned without ado, along with Moses. Paul, like Elijah, is considered one of those who have shaped the present; John, like the Baptist, augurs the future.[17] Peter's role remains obscure despite the repeated statement that "even Paul would be nothing without Peter".[18]

The point of view from which Schelling reflects on Church history is fundamentally an aesthetic one that does not lead to a consistent implementation of the authority principle personified by Peter. He does not even see the indissoluble relation between Peter and John, implied in the final chapter of John's Gospel. This is something that Joachim of Fiore also completely overlooked.

b. Realsymbolik

The history recounted in the New Testament is both spiritual and theological. It is far more than morally edifying. The relationship between God and the world, concretized as Christ's relationship to the Church, is offered to the contemplation of faith in real, incarnate episodes. Subsequent theology may derive valid principles from them but may not stray far from these concrete evangelical origins without becoming abstract and therefore untheological. Like Christ himself, Mary, Peter, Paul and John are not so much moral "examples" (how could Peter's denial be that!) as prototypes (*typos* Phil 3:17; only thus are they *synmimetai,* fellow imitators, cf. 1 Cor 11:1), forming the Church throughout history. Obviously this is valid even across the

[16] Ibid., 328.

[17] Ibid., 302–5.

[18] Ibid., 305. Soloviev will again refer to the image of the foundation but will give it another meaning: that which endures.

148

gulf which separates the pre-Easter, imperfect behavior of the disciples who have not yet received the Holy Spirit and the post-Easter Christians, filled with the Spirit of the risen Lord. The transgressions Peter committed before Easter, and the reprimands and correction these earned him, remain forever—with their distinctive features—signposts in the history of ecclesial office. Schelling is right when he says that "everything with which the Catholic Church is reproached finds its prototype in Peter's transgressions, about which the Gospels (particularly the Gospel of Mark) are anything but silent."[19] These episodes, which, particularly where Peter is concerned, invite criticism of Church office, are too well known to need discussing here. Yet, we regretfully have to admit that dogmatics as a "science" is not yet ready to integrate them but leaves them to homilies and contemplative prayer. Their proper integration requires a Catholic tact that knows how to preserve the difficult balance in the Petrine office (within the context of the Twelve) between that against which—on the basis of Jesus' promise and permission—"nothing will prevail" (Mt 16:18) and that which remains a very real, typically Petrine temptation for Peter's successors. It is the problem that can never be conclusively clarified: what is the standpoint of the Christian, of the Church? Is it before or after the crucifixion? Going toward the Cross (Jn 21:18–19) or coming from it (Rev 1:1–3)? On pilgrimage in the old eon or already surrounded, in anticipation, by the new one?

Simon Peter with his double name—"'You *are* Simon the son of John? You *shall* be called Cephas' (which means Peter)" (Jn 1:42)—is from the outset a dual figure, living at a period of transition. He attains to being Cephas only after the Resurrection, but even then he can commit faults that give Paul ground to "oppose him to his face"

---

[19] Schelling, *Sämmtliche Werke*, 2:311. But he mentions as examples only the reference to "Satan", the intensification of the three denials and the Lord's turning around to look at Peter.

(Gal 2:11–14). Even before the Resurrection, however, he was aware of the office entrusted to him: perhaps when he jumps out of the boat—with living but insufficient faith—to join Jesus; or when he wants to show himself to be the one who will never betray the Master; or when at the Last Supper he insists on knowing who the traitor is; or when he has the courage to draw a sword against the armed band to defend the Master; or finally when, out of a sense of responsibility, he enters the praetorium courtyard in order to find out about the Lord's fate. All these attempts that miscarry are undoubtedly motivated by his prerogative, whenever and however this was bestowed upon him by the Lord before Easter. Even the words with which he warns the Lord before the Passion or tries to protect him from it—and which earn him the sharpest rebuke as a tempter and an adversary—may be dictated by his as yet not-fully-conscious sense of responsibility. In other instances the Lord's reprimands are milder and more patient. Jesus sees, but at the same time overlooks, the discrepancy that still exists between Peter's intention and his ability. This holds even for the inevitable betrayal, but the Lord sees farther:

"Simon, Simon, behold, Satan demanded to have you (all), that he might sift you (all) like wheat, but I have prayed for *you* that your faith may not fail; and when you have turned again, strengthen your brethren." "Lord, I am ready to go with you to prison and to death!" He said: "I tell you, Peter, the cock will not crow this day, until you three times deny that you know me" (Lk 22:31–34).

It is remarkable that the Lord prays for "Simon" as the person in danger, but when he predicts the betrayal calls him "Peter", as the one who fails in his office. We find this same blend of perceptivity and patience in John 13:36: "Simon Peter said to him, 'Lord, where are you going?' Jesus answered: 'Where I am going you *cannot* follow me now; but you *shall* follow afterward.'" The Johannine parallel to

Peter's confession of the Messiah also has the same twilight atmosphere, except that Peter does not appear simply giving personal testimony but is closely bound up with the college of the Twelve. "Do you [pl.] also wish to go away?" Jesus asks the Twelve; and in Mark 8:29 (par) he asks the "disciples", "But you ... who do you [pl.] say that I am?" Peter (who in John's Gospel appears as if already irradiated by the post-Easter light) answers for all: "Lord, to whom shall *we* go? You have the words of eternal life, and we have believed, and have come to know, that you are the Holy One of God." Here, unlike the Synoptics, there follows no rebuke for Peter's wanting to prevent the Passion but a reference to Judas, an even greater disgrace to the Church: "Did I not choose you, the Twelve, and one of you is a devil?" (Jn 6:67–70).

In the "we" of Peter, who phrases his reply with collegial responsibility, there is a link with Jesus' reference to the one who will desert the *collegium* and cannot be included in Peter's confession. The conversation between Jesus and Peter at the washing of the feet also opens and closes with a reference to Judas (Jn 13:2, 11). Peter's startled question: "Lord, do you wash my feet?" becomes—after Jesus replies that Peter does not yet understand but will understand later—the exclamation: "You shall never wash my feet!" This is less a demonstration of the disciple's awareness of his office than consternation at becoming involved in something immense that overthrows all conventions (cf. Lk 5:8: "Depart from me, for I am a sinful man, O Lord"). Peter's exclamation about the three booths at the Transfiguration (Mk 9:5) proceeds from a similar reaction. The Lord tolerates this reluctance with the equanimity of one who has already decided to draw the disciple into his own ministry ("Henceforth you will be catching men", Lk 5:10) and thus into his own being ("If I do not wash you, you will have no part in me", Jn 13:8).

Three things about Peter must be kept in mind at all times. First, he is chosen for office even before he is enabled by the Holy Spirit to be a responsible leader. But this being chosen corresponds to a fundamental decision on the part of the disciple: "And when they had brought their boats to land, they left everything and followed him" (Lk 5:11). "Then Peter said in reply, 'Lo, we have left everything and followed you'" (Mt 19:27).[20] From this decision stems the disciples' (relative) openness to a growth in understanding of what Jesus really is. For "Christ did not enter Judea with the announcement 'I am the son of the living God.' Such an announcement would not have had the slightest effect. He waited until—by living with him and accepting his way of life—the disciples reached a loftier point of view, the expression of which came naturally at the first opportunity: 'You are the Son of the living God.'"[21] What has thus developed in them is not merely human good will (which, as far as Peter is concerned, mostly misfires). It is not "flesh and blood" that reveal the truth to them but "my Father who is in heaven" (Mt 16:17). And even if one postpones until after Easter the Lord's great declaration of Peter as the Rock of the Church, the Messiah-confession itself (Mk 8:29; Lk 9:20) undoubtedly takes place before Easter and represents something that is central, even though Jesus had to improve upon it and complete it to make it conform to the reality of God's Suffering Servant.

Peter's decision knows no return ("to whom shall we go?"). He gives a rudimentary though correct answer, as far as is possible before receiving the Holy Spirit. It is unbiblical to say that Peter, the sinner, the purely natural man ("flesh and blood") did everything wrongly, and only the grace of office enabled him to act rightly. Neither can the pre-Easter Peter be accused of presumption on the ground of his precedence in rank. It is not he who wants to sit at the right hand of the Son of Man but the brothers

[20] It is of no importance that this verse has been ascribed to the editor: it undoubtedly echoes a true state of affairs.

[21] Johann Adam Möhler, *Die Einheit in der Kirche,* sec. 68. Critical edition by J. R. Geiselmann (Cologne: J. Hegner, 1957), 231–32.

called the "Sons of Thunder" (Mk 10:36–37). On the contrary, Peter shows sincere signs of true humility. He has to hear many hard words from the Lord, and he accepts them. From here it is not very far to his being made the first pope within the community of his "fellow elders" (1 Pet 5:1).

The second point that emerges from the New Testament episodes is the utterly excessive demand made on the man Peter by the office he is to take on. How could a "sinful man" hold the "keys to the kingdom of heaven", so that his opening and closing on earth have eternal consequences? How could he "pasture" the "sheep and lambs" of Jesus, the only Good Shepherd—who as such represents God himself (Ezek 34:11–16)—particularly when, receiving pastoral authority, he is reminded of his threefold denial? How could he not sink when walking over such waves? How, in the panic of the "hour of darkness", could he resist reaching for the nearest handy weapon, which as a man (and familiar with the Old Testament) he knows how to use and which Jesus himself may have ordered him to carry (Lk 22:36, 38)? He is the representative both of mankind, for whose guilt the Lord suffers, as well as of a Church that will one day share her Lord's humiliation; how then could he appear as the magnificent confessor, beyond temptation, in the very hour when, according to God's most hidden design, the Lord is stripped of all power, even to abandonment by God? This hour of merciless truth reveals in purest objectivity what a Church might become, indeed, what she is, deprived of the fruits of her Lord's sufferings. The theological precision of the Passion scenes, in which Christians—traitors, deniers, cowards running away— stand more disgraced than Jew and Gentile, is so impressive that every Christian can recognize his own image in this primate, Peter, who first denies with a curse and then weeps bitterly.

Right in the middle of this bitter disgrace comes the incredibly healing and consoling promise of martyrdom for him, who as shepherd is to pasture the flock of the incomparable Shepherd: " ' . . . but when you are old, you will stretch out your hands, and another will gird you and carry you where you do not wish to go.' (This he said to show by what death he was to glorify God.) And after this he said to him, 'Follow me' " (Jn 21:18–19). The abyss that the excessive demands open between the man and his mandate, between the sinner who denies the Lord and his mission to pasture the flock of the Good Shepherd properly, is bridged by the grace of God. What seemed impossible, to follow in the footsteps of the One who is both priest and sacrifice, is granted him: tradition holds that Peter was crucified upside down. Even though reversed, the shape is the same. We should pay attention also to the words "where you do not wish to go". The similarity in shape is pure grace, so much so that it is brought about even despite recoil and resistance. At no time in world history will such resistance be strong enough to impair the grace that shapes likeness to Christ. Jesus' prayer has conquered Satan's "demand" (Lk 22:31); the "powers of death shall not prevail" against that which is founded on Peter (Mt 16:18).

The third point, which becomes evident from the Acts of the Apostles, is how matter-of-factly Peter takes his promotion in rank, until the imprisonments under Herod force him to depart for "another place" (Acts 12:17), leaving the leadership of the Jerusalem community to James, the brother of the Lord. Peter's sense of Catholic universalism, firmly founded on his vision at Joppa and openly announced at the "Council of the Apostles" (Acts 15:7–11), places him spiritually close to Paul's outlook. It is therefore logical that he, like Paul, should leave the burden of administering single communities and concentrate on mission. Being one of the Twelve, however, he was much closer to Jerusalem than Paul, and therefore he must have felt a greater inner conflict over the delicate, and at the time not tidily manageable, problems that arose between Jewish and Gentile Christians.

According to the Acts of the Apostles, Paul owed his arrest in the Temple to the Jews and his deliverance into Gentile hands to the

154

initiative of James, the leader of the Jewish Christians. As far as Peter is concerned, the letters of Clement suggest that he suffered his martyr's death as a result of internal strife among Christians, primarily Jewish Christians. "Peter, through unmerited jealousy, underwent not one or two but many hardships and, thus giving testimony (by his blood), departed for the place of glory that was his due."[22]

Just because Peter was much closer to the universalist views of Paul than to the followers of James (with whom, as one of the Twelve, and also because of the division of mission territories, Gal 2:7–10, he remained in contact), this does not imply a dependency or even a "subordination".[23] However, one may agree that Peter had "a much more difficult position (in face of the Jerusalem party) than the independent Paul, and that this conflict, regarding the dietary laws in Antioch, brought Peter . . . a particularly painful dilemma, which we can only surmise. . . . Mediators always have an especially difficult position."[24] The sword that cuts across Paul's entire existence—"To the Jews I became a Jew. . . . To those outside the law I became as one outside the law. . . . To the weak I became weak. . . . I have become all things to all men . . . for the sake of the gospel" (1 Cor 9:20–27)—must have pierced Peter even more painfully, battered as he was by jealousies (*zelos:* Clem 5,4) but

---

[22] Clement, *Letter to the Corinthians,* 5, 4, in *Ancient Christian Writers,* 1:12.

[23] As Oscar Cullmann feels obliged to conclude from the word *phoboumenos* (Gal 2:12) in *Petrus. Jünger–Apostel–Märtyrer* [Peter: disciple–apostle–martyr), 2d ed. (Zurich: Zwingliverlag, 1960), 57, 256f. Peter's "fear" of the circumcised, however, does not mean an underling's fear of his superiors, as Cullmann implies mainly on the basis of passages in the *Pseudo-Clementina* (257). Rather it has to do with the hard, intransigent party, the methods of which are sufficiently revealed in the Pauline epistles. Therefore one cannot take it as an "unambiguous" certainty that Paul's reprimand to Peter proved "that *to James,* whose people he feared, Peter played no leading role" (258).

[24] Ibid., 58; also 119–20.

remaining silent. One would almost want to add: "so that the (evil) thoughts of many hearts might be revealed" (Lk 2:35) in this sign of contradiction.

About the Antioch incident it is worth noting a few sentences of Ignaz Döllinger: "The worst was thus averted" (by this compromise of the Council of the Apostles), "and the Christian liberty of the Gentile converts secured; but the main difficulty remained unresolved and was purposely not touched upon at the Council. It was tacitly assumed that the Jewish Christians and the apostles themselves would continue to observe the law. . . . Without doubt the apostles intended the requirements of the Jewish laws to yield here to the higher duties of Christian brotherly love and the better claims of membership in the body of the Church." Peter, therefore, has "no qualms to live like a Gentile" and to share a table with Gentile Christians until James' people arrive, and he withdraws from that table-fellowship.

> This was no violation of the rule laid down by the Council, for the whole question was left unsettled there, and in any case whoever disregarded this part of the law was, in the eyes of all Jews, a complete breaker of the law. Peter, therefore, might well think that, being compelled to choose between the Gentiles and the Jews, he had better take the lesser evil of the two. As Paul says, he feared "those of the circumcision". This was no want of moral courage, of which he had given abundant proof more than once (in Jerusalem). . . . As the shepherd appointed by Christ for the whole flock, he belonged to both, but he had hitherto been primarily the apostle of Israel and was not yet willing to give up his labors in Jerusalem and Judaea . . . although he had already broken through the dividing wall of the ritual law by the baptism of Cornelius and maintained his right to do so against the scruples of others.

The present decision of Peter

> was intolerable to Paul as apostle of the Gentiles and preacher of evangelical freedom, and he thought too how the Pharisee zealots

who wanted to impose the whole law on the Gentiles would abuse this example of the chief apostle. He openly and sharply censured Peter for . . . acting now from fear of men against his better judgment; that was "hypocrisy". We are not told his reply; but there was not lasting quarrel, for in the thing itself both apostles were agreed. Paul never thought of urging Jews in general, especially those in Palestine, to renounce the law altogether. . . . Paul himself felt no hesitation about observing the law when it did not come into collision with the higher duties of his apostolate and his position toward Gentile Christians.[25]

This needs to be clarified somewhat more, lest the third aspect of Peter's function be limited merely to matters of Church leadership, mission and martyrdom. One might see in Peter's wrongdoing (Gal 2:11) in Antioch an epilogue to his pre-Easter transgressions, of which we said that they belonged to the *typos,* just as does Peter's pre-and post-Easter grieving about them (Mk 14:72; Jn 21:17). Nevertheless, this "offense" has a totally different quality from that of, shall we say, his denial. This is now unquestionably a product of his pastoral care to find the least harmful compromise solution for an objectively insoluble situation. How could such an "offense" be eliminated from the determining *typos* and symbolic reality found in Peter?

c. Present Reality in the Church

But before going farther, an objection must be dealt with. Our point of departure was the actual human constellation around the central figure of Jesus. At the very least, this includes the Baptist, the Mother of Jesus, the Twelve (with Peter and John) and Paul. This constellation appears, however, to belong entirely to the period of origins,

[25] Ignatz Döllinger, *The First Age of Christianity and of the Church,* 4th ed. (London: Gibbings & Co., 1906), 61–64 (altered — Tr.).

even if we do not deny its significance for the present-day Church. Only Peter seems to be an exception, insofar as he is still represented, in a special, personal succession, by the pope who exercises his office in today's Church. To envisage a succession for, let us say, the Baptist, for Mary or John or even for Paul seems absurd. Would it not be better if Peter, like the others, were limited to the founding period: while regarding him as historically unique, forever the "Rock" and "foundation", should we not let later Church leaders have their own special and different rank? Alone embodied in a present-day "successor", he seems an isolated phenomenon, for ever a stumbling block for all non-Roman Christians.

We must begin by pointing out that what first of all gives "scandal" is Peter's place in the theological structure. As shepherd who has to pasture the *whole* flock, he has a right to claim authority (in doctrine and leadership) and to demand unity. This prerogative is his alone. But it does not isolate him from the others who have founding missions and who, in their own way, have no less a continuing life and representation in the Church.

In his mission the Baptist faces in two directions. He personifies the past that is receding before the approaching new era, he withdraws and reduces himself to a mere fading "voice in the wilderness": "I am not the Christ, but I have been sent before him. . . . He must increase, but I must decrease" (Jn 3:28–30). On the other side, John steps into the new era as the "friend of the bridegroom" and as the last of the prophets who "perish" (Lk 13:33) and with whom Jesus declared his solidarity. Even the Twelve were sent by Jesus to go before him, and Paul is "nothing" (2 Cor 12:11). "Was Paul crucified for you?" (1 Cor 1:13). The apostle and disciple of Christ remains his herald, who by effacing himself makes room for the appearance of the one who is to come. It seems that the New Testament deliberately glosses over the end of Peter, Paul and John, while the Baptist remains a living presence in the Church.

Mary disappears into the heart of the Church to remain there as a real presence which, however, always gives place to her Son. We shall consider this further later on. To experience the reality of this presence one has only to look at the Eastern Church in which a living Marian principle permeates and perfumes the whole life of the Church. This is almost more potent than a separate, completely formulated Mariology. Catholics should note Mary's anonymous presence in the theology of the Church during the first centuries, where people are content to see in her the *typos* and the model of the "immaculate bride without wrinkle or blemish". Later, when dualism gives way to a growing interpenetration, and simultaneously an explicit Marian devotion begins, continual care has to be taken that a balance should be preserved, as is set forth in the closing chapter of *Lumen gentium.* The importance of the Marian presence for properly situating Peter's role shows best, perhaps, how real this presence is. We shall have to return to this later.

Indubitably, there is a real presence in the Church of the Twelve (with John) and the apostle Paul in what must be called the apostolic succession of the entire college of bishops. And the relation of primacy and collegiality, so hard to explain juridically, is the best proof that in the *Catholica* the office of Peter ought not to be isolated. As is well known, the fact that this nevertheless happened at Vatican I is the result of a historical accident which made it impossible to carry out the much broader plan of the Council.

The position of Paul, as one directly chosen by the Lord and accredited by the college of the Twelve, is unique in its own way and not open to succession except by remote analogies: there can be "charismatic" vocations, whose official recognition and acceptance into office are, so to say, compelled by divine evidence. Perhaps the ordination of Origen to the priesthood was one of these.

The Johannine presence, though not less evident, is more difficult to define. Even if a continuity of a Johannine office could be found (Ignatius-Polycarp-Irenaeus), this could not be the focus. The focus is

159

the "remaining" with which John's story of the first disciples begins (Jn 1:39) and his final chapter ends. "If it is my will that he remain until I come . . . what is that to you?" (Jn 21:22). This deliberately puzzling dictum has two facets: that the Beloved Disciple will really remain, for all times, in the Church, his presence not ceasing with his death; and that this presence, sealed by the will of the Lord of the Church, is exempt from Peter's control. The manner in which John first disappears from the Acts of the Apostles (leaving a place for the phenomenon of Paul), and how then (in John's third Letter) he is pushed to the sidelines by an ambitious member of his community (3 Jn 9–23), is characteristic of his "remaining".

Ever present is the concrete principle of love—intimate, holy love, closely bound to the life and attitude of Mary, love that humbly accepts Peter's preeminence but also knows that it is the "Beloved",[26] this love remains in Peter (Jn 21:15) yet also at his side (21:20–23), to draw attention to the presence of the Lord (21:7) or to mediate between him and the Lord (13:23–25; 21:20–23). This coexistence of "love" and "office", the theme which runs through the entire fourth Gospel and culminates in a huge, subtly complex fugue, is perhaps the most distinctly realized one in the entire "constellation", though it is quite different from the vision of Joachim of Fiore, Schelling or their followers.

[26] Cf. his being called before Peter, in Jn 1:37–39; the resting of the Beloved Disciple on Jesus' breast, so that Peter felt compelled to question the Lord about him (13:24); his entering the court of the high priest while Peter remained in the forecourt (18:15); his presence under the Cross, where Peter is missing; his arrival at the tomb before Peter ("first", 20:4); his recognition of the Lord first at the bountiful draught of fishes (21:7); the repeated reference to John's position at the Last Supper (21:20); and finally the fact that he outlived Peter (21:23). The "competition" in the fourth Gospel between "office" and "love" is almost naively indicated in the two apostles' "running together" to the tomb, with its deeply meaningful symbolic arrangement of the one who arrives first (love) and the one who enters first (office): great significance is laid on who yields place to whom, and when.

This interpretation can be gleaned directly from the Gospel and does not rest upon any abstraction or construction. It seems as if the writer of the last Gospel had foreseen the potential isolation into which the principle of office might be diverted on the basis of texts like Matthew 16:18–19, and hence, with all due respect to the "Rock" (Jn 1:42), he stressed the office's fatherly or motherly function. Not for nothing is *Bar-Jona* (Mt 16:17) rendered here as "son of John" (Jn 1:42 and particularly 21:15). This suggests to the one who has eyes to see it a far more intimate coexistence through all times than that between Peter and Paul, though in Roman tradition — and, as a result, in the liturgy — these two simultaneously martyred patrons are called the "founders" of the Church and are venerated as such (Irenaeus, according to Papias,[27] Tertullian[28]). Despite their closeness in the Jewish-Gentile conflict, there is that very distance between Peter and Paul which we find between ecclesial office and the gifted theological writer. The nod that "Peter" gives, at the end of his second Letter, to the "wisdom given" to Paul, is accompanied by a reservation that, of course, in Paul's letters "there are some things . . . hard to understand, which the ignorant and unstable twist to their own destruction" (2 Pet 3:15–16). In this regard — where Paul is thought of primarily as a "teacher" — the balance is in favor of a not unfriendly but reserved official attitude. In another context, where Paul exercises his office in concrete acts, his approach is supported by Peter: one may even say that Peter is immanent in Paul.

[27] Irenaeus, *Against Heresies,* 3, 1–3, in *The Ante-Nicene Christian Library,* vol. 5 (Edinburgh: T. & T. Clark, 1884): 258–60.

[28] Tertullian, *On Prescription,* 36, in *The Ante-Nicene Fathers,* vol. 3; *Scorpiace* 15, ibid., 648; *Against Marcion,* 4, 5 ibid., 429–74.

4. The Petrine Office as the Concrete Representation of Christ

a. Collegiality and Primacy

The real Christ, the risen Lord who wills to be present in his Church all days to the end of time, cannot be isolated from the "constellation" of his historical life, as outlined in the preceding sections. Iconography shows how aware the medieval Church was of this and how important it was felt to be to remind the faithful of it as they entered a church. At this point we are confronted with two aspects: there exists from the outset the idea (based on the words, "Where two or three. . . . ") that Christ is ever present in the Church's communion of love. And where this Church is understood in her integral wholeness, in her "catholicity" (as it has been called since *Ignatius of Antioch*)[29], the origin of this wholeness is seen in the loving community of the Twelve around Jesus, which is continually made present. Or else, the historical beginning of this community of love instituted by Jesus could be traced simply to his promise to Peter: "You are the rock, and on this rock I will build my Church." It is from this perspective that the Roman Church received the special distinction of "presiding in love",[30] that is, being the one who determines what is essential to Christianity and shows the way, as can be seen from the letter of *Clement* to the Corinthians.[31] She it is who was given definitive and authoritative teaching by the two princes of the apostles.[32] That is what Ignatius wrote to the Roman community, which was also visited by Papias,

[29] Ignatius of Antioch, *Letter to the Smyrneans,* 8, 2. Several times in *The Martyrdom of Polycarp* (Ignatius' student): in the salutation, in 8, 1 and 19, 2. Both in *The Fathers of the Church,* vol. 1 (New York: Cima Publishing Co., Inc., 1947).

[30] Ignatius of Antioch, *Letter to the Romans,* salutation, in *The Fathers of the Church,* 1:107.

[31] "You have been others' teachers", ibid., 109.

[32] "I do not command you, as Peter and Paul did. They were apostles; I am a condemned man." Ibid., 4, 3, pp. 109–10.

Polycarp, Hegesippus, and Abercius; Irenaeus stayed there. All expected to find there the deepest and clearest source of evangelical tradition. Like Paul (Rom 1:7) and Ignatius, Dionysius, Bishop of Corinth, praises the "custom" of the Romans, "known from the beginning", "of using all their means to do good to the brothers" according to "the tradition of your fathers".[33] This brings us to the witness of *Irenaeus* who, following in the steps of his predecessors,[34] undertook to defend against the gnostics the pure, integral, ecclesial doctrine, simultaneously adducing the demonstrable tradition of episcopal succession in all the communities and the teaching authority instituted by the apostles (*instituti sunt*) and handed down by them (*suum ipsorum locum magisterii tradentes*).[35] So as not to have to enumerate the lists of all the bishops of all the churches (as he could have done), Irenaeus is content with the list of the Roman church, as "with this church ... because of her more powerful founding authority (*propter potentiorem principalitatem*), all churches—that is all the faithful, wherever they may be and whatever their origin—have to agree (*convenire*), because the tradition handed down by the apostles was held in trust by her for all."

We leave this famous text without comment and proceed to one of its

---

[33] Eusebius, *Ecclesiastical History,* 4:23, 10. Dionysius answers a letter of Pope Soter and permits his letter to be read during public worship as "an exhortation", "like the earlier epistle Clement wrote on your behalf". Corinth had not only accepted Rome's first admonition of the year 96–97 but still honored it some seventy to eighty years later.

[34] Especially Hegesippus and Justin (the latter in his lost *Syntagma adversus omnes haereses,* from the method and content of which Irenaeus has drawn: *Against Heresies,* 4, 6, 2). Both are concerned with "the authentic account of the apostolic preaching" (Hegesippus, quoted by Eusebius, 4: 8, 2) and contrast its unity with the disunion of the heretics, who indeed call themselves Christians but who despite the multiplicity of their schools do no differently than the philosophers. Justin Martyr, *First Apology* 26, in *The Fathers of the Church,* vol. 8 (New York: Christian Heritage, Inc., 1948): 61–63.

[35] Irenaeus, *Against Heresies,* 3, 3, 2, pp. 259–60.

possible interpretations, primarily represented by *Cyprian*. In this, the previously described two elements become inseparably united. First of all, the Church, as well as her unity, is essentially *communio* in faith and love; but this union is manifested not only (as Ignatius wrote) by the unbreakable unity of the faithful with their bishop but also by the unity of the bishops with each other. Being the historical starting point of the entire episcopal *ordo*, the Bishop of Rome is the permanent exponent, the embodiment, the symbol, of this unity. The *ordo* by which the Church from Christ onward is articulated (as *plebs* and *clerus*) incorporates both the communion of love and the (strongly emphasized) legal authority that upholds the purity of faith and love as it did in the time of the apostles (through excommunication, for instance). And precisely through the unanimity of the bishops this brings about and demonstrates the loving communion of all churches: *"connexam et ubique conjunctam catholicae ecclesiae unitatem"*.[36]

The ideal realization of this unity of the episcopate— *"episcopatus unus est, cujus a singulis in solidum pars tenetur"*[37] —is guaranteed by Christ's having given first to Peter, and to him alone, the entirety (Mt 16:18–19) of that which he intended to entrust later to the Twelve collegially.[38] And when Cyprian speaks of the "one *cathedra*" of Peter—and of his

[36] Cyprian, Letter 55, 24, in *The Fathers of the Church*, vol. 51 (Washington, D.C.: The Catholic University of America Press, 1964): 149–50.

[37] Cyprian, *The Unity of the Catholic Church* 5, in *Ancient Christian Writers*, vol. 25 (New York: Newman Press, 1956): 47. "Cum sit a Christo una Ecclesia per totum mundum in multa membra divisa, item episcopatus unus episcoporum multorum concordi numerositate diffusus", Letter 55, 24. But this unity of the episcopate remains the foundation of the unity of the whole Church for which it was ordained, for the "plebs una in solidam corporis unitatem concordiae glutino copulata." *The Unity*, 23, pp. 64–65.

[38] "Hoc erant utique et ceteri apostoli quod fuit Petrus, pari consortio praediti et honoris [office] et potestatis, sed *exordium* ab unitate proficiscitur, ut Ecclesia Christi una monstretur." *The Unity*, 4.

164

primatus — on which the unity of the Church is built, he always has in mind this priority in time[39] that makes the Bishop of Rome the symbol and representative but not the legally empowered head of the college of bishops. However, the ideal "should" of the bishops' unity of mind (and that of their churches) is cruelly tried, during Cyprian's brief ten-year episcopate, by a harsh reality to which his vision proves inadequate. On some occasions he rises in revolt, asserting his direct episcopal relationship to Christ against the claims and actions of Rome (e.g., regarding the baptism of heretics), while on others he insists that the Pope intervene in disputes in which in other instances he, Cyprian, had himself made the decision.[40] Thus the consensus in love of the *episcopatus* proves to be an *abstraction,* unless in practice the legally accredited authority of the Roman primate supports it and gives it a concrete realization. We should note that the inadequacy of Cyprian's idea of collegiality (as the sole unifying principle) is amply illustrated in the Church today by clashes of irreconcilable opinions. We shall later examine this more closely.

But the idea of primacy we find in Irenaeus also leads to other consequences which become evident mainly (though not exclusively) in the Roman bishop's awareness of the responsibility of his office. When the Synod of Sardica (ca. 343–344) regards the Roman bishop as the legal court of appeal and "recourse"[41] in disputes and designates the "See of the apostle Peter" as the "head",[42] Pope Siricius feels the burden of this responsibility even though he does not carry it as an isolated individual: "We carry the burden of all who are burdened; or rather, it is carried in us by the blessed apostle Peter, who we trust

---

[39] Cf. Letter 59, 14: "ecclesia principalis". It makes little difference that these words can be found in one edition of *The Unity of the Catholic Church* (chap. 4), while they are not in the other. The two versions, adapted to different circumstances, are most likely by Cyprian himself.

[40] Letter 68, 239f.

[41] Denzinger-Schönmetzer, 133–35.

[42] Ibid., 136.

defends and nurtures us, his heirs, in all that concerns his stewardship."[43] The primacy that Cyprian deemed a temporal priority is now understood as though the "authoritatively" "judging"[44] head were Peter himself, "the original source from which the other churches continue to draw".[45] Thus, the office "weighed down with care" becomes the epitome (*summa*) of the priesthood; upon its decisions also depends the "very essence of things" (*summa rerum*).[46] The doctrine of the universal responsibility that the "heirs" of Peter received directly from Peter himself (and which concerns the Church as a whole) finds in *Leo the Great* a systematic, well-rounded and balanced expression, where collegiality in Cyprian's sense is taken into account, but where it is derived essentially from, and depends on, the fullness of authority (*plenitudo potestatis*).[47]

It is significant that the image of the "source" from which full authority in the Church flows, can change almost imperceptibly into the image of "motherhood", so that by the early Middle Ages Peter's concrete presence at the Church's beginning draws to itself the Marian form of presence also.[48] Here, the concrete reality of the clearly per-

[43] Ibid., 181.

[44] Innocent I, ibid., 217.

[45] Ibid., 217, cf. 218: "scientes quod per omnes provincias de apostolica fonte petentibus responsa semper emanent." A reappearance of the image of "head" as "fount" in Boniface I (422); ibid., 233.

[46] Ibid., 234.

[47] Pierre Batiffol, *Le Siège apostolique* (Paris: J. Gabalda, 1924), 349–451. See further references in Yves Congar, *L'Église de s. Augustin à l'Époque moderne* (Paris: n.p., 1970), 28f. Denzinger-Schönmetzer, 282, recognizes within the "dignitas communis" of the bishops (as formerly of the apostles) a "quaedam discretio potestatis" whereby all ecclesial office is understood as "sollicitudo", which finally converges "in the one See of Peter as care [*cura*] for the entire Church", and nothing should separate it from its head.

[48] *Mater et magistra,* in Denzinger-Schönmetzer, 774, 811. Other passages in Congar, *L'Église de s. Augustine à l'époque moderne,* 96, note. Also A. Mayer, "Das Bild der Mater Ecclesia im Wandel der Geschichte", *Pastor Bonus* 53 (1942): 33–47. See further Congar's introduction to the French translation of Karl Delahaye, *Ecclesia Mater* (Paris: Cerf, 1964), 9, note 5.

166

sonal origin is retained, but in such a one-sided manner that this *personal* authority tends to subordinate to itself the equally original concreteness of the Twelve (in the college of bishops) and is occasionally inclined to claim for itself even what was personalized in Mary, the reality of the pure and holy Church.[49]

This is not the place to trace the struggle of these two interpretations through all the centuries of the Church's history until, finally, in *Lumen gentium,* a reassuring and satisfactory balance was found. Only one aspect of the question concerns us here: it seems that from the beginning (cf. the letter of Clement), whenever the activity of the Roman bishop went beyond the boundaries of his diocese, it was linked to the task of arbitrating disputes. Here the (latent) juridical dimension and function emerge of themselves from the unanimity of a lived *communio.*

b. Love, Law, Power

The question that claims our attention was developed in the most convincing form by Johann Adam Möhler. From his early *Die Einheit in der Kirche*[50] to his mature work, *Symbolik,*[51] he carries it to a certain point, but there a further step becomes necessary. Influenced by his own inheritance, the Gallican, Febronian, "Enlightenment" idea of the pope as the "center of unity", as well as by his immediate Romantic sources, Drey and Schleiermacher,[52] he tends toward Cyprian's view of collegial unity: "For a long time it seemed doubtful to me that

---

[49] Pelagius I (556–561) already sees the "catholicae veritas *matris*" together with the "Church which abides in unity with him, in whom are all the apostolic sees which received the power to bind and loose, just as he received the keys", Denzinger-Schönmetzer, 446.

[50] Möhler, *Einheit.* Quotations from J. R. Geiselmann's critical edition.

[51] Möhler, *Symbolik,* 2 vols. Quotations from J. R. Geiselmann's critical edition (Cologne and Olten: Hegner, 1958).

[52] On Drey's influence: *Einheit,* introduction, 30ff. On Schleiermacher's influence, ibid., 586f.

having a primate should be a characteristic of the Catholic Church. Indeed, I resolved to refute this, because the organic relation of the parts to the whole—an idea that plainly applies to the Catholic Church and which she embodies—seemed to me . . . completely realized in the unity of the episcopate."[53] The pertinent texts of Cyprian about the *cathedra Petri* as the *ecclesia principalis* "from which the unity of the bishops derives" are favorably presented.[54]

For Möhler, the Church is essentially, as well as in her historical origin, a community of love, not by human achievement, but by the formative power of the indwelling Holy Spirit. Only those who love and labor within this bond of charity understand the Church,[55] just as the self-revelation of Jesus could not be forced on the disciples from without but had to be accepted and affirmed by them from within.[56] Looking at it this way, the ideal of the Church (namely, that she is pure *communio* of love) corresponds to her reality in the Holy Spirit: "Because all that is truly ideal is also real. The truly spiritual community was thought of by him, Cyprian (as by Paul), as always vigorously manifesting and forming itself. The truly spiritual community— spiritually alive, not merely conceptual—is therefore one in which we

[53] Ibid., sec. 67, 227.

[54] Ibid., sec. 70, 236.

[55] Ibid., sec. 7, 21; cf. the first introduction: "Therefore whoever now lives in the Church, and truly lives in her, will live also in the first period of the Church and will understand it. And whoever does not live in the present will neither live in nor understand the earliest, for both are one and the same. . . . Whoever is born of the Church brings nothing alien into her, because the Church has begotten him and has built into him her being and her essence. She has from the first established herself within him, and it is that which he now manifests." *Einheit*, 328.

[56] We have already quoted above the passage from Möhler's *Einheit* where he shows that Jesus had to manifest his most profound nature by living it in full view of his disciples, before his nature could find an expression through their faith (*Einheit*, sec. 68, 231f.). Jacques Guillet has based his work *Jésus devant sa vie et sa mort* (Paris: Aubier, 1971) on this principle. German translation: *Jesus vor seinem Leben und Tod* (Einsiedeln: Johannesverlag, 1973).

really *are* and not merely *think* we are: if we are aware of being members of the whole body and act as such, if we are in it and live in it. . . . The community of the faithful is therefore only as ideal as it is real, and it can become real only because it is ideal."[57] Truly lived unity has naturally sublimated pluralism as well as individualism within its unity[58] and is a dramatic embodiment of the spiritual.[59] (These are both basic principles of Romantic thought.)

Thus, after the first part—the main theme of which is the spiritual basis of the principle of unity—Möhler is able to develop in the second part the increasingly concrete steps by which manifest unity is built from below: unity (of the community) in the bishop, unity of the bishops in the metropolitan and in (local) synods and unity of the entire episcopate (Cyprian) summed up in the "unity in the primate" as the symbol of episcopal unity in its "living representative".[60]

Manifest unity developed historically and organically in the course of the first centuries. (Drey had suggested that this development be understood as the necessary gradual realization of a unity that hitherto existed only "virtually" as an ideal.[61]) But a realistic point of view had to appear that "disrupted sooner than expected" the ideal of a pure community of love, the pure "heavenly" Church. "Egoism" (that Möhler sees as the principle of heresy) "threatened to sever the bonds", and that is why, within the sphere of love, law became articulated: "The entire, otherwise divided strength will be concentrated in one (person), the more vigorously to resist all that hinders its

[57] Möhler, *Einheit,* sec. 31 (last edition), 101.

[58] Ibid., sections 39–40.

[59] Ibid., introduction, 74, on the primacy of the spiritual, which creates its own "corporeal expression". Cf. sec. 8, 23: "The letter . . . only an expression of the spirit" (ibid., 25). "The human body is a manifestation of the spirit which makes its presence known and develops within him" (sec. 49, 168).

[60] Ibid., sec. 67, 228.

[61] Cf. Geiselmann's presentation, *Einheit,* 34ff.

development."[62] But egoism is not only found outside the Church in self-isolating heresy. This is already the fruit of sinfulness within the Church herself. As a result, the bishop must "often proceed to act despite or *against* the wishes of the majority of the community", which is a sign that the "first love . . . has been abandoned".[63] And where this internal discord between the whole Church's "unity in love" (by now vanished) and the original expression that embodied this love (but is now compelled to stand on law and authority against it) reaches its climax, "law" becomes "power". And with this comes the threat of the great temptation—because the *communio* has grown cold and is endangered—that the one who possesses this "power" will misunderstand his role and misuse it despotically.[64] Law, according to Möhler, is love grown cold, and despotism is the consequence of law abandoned.[65]

[62] Möhler, *Einheit,* sec. 71, 239.

[63] Ibid., sec. 55, 192.

[64] Ibid., sec. 71, 241.

[65] Geiselmann (*Einheit,* 620–35) shows in a most enlightening manner the sources and parallels of this doctrine: first Drey, to whom the Church is primarily brotherhood, and only then "realm", whose power must oppose egoism and be "entirely oriented toward love". Therefore she can use her power only to mediate and reconcile; "but reconciliation is the daughter of suffering, and suffering must dissolve all rancor: through suffering it is changed into love." Then Franz von Baader (influenced by Saint-Martin) whose statements further clarify Möhler's: "Law comes to the fore (in the Church) only when love and concord are disturbed or injured. Similarly, attention is drawn to the scientific definition of a dogma only when this is attacked or threatened with misrepresentation. . . . Of course, society (civil as well as religious) can exist without authority evidently asserting itself as such, but it is there nevertheless. Three stages of society can be distinguished in this respect, the first of which describes the 'natural society' in which only *love* reigns; however, as soon as love is injured or is lacking and *law* speaks, the society changes into 'civil society'. Finally, when law is also transgressed, authority shows itself as *power."* E. von Moy as well as Bautain similarly derive authority and law from love, but the latter ties the original form of all law to *fatherhood.* See also Schleiermacher, *Glaubenslehre* (Leipzig: A. Deichert, 1910), sec. 161.

But apostasy as a movement that, from here on, seems to dominate Church history—and also, and in particular, the development from a nonmonarchical to a monarchical papacy that sees itself as such[66]—is for Möhler, who thinks organically, simply one side of the coin, taking into account the sinful reality of man in the Church. He does not disregard the other side: the action of the Holy Spirit of love, throughout the historical development of the Church, now as before, fashions an appropriate expression in the body of the visible Church. "Originally the bishop was hardly *discerned* as such by the faithful but merely *was* the one around whom others gathered, and so in the beginning was the metropolitan among the bishops of a wider area; so too was the primate in the assembly of all the bishops. But let us note the wonderful phenomenon: the fiercer the attack on the internal unity of all Christians, the stronger the latter expressed itself; the more egoism, the more love; the more disruptive an attack, the more concentrated and fervent strength it evoked."[67] From such a balanced perspective, law and authority (including "power") is not a foreign growth, a heteronomous principle imposed on love, but is inherent in the Church. However, it is only "noticed" and becomes an issue where the *consensus* and *communio* of love are disturbed. It has no other purpose than to preserve or speedily restore the unity in love.

This is why the mature Möhler did not want to commit himself either to an exclusive "episcopalism" or to an exclusive "papalism". When he discovered (in section 46 of *Die Einheit*) the important difference between fruitful "disagreement" within the Church and

[66] Cf. Möhler's slow development in the period between *Einheit* and *Symbolik* (which goes beyond "episcopalism" only in its fourth edition): *Symbolik*, 2:672–98. To begin with, he did not want to grant the pope "monarchical", i.e., legislative, but only executive powers in relation to the "universal laws of the Church", even though he affirms the papacy consistently as a divine institution.
[67] Möhler, *Einheit*, sec. 71, 239.

"contradiction", heretical opposition disturbing the unity of the Church, his road was clear to understand both forms of Church unity as "beneficial opposites",[68] both traceable to divine authorization.[69] Provided we note that in the end Möhler explicitly recognizes that the primacy was established by Christ, i.e., no longer understands it *merely* as the creative act of ecclesial love under the inspiration of the Spirit,[70] we can accept his basic principle: "The entire system of the Church is therefore nothing but the embodiment of love."[71] For this, however, Augustine has a more accurate explanation.

c. Office and the Holy Church

Möhler himself (in appendix 13 of *Die Einheit*) points to the teaching of the Fathers, particularly *Augustine,* that office in the Church can only represent unity, can only reconcile those who have fallen from the unity of love and can only receive new members through baptism because this Church of love really does exist, despite all her questionable earthly aspects. This is all the more remarkable as Augustine's

[68] "Hence, that which in the Church has the true character of a real opposition appears as being outside of her, isolated.... It cannot exist because it remains incomplete ... because an [isolated] contradiction cannot exist in reality ... love and egoism are not simple opposites", ibid., sec. 46, 154–56.

[69] Möhler, *Symbolik,* 2:697. One should not forget that for Möhler, the papacy's function of bringing about unity in isolation is exposed to the same temptations as that against which it struggles. Therefore he can state: "Protestantism is papism carried to the extreme, that is, complete egoism *in principle.* In papism each gives himself unconditionally to *one* person: in Protestantism, each *one* is in a position to oppose all others" (insofar as he makes of himself the principle of interpretation of revelation). Ibid., 698.

[70] Möhler, *Einheit,* sec. 49, 170; 168, note 1: "Building the visible Church is therefore the greatest act of the faithful", sec. 64, 215. "The episcopate, the constitution of the Church, is merely the external representation of the reality and not the reality itself"; cf. sec. 51, 178; sec. 55, 183.

[71] Ibid., sec. 64. 215.

principal struggle is with the Donatists and their unconditional demand for a "Church of the pure", against which he defends a "mixed Church, composed of good and bad", whose eschatological separation will take place only on Judgment Day, when the Church becomes the embodiment of the good alone. Still this does not prevent Augustine from holding on to the ideal of the first Christian generations, maintaining that "properly speaking, only the just form the true Body of Christ".[72] Moreover, he has the courage not to dissociate the true Church, hidden in this "mixed" Church, from the work of Christ, her head. Certainly he justifies his anti-Cyprian and now anti-Donatist doctrine, defended for the first time by the popes, that heretical baptism and perhaps even heretical ordination are valid (even though they do not confer the grace of the Spirit) because, irrespective of who the official minister is, it is Christ who acts through the sacrament. But Christ, who became man, is always "Head and Body", "Bridegroom and Bride". He does not act without that true Church which Augustine, echoing the Song of Songs, calls "the one and only dove" (*columba*), the "*communio* and community of the saints".[73] And because all Church law is originally rooted in love, Augustine—following Cyprian's line of thought—says that the keys, the power to forgive sins, are first given to the "dove", that is, to the Church, *insofar* as she is the unity of love, just as to her alone, primarily, "infallibility" is attributed.

"The Spirit is God. God therefore remits. . . . So then God dwelleth in his holy temple, that is, in his holy faithful ones, in his Church; by them (*eos*) doth he remit sins; because they are living temples."[74] This

[72] Augustine, *Contra Faustum,* 13, 16.

[73] Also Yves Congar, "Introduction générale à saint Augustin: Traités antidonatistes 1", in *Oeuvres de s. Augustin,* vol. 28 (Paris: n.p., 1963): 100–109. About the historical redemptive function of the Church as a whole in early patristics to Origen and Methodius, cf. Karl Delahaye, *Erneuerung der Seelsorgsformen aus der Sicht der frühen Patristik* (Freiburg im Breisgau: Herder, 1958), 142–93.

[74] Augustine, *Sermo* 99, 9.

thought is followed through so radically that the "loving unity" becomes a concept that is associated with the title "Rock" given to Peter, as well as with the power to forgive which was granted to the Eleven after Easter:

"Receive the Holy Spirit. If you forgive the sins of any, they are forgiven; if you retain the sins of any, they are retained." Therefore, if they [the apostles] represented the Church (*personam gerent Ecclesiae*), and this was said to them as to the Church herself, it follows that the community (*pax*) of the Church looses sins, and estrangement from the Church retains sins, not according to the will of men, but according to the will of God and the prayers of the saints who are "spiritual". "The spiritual man judges all things, but is himself to be judged by no one" (1 Cor 2:15). For the Rock retains, the Rock remits; the Dove retains, the Dove remits; unity retains, unity remits. But the peace of this unity exists only in the good, in those who are already spiritual or are advancing to obedience in the Spirit; it does not exist in the bad, whether they create a disturbance outside or are endured with sighs within the Church, baptizing or being baptized. But just as those who are tolerated with groanings within the Church—although they do not belong to the unity of the Dove and to that glorious Church "without spot or wrinkle or any such thing" (Eph 5:27)—if they are corrected and confess that they approach baptism most unworthily, are not baptized again but begin to belong to the Dove, through whose groanings sins are remitted (*per cuius gemitus peccata solvuntur*), while the sins of those estranged from her peace are retained; so even those who are openly outside the Church . . . are freed by the same law of charity and bond of unity.

The following quotation puts the issue acutely, assuming that those baptizing or admitting others to the Church are sinful bishops and priests:

For if "those only may baptize who are set over the Church and established by the law of the gospel and ordination as appointed by the Lord", were they in any wise of this kind who seized on estates by treacherous frauds and increased their gains by compound interest? . . . For the Lord would not say to robbers and usurers, "Whose soever sins ye remit. . . . " He is loosed who has made peace with the Dove, and he is bound who is not at peace with the Dove, whether he is openly without or appears to be within.[75]

According to this, there is no conflict between the official representatives of Holy Church (*personam Ecclesiae gerens*) and the Church herself if the former administer their office with the right attitude of love; but if they do not do this, conflict arises within them, as officials, and the Church of love that they are to represent. It is obvious that this conflict cannot exist between the Church and Christ, with whom she forms a common principle of love and forgiveness. Augustine's point of view here is clearly stated, in opposition to his own African predecessors, Tertullian and Cyprian.[76] *Tertullian,* who joined the Montanists, saw a chasm opening up between the hierarchical-legal Church of the bishops (*Ecclesia numerus episcoporum*), with their purely governmental succession to the apostles, and the Church of spiritual men who are the true followers of the apostles and to whom—as opposed to the former—is given the power to forgive even serious sins.[77]

Cyprian, as we have noted, represented the opposite tendency. He saw the unity of the bishops as being actually the original manifestation of the Church's unity (both official and spiritual) with Christ. *Augustine* accepted that Tertullian's differentiation occasionally might become necessary, when the office lapses from what it should be. But he also accepted Cyprian's conviction that office is rooted in the realm of primordial love. Augustine's position was in opposition to "the

[75] Augustine, *De baptismo contra Donatistas,* 3, 23. Cf. *Sermo* 71, 23, 37.
[76] See also: Joseph Ratzinger, "Volk und Haus Gottes in Augustins Lehre von der Kirche", in *Münchener Theologische Studien* 2, 7 (1954): 44–102.
[77] Tertullian, *On Purity,* 21, in *Ancient Christian Writers,* vol. 28 (New York: Newman Press, 1959): 118–22.

Donatist idea of priesthood, which places the minister of the Church not under but next to Christ, that looks upon this office not as *ministerium* but as *dominium* and requires personal holiness for sacramental holiness."[78] This enabled Augustine to locate the "sacrament" of ordination—as a specific participation by the officeholder in the ministry of Christ the Good Shepherd—in the innermost domain of ecclesial holiness, so that even in failure (in a bad priest) the fundamental effectiveness of the office was not allowed to be lost. Augustine's concept of the Church is sufficiently flexible (without falling apart) to see the innermost essence of the Church in the pure community of love. However, he does not (like Tertullian) relegate to the realm of the illusory or unreal the visibility of office and the sacraments, the unquestioningly maintained apostolic succession[79] *and the authority of the Church to define for the individual believer what is the Gospel's binding authority.*[80] While he designates the powers received in the sacrament of priestly ordination with the legal term of *jus dandi*,[81], there is no danger here of his interpreting this like the Romantics, as the first sign of the cooling or hardening of love. He means by it simply the close unity of the ordained with the Good Shepherd, which also involves giving his life for the sheep. "What is Peter? Is he not a shepherd, or is he a bad one? Let us see whether or not he is a shepherd. 'Do you love me . . . ?' And he answered, 'Yes, Lord; you know that I love you.' And you said to him, 'Feed my sheep.' You, you Lord, have by your own question, by the support of your own words, made him a loving shepherd." Peter had to reaffirm this three times with great sorrow to make amends for his betrayal.

---

[78] Fritz Hofmann, *Der Kirchenbegriff des heiligen Augustinus* (Munich: Huber, 1933), 426.

[79] Text, ibid., 94ff.

[80] "I would not believe the gospel if the authority of the Catholic Church did not move me to do so." Tertullian, *Contra Ep. Fund.*, 5, 6.

[81] Tertullian, *Contra Ep. Parm.*, 2, 13, 28 and 30.

And now he is a "shepherd and a good shepherd, of course nothing compared to the power (*potestas*) and goodness of the Shepherd of shepherds; yet he is a shepherd and a good one, and so are all others like him good shepherds."[82] They are such because they are "members of the Shepherd". "In that Head the apostles rejoiced; under that Head they were like-minded; they lived in one spirit, bonded in one body, and, therefore, they all belonged to the one Shepherd."[83]

Augustine carries the thought even farther: the good shepherds in the pure Church are bound in a particular manner to the One Shepherd who is the Head of the Church, hence they are not ultimately distinct from the Church, whose members they obviously are. Rather, the unity "Good Shepherd—good shepherds" also represents the union of Bridegroom and Bride. When Jesus entrusts his flock to Peter, "he stresses the unity; because there were many apostles but only to one is it said, 'Feed my lambs.' There are many good shepherds, but they are all in the One, they are one.... The friends of the Bridegroom do not speak on their own but are full of joy because of the voice of the Bridegroom." (Note how the Baptist is echoed here in Peter!)

> Jesus himself is the Shepherd who pastures through his shepherds. He can say "I feed them" because it is his voice that is heard through those who manifest his love. That is why he wanted to unite Peter—to whom he entrusted his lambs as man to man— so closely to himself that, despite having transferred the flock, he remained the Head. Peter is made the representative (*figura*) of the body, i.e., of the Church, and both become one flesh like Bride and Bridegroom. What did Jesus say, therefore, before transferring the flock, so that the transaction should not be like one between strangers? "Peter, do you love me?" ... He confirms the love

---

[82] Augustine, *Sermo* 138, 4; cf. 5.
[83] *In Jn* tract 46, 7; cf. 5.

to strengthen the unity. . . .Hence the shepherds may boast, but only in the Lord.[84]

Having presented this profound theology of office that sees its final meaning in the union of the officeholder with Christ, in whom office and devoted love are one and the same, Augustine, the anti-Donatist, can insist without hesitation that a bad shepherd, the "hireling", is not a shepherd in the Christian sense of the word. "For to be a true priest, a man must be clothed, not with the sacrament alone, but with righteousness", and even though the official acts of a bad priest are valid, "not only is he not a true priest, he is no priest at all".[85] "Therefore a bishop must be good; if he is not, he is not really a bishop. . . . Who is a bishop and yet is not one? He who is more concerned with his own honor than with the welfare of God's flock, and in this exalted ministry (*in ista celsitudine ministerii*) seeks his own interests and not those of Jesus Christ (Phil 2:21). He will be called bishop but is not one: he merely bears an empty title."[86] He is a "sham" (*fictus*[87]) even though he retains the *jus dandi*.

The office in its specific nature (as a pastoral office in union with the One Shepherd) is also anchored within the *columba* which, as a totality, according to Augustine, forgives sins in union with Christ.[88] But the office extends from the ideal Church into the Church of sinners: not only in order to forgive sins foreign to it but also to manifest its own weakness and sinfulness, and it represents unity (so to say *ex officio*) even in its existential estrangement and fall (Peter's denial!). Augustine was the first to recognize this. He concluded his conferences on John's Gospel with the famous parallel between Peter

[84] Augustine, *Sermo* 46, 13, 30.

[85] Augustine, *Contra Lit. Pet.,* 2, 30, 69.

[86] Germain Morin, *S. Augustini Sermones post Maurinos reperti* (Rome: n.p., 1930), 566. Cf. 568.

[87] Tertullian, *Contra Ep. Parm.,* 2, 11, 24.

[88] Augustine, *In Jn,* tract 124, 7.

178

and John: "Let no one, however, separate these great apostles. That which Peter symbolized (life among dangers and temporal evil), both shared; and what John symbolized (anticipating the bliss of the pure Church in the beatific vision), both will share in the hereafter."[89]

There are two thoughts, however, that Augustine has not quite fully developed: first, that this form of Church office which originates in "Johannine" love can and must effectively represent unity (which can exist only in love) beyond its origin, permanently imprinting the sign of the Cross on the Church in the world. The contrast between the "hirelings" (who are in the majority)[90] and the true shepherds who are "sons" creates a kind of structural fracture in the body of the Church, the pain of which is expressed by the *gemitus columbae* but is even more deeply suffered by the crucified Lord of the Church. Thus, it is not merely a consoling promise to Peter that in the end he may share the Lord's Cross. It is much more: the manifest expression of the fact that "office" is made possible only and entirely by the Cross. Who then, being "Peter" and "John", is not affected personally by this painful rent that characterizes ecclesial office? Who can call himself the "friend of the Bridegroom" except by effacing and losing himself in his work for the Lord? But if the sign of the Cross is firmly established in the Church in the sign of office, must not the *whole* Church become aware and approve of this Cross and share in the bearing of it? Not only the "pure Church of love", not only the holders of ecclesial office, but also (and particularly) the sinful Church, which specializes in being forever in revolt against the office and authority given to the Church?

A second point that Augustine did not fully clarify is whether by his time the distinct separation between the "pure Church of love" and the impure Church of sinners was already outdated. The ideal of the primitive Church that saw the Church as paradise restored had long been abandoned, and the opposite idea found its way increas-

---

[89] Ibid.
[90] Ibid., tract 46, 5.

ingly into Augustine's work, namely, that the segment of the *civitas Dei* that is on pilgrimage through historical time becomes the immaculate Bride-Church only in eschatological time.[91] Where then is this *columba immaculata* (Song 5:2) which, for Augustine, certainly did not mean only the heavenly Jerusalem but a real part of the Church on earth? Should not his Mariology have had a deeper influence here on his ecclesiology? Once we grasp that Mary, the Mother and Bride of the Lord, is the only member of the pilgrim Church to correspond to the Church's attribute *immaculata* (Eph 5:27)[92] and that Peter's office is founded on the "Church of love" (Augustine), must we not assume that Mary becomes just as really present in the visible Church at all times *within* Peter's presence in the current office-bearer and *within* the presence of the Twelve (and of Paul)[93] in all the holders of office?

[91] Augustine, *Retractationes*, 2, 18; cf. ibid., 1, 7, 5; *The City of God*, 18, 48; *De continentia*, 25; *Sermo* 181, 7.

[92] We are surely all predestined to be part of the eschatological Church as "immaculati"; Eph 1:4; Col 1:22; Jude 24 (the turns of phrase in James 1:27 are probably strongly influenced by the Old Testament concept of purity).

[93] For the sake of completeness it would have been necessary to treat thematically the continual and actual presence of Paul in the structure of the Church. Here we can only refer to the fact that all patristic literature (from the letters of Clement and Ignatius on) consistently traces the central Roman Church to the two princes of the apostles and that both now have the same feast-day and are thought of by the Fathers with similar dignity (Augustine's Sermons 295–99). (The historical question of whether Peter had been in Rome and the fact that Paul cannot be literally considered the founder of the Roman community is here totally irrelevant.) That they shed their blood together (*socium sanguinem ambo fuderunt*: Migne, PL 38:1361) is not irrelevant: in their martyrdom, they were drawn into the truth of the Cross, on which ecclesial office is grounded. Regarding their common feast, see: H. Lietzmann, *Petrus und Paulus in Rom* (Berlin, 1927); A. Baumstark, "Begleitfeste", in *Reallexikon für Antike und Christentum* 2 (1954): 90f., where it is shown that in Rome the two princes of the apostles were celebrated on June 29 and all the other apostles on the following day, until the 30th was assigned to the apostle Paul (at the latest by Gregory the Great). Despite this, however, the 29th was celebrated later again as a common feast for both Peter and Paul. Cf. also A. Chavasse, "Les Fêtes de S. Pierre et de S. Paul (6/30) au VIIème–VIIIème siècle", *Ephemerides theologicae Lovanienses* 74 (1960): 166–67.

The whole christological "constellation" that derives from the election of the Twelve—the Church of bishops and their communities—does not have sufficient weight without Mary to counterbalance the allegedly exclusive "claims" of Rome; her "claim" hinges on the same eschatological conditions as the Petrine "claim".

Before considering the question of the Marian Church, we should close our examination of Augustine's ideas by pointing out that the Petrine office is both central and "eccentric". Certainly, this office was placed in the "holy" center of the Church (hence the demand for a declaration of love from the first pope). From this center, however, it does not reach out only to the sinners who are displaced from it and thus "eccentric"; it is not only *for* them but rather *with* them (it is Peter, who denied the Lord, who is given office), in such a way that the personal guilt of the officeholder does not vitally affect the indefectibility of the office. Peter is *simul*—though not in the same respect—*justus et peccator, fallibilis et infallibilis* (both righteous and a sinner, fallible and infallible). This is the central "scandal" of Catholicism: that a sinner should claim an element of infallibility. In this regard "the other great Christian communities are largely proof against the kind of accusations which are leveled against the Catholic Church." But in Augustine's thinking, the Church is the very locus and organism of redemption; therefore, from a soteriological point of view, an eccentric position is *normal* for her. And the Petrine paradox—which Catholics do not attribute to "claims" by Peter but to Jesus' command and promise, and hence to obedience on the part of Peter—is, therefore, the normal center of the real, visible Church that preserves Christ's work in history. She should not desire to rid herself of this scandal; at most she must try as far as possible to make the "scandal of Christ" visible through it: "Blessed are you when men revile you and persecute you ... on my account (Mt 5:11). "Protestants take pride in the fact that in predominantly Reformed countries anticlericalism is unknown, while it flourishes in Catholic countries. This, they say, is because the former countries once knew the domination of clericalism.

There is some truth in this. A Church that lays such stress on her plenary authority—arrogantly, as some would say—is open to stricter criticism. And here lies the deepest reason for the well-known 'anti-Roman attitude'. . . . "[94]

[94] Yves Congar, *Vraie et fausse réforme dans l'Église* (Paris: Cerf, 1950), 69–70.

The All-Embracing Motherhood of the Church

Let us take Augustine at his word and agree that ecclesial ministry (which is completely misunderstood if viewed merely as the "common priesthood of all the faithful") is established within the all-embracing, holy, immaculate, truly loving Church. It belongs there by birthright, though the Church does not lay claim to it because, being an entity of such pure selflessness, self-surrender and docility, the very thought of any kind of claim would be foreign to her, and the explicitly masculine function of office would not suit her. Nevertheless, again according to Augustine, the office is not relegated to a *penultimate,* purely "structural" sphere. Christ himself, by his own act, founded it and incorporated it into the *ultimate* sphere, where office is represented and exercised for the faithful. Hence, the question cannot be avoided: what or who, then, is this encompassing sphere? Biblically, both in the Old and New Testaments, and also in the symbolic pattern of thought in antiquity—current up to the time of the Church Fathers and well into the Middle Ages (with offshoots reaching into the Baroque period)—the Church is perceived as the sphere of the feminine in all her essential characteristics: Virgin, Bride, Mother. By contrast, a distinctly masculine character is ascribed to office. This is a matter of historical knowledge. It remains to be seen whether this view will continue to be viable in our day; or will this inclusive sphere—which used to be designated, as a matter of course, by the compound word *Maria-ecclesia* and was part of a total view—disintegrate under the relentless assaults of theological questioning until only fragments of it are left in the consciousness of modern

Christians? Anyone can test this by asking himself: Do we still experience the Church as the ideal of all that is feminine? Do we see her as the second Eve, created from (the "wound" in) the side of the new Adam to complement him; as the paradisal Virgin, who in her union with Christ and in her fruitfulness by him does not cease to be a virgin; and who, as Origen says (quoting Revelation 14:4), makes all those who belong to her spiritually virginal? Finally, do we see this Virgin as the archetype of the Mother who carries, bears and rears her children? The Church Fathers pondered thoroughly each and all of these traits and interwove them into a rich symbolism.

The question is a grave one for us, because a Church stripped of this all-embracing sphere is in danger of being reduced to a purely sociological entity or, at best, is far more vulnerable to sociological criticism than a Church conceived in terms of the ancient *mysterium* vision. As long as this earlier vision was predominant, the clerical aspect and, at its center, the Roman aspect stood in a right relationship to the more inclusive feminine sphere. Within this, from Gregory VII on, the office asserted itself more and more energetically. Let us face the fact: balancing *Petrus* with *Maria-ecclesia* is primarily an internal concern of the Catholic Church (leaving the Orthodox Church aside for the moment). The Reformation churches will undoubtedly see this as an attempt to cast out the devil by Beelzebul. On the Protestant side it has also been remarked, not without malice, that it was not by chance that the same popes (Pius IX and Pius XII) emphasized both the role of Peter and that of Mary. Let us not be disturbed by this. Primarily our aim is to understand as clearly and as fully as possible the *Catholica* as she has *legitimately* understood herself, both objectively and historically (disregarding any deviations), and as she still must understand herself today.

Granted that the feminine image characterizes the all-encompassing Church, one thing does become evident: according to the Bible (in conformity with general anthropology), woman must conceive from man if she is effectively to bear and develop what she has received. It

184

follows that the all-inclusive feminine *ecclesia,* like the masculine ministry that is rooted in her, is obviously dependent upon something beyond her, on the grace given by Jesus Christ, through whom the trinitarian life is mediated to the Church and to her children. If the Church as a whole is characterized as feminine, and if the masculine ministry is fundamentally anchored in *this* sphere, a twofold danger is avoided at a single stroke:[1] first, that the Church might become a self-sufficient entity, interposing herself as an "intermediary" between the believer and Christ, whereas she is primarily an open womb and teaches mankind, in her and with her, to be similarly open; and secondly, that the clergy might equate their paternal role with the divine, paternal authority of God instead of recognizing that their exercise of authority is pure service,[2] the pure communication of the authority that belongs solely to God. And if it is true that the Church's womb receives, not a "perishable seed, but . . . imperishable, through the living and abiding word of God" (1 Pet 1:23), and this by God's own completely free will (James 1:18), then neither the all-embracing maternal Church nor the paternal ministry rooted in her can claim to receive that seed of God—which is in his "Word" and the "gospel" (1 Pet 1:25)—as if it were a gift received at one point in time, instead of remaining continuously open to receive it.

That the paternal ministry is rooted in the Church's maternity[3] becomes evident from Paul's fatherly attitude toward his communities

---

[1] See also: Henri de Lubac, *Les Églises particulières dans l'Église universalle* (Paris: Aubier, 1971), 115–209; Louis Bouyer, *L'Église de Dieu* (Paris: Cerf, 1970), 317–18 and *Le Trône de la Sagesse: Essai sur la signification due culte mariale* [The seat of wisdom] (Paris: Cerf, 1957), passim.

[2] *Lumen gentium,* chap. 3, no. 24, with New Testament texts pertaining to ministerial "diakonia".

[3] However, we do not wish to give the impression that we agree with Scheeben's presentation which equates the motherhood of the Church with the office of the priesthood. Matthias Joseph Scheeben, *The Mysteries of Christianity* (St. Louis: Herder, 1946), sec. 79, 545ff.

(1 Cor 4:15), which he has begotten "through the gospel" and whom he addresses as his "children" (2 Cor 6:13), "whom we have exhorted, encouraged and charged" (1 Thess 2:11). But this apostle whom some have called a "misogynist" uses largely feminine images: he boasts of being a mother who suffers "in travail" (Gal 4:19) for his children, and with those to whom he has given birth he is "gentle ... like a nurse taking care of her children ... sharing (his) own self" (1 Thess 2:7–8). Contrasting the father's role and that of the mere "pedagogue", he shows that there is more to it than a simple image. In the domain of the gospel, to beget and give birth spiritually are realities rooted in the depth of the *mysterium* of the divine birth (Jn 1:13; 3:3–5; James 1:18; 1 Pet 1:3, 23–25; 1 Jn 3:9). This is echoed by the first Church Fathers and well into the Middle Ages[4] and is closely linked to the image of "Mother Church", conceiving, carrying, giving birth and nurturing. "The Church gives birth daily to Christ by faith in the hearts of those who can hear", says Albert the Great (and innumerable other authors).[5]

1. Mother Church: A Fading Image

To begin with, we must ask ourselves: Is the image of "our Mother the Church" (that has become alien to us, and that we prefer to replace with the more popular expression "People of God") anything more than an analogy which was once appropriate, on the basis of prevailing cultural conditions, and which is no longer appropriate since it no longer corresponds to our changed ways of thinking and

---

[4] Hugo Rahner, "Die Gottesgeburt: Die Lehre der Kirchenväter von der Geburt Christi im Herzen der Gläubigen", in *Zeitschrift für katholische Theologie* 59 (1935): 333–418.

[5] Albert the Great, *In Apocalypsim,* 12, 5. *Opera Omnia,* vol. 38 (Paris: Borgnet, 1890–1899): 656.

feeling? Even though we cannot deny that this image has some biblical foundations, are these convincing enough to bind us—despite our resistance and lack of understanding—to the ideal of the all-embracing "maternal love of the Church" that was so dear to the minds and hearts of Christians of past generations? Would it not suffice to extract certain essentials from this "ideology" of the maternal Church, which has been lost as a coherent image, and fit these elements into our changed emotional world?

Karl Delahaye has undertaken this task in a well-known work that is more nuanced that we can show here in a brief summary. He hopes to stimulate a "renewal of pastoral methods along the lines of early patristics"[6] by selecting and adapting elements that were intrinsic to the image of "Mother Church" and were lost when the latter faded. The Church does not comprehend her own greatness fully because she knows herself only through analogy, in images, and also "because the richness of her existence unfolds only in the course of history".[7] It is therefore quite possible for an image that was formerly central now to find itself relegated to the periphery, particularly when an ancient civilization that contemplated and assimilated truth in images has given place to an era that thinks, abstracts and infers in concepts. For the Greeks, and also for the ancient Near-Eastern and biblical peoples, an image was not a representation of, or a correspondence to, a thing, independent of reality, but a manifestation of the thing itself.[8] Thus for Paul, the invisible God is not deduced from creation but is "clearly perceived" in it (Rom 1:20). The extent to which we have abandoned such

---

[6] Karl Delahaye, *Erneuerung der Seelsorgsformen aus der Sicht der frühen Patristik* (Freiburg im Breisgau: Herder, 1958). Already in a dissertation written in 1952 by F. X. Arnold, whose concern was to present the work and apply its categories, such as differentiating between the (mere) "process of salvation" (by God, but also using worldly instruments) and "the mediation of salvation" (through human beings understood in a personalist sense).

[7] J. Bernhart, *Kosmos, Hierarchie, Kirche* (Vienna: n.p., 1936), 81–82.

[8] Delahaye, *Erneuerung*, 10.

symbolic thinking is evident from the failure of the phenomenological movement.[9] The Bible frequently speaks in images (e.g., the Lord's parables) that have successfully made the transition from an Old Testament to a New Testament meaning, made possible by the theological doctrine of type and antitype. Christ is *eikōn theou* (2 Cor 4:4; Col 1:15), not to be translated in modern terminology as image or copy, but as "visible manifestation of the reality, substantially identified (*metochē*) with the subject".[10] Starting from biblical foundations, the Church Fathers created "meaningful archetypal images" of the Church, such as "body" and "woman".[11] In the New Testament, Paul made a masterful synthesis of "woman" (as *daughter* of Zion, as *spouse* of Yahweh, as Jerusalem the barren *mother* made wondrously fertile, as the Shulamite of the Song of Songs) and "body" by referring back to the "two in one flesh" of Genesis (2:24) and applying this to the mystery not only of the Incarnation but also of the Passion of the Son of God. Thus Ephesians 5:25–33 almost anticipates the patristic *ecclesia ex latere Christi* (corresponding to the first Eve from the side of Adam). The bridal imagery of the Gospels is reflected in Paul (2 Cor 11:2; Rom 7:2–4). Among these, "the Jerusalem above", "our mother" (Gal 4:25–28), acquires particular importance because, while the earthly Jerusalem will not let "her children" be gathered together (Mt 23:37; cf. Lk 19:44), the heavenly Jerusalem (in the concluding image of the New Testament) descends like a bride adorned for the wedding feast of the Lamb (Rev 21:1–3). This is preceded by the image of the woman in pangs of childbirth: between heaven and earth she gives birth to the Messiah and to those who "bear testimony to Jesus" (Rev 12:17).

Moving from this rich material to the even richer "Mother Church" theology of patristics, we must again take the ancient world and

[9] Whose attempt was well regarded by Delahaye.

[10] H. Kleinknecht, article *Eikon,* in Kittel, *Theologisches Wörterbuch zum Neuen Testament* (1935), 386.

[11] Delahaye, in reference to J. Bernhart and E. Commer.

particularly the Hellenistic milieu into account. Here we find the image of the earth, the *magna mater,* both virgin and bountiful mother. For Plato, matter (space) is mother and nurse of the universe (the All-Becoming). Personifications—feminine by preference—abounded in late antiquity.[12] Gnosticism adopted, multiplied and intensified them by making them *hypostases* with dramatic destinies. It is in this ambience that the circuitous meandering of the Church Fathers' thought arrived at *Ecclesia Mater* which, according to Delahaye, is merely a personification, supported by the ancient belief that redemption is always a restoration to original perfection. Hence the Church, Bride and Mother, can be a virgin, like the heavenly Eve.[13] Accordingly we see an imposing series of grandiose literary monuments—hymns glorifying the "mystical Mother and Virgin", wedded to her Bridegroom on the Cross and in the Resurrection and reigning on earth as in heaven—such as Hugo Rahner, with a preference for "triumphant language" (Zeno of Verona), has presented to us.[14]

Delahaye dispassionately asks what importance such an image might still have for us. For him, it was merely one attempt among many to present graphically the unfathomable mystery of salvation.[15] The rich content of the image is reduced to the Church's pastoral activity, which always presupposes a prior *reception* of the salvation offered by God (in word and sacrament), which is then *transmitted* partly as an "object", instrumentally (corresponding to the ancient view of woman), and partly by active personal participation (in the modern understanding). It is always the entire holy people who participate in this communication of salvation to each individual, corresponding to the

---

[12] Literature in Alois Müller, "Ecclesia-Maria: Die Einheit Marias und der Kirche", in *Paradosis* 5 (Fribourg, 1951): 10–11.

[13] Delahaye, *Erneuerung,* 34.

[14] Hugo Rahner, *Lobpreis der Kirche aus dem ersten Jahrtausend christlicher Literatur* (Einsiedeln: Benziger, 1944).

[15] "Our thought categories are not in a position to grasp adequately what is set forth in early patristics." Delahaye, *Erneuerung,* 89.

priority of the "mother" vis-à-vis the children in the ancient image. Here Delahaye does not intend to equate the priestly office of service with the common priesthood of the People of God but rather tries to determine its proper place in the more inclusive context: "By accepting office, the officeholder does not surrender his maternal function of mediating salvation as a believer, but this becomes secondary to his newly received paternal duty."[16]

It seems premature to discard the ancient image as unusable. The patristic writings themselves can justify its significance even for our age. Undeniably, the image of "Mother Church" expresses certain fundamental "tensions" inherent in the mystical character of the reality that underlies the image, namely that the Church is to be virginal and pure (cf. 2 Cor 11:2) while yet being united with her Spouse (Eph 5:25–33) and a fruitful mother (cf. Gal 4:26; Rev 12). But this very image is intended to reconcile these apparent contradictions. Thus the Church Fathers state that the Church that gives birth to her children in baptism does not release them from her body but on the contrary accepts them into her body.[17] Furthermore — a more important point — the Church is both cause and effect of the sanctification of the faithful. Hippolytus especially emphasizes that the Church is the Mother of the faithful, while she is also "the holy assembly of those who live in righteousness",[18] and that the Word of the Father, by becoming man, "continually raises up saints who in turn bring him forth ever anew".[19] Applying this to the Church and saying that she

[16] Ibid., 154. Yves Congar expresses a similar view in "Mutter Kirche", *Kirche Heute, Brennpunkte* 2, 2d ed. (Frankfurt am Main: Kaffke, 1969), 30–37.

[17] For instance Irenaeus, *Against Heresies* 5, 20, 2, in *The Ante-Nicene Christian Library,* vol. 9 (Edinburgh: T. & T. Clark, 1883), 109–10; Cyprian, *The Unity of the Catholic Church,* 23, in *Ancient Christian Writers,* vol. 25 (New York: Newman Press, 1956): 64–65.

[18] Hippolytus, *In Daniel* 1, 17, 6–7.

[19] Ibid., 1, 9, 8.

"never ceases giving birth to the *Logos* from her heart",[20] the question arises whether the already existing Church engenders the *Logos* in the hearts of the faithful or whether the "saints" engender the *Logos* and thus also the Church, which Hippolytus thought entirely possible. As Bede put it: *"Ecclesia quotidie gignit ecclesiam"*[21] But Augustine already concedes that the Mother exists in the assembly of her children.[22] This may be true theologically, but it destroys the coherence of the mother image. The same thing occurs in the Fathers, insofar as priority is given to Mother Church over her children (as the Church of the sacraments and of the word, of authority and teaching), yet she only exists in her children and nowhere else. "In carnal wedlock, mother and child are distinct, while in the Church, by contrast, Mother and child are one."[23] However, we still have not mentioned the most serious contradiction. The early Church Fathers refer as a matter of course to Mother Church as the "bride without spot or wrinkle or any such thing, that she might be holy and without blemish" (Eph 5:27). We encounter this wholly loving, all-holy Church in Augustine too, who inclined more and more to locate the reality of this immaculate Church in eschatological time. This, however, throws a critical light on the certitude (never doubted, though never reflectively explored) which was based on the data of Scripture and the contrast between the (never altogether spotless) synagogue and the Church wholly cleansed by Christ's blood: who is or who are this pure Church or Church of the pure, rightly called the *real,* the *true* Church, suffering the falsehood and hypocrisy of the Church of sinners, whom she makes righteous, elevates and reconciles with herself?

---

[20] Hippolytus, *Treatise on Christ and Antichrist,* 61, in *The Ante-Nicene Fathers,* vol. 5 (New York: Charles Scribner's Sons, 1919): 217.

[21] Bede, *Explan. Apoc.* 2 (Migne: PL 93:166d).

[22] "Cum ex ipsis filiis congregatis constet ea quae dicitur mater." *De div. quaest.* 83: Q 59, 4.

[23] Augustine, *Enarr. in Ps.* 127, 12.

We know that in the New Testament the members of the Church are called saints in accordance with the Old Testament meaning of election and consecration to God, now deepened by Christ's work of reconciliation.[24] This applies particularly to the original core of the Church, the "saints of Jerusalem" (2 Cor 8:4; 9:1, 12; Rom 15:31), the ever-holy city.[25] However, it is obvious that this collective consecration of the community by no means makes the individual members "pure", as they should be in virtue of their election. The *Shepherd of Hermas* already sees "all these saints" as "sinners" who should do penance and for whom one should pray.[26] The title of "saints",[27] which remains valid for the Christian community as such, does not guarantee that in her visible existence she will reflect the "pure virgin" (2 Cor 11:2), the "glorious" spouse "without blemish" (Eph 5:27).

Surely, in contrast to the synagogue (the "present Jerusalem", Gal 4:25) and in contrast to all earthly reality, the "Jerusalem which is above", the "new Jerusalem" (Rev 21:2) which eschatologically comes down from heaven, must be without blemish. Paul actually calls it "our mother" (Gal 4:26); we have come "to the city of the living God, the heavenly Jerusalem" (Heb 12:22). The whole of patristic literature— from the second letter of Clement through Origen to Augustine's *City of God*—is pervaded by the yearning for this heavenly, archetypal, primitive Church, often described as preexisting. The earthly Church is merely her imperfect image, bound to her while she humbly wanders through a world that is far from God. Where this preexistent Church is presented as real, she resembles a gnostic *aeon* (cf. Origen and Methodius) that has fallen into the realm of time, whither her

[24] Hippolyte Delehaye, *Sanctus. Essai sur le culte des saints dans l'antiquité* (Brussels: Societé des Bollandistes, 1927).

[25] Lucien Cerfaux, " 'Les Saints' de Jérusalem", in *Ephemerides theologicae Lovanienses* 2 (1925): 510–29; now in *Recueil L. Cerfaux,* vol. 2 (1954): 389–413.

[26] *The Shepherd of Hermas,* vision 1, 9, in *The Fathers of the Church,* vol. 1 (New York: Cima Publishing Co., Inc., 1947): 234; Vision 2, 2, 4, ibid.

[27] Examples in Hippolyte Delehaye, *Sanctus,* 29.

spouse, Christ, pursues her to bring her home.[28] But this is not the Church that Paul has in mind when he speaks of the bride cleansed with water, or of the "pure bride" that is vulnerable to seduction by the serpent; the reality he is thinking of is earthly and concrete.

In the second century it was common to call the (pure, intact and ecclesial) faith "our mother". Thus Polycarp in his letter to the Philippians says that the faith given(!) to us "is the mother of us all".[29] Similarly, in an early interrogation of a martyr, in response to the proconsul's question as to the martyr's parents, the latter replied: "In truth, our father is Christ, and our mother is faith in him."[30] All the Church Fathers' writings on heresy equate falling away from the true faith of the Church, and the consequent separation from her, with the Old Testament "harlotry", so that, in retrospect, perseverance in the true faith of the Catholic Church becomes the mark of the faithful spouse of Christ.[31] But this faith is only one of the essential traits of the spouse's spotlessness. What corresponds to it, namely, love within the Church, is assumed rather than explicitly stated as concrete.

Should the martyrs be considered the core of the holy Church? They may be holy, but all the same they have died and are no longer part of the earthly community; they can be venerated, and people can have themselves buried in places associated with them. Or what of the confessors, those who, while they suffered for the faith, yet escaped with their lives and, on the basis of this, "have merited the priestly dignity be-

[28] Origen, *Comm. in Mt.* 14:17; Methodius, *The Symposium,* 3, 8, in *Ancient Christian Writers,* vol. 27 (New York: Newman Press, 1958): 63–65.

[29] Polycarp, *Letter to the Philippians,* 3, 3 in *The Fathers of the Church,* vol. 1 (New York: Cima Publishing Co., Inc., 1947): 137.

[30] "Mart. S. Justini et Soc.", in Rudolf Knopf, *Ausgewählte Märtyrerakten* (Tübingen: J. C. B. Mohr, 1929), 17.

[31] For example: Cyprian, *The Unity,* 6, in *Ancient Christian Writers,* 25:48–49. For texts on heresy as fornication, cf. my study "Casta Meretrix", in *Sponsa Verbi* (Einsiedeln: Johannesverlag, 1960), 251–57.

fore God"?[32] Yet Cyprian raises bitter complaints about their arrogance and presumption in that they circumvent the Church's path of penance and, on their own authority, reconcile apostates with the Church.

And what of the "Church structure" established by Christ? Should it, perhaps, be regarded as the "infallible" element, as against the existential aspect, which, although it is lived out within this structure, is at best an approximation of it? This would be to introduce a totally modern distinction into the ideas of the ancient Church. Y. Congar in particular favors this distinction of the Church as institution— to which "the faith, the sacraments and the exercise of authority received from Christ" belong[33]—from the Church as *congregatio fidelium*(made possible by the foregoing). However, we have seen that even a "hierarchist" like Cyprian never separates the "institution" (*ordo*) of the bishops from their *communio,* their loyal unity in faith and love; both stand or fall together. And where this principle is proven inadequate, as later in Donatism, both aspects become questionable.

[32] Hippolytus, *Canones Ecclesiae,* Canon 6, Migne, PG 10:959–62.

[33] Yves Congar, *Vraie et fausse réforme dans l'Église* (Paris: Cerf, 1950), 95. Likewise in *Jalons pour une théologie du laïcat* [Lay people in the Church] (Paris: Cerf, 1953), 46ff., where again the aspect "institution of redemption" precedes and makes possible the aspect "community of redemption". René Laurentin thinks similarly and assigns Peter to the first and Mary to the second aspect: "The first aspect is the official representation of Christ; this is embodied in Peter and his successors. The second is the mystical communion with Christ; it is summed up in Mary." *Court traité de théologie mariale* [Queen of heaven: a short treatise on Marian theology] (Paris: Lethielleux, 1953), 109. Charles Journet's profound theology of the Church rests on other grounds. For him, the real Church, immaculate and infallible— indwelling all her sinful members—is the "gratia creata" which by the presence of the Holy Spirit confers on her the "anima creata", that is "the sacramental character, sacramental grace, and with it the orientation toward the power of jurisdiction." *L'Église du Verbe Incarné* [The Church of the Word incarnate] (Paris: Desclée de Brouwer, 1951), 2:522. To this grace the imperfect members of the Church come closer "asymptotically" (ibid., 393); but they belong to the Church only insofar as they are not sinners and partake of her holiness (ibid., 488). Elsewhere we have criticized this concept, that became possible only after High Scholasticism.

194

Should we therefore see the perfection of the Church entirely due to and contained in Christ's perfection yet, insofar as the members are distinct from Christ, regard this perfection as being sufficiently expressed by a certain "striving" for the perfection of the Head, by an approximation of the "spotless" ideal which, in itself, is unattainable on earth?[34] This seems to be the only solution left and is the inevitable conclusion if we accept the Platonic hypostatizing of a "spotless Church" (which is the "true" Church)[35] existing only in heaven or eschatologically, whereas the empirically real Church is the "sinner" striving toward conversion.[36] Thus the concept of the Church's perfect holiness, upheld by the Fathers, could be abandoned from time to time in the Middle Ages in favor of mere "freedom from grave sin".[37] This was a Church that had already resigned herself to not being spotless and was already on the way to the "sociological" Church of the present day. There could be no going back to the patristic "hypostasis" of the pure Church, except perhaps in the echo of it which we find in the newly found delight in symbols and images of the Romanesque and Gothic periods.[38]

However, the dilemma which we have illustrated by reference to Karl Delahaye is artificial. The facts will not justify a separation of the

[34] In reference to Eph 4:13, cf. Hippolytus, *Against the Heresy of Noetus,* 17, in *The Ante-Nicene Library,* vol. 9, pt. 2 (Edinburgh: T. & T. Clark, 1883), 68. "For there is also one Son (or servant) of God, by whom we too, receiving the regeneration through the Holy Spirit, desire to come all unto one perfect and heavenly man." *On the Antichrist,* 3.

[35] "Kyriōs ecclesia": Origen, *Treatise on Prayer,* 20:1, in *Ancient Christian Writers,* vol. 19 (New York: Newman Press, 1954): 70–71.

[36] Gregory the Great: "Dicat ergo ecclesia: inde sum fusca, inde peccatrix, quia sol me decoloravit, quia creator meus, dum me deseruit, ego in errore lapsa sum." *Homilies on the Canticle of Canticles,* 1, 5; ed. Heine, 138.

[37] Helmut Riedlinger, *Die Makellosigkeit der Kirche in den lateinischen Hohenliedkommentaren des Mittelalters* (Münster: Aschendorff, 1958), 99, cf. 107, 110f; 117, 122, 123, etc.

[38] Cf. primarily Yves Congar, *L'Ecclésiologie du haut moyen-âge* (Paris: Cerf, 1968), bibliography, 41–52. Wolfram von den Steinen, *Homo coelestis* (Munich: Francke, 1965).

concept "Virgin-Mother-Church" from that of "Virgin-Mother-Mary". Both of these themes are so intertwined in the Bible and in patristics — at least since Justin and Irenaeus — that they cannot be dealt with separately. It must be generally acknowledged that in the very period when the alleged "hypostasis" of the (pure) Church is losing its previously unchallenged credibility (roughly from the Carolingian period),[39] the historical person of Mary begins to come into greater prominence as the *Realsymbol* of this (pure) Church. To the extent to which the immaculateness of Mary becomes theologically confirmed during the course of the Middle Ages, it can become the original core of that Church which remains virginal in relation to her Lord, even in wedded fruitfulness, and which has an all-embracing motherly role within the Church's paternal and official sphere and in relation to the people as a whole.

2. *Mother Church: The* Realsymbol *Regained in Mary*

It is unnecessary to reintroduce here the oft-described development of the doctrine of Mary as the archetype of the Church. This can easily be found elsewhere.[40]

[39] L. Scheffczyk, "Das Mariengeheimnis in Frömmigkeit und Lehre der Karolingerzeit", in *Erfurter theologische Studien* 5 (Leipzig, 1959). How lively the sensitivity to the Church's motherhood can remain even up to modern times is shown in Newman's farewell sermon to the Anglican Church: "O mother of saints! ... O nurse of the heroic! ... O virgin of Israel! ... O my mother." *Sermons Bearing on the Subjects of the Day* (Westminster, Maryland: Christian Classics, 1968), 406f.

[40] To mention only the most important: Matthias Joseph Scheeben, *Dogmatik,* vol. 3 (1882), sec. 274–82; Heinrich Maria Koester, *Die Magd des Herrn,* 2d ed. (Limburg: Lahn-Verlag, 1954); Otto Semmelroth, *Urbild der Kirche* (Würzburg: Echter Verlag, 1950); Hugo Rahner, *Maria und die Kirche* [Our Lady and the Church] (Innsbruck: Marianischer Verlag, 1950); Alois Müller, *Ecclesia-Maria,* 2d ed. (Fribourg: Universitätsverlag, 1955); Georg Schückler, *Maria im Geheimnis der Kirche. Zur Mariologie der Kirchenväter* (Cologne: Wort und Werk, 1955); Louis Bouyer, *Le Trône de la Sagesse* (Paris 1957). More recently, Gérard Philips, "Marie et l'Église", in *Maria* 7, ed. H. du Manoir (Paris: Beauchesne, 1964), esp. 375.

It will be obvious to anyone who considers with an open mind the relationship between a human mother and her child—particularly if this is done from a Christian point of view, free from the antifeminine bias of antiquity—that the Mother, Mary (particularly as the Gospels present her unequivocally as a virgin), belongs to the innermost circle of that human "constellation" around Jesus which is of theological significance. To regard her merely as a mother in the physical sense, without a spiritual relationship to her child, is untheological because it is inhuman. The infancy narratives, particularly those of Luke, are clearly full to the brim with theological symbolism—leading from the Old to the New Testament—that has a real foundation in the simply told events. As could be expected, the Marian episodes of the fourth Gospel are essential to its understanding.[41] The Letter to the Ephesians forcefully presents the relationship of Christ and Church as that of man and wife, and since Paul shows Christ to be the second and final Adam, the Church automatically assumes the role of the second Eve, without reference to her relationship to Mary. The image in Revelation of the woman in labor remains unexplained: who is she who bears the Messiah (Rev 12:5) as well as all the others who are her descendants (12:17)?

Later reflection follows the path opened up by Paul. In Hermas and in the second letter of Clement, the Church appears as Virgin, Mother and immaculate Bride. The theme is developed from here on. But it is in Justin (ca. 150) that we find for the first time the parallel of the disobedience of the virgin Eve and the obedience of the Virgin Mary—no doubt based on the *protoevangelium* (Gen 3:15). Irenaeus

[41] A. Feuillet, "La Vierge Marie dans le Nouveau Testament", *Maria* 6 (1961): 15–69. With respect to Luke, see: René Laurentin, *Structure et théologie de Luc I–II* (Paris: J. Gabalda, 1957); Heinz Schürmann, *Das Lukasevangelium,* vol. 1 (Freiburg im Breisgau: Herder, 1969). With respect to John: François Marie Braun, O.P., *La Mère des fidèles. Essai de théologie johannique* [Mother of God's people], 2d ed. (Tournai and Paris: Casterman, 1954).

deepens the theme and builds it into the foundations of the theology of redemption. Two parallels go side by side: Adam is created from the virgin earth, Christ from the Virgin Mary (so as to receive his body from Adam's seed);[42] then the Virgin Mary's obedience "compensates for" the disobedience of the virgin Eve,[43] and by this obedience she "becomes the cause of salvation . . . for the whole human race".[44] In addition, there is further development of the image of the Church's motherhood.[45] Is there a relationship between the virginal fruitfulness of the Church (the baptismal font) and the virginal fruitfulness of Mary? The dispute goes back and forth concerning the text of *Adversus Haereses* IV, 33, 4 and 33, 11: Does it refer to Mary or the Church? Even if it means the maternal womb of the Church from which "new birth" comes "through faith", Irenaeus points for confirmation to the extraordinary salvific sign given by God: the birth from the womb of the Virgin (Mary). The recently published critical edition in *Sources chrétiennes* favors this interpretation unequivocally.[46] Hence the subsequent passage (in no. 11) must also be understood as referring to Mary: "They (the prophets) preached about the Emmanuel who was to be born from a virgin (Is 7:14), indicating the union of God's Word with the 'work of his hands'. The Word became flesh, and the Son of God became the Son of Man. He, the Pure One, purely opened the Mother's pure womb, which he himself had made pure and which gives mankind new birth to God. Thus he, the 'strong God' whose birth is ineffable (cf. Is 53:8), becomes what we are." Alois Müller is right: the insight of "Mary's *identity* with the

[42] Irenaeus, *Against Heresies,* 3, 21, 10 (=Epideixis 32–2); 5, 21, 1.

[43] Ibid., 5, 19, 1; Epideixis 33.

[44] Irenaeus, *Against Heresies,* 3, 22, 4; quoted in *Lumen gentium* no. 56.

[45] Cf. Müller, *Ecclesia-Maria,* 54.

[46] "There is no possible doubt that the "gennēsis kainē" of which Irenaeus speaks here is the virginal birth by which the Son of God is born from the womb of Mary." *Sources chrétiennes,* 100/101:269.

Church" strikes us like a lightning-flash.[47] "Mary is *analogously* the concrete universal of the 'Church', just as Christ is the concrete universal of divine Sonship".[48] It may be that the reference to Mary's womb which "gives new birth" implies no more than the "cause of salvation" (in the earlier text); one must not over-interpret Irenaeus' flash of intuition;[49] but for posterity, which will always speak somewhat hesitantly of Mary as the *typos* of the Church, the principle is established here that Mary is more than simply a symbolic, anticipatory embodiment of something that takes place spiritually in the Church (as, for instance, according to Cyprian, Peter's priority over against the other apostles was *only* symbolic): first and foremost what Irenaeus sees in Mary is the spiritual power of her obedient consent, which has archetypal efficacy for salvation.

Let us move on to the fifth century, though in the intermediate period the concept of the Church was much discussed (e.g., her origin from the wound in the side of the Second Adam), and Revelation 12 was occasionally applied to Mary, an interpretation rejected by Methodius. Here we find Augustine preoccupied with the parallel of the symbol (bodily birth from Mary) and the reality (spiritual birth from the Church), though he shrinks from going as far as Irenaeus. Only exceptionally does he venture to make a statement such as: "Mary is Mother and Virgin not only in spirit but also in flesh. She is not the spiritual mother of our Head who is himself the Redeemer; rather, she is born spiritually from him, because all the faithful, of whom she is one, are rightly called sons of the Bridegroom. But she is in truth the Mother of his members (and such are we) because by her love she cooperated in the birth of the

---

[47] Müller, *Ecclesia-Maria,* 71.
[48] Ibid., 73.
[49] Philips, "Marie et l'Église", 379.

199

faithful who are members of the Head."[50] Thus the West gained the insight, though not without pains, with which Cyril of Alexandria capped his fulminating sermon at the Council of Ephesus: "Let us praise the ever-virgin Mary, and that means, indeed, the Holy Church as well as her Son and immaculate Bridegroom. To him be glory forever. Amen."[51]

This is an acknowledgment in principle of what Scheeben refers to as the *perichoresis* between Mary and the Church, which is so close that "one can be fully understood only in and with the other".[52] This intermingling is clearly illuminated by Haymo of Auxerre, who says that Mary as the Mother of God is the "personified representation of the Church".[53] Thus, any suspicion that the Church is formed after the pattern of an *hypostasis* (in the mode of thought of the ancients) is dispelled. It enables the Church, on the basis of the historical reality of Mary (whose viriginal motherhood is universally accepted at this time), to be understood and loved in her authentic femininity and all-embracing maternity, because Mary's "personal portrayal" does not imply a narrow devotion to her as a private person. We must see her expropriated and given to the whole Church, from the Annunciation in Luke 1 to her shocking "public exposure" in Revelation 12,

[50] Augustine, *On Holy Virginity,* 6, in *The Fathers of the Church,* vol. 15 (Washington, D.C.: The Catholic University of America, 1955), 149. Cf. an analogous Syrian text from the end of the fifth century in Anton Wenger, *Vatican II,* vol. 2, *Chronique de la deuxième session* (Paris: Éditions du Centurion, 1963), 124–25: "You are the fullness (head and body). I first bore you and then all who hope in you."

[51] Cyril of Alexandria (Migne, PG 77:996c).

[52] Scheeben, *Dogmatik,* vol. 3, no. 1819, 618.

[53] Among the works of Haimo of Halberstadt, *In Apoc.* 3, 12 (Migne, PL 117:1081a). However, the same formula was applied by the Church Fathers, much earlier and for a long time, to women mentioned in the Old and New Testaments.

where she is shown as giving birth between heaven and earth.[54] Thus Mother and Church reflect each other.[55]

We do not need to follow the development of the Marian idea in detail. In the early Middle Ages, Mary came to the fore in the consciousness of the Christian people, and her feasts and liturgies multiplied rapidly. But the person of Mary took over the theological place formerly occupied by the (unreflectedly) "hypostatized", pure Church; in the commentaries on Revelation 12 (Ambrosius Autpert) and on the Song of Songs (Paschasius Radbertus), Mary becomes more and more recognized as the one who has been given the "fullness of grace"—*gratia plena*—an archetype of that fullness of grace which Christ has given to the Church (Abélard, Alan of Lille, Albert the Great).[56] The role of Mary at the foot of the Cross, where, according to ancient teaching, the Church was born from the wound in Jesus' side, was brought into sharper focus (e.g., by Rupert of Deutz), emphasizing her motherhood with regard to the Church. With her own conception and birth, the seed of the Church has already been planted "because the first person in the Church was

[54] This "public exposure" does not mean that Mary's function is absorbed by the people as a whole, as Altfrid Kassing assumes in *Das Verhältnis von Kirche und Maria im 12. Kapitel des Apokalypse* (Dissertation, Louvain University, 1957): "The question is not that Mary as an individual permeates the whole Church, . . . rather what matters is the *mutual* relationship of *all* members of God's community *with one another* . . . the birth of the 'male child' is seen in Revelation 12 as an act of the *community*," 154.

[55] "Ipsa (Maria) in Ecclesia, et Ecclesia in ipsa figuratur." Serlo of Savigny, O. Cist., *In Nativitate Beatae Mariae* 1, *Bibliotheca Patrum Cisterciensium,* vol. 6 (Paris, 1664), 117. Also the well-known discourse of Abbot Isaac of Stella, Sermon 31 (Migne, PL 194:1963a).

[56] The principle that all graces given to the Church (e.g., including those of the priesthood) were abundantly (*eminenter*) present in Mary is unduly emphasized by the *Mariale* that, until recently, was attributed to Albert. This work had a great and continuing influence up to the Reformation. Its principle rests on the concept of hierarchy of the Pseudo-Dionysius, whose system was then very influential.

born".[57] In modern times the insights gained in the Middle Ages have been classified and systematized, sometimes too much so, because the delicate *mysterium* of Mary cannot be rendered in rigid conceptualizations. This is why the Magisterium continually has had to set limits to the incautious developments of unenlightened devotion. The essential thing is that, in the history of the *ecclesia immaculata,* the core, i.e., the *Realsymbol,* Mary, came into prominence at the right time to prevent that idea of the Church from disintegrating into mediocrity and ultimately into sociology. The period of one-sidedly private devotion was a prolonged transition, mistaken in its cramped approach but not in its essence. Its persistence right up to the present time has enabled *Vatican II* once more to relate Mariology and ecclesiology. In *Lumen gentium,* the account starts with Mary's motherly and maidenly role in the life of her Son (*Lumen gentium* 55–59); then, continually reiterating the *leitmotif* of "motherhood" and "motherliness", it ponders the comparison between Mary (the archetype of the Church) and the earthly, sinful Church that strives for holiness (60–65). It ends by commending devotion to Mary as a sign of hope and consolation for the pilgrim People of God (66–69). The theme in the central section begins with the "motherly duty of Mary toward mankind". In no way does this obscure her Son's unique mediatorship; rather, the active freedom of her faith and obedience redounds to the praise of God (56). Only after describing her role at the Cross (where the Church is born) (62) does the document speak about the Church whose *typos* she is: "For in the mystery of the Church, which is herself rightly called mother and virgin, the Blessed Virgin stands out in eminent and singular fashion as exemplar both of virgin and mother."

[57] Godfrey of St. Victor, *In Nativitate Beatae Mariae;* see H. Barré, "Marie et l'Église, du vénérable Bède à St. Albert le Grand" (Société Franç. Étud., March 9, 1951), 59–125 (quotation on 93); cf. H. Coathalem, S.J., "Le Parallelisme entre la S. Vierge et l'Église dans la tradition latine jusq'à la fin du XIIème siècle", in *Analecta Gregoriana* 74, Ser. Theol. 27 (Rome: 1954).

As a virgin she gave birth to Christ, "the firstborn among many brethren" (Rom 8:29) "in whose generation and formation she cooperates with a mother's love" (63).

By the time of Vatican II the Church had lost all vestiges of the pseudo-gnostic *hypostasis* and had attained virginal holiness and motherhood by "contemplating" Mary (64). For, "while in the most Blessed Virgin the Church" — of whom she is a "member" (53)[58] — "has already reached the perfection whereby she exists without spot or wrinkle (cf. Eph 5:27), the faithful still strive to conquer sin and increase in holiness." "They turn their eyes to Mary" and become more and more like Christ, also, and particularly, in "apostolic work" (cf. *Constitution on the Liturgy,* 5). Hereby the office of ministry is also assigned its place in the Virgin-Mother-Church, whose motherliness is specially emphasized (65).[59]

Lastly, in summarizing the principal themes of the *Maria-Ecclesia* tradition, the Council points out the differences in Mary's relationship to the three Persons of the Trinity (*Lumen gentium* 52–53: "Mother of the Son, therefore . . . daughter of the Father and the temple of the Holy Spirit", 65). Contemplating this mystery that is specially revealed in Mary (Lk 1:28, 31, 35), all that appeared previously as a disturbing contradiction in the "image" of the patristic "Mother Church" becomes

[58] We are not concerned here with the problem of understanding Mary's status which arises from her being simultaneously Mother and Daughter of the Church. Henri de Lubac, in *Paradoxe et mystère de l'Église* (Paris: Aubier, 1967), 110, points out that Paul VI prudently adapted his manner of expression to that of the Council, but that this question had been known to tradition for a long time. Thus, in the eighth century, Berengaudus said in his commentary on the Apocalypse (Migne, PL 17:960b), "Mary is the Mother of the Church because she brought into the world the Head of the Church; she is daughter of the Church because she is a member of her, the most exalted member". German translation: *Geheimnis aus dem wir leben* (Einsiedeln: Johannesverlag, 1967), 122.

[59] On this whole question, see the representative commentary on *Lumen gentium* by Gérard Philips in *L'Église et son mystère au deuxième Concile du Vatican I–II* (Paris and Tournai: Desclée, 1967).

clear. Moreover, the apparent contradictions are reconciled in the indissoluble reciprocity of Mother and Son, in that the Mother can (and must) have a "prerogative" only because this was given to her for her motherly task by the grace of the Father and the merits of the Son. Most of all, however, Mary's work as a "helpmate" of the New Adam is focused wholly beyond herself and subordinated to his trinitarian work of salvation: to make men, i.e., his brothers, be children of the Father by the gift of the Holy Spirit and thus gather them into a community founded on trinitarian life. Likewise, the Church's work of announcing the word and dispensing the sacraments is focused beyond herself on that same work of Christ, the aim of which is to rebuild the Church—with the Church's help.

3. Mary and Peter

It is difficult to set forth adequately the relationship that exists between Mary, the prototype of the Church's maternal love (that we have just described), and the Petrine office within the apostolic college. Before attempting to do so, we must clearly recall what we have been taking for granted all along, namely, that we are dealing here with only two *Realsymbols*—albeit two of the most important ones—within the "constellation" of Jesus Christ. He alone is the Lord of the Church. Mary is his handmaid; Peter, the first person entrusted with office, is assigned to the "lowest place", to be "the least" and the "servant of all" (Lk 22:26; 14:9); Paul says this applies to all the apostles (cf. 1 Cor 4:9). This creates the Christian dialectic: Jesus alone, naturally, is "above" and "from above" (Jn 3:31), and all the rest are naturally "from below" (Jn 8:23). Also we must understand that since he whom we rightly call "Teacher and Lord" (Jn 13:13) humbled himself by taking the form of a servant, we who are by nature inferior should not try to take a higher place than our Master (Jn 13:16). Yet, all the same, Christ's humiliation becomes the measure of our attitudes and practical action, through the grace of God's love, which humbles itself and bears our weaknesses and sins. This is clearly seen in the Lord's Eucharist, which establishes and sustains the Church's very being; since she is *communio* with the Lord who gives himself for all, she imparts to us an inner grasp of what *communio,* Church, means, both in terms of attitude and of practical action. The eucharistic Lord—the concrete presence of trinitarian life—is himself the foundation of the Church's unity. When Mary and Peter enter into relation with this unity in their particular ways, they do so as commissioned by the Lord and for his service. It is only because Christ unceasingly offers himself to, and within, the Church in the Eucharist, that she is called the "fullness of him who fills all in all" (Eph 1:23); naturally, therefore, the Marian motherliness as well as the Petrine pastoral care must be patterned after this christological model of self-sacrifice.

a. The Liberating Embrace

Both the Marian and the Petrine principles are coextensive with the Church: "The entire Church is Marian".[60] As interpreted by Vatican I and Vatican II, she is also Petrine,[61] insofar as Peter, and his successor, "represents the Church in his person" (*persona ipsam ecclesiam gestante*).[62]

---

[60] Journet, *L'Église du Verbe incarné,* 2:438–46.

[61] Denzinger-Schönmetzer, *Enchiridion Symbolorum,* 3064; *Lumen gentium,* no. 25. An important topic ought to be thoroughly discussed here, namely, the relationship between Mary and the office of the priesthood in general. René Laurentin dealt with it historically and systematically in the two volumes of his comprehensive work *Marie, l'Église et le sacerdoce* (Paris: Lethielleux, 1952–1953). But since it is complicated and moreover does not pertain directly and expressly to the Petrine office, we have disregarded it. We only indicate that the relationship cannot be dealt with in the ordinary categories of "clergy-laity", but the special status of Mary may throw light on the problem involved in this pair of categories.

[62] D'Avanzo at Vatican I (Mansi 52, 762d).

Moreover, "in his relation to the universal Church he is, as a public person, the head of the Church" (*persona publica, i.e., caput ecclesiae in sua relatione ad ecclesiam universalem*).[63] "He can no more be separated from the universal Church than the foundation can be separated from the edifice that it is intended to support."[64] But precisely this image, based on Matthew 16:18, indicates that each is coextensive in different ways.[65] Not only did the Marian Yes precede the Incarnation of the Church's Head (and hence of her members), whereas the appointment of the Twelve under the leadership of Peter is a single act — though weighty in its consequences — on the part of Jesus; qualitatively, the form of the Marian faith (consenting to God's activity) is offered to the *Catholica* as the model of all being and acting, while the catholicity of Peter's pastoral care, though all-embracing in its object, is not communicable in its specific uniqueness.[66] For both these reasons the Petrine universality is subject to the formative influence of the Marian, but not vice versa. Admittedly it is difficult to understand how the Marian all-embracing universality, which is emphatically not "official" but, like everything in the Church (*including* the official side), consents, "lets be", "sets free", can yet exercise a formative influence on the official, Petrine universality, which has the task of "holding together" and "administering" and thus cannot "let be" in the same sense.[67]

The Marian *fiat,* in its truly *unlimited* availability, is, by grace, the

[63] Gasser, in his commentary on the definition (Mansi 52, 762d).

[64] Ibid., 1213bc

[65] A similar limitation is felt when Gasser takes up Cyprian, and again the Gallican-Febronian image of the center (toward which the individual churches converge): "in centro constitutus" (ibid., 1214b), "Centrum unitatis ecclesiasticae" (ibid., 1213b).

[66] Naturally, in analogy, but only in analogy, this is shared by the pastoral care of all the bishops and their priests — and again in analogy (but in greater dissimilarity) by all the faithful.

[67] The text so often applied by the Fathers to Mary and Jesus, "femina circumdabit virum" (Jer 31:32, LXX) can also be applied here to Mary and Peter.

bridal womb, *matrix* and *mater,* through which the Son of God becomes man, and thus it is by this *fiat* that he also forms the truly universal Church. By the power of the boundless, triune God, this *fiat* opens up the boundaries of earthly time "in advance" (in "anticipatory redemption" in the case of the "Immaculate Conception") so that what is earthly and temporal—whether Mary, her Son or the Church—should not place any fundamental obstacle to God's indwelling but should be *infiniti capax.* What is basic to the infinite elasticity of the Marian Yes is that it again and again stretches beyond understanding and must consent to what is not within the domain of the humanly possible, foreseeable, bearable or fitting. It must embrace virginal conception by an already married woman, her "not understanding" the reply of her twelve-year-old, to her being painfully rebuffed by her Son (some twenty years later) and finally her being abandoned at the foot of the Cross and committed to "another son", John. . . . These events repeatedly challenge her understanding and demand an endlessly growing readiness (without any resistance). In all this, Mary shows herself to be "truly *blessed*" because she has believed (Lk 1:45; 11:28, cf. Jn 20:29), and thus she becomes the "seat of wisdom". This is the mold in which the Church is formed. It is to that end that Mary's availability to God and to his Son is channeled through the disciple to whom Jesus entrusted her as mother (Jn 19:26–27). From the beginning the Marian principle is thus the exact opposite of any "partial identification" where discipleship depends on the measure of one's personal comprehension or "responsible" evaluation. But it is equally the opposite of the passive indifference of a mere instrument that can be manipulated at will. In fact, Mary keeps alert to find at any moment the correct response to a new demand (Lk 1:29, 34; 2:19, 51). At Cana she shows a sensitive solicitude for the poor. Her suggestion, "Do whatever he tells you" (Jn 2:5), reveals once more her *fiat,* her detachment, in the midst of this care. It is not simply a matter of "submission to the will of God", still less of cluttering up the space with conventional well-wishing; rather it is the will to retreat into the background and make possible the encounter between human need and divine grace. "Letting it be" is not the same as letting things go. It is not bursting through restraints; rather it is making room for the other (be it God or man or both) to act freely. The unmistakable uniqueness of Mary's alert generosity shows how close she is to the Holy Spirit—whose chosen vessel she is—to that Spirit who, as Divine Person, ever active but "hidden", discreetly yields to the mutual love of Father and Son, to which he owes his being, to which he testifies and which he *is*. When Mary, filled with the Spirit, becomes the archetype of the Church, she appears as the temple of the Holy Spirit who breathes through her whole being and who, without drawing attention to himself, initiates her into the truth of the Father and the Son—which, again, he *is*.

The Marian *fiat,* unequalled in its perfection, is the all-inclusive, protective and directive form of all ecclesial life. It is the interior form of *communio,* insofar as this is an unlimited mutual acceptance, far more than a human "getting along together" or fraternization.[68] The space and time limitations of the human condition remain external to this (ideally) unlimited receptivity. Here, even an abuse of trust does not result in mistrust in return. Mary suffers from the sinfulness of her fellow humans; but in order to meet this sin, she does not have to abandon her own center, she does not have to adopt the standpoint of the periphery. As sin closes in on her—actually on her Son, and, through his suffering, on her—she knows all that she needs to know about sin, and she has no other remedy than her own availability. Thus her attitude becomes foundational for the Church of the faithful, the Church that is pure *communio,* the Church of the "priestly people" who suffer with Jesus Christ.

---

[68] "Do nothing from selfishness or conceit, but in humility count others better than yourselves" (Phil 2:3). This is Paul's premise for putting into practice the many demands for unity and for the possibility that all might "bear one another's burdens" (Gal 6:2).

How is this Marian disposition related to the masculine ministry received by Peter (within the college of the Twelve) from the Chief Shepherd, Jesus? This ministry is to tend the flock as Jesus, the divine Shepherd, did (Ezek 34:11–16). But the salvation of the flock cannot be accomplished without the judgment (Ezek 34:17, "I will judge between sheep and sheep, rams and he-goats") when the world ends (Mt 25:32–34). The keys that Peter holds can open or close: this demands discretion, discernment, examination of the particular case and the giving of judgment. Peter must be concerned with the position of the sinner who stands outside the Marian center of love; he must find his way to the Church's law both from his own standpoint and from where the outsider stands. How is this law, that arises more or less abstractly from the concrete reality of the *communio*, to be employed for salvation in Christ? The "eccentricity" of this office, which, as we have seen, was given to a (former) sinner, lies in the fact that law is elicited from within the *communio* of love as a result of sin in the world.

It would not be correct to say, on the basis of our remarks concerning Möhler, that this "eccentric" aspect is nothing but a deficient realization of the Marian *communio* in the Church. In fact, it has its roots in the divine sovereignty and in the office of Judge that Christ, the Redeemer of the world, received from the Father. This is clearly and frequently stated in the Gospels, the apostolic Letters and Revelation (where the latter's visions entirely mask the loving aspects of this judgment). This aspect of judgment in the work of redemption, though "eccentric", is constitutive, for redemption is concerned with a "critical" process of discrimination as regards the ungodly "world" (hence the aspect of "conviction" in the legal sense in Jn 16:8–11). Jesus' sovereignty and judicial authority (always representing that of God the Father: Jn 5:22–23) may be described as "eccentric" only because in the relationship between God and the truly redeemed, who have received the "spirit of sonship" and can boldly call God "Abba, Father", abstract law is absorbed back into love's intimacy. All that remains of it is a loving respect (*timor castus:* 1 Pet 3:2; Sir 1:11–20, that, according to the Fathers, is an interior form of the love of God) that looks up to the Father who is "greater than I" (Jn 14:28).

Just as Mary received the unconditional quality of her Yes from God (who in Jesus is "always Yes": 2 Cor 1:19), Peter received his keys from the same Lord who irrevocably opens and closes (Rev 3:7)—but only in such a way that he opens a door that "no one is able to shut" (Rev 3:8). Whereas, in the Old Testament, authority was given "to destroy and to overthrow, to build and to plant" (Jer 1:10), in the New Testament the first alternative is expressly dropped: "the authority which the Lord has given me for building up and not for tearing down" (2 Cor 10:8; 13:10). Thus in the New Testament God's paternal face becomes evident throughout the judgment by the Father, Christ and the Holy Spirit (in which office in the Church also has a part). This is not the face of the ancestral God of ancient times but the face of the Father of Jesus Christ, in whom Jesus "rejoiced in the Holy Spirit" (Lk 10:21) and of whom he says, "the Father himself loves you" (Jn 16:27; 14:21, 23). To this Father we can turn without fear. It is therefore not an aberration when the name of "Father" reflects on Peter and his successors, even though they cannot bear it with the same right as Mary can bear the name of Mother. In the first centuries the appellation "Father" was commonly given to the divine Son, insofar as he represents and makes visible the Father and manifests his creative power in founding the Church through word and sacrament. Though this title was, so to say, forbidden in the circle of the Marian *communio* (Mt 23:9), still it is not inappropriate where the Church's authority is exercised, because for the one who seeks reconciliation, this authority can be none other than paternal.

Peter remains, nevertheless, a member of the Marian Church, which, as we have seen, is equally characterized by the Yes of God who reconciles the world to himself. All leadership in the Church should be *diakonia;* it is even described in terms of "slavery" (Mt 20:25–27 par). And the higher the office, the more it should be this, in contrast to "the rulers of the Gentiles (who) lord it over them". Thus in Jesus himself we see the perfection of this service in his "giving his life as a ransom for many" (Mt 20:28). Peter, therefore, must also follow the Marian path of "letting it be", of helping to free people from all kinds of spiritual shackles. His following of Jesus to the Cross will be the pinnacle of such liberating service on his part. Moreover, Peter's physical crucifixion is only the end of his prior spiritual one: his central (yet "eccentric") ministry requires him to make laws and enforce them, and while this juridical aspect proceeds from the very midst of love and is "covered" by it, as far as those are concerned who are still learning how to love (and who is not, apart from Mary?), it is in danger of being taken as abstract law. Thus "authority" can be mistaken for that "power" by which the great of the earth lord it over the people.

Peter *has* to step forward as an individual, over against the others, be they the people with whom he is in *communio* or the bishops with whom he forms a *collegium,* not by "domineering" (1 Pet 5:3), but as a servant who does not detach himself from *communio* or *collegium* but rather "strengthens" them (Lk 22:32), frees them to be themselves in true liberty.

To do this, Peter really needs the freedom that has had to be fought for down the centuries in the face of Conciliarism, Protestantism, Gallicanism, Jansenism, Josephism, Febronianism, etc. All these placed his office in shackles in order to claim for themselves, by stipulating conditions for "consent" or "reception", the authority to "set free"; in reality their aim was to give authoritative freedom to themselves. Whereas, if the primacy was taken seriously, there seemed to be a danger of inviting the bearer of this office to use this authority irrespective of *communio* and *collegium,* the conditions demanded by these movements actually *accomplished* a break in *communio* and *collegium* by restricting the exercise of the primatial ministry and denying the primate his liberty to perform his—Marian—liberation. These were the factors that made Vatican I necessary, no matter how "inappropriate" or incomprehensible its definitions regarding primacy may seem to the spirit of our age. And even though Vatican I may have been regrettably one-sided (before the broadening interpretation of Vatican II), it responded to a critical situation in the Church.

b. Immaculate—Indefectible—Infallible

Everyone knows or should know what the biblical word "immaculate" or "without blemish" means when referring to the ideal Church (according to God's plan: Eph 1:4; the hope of all the redeemed: Jude 24) and to her real archetype, Mary: the perfect bridal correspondence of the Church, in her objective consecration and subjective self-gift, to the Bridegroom (*ut sit sancta et immaculata:* Eph 5:27). Before defining the Immaculate Conception, Pius IX enquired as to the sense of faith of the whole Church. The answer he received was that the whole people, made up of fallible and sinful individuals, was convinced that it possessed such an "unblemished", real and personal center in the person of the Mother of the Lord.[69] When the time came to guarantee the integral and ever-present reality of this genuine personal center (in the dogma of the bodily Assumption into Heaven), Pius XII sent out an even more inclusive questionnaire to collate and evaluate the sense of faith of the whole Church in all her parts. Where the whole Church has an awareness of the perfect correspondence (not only preexistent and eschatological but also historical) on the part of the "bridal" Church vis-à-vis the work and will of Christ, the explicit formulation of this in the allegedly "new" Marian dogmas proves to be nothing more than the definition by the Magisterium of something that already existed.

This does not mean that the Christian people regards itself as being

[69] John Henry Cardinal Newman, "On Consulting the Faithful in Matters of Doctrine, in *Rambler* (July 1859).

the "democratic" guarantor of infallible orthodoxy. Rather, its awareness is supported in its faith from two directions at different levels of perception. First, by what the Fathers called the "holy Church" or the "Church of the saints" (in which Mary came to be seen more and more clearly as her innermost personal core), seen preeminently as the vessel and instrument of the Holy Spirit; and secondly, the apostolic succession of the pastoral and magisterial office, which from the beginning had been the incontrovertible point of reference for orthodox faith. In other words, the *sensus fidelium* to which, with Newman—who relied mostly on Perrone (and his authorities) and on Möhler—we can attribute indefectibility in faith, is from its very first appearance a *consensus,* i.e., a "feeling with", a being-of-the-same-mind. Both points of reference, that is, in personal terms, Mary and Peter (in the midst of the Twelve) belong together in the undisturbed Catholic consciousness. But the presence of sin, of self-righteousness—*ubi peccata, ibi schismata*[70]—causes the factor of law to make a one-sided appearance within the *communio* and challenges the Petrine office not only to act as judge and arbitrator but also to limit and define its powers in this regard.

To understand this development, which reached a provisional conclusion in Vatican I, we need to see its premises clearly; first of all the particular "eccentric" nature of the Petrine office (which, in a way, could be generally applied to all Church office); secondly, its exercise in an "eccentric" situation that we described (at the end of the previous section) as "critical".

To start with the latter, this crisis did not exist in the beginning. It was brought about by the Church's efforts to gain an understanding of the problems that arose in her structure from the awareness of the charism of indefectibility. This was a second phase of consciousness,

[70] Origen, *In Ez.,* hom. 9, 1.

no longer naive, that had to be gone through.[71] Attempts have been made to show that it was connected with the development of modern thought as a whole in its philosophical need to establish "proof".[72] This helps to explain the first point, namely, the fact that the Petrine office has been defined, delimited, precisely in its (constitutive) eccentricity. To put it more clearly: it has been defined, not in the *normal* situation (christianly speaking) of *communio* with the whole Church and her indefectibility, but in that special situation in which contradiction obliges it to act as judge, where it is a question of the pure right to make decisions.

The crisis of which the Council Fathers were all aware[73] made them take the eleventh of the fifteen chapters of the first draft and put it first; because of the war that interrupted the Council, this chapter was the only one considered. In the prologue they briefly indicated the parts they regretfully had to leave undone: "The Church . . . the house of the living God, wherein all the faithful should be united in the bond of one faith and one love"; "the unity and indivisibility of the episcopacy . . . should safeguard the multitude of the faithful in unity of faith and *communio*", and hence, "the permanent principle of unity and its visible foundation", the office of Peter which serves the Church, built on it, to grow and rise to heaven . . . .

[71] "The concept of infallibility belongs to a set of problems which arise in human reflection, in a second, psychological stage where the knowledge of objective reality is paralleled by consideration of the conditions of this understanding. But for the one who has arrived at this stage—and modern man obviously has—it becomes clear that the immediate motivation which directs the mind of the Catholic to accept certain doctrines . . . (is) the fact that revelation has transmitted these doctrines to him through this ecclesiastical Magisterium which is their legitimate interpreter (cf. Newman, *Certain Difficulties,* vol. 2 [1885]: 313)": Jean Stern, "L'Infaillibilité de l'Église dans la pensée de Newman", *Révue des sciences religieuses* 61 (1973): 177.

[72] Karl Lehmann, "Von der Beweislast für 'unfehlbare Sätze' ", in *Zum Problem der Unfehlbarkeit. Antwort auf die Anfrage von Hans Küng,* ed. Karl Rahner, *Quaestiones disputatae* 54 (Freiburg im Breisgau: Herder, 1971), 368.

[73] Clearly stated in the last part of the prologue: Denzinger-Schönmetzer, 3050.

Let us not be concerned about who was responsible for the crisis—whether the exaggerated demands of Rome brought forth resistance, or the challenge made the exercise of Rome's rightful authority necessary; or perhaps it was that the failure to take responsibilities at the periphery contributed to overburdening the "central office".[74] The fact is that, in all its essential premises, the Council always considers "both unities"—that of the faithful People of God as a whole and that of the episcopate as a whole—and accepts their indefectibility (or infallibility) as a matter of course, provided they are both seen in connection with the Roman "head", and do not regard the latter *merely* as an integrating factor that, together with the *collegium* and the *communio,* forms the body of the Church, but see this "head" *within* the *collegium* and the *communio* as the element instituted by Christ to represent and (what is more) to determine unity.[75] In this latter capacity, the "head" must be able to exercise his legal authority

[74] This was the point of view that I emphasized, somewhat one-sidedly, in the short essay "The Pope Today" in *Elucidations* (London: SPCK, 1975), 99ff., and which is considerably supplemented here. On the overburdening of the clergy, see also Karl Delahaye, *Erneuerung,* 192.

[75] Cf. the collection issued, for the jubilee of the Council, of the best and (after Vatican II) most relevant treatises on the subject of the Council: *De Doctrina Concilii Vaticani Primi studia selecta annis* 1948–1964 *scripta, etc.,* selected by R. Aubert, U. Betti, et al. (Rome: Libreria Editrice Vaticana, 1969, abbreviated as DCV). Of primary interest are the following contributions: Walter Kasper, "Primat und Episkopat" (from *Theologische Quartalschrift* [1962], 47f.); J. P. Torrell, "L'Infaillibilité pontificale est-elle un privilège personnel?" (from *Révue des sciences philosophiques et théologiques* [1961], 229f.); G. Dejaifve, "Ex Sese, non autem ex consensu Ecclesiae" (from *Salesianum* [1962], 283ff.); G. Thils, "L'Infaillibilité de l'Église 'in credendo' et 'in docendo'" (from *Salesianum* [1962], 298f.); A. Chavasse, "La Véritable conception de l'infaillibilité papale d'après le Concile du Vatican" (from *Église et unité* [1948], 57ff.).

throughout the whole of the united body[76] without being limited by the rights of his fellow bishops. Canon DS 3064 rules out any curtailments of the *suprema potestas jurisdictionis* and its *tota plenitudo,* making all conciliar and Gallican theses past history, once and for all, in the Church. Such ideas of a merely collegial infallibility had been proposed, initially with effect, at the Council not only by the French (Maret) but also by such serious theologians as Hefele, Ketteler and Strossmayer, who argued on the basis of Church history (the *communio* of the constituent churches was always the foundation of orthodoxy in faith), from the factor of consultation, implied in the principle of *communio,* and from considerations of ecumenism. But these reasons, reflecting the ideal of the Church, had to give way before the reality of the Church militant—a Church that was involved in battles even within herself—where there was the most persistent need to establish the final legal court of appeal, beyond which no further appeal could be made. Who, asks Gasser, passes the definitive judgments (*dando definitivam sententiam*)? Or, to put it more simply, who defines (*definit, seu . . . definitiva ac terminativa sententia proponit*)?[77] Here "irreformable" means the same as "unappealable".

The emergence of the purely legal point of view in distinguishing the "duties" and "rights" of the pope becomes nearly too articulate in the answer to Bishop Freppel of Angers, who wanted to reconcile the contending parties; questioning the bishops and the people before issuing a definition, calling upon the Holy Spirit, and so forth, belong to the pope's "moral obligations", whereas the issue being raised, it was said, was purely one of rights.[78] This distinction within the *con-*

[76] In the postscript to chapter 11 (about papal infallibility) presented to the Fathers on March 6, 1970, is the following: the pope cannot fail because of divine support (under certain conditions): "et hanc Romani Pontificis inerrantiae seu infallibilitatis praerogativam ad idem objectum porrigi, ad quod infallibilitas Ecclesiae extenditur" (Mansi 51, 702a).

[77] Mansi 52, 1227b.

[78] Ibid., 52, 1041ac.

sensus of the whole Church between what is appropriate and what is strictly necessary could not have existed in the early Church's idea of *consensus;* it was made inevitable by the one-sided insistence on rights on the part of the Gallicans.[79] As a result, the Council early (June 18, 1869) called for a qualification: *"antequam ecclesiae consensus vel independenter a consensu ipso".*[80] This wording was included at the end (practically unnoticed) in the definitive text: *"definitiones ex sese, non autem ex consensu Ecclesiae, irreformabiles esse".*[81]

In order to get beyond the question of "rights" and to grasp the nature of the papal act of leadership in its absolutely pure form, two things were necessary.

First, a most precise focusing of the microscope on this single act, excluding everything that was not directly pertinent to it. Obviously, Peter's successor is not "impeccable", sinless; and so to avoid misunderstandings—particularly when it comes to translations into other languages[82]—one should not speak of the "infallibility of the pope" but "of the Magisterium exercised by him". What was more difficult was deciding whether, in the exercise of this office, he could be designated "personally" infallible. On the one hand this seemed desirable to put a stop to the Gallican equivocation that distinguished between the (abstract) "see" (*sedes apostolica*) and the one who occupies it (*sedens*), which was an "awkward, indeed, an absurd distinction".[83] Obviously, infallibility pertains to the concrete person. On the other hand, the charism is not given to the pope as a private person because as such he is by no means infallible. Ever since the Middle Ages the possibility has been envisioned that a pope could become a heretic.[84]

[79] G. Dejaifve, DCV, 518.

[80] Mansi 49, 712a.

[81] Denzinger-Schönmetzer, 3074.

[82] Mansi 52, 1218d–1219a.

[83] A. Chavasse, DCV, 561.

[84] Yves Congar, *Ministères et communion ecclésiale* (Paris: Cerf, 1971), 79f. Text 80, footnote 84.

Yet it would be too little (and again abstract) to grant infallibility, not to the person, but to the "function";[85] rather it is a question of the public person who expressly represents the whole Church.[86] But even to him (who is always the "highest judge in matters of faith and morals"), infallibility is not granted as an inherent characteristic. It is strictly limited to the act by which, with the help of the Holy Spirit, he explicitly exercises the office of judge in matters concerning the whole Church.[87] Hence there is no question of a permanent attribute attaching to the person; this places the pope's infallibility in distinct contrast to the "indefectibility" promised to the Church as a whole, equally with the support of the Spirit. Finally it has to be emphasized that this personal infallibility also has a relational quality, insofar as it is the "public person" of the pope—and the same applies, analogously, in the case of the bishops—who performs the act of decision *"in relatione ad Ecclesiam universalem"*.

These qualifications were made with minutely detailed care and conscientiousness, but the same could not be said of those *silences* concerning the conditions required of the *communio*. The reason given for this was that it was necessary in order to establish the purely legal point. Assurances were given again and again that these conditions would definitely not be omitted or forgotten; they only had to be temporarily deferred for the sake of precision. In answer to the exaggerated papalists, like Manning (who spoke of a papal infallibility "apart from the bishops"), it was emphasized:

> We did not separate (*non separamus*) the pope from the right and proper relationships within the Church. The pope is only then infallible when he exercises the office of teacher of all Christians, and when representing herewith the whole Church in judging and defining what should

[85] Cf. J. P. Torrell, DCV, 501–2.

[86] "Si igitur *personalis* accipitur in sensu privatae personae, unde odiosa illa vox *personalitas*, et tunc est rejicienda; sed si accipitur pro persona ipsam ecclesiam gestante, tunc est personalis." D'Avanzo (Mansi 52, 762d).

[87] Gasser, ibid., 52, 1213a.

be believed or repudiated by all. It is as impossible to separate him from the whole Church as it would be to separate a building from its supporting foundation. Furthermore, we do not separate (*non separamus*) the infallibly defining pope from the collaboration and assistance of the Church, at least in the sense that we . . . do not exclude it.[88]

"We do not exclude (*non excludimus*) collaboration, because infallibility is not an inspiration or revelation but is granted the pope as a divine support. Therefore the pope has to employ (*tenetur*)—considering his office and the importance of the matter—all appropriate means to ascertain the truth and express it suitably."[89] His having to avail himself of collegial and communial inquiry involving the whole Church highlights the latter's prior indefectibility. The ninth chapter of the first schema on the Church was dedicated entirely to this. "When we say that the Church cannot err, we mean that this applies to the whole body of the faithful as well as the college of bishops. The statement 'the Church cannot err' thus means: what all the faithful regard as belonging to the faith is necessarily true and *de fide;* similarly, what all the bishops jointly proclaim as belonging to the faith is necessarily true and *de fide.*"[90] "The center of unity", the papacy, must necessarily refer to this unity in faith—of the whole Church and the whole episcopate—because, with all its privileges, its role is nothing else than that of guaranteeing unity in faith and love.[91] The circular letter issued by the German bishops in 1875, and approved by Pius IX,[92] amply stresses this aspect and concludes by explicitly highlighting the pope's obligation to Scripture and tradition (which the Council had itself emphasized);[93] it is they which he interprets, after having taken

[88] Ibid., 1213bc.
[89] Ibid., 1213d.
[90] Ibid., 51, 579c.
[91] Denzinger-Schönmetzer, 3050–3051.
[92] Denzinger-Schönmetzer 3112–3116.
[93] Denzinger-Schönmetzer, 3069.

the necessary steps to arrive at an interpretation—an ecumenical council or an enquiry of the whole Church or special synods, etc.

But even when the balance has been restored and an integration seems to have been achieved, it remains true that Vatican I shows the office of unity primarily in its eccentric nature, as witness the abstract deduction of law from the *communio.* The office is revealed in its dynamic function of leading what is *not united* in the Church, by the accredited representation of unity (which resides less in the office itself than in the Church of the saints, the Bride without wrinkle or blemish) to the pastures of true unity. And yet the latter unity has already been given to the faithful as a "pledge": inwardly and outwardly in the unity of grace, faith, hope, love, the sacraments, Church office, the path to the one God, "who is above all and through all and in all" (Eph 4:4–6).

Vatican II endeavors to express more articulately and more fully the achievements of Vatican I, such as the unique correlation of Church unity in *communio,* collegiality and primacy. Yet, in the epilogue of the *nota praevia* (for which the Theological Commission is solely responsible) attached to the chapter on bishops in *Lumen gentium,* it could not avoid the danger of once more upsetting the balance of "truth and love, of *logos* and *ethos*".[94] While it is necessary to justify the

[94] Joseph Ratzinger, "Die bischöfliche Kollegialität nach der Lehre des zweiten vatikanisches Konzils", in *Das neue Volk Gottes* (Düsseldorf: Patmos, 1969), 198: "A certain climate of suspicion and anxiety . . . is distinctly reflected in the painstaking and detailed explanations of the text" in the third and fourth points. The statement that the pope "as highest shepherd of the Church may exercise his full authority at any time according to his discretion (*ad placitum*)" and may follow "his own judgment" (*secundum propriam discretionem*) "has not been stated up to now in this form by any document of the Church" (196). Furthermore it is pointed out that the college of bishops can act only at certain times "in strict collegial action, and then not without the consent of the head". Ratzinger says (ibid.) that within the universal collegiality of the Church, such a distinction between what is strictly collegial and what is not can only lead "into a blind alley". "It is difficult to find positive meaning in the *plena potestas* of a collegiality that only has such because denying this would lead in the end to an infringement of papal *plena potestas.*"

eccentricity of the Petrine office, it can only be done without danger if this office manifests its function (of effectively embodying unity) in practice at the heart of the *communio* and the *collegium,* making for liberation through integration. This now has a good chance to succeed, as the last two Councils have directed the whole *communio* of the Church, as well as the entire college of bishops, to allow the Petrine office space in which to exercise its function. If both things take place in the spirit of mutual eucharistic *communio,* the pilgrim Church will be able to be an anticipatory reflection of the perfect Church, without overplaying her role (i.e., in eschatological-pneumatic exaggeration) as pilgrim and penitent. Let us say it once again: the authoritative form of office that Christ established in the pilgrim Church is not an obstacle to her but the indispensable prerequisite if she is to be *communio* in the Spirit of Christ here on earth. What took place in the two Vatican Councils is nothing less than the liberation of the *Catholica,* enabling her to fulfill her unique potential of living under the headship of Christ in his Spirit.

It seems to me that, once the intention of the Councils is understood and unconditionally affirmed, it can be freely discussed whether the meaning was best communicated by the term "infallible". The confusing associations of the word were not unjustly noted,[95] taking into account the sensibilities of modern people, who, whether Christians or not, are not versed in the more subtle distinctions of theology. Just as the terminology of the Council of Ephesus underwent a decisive revision at Chalcedon, in order to express the *same* thing with *even less misunderstanding,* it is not inconceivable that what the

---

[95] Hans Küng, *Unfehlbar? Eine Anfrage* [Infallible? An inquiry] (Zurich, Einsiedeln and Cologne: Benziger, 1970), 148; H. Fries, "Das missverständliche Wort", in *Quaestiones disputatae* 54 (1971): 216–32. There are analogies to the "ex sese" that (as the article by Dejaifve shows) may be completely defensible, yet they could lead to misunderstanding: H. Fries, "Ex sese, non ex consensu Ecclesiae", in *Volk Gottes. Zum Kirchenverständnis der katholischen, evangelischen, und anglikanischen Theologie,* ed. R. Bäumer and H. Dolch (Freiburg im Breisgau: n.p., 1967), 480–500.

last two Councils expressed in distinctive terminology might at some time be formulated with other, more easily understood words. Heinrich Fries' suggestion of *Verbindlichkeit* (binding power), which, "at the highest level can become an *ultimate binding power*" (*Letztverbindlichkeit*), seems to me certainly worth considering.

c. Uniting and Vanishing

Before we turn to the practical questions connected with Peter's duty, as a sinner, to represent the Church of the saints by his unifying office, we should at least take a brief look at another of the Twelve, whose express task is to link the two *Realsymbols* of the one Church of Christ. From the end of the second century, the tradition of the Church has held that the "disciple whom Jesus loved", mentioned in the fourth Gospel, is the author of that Gospel and identical with the John "Son of Thunder" found in the Synoptics.[96] He who, with his brother, was assertive and tempestuous, wanting to call fire from heaven on the Samaritans and aspiring to sit on the right and left of the Lord in the kingdom of God, has now retired into complete anonymity. The "thunder" transferred itself to the majesty of the Master's voice, to his incisive and resounding pronouncements in disputation, but also to the utterly unsentimental sublimity of his words of love; and the voice of the Father, as it speaks to him, seems like thunder to the uncomprehending crowd. Thus he gave back to the Lord the name he had given him, and he gave his own name (as we have already seen) to Simon Peter, with whom he appears in close relationship in the Acts of the Apostles and whom he calls "Son of John". Not only does he give Peter his name; he also gives him his prerogative of the "greater love". So he allows what is personal to him

[96] Selections about the question of authorship in the careful introduction of Rudolf Schnackenburg, *Das Johannesevangelium* [The Gospel according to St. John], pt. 1 (Freiburg im Breisgau: Herder, 1965), 60–68 (review of the entire literature).

to be taken up into the Church, which is why one cannot ask why Jesus, who loves John more, wants to be loved more by Peter.[97] The fact that, deprived of his prerogative in favor of Peter, John nevertheless "remains" (and as such becomes a vexing puzzle for Peter) is not due to himself but to the Lord's good pleasure. He "remains" and becomes anonymous and is even pushed into a corner by an ambitious Church leader, but he is not inactive; he will confront "Diotrephes, who likes to put himself first" and who drove the brethren "out of the Church" (3 Jn 9–10).

From the first chapter of the Gospel to the twentieth, and thence to the postscript of chapter 21, one can follow the unbroken symbolism which links the Beloved Disciple with Peter, the man in office. John's presentation does not reflect merely sympathy and respect but deep down also something like maternal care not only toward the person (Peter had been dead for some time) but also toward the principle he represents. He outlines and brings into relief Peter's office but also accompanies him in a human and loving way. Far from treating the limitations of Peter's office ("What is that to you?", Jn 21:21–23) with irony, he affirms it and elevates it ("Follow me . . . ", Jn 21:19–22). In his Gospel of love, John is a paradigm of "being in touch with the (Petrine) Church". From the isolated sentences in which Peter appears alone (1:41–42; 6:67–71; 13:36–38; 18:10–27) or with John (1:37–39?; 13:22–30; 20:1–10; 21:1–23), one could easily compose a whole series of "rules for cultivating an ecclesial attitude".

Still, it is the Beloved Disciple to whom Jesus on the Cross entrusted his Mother and who henceforward lived with her as a son. He understood Mary's role in the work of salvation at the foot of the Cross and in retrospect also at Cana. To him was given the guardianship of everything Mary meant to Jesus; he was not a private person but a privileged witness of the decisive event of God's love that none of the others among the Twelve had seen: "He who saw it has borne

[97] Augustine, *In Jn,* tract 124, 6.

witness—his testimony is true, and he knows that he tells the truth—that you also may believe" (19:35). Hence Heinz Schürmann's interpretation: "The Mother of Jesus stands here"—not alone but in a group of women—"representing in a particular way the community of those who are destined to receive Christ's salvation. But the unity of the Church is guaranteed by the word of Jesus that is given in canonical form in John's Gospel. From the Cross, the One 'lifted up' established the unity of the Church by referring all who seek salvation to the Word."[98] We would simply add that this is the Word of the Father's and his Son's love for the world, authentically witnessed by the one who was privileged to be the Beloved Disciple.

In none of the Gospels do the Marian and Petrine spheres touch directly (although Mary and Peter were certainly together in Cana and again in the community waiting for the Spirit). But John is intimately linked with both of them and understands this bond as something laid upon him. It is important to recognize that neither Mary nor Peter is the sole representative and *Realsymbol* of Church unity. It is John who actually has the mediating role that prevents the Church from falling into two separate parts (as Tertullian saw her fall apart before his eyes). Now John understands that his "ministry of the center", of mediatorship, means that he must retire into the background. He "remains", but in the background; he is given no privilege of immortality (21:23). The range of his unifying action is eminently "catholic", because he brings together both ends, one of which is frequently dropped, often in his name. He is the one who can point out the exact locus of the Petrine office *within* the whole edifice founded by Christ, without the slightest anti-Petrine feeling (there is no "opposing him to his face" here in the name of Church unity, as in the Letter to the Galatians). And since he, the vanishing one, is

[98] "Jesu letzte Weisung", *Sapienter Ordinare: Festgabe für Erich Kleineidam* (Leipzig: *Erfurter Theologische Studien,* 1969): 120.

expressly commanded by Jesus to "stay", his place as a *Realsymbol* cannot be left vacant and without succession. This place is filled primarily by the saints who have, as it were, an unofficial ecclesial mission and whose authenticity can be recognized by the fact that they always represent the link between the Marian and the Petrine in the Church, supporting both even when this seems to lead nowhere. The truly Johannine Church is not a "third", spiritual Church, supplanting the Petrine and the Pauline, but the one that stands under the Cross in place of Peter and on his behalf receives the Marian Church.[99]

---

[99] One might mention at this point the vision of Gregory Thaumaturgus, described in the biography of Gregory of Nyssa (Migne, PG 46:909c–913a): An old man appeared to him, with an extended hand bringing to his attention another figure, a woman of unearthly beauty. From the way they spoke to each other, Gregory gathered that they represented John the Evangelist and the Mother of the Lord. She asked the disciple to explain "the mystery of piety" (1 Tim 4:6). John gladly responded to the Mother's request and introduced Gregory in clear language into the mystery of the Trinity, in words that Gregory wrote down and according to which he later preached. John appeared here as a *theologos katexochen* — significantly — at the bidding of Mary.

The Historical Peter in His Successors

In order to proceed to a practical discussion of Peter's office in the Church, we must summarize the preceding chapters from a specific point of view. Before speaking of "Christ in his constellation", we stated that he is the only one who reveals the triune God. Hence, what this "constellation" indicates is that Christ chooses to accomplish his work of revelation and reconciliation together with those whom the Father has sent him or whom he himself has called, despite the essential distance between him and them—for he has to shape them so that they can comprehend the meaning of his mission. As revealed in the High Priestly Prayer, the order is: first Christ himself, then those whom he calls and finally those who are reached and incorporated. If these are the people with whom Christ assembled and established a Church, then this whole Church, as *communio,* participates in the essential nature of his mission, namely, mediation, being a link in communication with the triune God. The *communio* of the Church cannot be a self-contained, self-fulfilling entity that experiences the "presence of the Divine in the world" in a complacent enjoyment of love, nor can it interpret ecclesial office as a mere structural principle of a self-sufficient "organism" (as Romantic theology tried to do).

Like Christ, the "Lord and Master", who took on the form of the "Suffering Servant", all members of the constellation (all of whom were made "structural principles" of the Church) must participate according to the call they have received in his service, which leads "away from self to God". The Baptist is not the Christ (cf. Jn

226

1:20–21) but *only* a voice proclaiming the way; he "must decrease" (Jn 3:30) as the Word reveals himself. Mary is *only* the "handmaid of the Lord" who surrenders her whole self: "Let it be according to your word." John is *only* the anonymous disciple whom Jesus loves, who, effacing himself, connects the two great symbolic realities of Church unity. Paul is *"nothing"* (2 Cor 12:11), "what we preach is not ourselves" (2 Cor 4:5), he is *only* sent as an ambassador "in the ministry of reconciliation" (2 Cor 5:18, 20). And Peter, time after time humbled and corrected, is *only* an administrator admonished to pasture, not his own flock, but Christ's flock, according to Christ's intention. Through these mediating figures the form of Christ (cf. Gal 4:19) is impressed on the whole People of God.

But this manifest withdrawal is not a leave-taking: it is a mission. Inherent in it is the burden of authority through which the Divine Sovereignty wishes to be directly represented. When Jesus sent the newly called Twelve, who "are to be with him", on their first mission to proclaim the "Good News" (and hence to be guardians of the purity of the teaching), he almost immediately gave them the "authority to *cast out demons*" (Mk 3:14–15). These demons are spirits perpetually opposed to Jesus' intentions: they "know" (Mk 1:24–26) rather than have faith, they "scatter" rather than "gather" with Jesus (Mt 12:30); they respect men rather than God (Mt 16:23), they ravage the flock of Christ, "speaking perverse things, to draw away the disciples after them" (Acts 20:30). It is against these demons that Jesus gave "full authority", *exousia,* to his disciples. As Paul powerfully describes: "For the weapons of our warfare . . . have divine power to destroy strongholds. We destroy arguments and every proud obstacle to the knowledge of God and take every thought captive to obey Christ" (2 Cor 10:4–5). Yet Paul speaks specifically of this antidemonic authority— given for counteracting, in the service of Christ, the autonomous positions of rebellious and insubordinate reason—that it is from the Lord only "for building up and not for tearing down" (cf. 2 Cor 10:8;

13:10). And as truly Christian authority, it does not fight with the same worldly weapons as demons do: "For though we live in the world we are not carrying on a worldly war, for the weapons of our warfare are not worldly but [according to God's plan of redemption] have divine power" (2 Cor 10:3–4). Paul spoke these strong words against the *pneumatic* Corinthians to whom he also said that *gnosis* puffs up, "while love", the Christ-like love (1 Cor 13), alone "builds up" (1 Cor 8:1). "Rationalism" and "pneumaticism" of any kind imagine that they are self-sufficient and that they have an exclusive hold on resurrection in the *parousia.* But "what have you that you did not receive? If then you received it, why do you boast as if it were not a gift? Already you are filled!" (1 Cor 4:7–8). It is for rooting out such proud defenses against Christ's poverty and humiliation that apostolic authority has been given in a central form.

What Paul is analyzing here is the office given collegially to the Twelve and their successors, and more "personally" (in the way we have described) to Peter in their midst. This is not what unifies, because unity is in Christ alone and through him in the triune God; however, it is an indispensable, visible service, mediating unity.

Exactly because it is limited to a pure act of service (arriving at judgments and giving verdicts), the authority of office that has been granted to the Church stands in stark contrast to the spiritual bulwarks that rely on their own light of rational "evidence" or pneumatic "experience". Consciously or not, these cannot surrender their own natural point of view and become "captive to obey Christ", accepting Christ's supernatural viewpoint and thus becoming aware that experience and obedience are inseparable. In contrast to the "bright" light of rational evidence and pneumatic experience, the "limited" Petrine authority is like a stroke of lightning by which the divine and sovereign "totality" strikes the individual components and finite limits of the human mind, melting down the hardened parts and fusing them into a transcendent whole.[1]

1. *The Office of Peter in Tension*

a. One for All

Thus we have once more situated the office of Peter and the function of his successors within the total context. But it must never be forgotten that nothing can be *deduced:* everything rests on the paradoxes of the historical gospel, namely, that a man is addressed as "Rock", that the "keys of the kingdom of heaven" are handed to him and that he is charged with pasturing Christ's flock and strengthening his brothers. It is said to him, along with the other apostles: "He who hears you hears me" (Lk 10:16). The understanding of these words and of their consequences is also historical; it unfolds its content gradually and to the extent that is necessary. The form emerges slowly, in balance with actual conditions in the Church. This balance can only come about where the Church understands herself as a *mysterium* that has its center in Christ and the triune God.

As a result, the balance between the aspects of the Petrine office itself also has the quality of *mysterium,* and it can be neither reached nor understood by others apart from a living faith. As far as the particular *person* of Peter's successor is concerned, the equilibrium of

[1] It is obvious that we do not intend to give a thorough description of the papal leadership, which, through the centuries, has shown itself to have enjoyed positive, enduring support from God. We are concerned only with its sharp cutting edge that was specifically isolated by Vatican I as formal authority.

his personal office and the offices of his colleagues (and the same applies to the relationship between bishops and priests and all who share in any way in the diversified ecclesial office) can only be discovered in faith and love. Insofar as Peter's successor represents unity officially, he creates space for the others, enabling them to share in unity in their own way. Thus he possesses to the highest degree what today is called the *apostolat de présence*. As pope (not as Bishop of Rome) he does not need continually to remind others that he is there, by issuing encyclicals, etc.: his very existence provides a focus for orientation, reminding everyone that they are all members of a higher totality (to which the pope equally belongs). Thus they are rescued from the sense of isolation and the culs-de-sac of "pluralism". It is not a case of seeing one's own point of view relativized and being resigned to the fact that there are others in humanity and in Christendom who have opposing views; rather, one can be joyfully aware that, with one's own views, to the extent that they contain truth partially, one is making a contribution to the living organism of unity. In the former case, we have contradiction; in the latter, as Möhler taught,[2] simply (fruit-ful) antithesis. However, this enabling function that creates unity presupposes the aspect of authority, i.e., the unique aspect that does not merely advance one particular opinion in opposition to

[2] Johann Adam Möhler, *Die Einheit in der Kirche,* critical ed. by J. R. Geiselmann (Cologne: Hegner, 1957), sec. 46.

others.[3] We shall see what weighty consequences follow from this with regard to the relationship between the teaching office and theology.

An example of this "enabling function" would be a synod of bishops in which the Holy Father participates but does not enter into the discussion by expressing a particular view. Such silent participation and taking cognizance must not be interpreted as arrogance but as facilitating free expression in the presence of visibly personified unity. In human terms, the way particular popes exercise this office of facilitating unity may vary greatly. But it is less important whether the person of the pope presents an official face or projects an image of Christian kindliness or of personal humility: for here too there is a fruitful plurality in the various ways of responding to the same mission.

---

[3] Erich Przywara stressed this most strongly—though relying somewhat one-sidedly on Vatican I—in "Reichweite der Analogie" (first published in 1940) in *Analogia Entis, Schriften,* vol. 3, 2d ed. (Einsiedeln: Johannesverlag, 1962), esp. 274–84. Cf. also Przywara's articles collected by Bernhard Gertz, *Katholische Krise* (Düsseldorf: Patmos, 1967). Here, as early as 1925, "the fatal direction toward self-destruction and self-laceration" of the Church was identified, "and the end seems to be chaos" (20). In 1929 he advances the saving principle against the attempt "to found the Church from below", namely, an "objective prolongation of the life of Christ, independent of either the soul or the community, a prolongation that is thereby juridical in character" (56), and "an emphasis on the Church's unconditional primacy" (68) in terms of the *"successio apostolica":* "The so-called 'juridical formalism' of the Church is ... actually her spiritual aspect and therefore her inmost form, as the soul is the form of the human body. As the Church is the organism of the Mystical Body of Christ, the power of this organism (as that of the organism of an individual) is tied to the power of organization, the conscious and freely willed cooperation of superior and subject for the benefit of the one body" (78).

b. Mysterium and Definition

With regard to the mission itself, its content, too, is situated in that tension which is created by the pope's position in the Church. He is the final point of reference when it comes to that unity in the content of faith that is necessary for the Church's unity (*"one* Lord, *one* faith": Eph 4:5). The unity of faith's content can only be grasped at a transitional median point, namely, where, proceeding from the brilliance of historical revelation that is witnessed in Holy Scripture, it is articulated in intelligible words, neither lost in the obscurity of the deep *mysterium* in which it is rooted and which it expresses nor disintegrating into the multiplicity of personal views of individual believers. There is such a median point: biblical revelation, of itself, does not splinter necessarily into pluralism. Rather, God's word, which, as Heinrich Schlier says, has "event-quality",[4] is articulated as intelligible speech, all its manifold aspects constituting an integral whole. This is something we presuppose here, yet in no way can it be put forward completely independently of the unity of the *Magisterium*. For the formulation of the Canon and the substantial unity of all early Christian creeds testify to the objectivity of the early Church's understanding of the Christian faith and to the agreement of the constituent churches with regard to this unity of faith. But just as ancient as the awareness of the intelligibility of the unadulterated tradition and interpretation found in the Creed (on the basis of Scripture and its intact transmission, guaranteed by apostolic succession) is the conviction that every "article of faith" is rooted in the divine *mysterium*. This does not cease being mysterious, even when revealed. Fundamentally, the understanding which comes by faith embraces more truth than it can understand—for in faith, after all, it is God who is embraced.

[4] Heinrich Schlier, *Besinnung auf das Neue Testament* [Relevance of the New Testament] (Freiburg im Breisgau: Herder, 1964), 15, 42ff.

Mary's faith could accept the unfathomable, not because she did not try to comprehend (Lk 1:29, 34; 2:19, 51), but because, for her faith, darkness was more essential than clarity. The mission of Peter, as of all who proclaim the gospel (cf. Paul, 2 Cor 12:1–4; Eph 3:4), is different: he must understand, and will, as far as he is able. What Peter does not understand at first will become clear to him later (Jn 13:7; cf. 13:13, 37). After the Resurrection, Jesus introduces him and the other ten to the meaning of all revelation, the law, the prophets and the Psalms (Lk 24:44). Thus the basic understanding of the proportions of the divine plan of salvation is impressed once for all on the mind of the Church. One is inclined to compare this infused knowledge given to the Church (and especially to the teaching Church) to the vision of St. Benedict when "the whole world was presented to his eyes as if united in a single ray of sunlight",[5] or to the insight given St. Ignatius beside the River Cardoner: he could not put into words what he had grasped, but his spirit was filled with such clarity that it seemed to him that, if he were to bring together all the grace he had received through his life and all that he knew, it would not equal what he was given on that one occasion.[6]

The infused understanding that the teaching Church has received is not theology in the technical sense, even when good theologians are made bishops and popes. Obviously they need the reflex understanding of theological knowledge if they are to interpret, defend and proclaim specific articles of faith. "Instruction in the word" has not ceased with the conclusion of Holy Scripture: it remains a task and a charism of the Church for all time.

[5] Gregory the Great, *Dialogues,* 2, 33. Gregory adds: "But when it is said that the world was made comprehensible to him, that does not mean that heaven and earth were diminished but rather that the soul of the seeker was expanded by God so that, enraptured, he could perceive all that is lower than God."

[6] Ignatius of Loyola, *Lebenserinnerung* [St. Ignatius' own story], ed. Feder (Freiburg im Breisgau: Herder, 1922), no. 30, p. 48.

Still, systematization of the doctrines of the faith, for which theologians strive, is different from defining a particular point of doctrine, which in certain situations is the duty of the Church's Magisterium, be it for the defense of orthodoxy or to clarify an essential aspect of faith of special concern to the whole body of the Church. A given statement by a single theologian has a relative value within his particular understanding of the faith (which might be shared by several theologians or by the general theological opinion of the era); but even in the case of the most brilliant, this understanding will be subjective and limited. One could say that the individual theologian's primary concern is "propositional coherence" defined by the context of his understanding. In contrast, the Magisterium has no "system" but a somehow habitual knowledge of the overall proportions of revealed, divine truth. When it makes a pronouncement, it is sufficient for it to find the "most appropriate" form of words, in the particular historical situation, to express the abiding *mysterium*.[7] It is not a question of "propositional truth", if there can be such a thing isolated from the intention of the one who is speaking; rather, an expression must be found which is transparent enough to open up the new horizon in revelation, manifested to the Magisterium in the moment of a definitive decision, transparent enough to allow what is indicated by the words to show through within this horizon. Qualitatively this goes beyond the limits of any theological system, which is always colored by a particular perspective, a particular "formal object", a particular cast of thought, and where inner coherence and evidence must be the criteria for the correctness of its individual propositions. But these very perspectives and modes of thought are necessarily subject to the judgment of the Church's Magisterium when it is a question of

[7] " . . . quam quidem conversionem catholica Ecclesia aptissime transsubstantionem appellat." Denzinger-Schönmetzer, *Enchiridion Symbolorum,* 1652; cf. 1642: "convenienter et proprie".

whether and how far they can (objectively) open up to the "complete vision" of revelation and (subjectively) are ready to do so. Clearly, this judgment can and must extend to individual statements within these theological systems if there is a question of their consistency with the "complete vision" of the Church (which is never systematic).

Ordinarily, the Church cannot demand that a personal or scholastic system should open its own horizons toward those of the Church, as an act of blind obedience. There must be a conversation in which the theologian explains his views and the Church's representatives (who do not possess infused, total theological knowledge) are obliged to take careful note of these explanations. Frequently the view of a theologian enriches the empirical grasp that the Magisterium—and in general any teacher in the Church—has of a particular aspect of revelation. There should be a lively exchange in the Church between theology and the Magisterium, yet not as between two opposing *cathedrae* with different, divinely given missions. Rather, with Newman, it would be right to say that "Theology is the fundamental and regulating principle of the whole Church system. It is commensurate with revelation"[8] and is authorized to determine what is genuinely infallible in Church definitions.[9] Yet he does not locate the competence of theologians on the side of

[8] John Henry Cardinal Newman, *The Via Media of the Anglican Church,* vol. 1 (London: Longmans Green and Company, 1918): xlvii.

[9] John Henry Cardinal Newman, "A Letter Addressed to His Grace the Duke of Norfolk", in *Certain Difficulties Felt by Anglicans in Catholic Teaching,* vol. 1 (London and New York: Longmans Green and Co., 1891), 321.

the teaching Church but in the "sense of faith" (infallible in its totality) of the faithful.[10]

Because the two partners speak on different ecclesial levels, the Magisterium's *final* decision is not open to appeal and cannot be changed. Nevertheless, as all human words, even the clearest, need an interpretation, and as any true statement can be seen in a new light in a new and wider context, the work of the theologian is by no means ended by a definition. While no solemn definition is ever invalidated — as, by analogy, no word of Scripture can be erased — its range of applicability can be examined at any time. In doing this, theology

[10] Letter to Miss Froude, July 28, 1875, in Wilfrid Ward, *The Life of John Henry Cardinal Newman,* vol. 2 (New York: Longmans Green and Co., 1912): 564. Here Newman somewhat misleadingly called the sensus fidelium "passively" inerrant: "Here on the one hand I observe that a local sense of a doctrine, held in this or that country, is not a *sensus universitatis,* and on the other hand the Schola Theologorum is one chief portion of that *universitas* — and it acts with great force both in correcting popular misapprehensions and narrow views of the teaching of the active *infallibilitas,* and, by the intellectual investigations and disputes which are its very life, it keeps the distinction clear between theological truth and theological opinion and is the antagonist of dogmatism. And while the differences of the School maintain the liberty of thought, the unanimity of its members is the safeguard of the infallible decisions of the Church and the champion of faith." We find the division of the Church into a "teaching" and a "listening" part outdated and prefer a much more nuanced scale of ministries (*ministeria*) in the Church, for example, deriving the ministry of the theologian from the ancient triad of "first apostles, secondly prophets, thirdly teachers" (1 Cor 12:28), or from the later triad (presumably after the death of the "apostles and prophets"), "evangelists, pastors, teachers" (Eph 4:11). But aside from the fact that such direct transference of biblical offices to postbiblical times is questionable — notwithstanding the high respect for theologians through-out the centuries — it has no demonstrable theological tradition. What is more important is fully to understand Newman's concept of the so-called "listening" Church. For him, this concept is in no way passive but means the sphere of common faith that also embraces the teaching office itself. According to Newman, the fact that the theologians arise from this sphere means that they are able to correct an occasional deviation on the part of the teaching office. Cf. Louis Bouyer, *L'Église de Dieu* (Paris: Cerf, 1970), 150.

encounters two things: the historically determined limits of the definition and, within it, an ultimate directive transcending these limits, intended as at least an ultimate signpost. Of course, a signpost is not the same as traveling the whole road to the very end; but it shows the right direction for the pilgrim Church: "This is the way; if you go left or right at this point, you will be going astray." But such an orientation is given *within* the life of faith, which only sees *per speculum in aenigmate* and where knowledge is "partial" (1 Cor 13:12). Theologians as well as the Magisterium would do well to take this to heart.

Shortly before Vatican I a critique of Frohschammer was put in these terms: "Reason based on its own natural principles is not able to deal with such (supernatural) truths (dogmas)" because "mysteries revealed for us in Christ transcend not only human philosophy but also the natural reasoning of angels. Even when accepted in faith they still remain (for the time being) hidden in impermeable darkness by faith itself as by a holy veil during our pilgrimage in this mortal life far from the Lord."[11] It is precisely Vatican I, which people like to accuse of theological rationalism, that admitted in its first statement the "unfathomable nature" of God (DS 3001). By distinguishing between the orders of faith and reason, it emphasized that it is to faith that "the mysteries hidden in God are revealed to be believed". The meaning of these, according to the words of Jesus, are hidden from the wise and clever and revealed to the simple (DS 3015). And although "reason enlightened by faith, when it seeks piously and soberly, by God's gift, can reach a certain understanding of the mysteries . . . yet it will never be able to penetrate them as it can the truths that are in its own domain. Because the divine mysteries, by their very nature, transcend the created mind, so, despite revelation and the pious acceptance of it, they still remain enveloped by faith in darkness as by a cover during our pilgrimage in mortal life far from the Lord. For we walk by

---

[11] Denzinger-Schönmetzer, 2856–57; cf. also the succeeding numbers as well as the relevant parts of the *Syllabus.*

faith and not by sight" (DS 3016). This defines, beyond all appeal, the fact that dogma *cannot* be defined in the same way as one would a scientific statement. In this sense, too, Vatican I finally closes a door and creates a new situation, as it were, a new atmosphere, for all dialogue between Magisterium and theology. However, the thoroughly apposite reference to the faith of the simple does not dispense the Church's Magisterium from the duty of living in the tension between having to teach and not being able to arrive at ultimate definitions.

c. Consent and Risk

A final tension becomes evident here, inherent in the problem of *consensus,* of the consent not only of theology but of the whole believing Church to the pronouncements of the Magisterium.[12] We have advanced beyond the Gallican interpretation of this consent, condemned by Vatican I, which made it a condition *sine qua non* for acceptance. Thus the door is once more open for a consent which is based not on merely legal considerations but in the concrete Church *communio* (which, of course, integrates legal aspects within itself). Therefore it hardly seems fruitful a priori to proceed from a historico-juridical interpretation of the *reception* concept, because juridically speaking there is only "genuine *reception*" where there are two distinct or separate partners who can thus enter into the relationship of giving

---

[12] Cf. the above-mentioned works of H. Fries as well as Aloys Grillmeier, "Konzil und Rezeption", in *Philosophie und Theologie* 45 (1970): 321–52; Yves Congar, *Ministères et communion ecclesiale* (Paris: Cerf, 1971) and "Reception as an Ecclesial Reality", in *Concilium,* vol. 77, ed. Alberigo Weiler (New York: Herder and Herder, 1972): 43–68.

and receiving.[13] In the Church, where all share the same faith and together constitute the Body of Christ, this is unthinkable. However, if we proceed from the realistic image of the Church as a community of sinners striving toward the good, and accordingly see the Magisterium in its "eccentricity", the tensions and difficulties in the exercise of the Magisterium clearly stand out. On the one hand the Magisterium is a function integral to the *communio;* to that extent, not only is it rooted in Scripture and tradition, it must also consult the Church community with regard to its faith, as Vatican I emphasized (DS 3069) and as Bishop Gasser underlined even more explicitly.[14] On the other hand, it is also the task of the Magisterium, for various reasons, to bring about a clearer recognition of the importance of particular aspects of the doctrine than is generally prevalent. John grants that his community has sufficient knowledge of the faith because of its "anointing" (having received the Holy Spirit in baptism and confirmation): "But you have been anointed by the Holy One, and you all know." (Or, "you know everything".) "I write to you, not because you do not know the truth, but because you know it and know that no lie is of the truth . . . and you have no need that anyone should teach you" (1 Jn 2:20–27). Nevertheless, he *does* write to them. He emphasizes what they know and highlights it, aware that it is not superfluous to do so. Perhaps only by hearing his words will they become aware of what they know or will become fully convinced of things that up to now seemed not quite certain. What has been habitual (and thus partly or totally unconscious) becomes real to them. Uncertainty is replaced by certainty. Thus, despite the funda-

[13] Grillmeier, "Konzil und Rezeption", 331. Grillmeier's legal approach to the theology of reception has the advantage of working with highly differentiated concepts that can also be applied in a differentiated manner to diverse situations in Church history. This makes it obvious that within the Church *communio* one can only speak of "reception" in an oblique sense.

[14] See above, 215ff. [manuscript].

mental identity between the antecedent agreement (in the *sensus fidelium*) and the subsequent agreement (in the *consensus fidelium*), there can be an accidental difference between the two. For an illustration one might turn to the perfect example of Mary's obedience in faith. She was in harmony with God's will even before the angel's appearance (for "the Lord is with you"), yet she can still be frightened by the angel's salutation, must reflect on "what this greeting means" and has to ask "how shall this be?" before giving her final consent.

One could also take an example from the Church of sinners: a person who has made a vow of obedience to his spiritual guide can be so surprised by an unexpected and perhaps very difficult demand that he becomes frightened and cannot see how he could comply with it. We are assuming that this demand is right in the eyes of God, even if its purpose is only to lead the person beyond the limits that he (like everyone else) unconsciously sets to what might be expected of him. This example is not chosen to suggest that the Magisterium's purpose is to train the Christian people to obey blindly but only to indicate that there can be cases where an official decision of the Magisterium may seem to the ordinary believer to be "asking too much". He might react prematurely by objecting that to define faith in this or that degree of detail is "ill-timed" or does not fully correspond to the "sense of faith" of believers and should therefore be contested from the outset or, at best, be turned in the direction of a higher synthesis. Later on we shall discuss the legitimacy of contesting Church decisions; here we are concerned with the empirical gulf which yawns between what is habitual and what is actual in faith: we hold that it is the special duty of the pastoral office, following the Twelve and Peter, to lead the faithful to the highest level of their own faith. And it must be said that there is the element of *risk*, both in existing faith and in being led to a deeper faith. Every believer takes the risk of faith at the word of Christ ("Help my unbelief", Mk 9:24), yet imperceptibly and almost inevitably he grows accustomed to taking the criteria of his own experience as the basis for his faith, and these, for a sinner, are inherently minimalistic. Since the measure of personal risk where faith is concerned varies greatly among individual Christians, the pastoral office is faced with an equally great risk in trying to anticipate what degree of risk Christian people as a whole are willing to take for their faith. Is it realistic (to speak for once, not ecumenically, but just among Catholics) to expect the faithful as a whole to believe in Mary's bodily Assumption into heaven when they are too spiritually slothful to discern the deep relationship between Mary and the Church and hardly perceive the necessity, if all eschatological hopes are to be brought to fruition, of a "marriage of the Lamb" which, at the center, has already been consummated? Their grasp of things remains on the surface, a surface which distorts the underlying reality.

Our primary concern here should not be to criticize or seek to limit the "Roman tendency to dogmatize" or to present a (would-be infallible) exposure of "tendentious explanations". What is needed is a truly pastoral judgment as to that point where, for the average member of the "flock"—and for the growing number who are only "partially identified" with it—the "better" becomes the enemy of the "good". The question is rather whether the continual attempts to explain the *mysterium* of faith, in this pilgrimage on earth, do not in fact threaten to profane it instead of leading to a deeper worship.

Of course there has been (more among theologians and the laity than in the pastoral office) a naive view, carried along on the current of popular evolutionism, that by increasing the number of definitions the "knowledge of faith" is advanced, hence becoming more available to the pilgrim Church. This was one of the numerous chiliastic temptations, and it has only been left behind today because it has been replaced by other and more virulent forms of the same temptation. We know how inextricably and deeply all aspects of the *mysterium* are interwoven, so that even the attempt to formulate one single aspect in isolation endangers perception of the interrelated whole—and no proposition can be formulated without isolating parts. The clarity of detail thus achieved can obscure what is more important: integration into the whole organism. This is evident in the attempts to define, for example, concepts such as *communio sanctorum, réversibilité des mérites,* "coredemption" (of whatever kind) and the term "coredemptrix" as applied to Mary. The problem is not primarily that of isolated statements; it is more intrinsically the problem of illuminating particular aspects of the deepest mystery of a God who remains (forever!) beyond our comprehension and yet approaches us and breaks in upon us in a "for us" that demands an ever-deeper identification with him (cf. the intensification: *per* ipsum → *cum* ipso → *in* ipso). There is a tension here which the Church's Magisterium must keep in mind: on the one hand, the primary articulation of this *mysterium* in the word of Holy Scripture, while there is nothing vague about it, is in many ways a first approach; and as regards the secondary extrapolation of this word in dogmatic statements (whether "defensive" or "explicatory" or both), there is the danger that it will cause people to lose sight of the arcane character of all Christian truth—even, indeed particularly, when it is uttered in the public forum.

2. *The Charism of Leadership*

a. The Beginnings

The tension between office and theology leads directly to one of the central issues: in the "christological constellation" in which the Catholic Church stands, what is the specific, unambiguous status and function of the Petrine office? One look—occasionally a very painful one—at the history of the Church and the papacy proves two points: first, though there were many exemplary popes who were personally holy, yet their distinctive charism is not on the Marian-Johannine model of subjective holiness. But, as if it had to be hammered into our minds, we also see a large number of popes who, from a Christian point of view, are highly questionable and under whose rule the function of the office did indeed shrink to the guaranteed minimum explicitly adumbrated by Vatican I. Secondly, and equally evidently, although a number of outstanding theologians have occupied the See of Peter, the Petrine charism is not found in the field of deep or specialized theology in the Pauline line, not even where definitive instructions are issued by Rome regarding the direction that theology should take. This often happened in the first centuries, for instance in the astonishing letter of Pope Dionysius (ca. 260) to the Church of Alexandria (DS 112ff.), in Leo the Great's letter to Flavian, which played a decisive role in determining the direction of the most important dogmatic council, that of Chalcedon (DS 290ff.), or in the letter of Agatho (in 680) to Constantine IV against the Monothelites (DS 542ff.). These three examples are cited as a series by Harnack,[15] but the list could easily be extended to include the Creed of Damasus I (DS 144ff.) and that of Leo IX in the eleventh century (DS 680ff.). A typical and worthy link in the chain (and the most recent) is the *Credo* of Paul VI.

Harnack says about Pope Dionysius—who had to reprimand the Bishop of Alexandria, a highly intelligent student of Origen—that "the Roman Bishop did not trouble himself with the speculations of the Alexandrians . . . and simply focused on the conclusions" and their consequences. The same may be said of the writings of Leo and Agatho: "Starting with these deductions, they refuted doctrines of the right and of the left and simply proposed a middle line. This they based formally on their ancient creed."[16]

The distinctiveness of the two modes, i.e., Mary/John and Paul, provides us with a clue, the same clear clue we discovered in the *early history of the papacy.* Everything began (before reflex thought was necessary) with a charism of leadership that was lived "instinctively"

---

[15] Adolf von Harnack, *Dogmengeschichte* [History of dogma], vol. 1, 4th ed. (1909): 772.

[16] Ibid., 771–72. Harnack's polemical interpolations are omitted.

from the very center. Very touchingly, the martyr-bishop Ignatius speaks of the Roman community as "presiding in love", which does not refer to the legal presidency of a "loving alliance" of individual churches but to the central reality of that love which creates "Church". "Precedence" here means more than mere "moral excellence in the approach and practice of charity", particularly since, immediately following this, the Roman Church is called *christonomos,* the one "observing the law of Christ".[17] The extraordinary charitable care of the Roman community, not only for the numerous poor of the capital city but even for those in the remotest Asiatic communities, is mentioned often and with high praise as late as the third century.[18] Listening carefully to the tone of Pope Clement's reprimand from Rome to the Corinthians—which was no doubt written during the lifetime of the apostle John (96 A.D.) and is a most important document regarding the early stages of the Roman "claim"—it evidently arises from a concern, in Ignatius' sense, for the integrity of love, which is the essence of the Church. Externally this may appear in the garb of the old Roman concept of "cosmic order", but in fact it expresses the Pauline readiness for loving (Marian!) submission to the *form* of the Church instituted by Christ through the apostles. The reprimand itself, issued from Rome, is understood in the spirit of the apostolic Church as a function of *agape.*[19] Together with the reference to the tradition of office, it is unhesitatingly accepted by this allegedly "purely charismatic" community and even a hundred years later is being read out with reverence at public

[17] Joseph Fischer, *Die apostolischen Väter* (Munich: Kosel-Verlag, 1936), 129f. Eleven words before *prokathēmenē* there is a reference to the "presidency", "pre-eminence" of Christ (*prokathētai*) within the area of the Romans.

[18] Texts in Gustave Bardy, "La Théologie de l'Église de s. Irénée au Concile de Nicée", *Unam Sanctam* 14 (Paris: Cerf, 1947): 225–26.

[19] Heinrich Schlier, "Die Eigenart der christlichen Mahnung nach dem Apostel Paulus", in *Besinnung,* 340–57.

worship[20] and will continue to be circulated to other areas, especially in the East.[21]

Subsequently the Petrine function asserts itself only — but then very definitely — when there is vital need for it: when the "unity in love" is imperiled or when people turn for advice or arbitration to the acknowledged center of unity, the concrete focus: Rome. The See of Peter has become the recourse of those seeking justice, which demonstrates that law expresses love. Irenaeus accepts without question the existence of this focal point, this center, both because it is generally accepted and because it has accredited apostolic origins. The specifically Petrine succession, says Henri de Lubac, "is exercised in the beginning quietly, by simply taking place, without theoretical expositions, claims or an arsenal of proofs — and that is what could rightly be expected. The opposite would be suspect, implying that acceptance of an innovation had to be forced on those who were reluctant. The sober practicality of the beginning simply accords with life. Reflex thought always comes later and gains importance as contradictions arise. Theological justifications do not by themselves change a hitherto unjust fact into a right but only uncover the underlying law inherent in the fact."[22] Perhaps it is providential that the Rome of the second and third centuries had not one significant theologian — with the exception of Hippolytus, who caused a schism — while great theologians arose in Alexandria, Gaul, Carthage, Palestine and the Middle East. We might be inclined to think that Rome, guarding the apostolic tradition in its rather simple way, was always behind the times in its interventions, which were all the more embarrassing, the more they were presented with

---

[20] Eusebius, *Ecclesiastical History* 4:23, 11.

[21] Louis Marie Olivier Duchesne, *Églises séparées* [The churches separated from Rome], 2d ed. (Paris: A. Fontemoing, 1905), 131f.

[22] Henri de Lubac, *Les Églises particulières dans l'Église universelle* (Paris: Aubier, 1971), 194. German translation: *Quellen kirchlicher Einheit* (Einsiedeln, Johannesverlag, 1974). Duchesne, *Églises séparées,* 107.

the weight of authority; but the astonishing thing is that these interventions (which were by no means frequent initially) prove the very opposite: Rome's responses, although they refer back to the faith handed down, regularly point beyond the ecclesial horizon of the "committed" and "speculative" theologians.

This might not always be apparent, as for example in the forceful Pope Victor's (189–198 A.D.) authoritarian ruling regarding the time of Easter—about which even Polycarp and Anicetus had not been able to agree—which was not a question of dogma but a purely disciplinary matter.[23] Nevertheless, Victor was objectively correct. The Council of Nicaea later upheld the excommunication pronounced by Victor (which at the time had been obstructed): the old Quartodeciman tradition, which insisted on the celebration of Easter simultaneously with the Jewish Pasch (14 Nisan) instead of on the subsequent Sunday (the Sunday of the Resurrection), had to be abandoned as a judaizing vestige. To Victor's credit it should be mentioned that, before issuing his edict, he held synods in all regions of the Church, which, with the exception of Asia Minor, "unanimously"[24] approved his decision. A more important example is the bitter dispute between Cyprian (unquestioned leader of the numerous African episcopate) and the Roman Bishop Stephen I (254–257) about the validity of baptism administered by heretics. In an earlier dispute about the reconciliation of *lapsi,* Cyprian showed both pastoral shrewdness and tolerance.[25] Here, however, he insisted on his theo-

---

[23] Thus Irenaeus "respectfully and insistently" brought this to his attention to prevent him from excommunicating the Asiatics, which would have had serious consequences. "The whole Church was at peace, both those who kept the day and those who did not." Eusebius, *Ecclesiastical History,* 5:24.

[24] Ibid., 5, 23

[25] In the earlier conflict under Pope Cornelius about the reconciliation of the great number of apostates as a result of the Decian persecution, Cyprian's adversary was not Pope Cornelius, with whom he objectively agreed, but the antipope Novatian against whose rigorism Cyprian fought.

logically polished idea of a "holy Church", outside of which (i.e., outside her visible limits, defined by the unity of the episcopate) there can be "no salvation"—this is the traditional ideal of the second century. Cyprian feels that he is being progressive, by contrast with the unenlightened traditionalism of Rome.[26] But Pope Stephen's decision shatters Cyprian's closed concept of the Church in favor of an opposing, "eccentric" view: valid baptism can also be administered outside ecclesial unity, even by Marcionites and Montanists,[27] because the scope of ecclesial authority and love does not simply coincide with the action of God. At the time this decision had no theological backing;[28] it pointed to the future. While the great Cyprian's position— "one must possess the Holy Spirit if one is to transmit him"—gave birth to the Donatist sect, Stephen's position was developed theologically by Augustine against the Donatists and has become the foundation of the Church's theology and practice up to the present. Without it, any ecumenical attitude and theology would be impossible.

Stephen, like Victor, spoke with authority: "He does not discuss, he commands."[29] This enraged Cyprian: "Stephen, who claims Peter's seat by succession!"[30] Bishop Dionysius of Alexandria, a friend of the Pope, had to conciliate by pointing out that the Roman usage had been practiced in other places also since ancient times.[31] But then it was Dionysius who provoked the third occasion of Roman intervention,

[26] Cyprian, "For custom without truth is the antiquity of error": Letter 74, 9, in *Fathers of the Church,* vol. 51 (Washington, D.C.: Catholic University of America Press, 1964): 292. "In vain do some who are conquered by reason oppose custom to us as if custom were greater than truth", Letter 73, 13, ibid., 275.

[27] Text in Bardy, *La Théologie de l'Église,* 43, 55.

[28] Stephen appealed rightly and fittingly to another older tradition that supported him, and Alexandria and Palestine sided with him, while the Church of Antioch and its dependencies were in accord with Africa.

[29] Bardy, *La Théologie de l'Église,* 218.

[30] Cyprian, Letter 75, 17.

[31] Eusebius, *Ecclesiastical History,* 7:7, 5.

and this time it was even more fundamental and concerned Christology, which the Bishop of Alexandria, a pupil of the master theologian Origen, had defended, in the spirit and sense of Origen, against the Sabellians (who dissolved the distinction of the three Persons in the divine Oneness). But had not Origen already gone too far in the other direction?[32] His pupil was accused before Pope Dionysius. The Pope does not feel pressured. He sends off two finely tuned letters, a personal one to the Bishop, inviting him to explain his view in more detail, and a peremptory one to the Alexandrian Church, condemning both Sabellianism and, "so to speak, its diametrical opposite", without naming names. He does this in straightforward terms, which are all the more amazing since they clearly rule out, in anticipation, the Arianism that will develop from Origen's subordinationism just as logically as Donatism will spring from Cyprian's view of the Church. To say that there was a time when the Son did not exist, when God was without him, is "totally absurd" (DS 112–115). The Pope does not base his plain exposition on the profundity of a philosophical school but simply on the Bible and tradition, which were not subject to the temptations to which the late Hellenist schools of theology were liable, namely, to bring everything (in one way or another) into a unity without multiplicity. The Pope is in harmony with revelation as well as with the faith of the people; his position is both earlier than, and more advanced than, that theology which is prone to heresy.[33] Moreover, he speaks the language of respect (this is even clearer in the case of Leo I) regarding the *"mysterium";* to him, the kerygma of the triune God is "sublime", worthy of veneration (*semnotaton*); its subject is wonderful (*thaumasten*), involving "the superabundant greatness and majesty of the Son of God" (*to axioma kai to hyperballon megethos*

[32] Cf. his observations recorded in conversation with Heraclides, *Sources chrétiennes* 67 (1960).

[33] J. Lebreton, "Du désaccord de la foi populaire et de la théologie savante dans l'Église chrétienne du IIIe siècle", in *Révue d'histoire ecclésiastique* 20 (1924).

tou kyriou). Bishop Dionysius did not protest; he developed an answer in four books, the orthodoxy of which is confirmed by the extant fragments.

By that time, the Bishop of Rome was wholly accustomed to settling controversies and requested people to have recourse to him. Strangely enough, Cyprian himself, in a case that deserves attention, indicates him as an ultimate instance.[34] The Council of Sardica would solemnly advert to this custom (DS 133–135). Siricius could already say, "We carry all the burdens, or rather, the holy Pope Peter carries them through us" (DS 181). Innocent I asked with surprise, "Do you not know that answers go from the apostolic source to petitioners in all the provinces" (DS 218, cf. 217)? And for Boniface I (422 A.D.), Rome's answers were always definitive: "It was never permitted to question a ruling once delivered by the Apostolic See" (DS 232). Celestine I ratified Nestorius' exclusion from the Church as pronounced by the Council of Ephesus; and Leo I prepared the condemnation of Eutyches in his Letter to Flavian (the *Tome*) as well as approving the relevant teaching of the Council of Chalcedon. Again we notice the antirationalistic language which is profoundly aware of the *mysterium* which is to be guarded; the word "sacrament" is everywhere; writing to the Emperor Leo, he complains that in Alexandria (because of the activities of the presbyter Timotheus Ailuros) "the light of all heavenly mysteries has been extinguished".[35]

---

[34] Pierre Batiffol, *L'Église naissante* [Primitive Catholicism], 2d ed. (Paris: Cerf, 1971), 454ff.

[35] Text in Hugo Rahner, *Kirche und Staat im frühen Christentum* (Munich: Kösel-Verlag, 1961), 245.

b. The Narrows

Once the Roman bishop's charism of leadership in matters of faith was established—setting to one side the few borderline instances where a vacillating individual reigned (Liberius), or one unduly weak in facing lengthy intimidation (Vagilius), or a naive man who was easily deceived (Honorius)—it remained unchallenged. What was harder for the popes was to find their way through the long, drawn-out fascination exercised by the theocratic ideal (both of antiquity and of the Old Testament) on ancient times, the Middle Ages and modern times. This fascination lasted from Constantine, Theodosius, Justinian, Charlemagne and the Ottonians right up to seventeenth-century absolutism.

We cannot write the whole Church history of a millennium here, so we shall simply set down and illustrate three summary observations.

1. No age can go beyond its spiritual horizons. Hence it is senseless and unjust negatively to criticize an age for trying to present God's reign in the world of its time through the unity or the convergence of Church and state. Nor should we forget that the ancient, sacral idea of the *polis* (with its priest-king) as well as the Old Testament idea of the reign of God (which involved a relationship between priesthood and an *anointed* monarchy) were by no means simply untranslatable into New Testament terms. Least of all where there was a broad and serious view of the Church's openness to the redeemed world, as in Origen's "Dream" of a completely converted Empire[36] or in Augustine's *City of God,* which bears no trace of caesaropapism yet nevertheless projects the image of a truly Christian emperor.[37] Although its deepest intention was not grasped, Augustine's work became the "textbook" of the Christian Middle Ages.

[36] Origen, *Against Celsus,* 8, 74, in *The Ante-Nicene Fathers,* vol. 4 (New York: Charles Scribner's Sons, 1913), 668.

[37] Augustine, *The City of God,* 5, 24–26.

2. Within the Western Church—the Byzantine Church having fallen prey to the state—the important issue, from the outset, was freedom. However, while it was still possible to exercise freedom in the West at the price of deep humiliations, persecutions, ill-treatment and exile, it became much more difficult as the young Germanic peoples erected a new, mythic-sacral mode of thought on the tradition of antiquity and the Old Testament. Charlemagne, the Ottonians and the Hohenstaufens developed this approach on a grand scale. And when, as far as the Church was concerned, the dream of a theocratic union of Church and state collapsed, and the Church freed herself, under Gregory VII, from the embrace of the "Holy Empire", there seemed to be no other choice but the same in reverse: a Church, conceived in the juridical categories of the state, that with God-given *potestas directa* encompasses the state. What might appear to us as making the Church "legalistic", and thus abandoning her original ideal, was merely the attempt to do what was as yet impossible, namely, to disengage from the model of an earthly kingdom of God. The "Secularization", through Frederick II, the bourgeoisie and the developing sciences, which will bring the solution, would have seemed to the preceding period a betrayal of the Church's mission to the world.

3. Yet through all these tragic times, continuing through Napoleon's battle for the Church state (the *Patrimonium Petri*) and up to 1870, the words of Jesus and Paul were there, sometimes oblique and open to various interpretations, in principle demythologizing the sacred state, as the Christians of the first persecutions clearly understood. These words could always provide a new stimulus, even though the biblical texts do not give a ready-made prescription for the relationship of state, Church and the kingdom of God. But even less do they permit a gnostic dualism between the world and God's reign, and hence an indifference by Christians toward the state, which frequently leads, in a dialectical about-face, to the Church being subservient to the state.

A few illustrations must suffice here. Christians, who are "aliens

251

and exiles" in this world (1 Pet 2:11) have the complete freedom of the children of God, yet they are advised by Jesus to pay taxes (Mt 17:26–27). Paul tells them to obey the God-given authority of the state (Rom 13:1), to pray for kings, princes and "all who are in high positions" (1 Tim 2:2). We have evidence of this prayer for the state since the time of Pope Clement.[38] Tertullian, Aristides, Justin, Origen and Dionysius of Alexandria also commend it, even in periods of actual persecution, when the other image of the state—the great adversary of God, the "beast" of Daniel and of Revelation—is alive, as evidenced in Hippolytus' commentary on Daniel. The prayer of Christians and their blameless lives sustain the world order (Aristides, Justin); they are the soul of the world (*Epistle to Diognetus*), the salt of the earth and hence also of the secular state. They "do more good for their fatherland than all the others, for they are examples to the other citizens, teaching faithfulness to God who is above the state. In this way they carry with them their fellow citizens—if these have lived a morally good life in this small, earthly state—to that mysterious, divine state in heaven. To these Christians it may be truly said: 'You have been faithful in the small state, now enter into the Great State' " (Origen).[39]

The Catholic Church never completely forgot the lessons of the persecutions. These remained alive in her memory during the popes' great freedom struggles with the "Holy Emperor" (first of the West, then of the East), whose power had summoned the councils but also given virulence to many of the great heresies. The monarchism of the emperors tended intrinsically either to Arianism (only one can be the

[38] Clement of Rome, *Letter to the Corinthians,* 60, 4; 61, 1–3, in *Ancient Christian Writers,* vol. 1 (New York: Newman Press, 1946): 47.

[39] Origen, *Against Celsus,* 8, 74; cf. already 63–70. Origen also attempts to meet the objection how Christians could pray for a state that plans their demise: the authority of a state comes from God, but it is abused by men. *Commentary on the Letter to the Romans,* 9, 26–30.

highest God), monophysitism (only the divinity is manifested in the humanity of Christ) or monothelitism (there is only one will!). This stiffened the resistance of the Roman bishops: as guardians of the true faith, the best of them were compelled to defy the emperors face to face. From time to time (and this was inherent in the structure of the Church's constellation), a great and solitary saint — like Athanasius, Ambrose or Maximus Confessor — strengthened the popes in their stand (Julius, even Liberius,[40] Damasus, Martin I). As yet, the fight was only with spiritual weapons. In the Basilica of Milan, which was surrounded by the emperor's soldiers, Ambrose exclaimed in a sermon (385): "I too have a weapon, but it is in the name of Christ. I too can give my body to death. We too have our 'tyranny': the tyranny of a bishop lies in his weakness, for it is written: 'When I am weak, then I am strong.'"

Against the emperor's claim to be the highest authority in the Church, able to change the face of the Church according to his own wishes, there arise those great documents that guaranteed both the freedom of the Church and the supreme leadership of the Roman authority. They ranged from the decree of the Roman synod of 382 under Damasus,[41] through statements of Innocent I and Leo I, to Pope Gelasius' (492–496) balanced formulation of the separation of spiritual

[40] Though later crushed and weak, he once stood before the imperial court courageously testifying to the faith, as recorded in Theodoret's *Ecclesiastical History* 2, 16 (London: Bohn, 1854), 99–100. When the Emperor mockingly asked him "What portion do you constitute of the universe, that you desire to destroy the peace of the whole world in order to defend one solitary wicked individual [Athanasius]?", the Pope answered, "If I were standing alone, the cause of truth would not be less important. There was once a period when only three persons [the three young men in the Old Testament] could be found sufficiently courageous to to resist the royal mandate." And when the Emperor threatened him with banishment, "I have already taken leave of the brethren who are in that city [Rome]. The decrees of the Church are of greater importance than a residence in Rome." He refuses any interruption of the journey and goes into that exile which finally demoralizes him.

[41] Denzinger-Schönmetzer, 350. For its authenticity see the foreword by Schönmetzer.

and worldly powers.[42] "The emperor is in the Church, he is not above the Church."[43] At that time, in the West, the predominant image was of a pope who was fighting for the freedom of the Church with the bishops firmly gathered around him; while in the East the bishops, with few exceptions, surrendered slavishly to the emperor. It is the prudent, restrained theology of the Augustinian *City of God* — two realms, two authorities — which strengthened the morale of Leo I, Gelasius and Gregory I (who was also inspired by Benedict). Byzantium never accepted this distinction. But neither could Rome accept the wish of "New Rome" to have the patriarchal see which had been erected there granted equal dignity (and that for political reasons) to that of the "Apostolic See" founded by Peter and Paul.

However, in 774 the pope and the emperor — Hadrian I and Charlemagne — embraced on the steps of St. Peter's. In 800 Leo III surprised Charlemagne with an emperor's crown; Charlemagne: the very man who saw the pope merely as the senior bishop and himself as the overlord of the Church. Shortly before this coronation, monks from Jerusalem had paid him homage and handed over to him, in the name of the Eastern Roman Patriarch, the keys of Jerusalem.[44] The measures the Church took to extricate herself from this new embroil-

[42] Denzinger-Schönmetzer, 347.

[43] Ambrose, *Sermo contra Auxentium,* 386. (Migne, PL 16:1018).

[44] Nicholas I (858–867) protested against a new sacral kingship that was feasible in the Old Testament as well as in pagan Rome. These were pre-Christian "types" of the "true king and high priest" Jesus Christ, whose coming made it completely impossible from then on for the same person to be both emperor and pope (Denzinger-Schönmetzer, 642). This protest remained unheard. Based on the famous text of Gelasius about the separation of these two offices, Nicholas deepened the thought christologically: "The one intermediary between God and humanity, the man Jesus Christ — who himself only wished to be exalted by his healing humility and not be demeaned again by human pride — arranged such a separation of the two powers because of their different competencies and separate dignities, so that the Christian emperor be in need of the pope for his eternal salvation while the pope should follow the emperor's laws in purely temporal matters" (ibid.).

254

ment, namely, the Donation of Constantine (ca. 816) and soon afterward the Pseudo-Isidorian Decretals, were to forge her own chains; she embarked on a course that was worldly and not spiritual. It was then that episcopalism came on the scene as the alternative to papalism, isolating Rome (with her curia) from the organism of the Empire, in which the bishops functioned as high officials. The ethical center of gravity lay with the Ottonian emperors; Rome sank for a century into scandalous and bloody outrages. We have already mentioned that it was an archbishop, later to become Pope Sylvester II, who first called the papacy the seat of the Antichrist. True, Rome recovered, aided by the Herculean strength of Hildebrand, and subsequently rose to great heights under Alexander III and Innocent III, in whose reign the term *plenitudo potestatis* (DS 774) is employed, a term which will constantly recur until Vatican I. But while, in the dark century for the popes, Christianity blossomed in the Empire due to the expansion of innumerable monastic orders, and the charisma of leadership did not seem to be absolutely essential, from now on, since spiritual authority was attempting to use secular means to free itself from secular authority, the energetic exercise of spiritual authority was bound to bring it into conflict with the countless evangelical and charismatic reform movements which were making themselves felt "from below". Lacking the necessary leadership and mediation from hierarchical government, the latter were vulnerable to distortion and consequently had to be condemned as chaotic movements, not amenable to a Church authority that seemed to them superfluous. The meeting between Francis and Innocent was, for all practical purposes, an exception, a golden moment already over by the time the Franciscans were sucked into the undertow of the antipapal, spiritualistic current which drew on Joachim's ideas. The spiritualistic movement could stretch out a hand of welcome to the *Defensor pacis* (1324) of the Paris doctors Marsilius of Padua and Jean of Jandun, which was anti-Roman and claimed to be evangelical but which rejected any concrete authority.

With the defeat of Boniface VIII by Nogaret, the French exile of the popes and, finally, the Great Schism which involved three simultaneous popes and deeply disturbed all Christendom, the power of leadership once again became sharply separated from spiritual renewal. This time it was much more painful than in the tenth century: then the Empire had been there as an all-embracing reality; now its place had been taken by the middle class and nationalism. As a result, the Rhineland mysticism became otherworldly and introverted, orthodox spiritualism lacked a real ecclesial dimension, and Catholic unity was fundamentally threatened by an aggressive Wycliffism. The watchword was now to "save both Church and papacy from the popes",[45] and so conciliarism, as represented by Constance and Basel, seemed the only way to give the Church a worthy and unifying head; Anglicanism, Gallicanism and the *Gravamina Nationis Germanicae* were the fruits of the disturbed balance that had prevailed within the hierarchical system since the Middle Ages. Only a few thinkers, among them Nicholas of Cusa (in his *Concordantia Catholica*), were able to achieve a balance between collegiality and primacy. Far from being healed, the breach deepened under the Renaissance popes and the Reformation, which was the inheritor of centuries of freelance attempts at Church reform. Chieregato's admissions before the Nuremberg Reichstag came too late, and Adrian VI died too soon. In the *Sacco di Roma,* the plundering German soldiers, dressed in papal robes in front of the Castel Sant'Angelo, mocked the imprisoned Clement VII, held a "council" and proclaimed Luther pope.

Considering the immense gulf separating the different principles of Church life which needed to be united at the beginning of modern times, the achievement of Trent is remarkable. For, taken as a whole, it restored to the Catholic Church a papacy that has continued sound and irreproachable down to the present day. Moreover it fundamentally integrated the papacy into the early Christian collegial unity. A

---

[45] Joseph Bernhart, *Der Vatikan als Weltmacht* [The Vatican as a world power], 2d ed. (Munich: List, 1949), 191.

start was made with the decision that bishops were duty-bound to reside in their dioceses. This was followed by the reorganization of the seminaries and the fostering of an ecclesial spirit, which was spread among the young and the clergy by the order founded by Ignatius Loyola. Much lagged behind. The Inquisition was still at work, and wars of conquest across the ocean were still tolerated. Nepotism continued to flourish, and the worst evil, least recognized and most vehemently defended, the Church state, was the last to be wrenched from the papacy.

How many unnecessary humiliations could have been spared the papacy in more modern times, such as the absurd situation where the rigid Caraffa Pope invoked the aid of the Sultan against the equally rigid Spaniard, Philip II, or Gregory XIII's sanction, expressed to the same Philip, of political assassination in the confessional wars. (The humiliation of the Enlightenment Pope, Pius VI, by the freethinkers, particularly when he visited Vienna, does not belong in the same category.) But much of the tragic struggle of his successor, Pius VII, with Napoleon could have been avoided; for the latter, in his brutal resurrection of the ideas of Justinian and Charlemagne, was not concerned solely with the notion of the state Church: he continually returned to the Church state. In the Schönbrunn Decree of 1809 Bonaparte revoked the Donation of Charlemagne, "to put an end to the quarrels that were so damaging to the welfare of religion as well as of the Empire"; as a result, by his Majesty's will, "the popes are to be made what they always should be; the emperor is the one who protects the spiritual power from the passions to which secular power is subject. Jesus Christ, of the blood royal of David, did not desire to be King of the Jews. . . . 'My kingdom is not of this world', he said, and thus condemned forever any attempt to mix religious interests with worldy inclinations." Thereupon the Pope signed the Bull against the "robbers of the *Patrimonium Petri*" which had long been prepared in the chancellery. Before daybreak ladders were set up against the Pope's window, and a French officer climbed up and presented him with the summons to renounce all secular power. The Pope replied calmly, "We cannot renounce something that does not belong to us. Secular power belongs to the Roman Church; we only administer it." Then he was dragged to Savona, where everything was done to wring concessions from him. After the Emperor was defeated, he visited his sick prisoner (meanwhile transferred to Fontainebleau) and called him his "father", laying before him his fantastic vision of a Europe united under emperor and pope. And at the Congress of Vienna, the faithful, resourceful Consalvi succeeded in trading back the Pandora's box that the Church had been well rid of!

After 1870 such incidents could not recur. The "narrows" were finally left behind. The papacy was now free to devote itself to its particular, hereditary task of protecting the Church—and her shepherds first and foremost—from all state interference, a task of which it had always been conscious in the first centuries, in its confrontation with both state persecution and state flattery.

c. Toward Balance

The two outlets from the historical "narrows" did not coincide in time. The first outlet opened through the shock of the French Revolution, with the physical and moral humiliation of the papacy under Napoleon (to which belongs the collapse of the old imperial Church of Germany, seen in the 1803 Reichsdeputationshauptschluss), and then with the flight of Pius IX to Gaëta and the final breakdown of the concept of the Church state. Even after this catastrophe, the papacy was reluctant to accept the situation, with its almost pathological *"Non possumus!"*

The second way out was what we have called the papacy's self-affirmation in the emergency conditions of 1870–1871, a "victory" that can only be seen as the belated conclusion of centuries of strife, now making way for something quite new. This new thing has apparently been made more difficult because of that "victory", but it is something that Vatican II kept resolutely in the center of its attention, namely, to take a function that had become isolated from the whole and reintegrate it into the "People of God"—which the last Council explicitly described as the comprehensive, all-embracing framework.

If all members of the Church would comprehend this all-embracing whole, the integration would not be difficult. Then the office of Peter (in the context of collegiality) would exercise solely that most important ministry of maintaining unity within a common will for such unity, within the ideal consensus of ecclesial love. For the more the members aspire to integrate their personal missions into the mission of the whole Body, the less reason there is for the governing office to step in with legal measures. This goal is clearly manifest since Vatican II (which does not mean that the majority of members of the Body effectively strive for it, let alone attain it); but the road from the "narrows" to this insight has been a painful one. It begins with the period of the Restoration in Rome, started with Leo XII and Gregory XVI, and includes Pius IX's initial openness as well as his later period which was determined by Secretary of State Antonelli. Despite the political reorientation by Leo XIII and later by Pius XI, this transition within the Church continued until John XXIII. As yet, Rome could not adapt her spiritual horizon to the radical changes brought about by the French Revolution and particularly by German Idealism and its incalculable consequences.

Hence, fear expressed itself in conservative defensiveness toward the "outside" (the "Syllabus") and by mistrust turned inward. This fear, nourished by an insufferable, sycophantic and informer spirit, manifested itself in consistent rejection (practically without exception) of all Catholic attempts to meet the modern intellectual world with empathy and dialogue. In an earlier time, the Inquisition prepared stakes for the burning of heretics: now it methodically burned that Catholic spirit which was attempting, in continuity with the Church Fathers and even with High Scholasticism (in its dialogue with Islam

259

and Judaism), to make contact with the spirit of the new age. This brought about an atmosphere of terror, an artificial, paralyzing quiet. But embers continued to glow under the ashes. A long list of unnecessary human tragedies attested to the uneasy and unclarified relationship between theology and the Magisterium. This sickness had three crises: the first was around the time of the "Syllabus" (1866), the longest and most important was that of Modernism, which outwardly was put down by the encyclical *Pascendi* (1907); and finally, as epilogue, the false alarm concerning the *Nouvelle Théologie* to which *Humani generis* (1953) intended to put an end. The secret proceedings of the Holy Office—denounced by Cardinal Frings at Vatican II as infringing all natural rights guaranteed to the human person—and the associated practice of cowardly denunciations, poisoned the intellectual atmosphere of the Church for more than a century.[46] It required almost superhuman spiritual heroism on the part of individuals if they were not to become embittered. This is well illustrated by citing only four names (and there were many others) whose bearers narrowly escaped condemnation: Newman, Blondel, de Lubac, Teilhard.

The genius who could have given a complete Catholic answer to the giants of German Idealism had not yet been born. Hence an answer had to be struggled for piecemeal. The ideal solution would have been the establishment of academies in which Rome would participate in the thinking and learning process. Instead, philosophers and theologians worked mostly on their own, producing only partial answers, and, as isolated individuals, they could easily be disposed of. Their corpses bestrew Denzinger for more than a century: the

[46] Félicité de Lamennais, *Affaires de Rome: des maux de l'Église et de la société* (Paris: P. D. Cailleux, 1836–1837), 88. "I shall never understand a form of justice where the accused is not informed of the accusation, without investigation, without debate, without any defense. So monstrous a judicial proceeding would be revolting even in Turkey".

traditionalists, Bautain (DS 2751–856, 2765–2869), Bonnetty (2811–14), Lamennais (2730–32) and the "rationalists", Hermes (2738–40), Günther (2828–31), Frohschammer (2850–61). In a special "grave" lies Döllinger (2875–80) and in another, the noble Rosmini-Serbati (3201–41), condemned in detail posthumously, whose *Five Wounds of the Church* was placed on the Index as early as 1849.

In retrospect it must be admitted that these condemnations were justified. In fact, neither the "traditionalist" nor the "rationalist" road led anywhere. Moreover, as well as issuing the condemnations, Vatican I actually put forward a short positive guideline (DS 3000–3045). The Modernist excesses also needed to be trimmed, for they were destroying central mysteries of revelation. Still, condemnation itself did not show a positive way forward, and many an intellect which should have been encouraged to find such a path was in fact disheartened, intimidated or embittered.

In this fateful period, what stands out most is perhaps the limited nature of the Petrine charism of leadership. It could deliver hard blows to those who departed from the center line but was unable to contribute much that was constructive toward solving the problems presented by the times. We do not mean to say that this must always be so. Considering the integration that is today's task, things could be very different now. Nor should we forget the great positive impulses which have come from several strong encyclicals of Leo XIII and Paul VI which were themselves products of collaboration.

Blondel, deeply religious, always trying to defend the Church, writes on the occasion of the condemnation of Loisy: "Oh, how much better it would have been, instead of ostracizing him, to publish a directive clarifying what is unacceptable and what acceptable. That would have served truth and charity in an appropriate way. But now what can I say to one of my colleagues when he says, 'Freedom of research in the Church is an illusion, because authority is in the hands of incompetents'?" Blondel's embarrassed answer, that the Holy Spirit

261

can make use of any means, no doubt satisfied neither his colleagues nor his own heart.[47]

It was *Laberthonnière* who, in his meditations on the form of ecclesial authority, came up with the most profound and prophetic insights. We can leave to one side his one-sided polemics—which provoked the Magisterium—against all (Thomistic) application of an impersonal Aristotelianism (but also of Platonism, Stoicism and Neoplatonism) in the development of a personal and Christian world view, which essentially is based on the gospel of *Deus caritas.* His skirmishes with Greek philosophy are totally irrelevant to his analysis of what authority should be in the Catholic Church, what it could be and what it unfortunately was in his time. "The question is: In what spirit and in what manner should leadership and instruction be given, to be truly human and Christian? And, in turn, how should a person who is progressing in faith prepare himself to receive guidance and instruction? Authority per se is never in question. . . . An established authority is only attacked with troops that are in the service of some other authority. And as everyone knows, there is no more severe, ruthless and tyrannical discipline than that of revolutionaries."[48] Because, for Laberthonnière, the triune and incarnate God is essentially total self-giving, his Church can be in her essence only "a unity through *communio*"[49] of free persons who, by their freely willed love, are moved to build a unified Church. Again, Church as "organization" implied from the very beginning "a hierarchy and hence a jurisdiction . . . , for to be able to live in a society, authority, organization and jurisdic-

[47] Maurice Blondel to Wehrlé, *Correspondence de Maurice Blondel et Joannès Wehrlé,* vol. 1, commentary and notes by Henri de Lubac (Paris: Aubier, 1969): 130.

[48] Lucien Laberthonnière, *La Notion chrétienne de l'authorité. Contribution au rétablissement de l'unanimité chrétienne* (Paris: Vrin, 1955). This book, as the others in *Oeuvres de Laberthonnière,* edited by Louis Canet, is put together from many disparate fragments, the editorial arrangement of which could be criticized but which as a whole clearly presents the central teaching from various aspects. The quotation is from 98–99.

[49] Ibid., 119.

262

tion are indispensable."[50] But in the Church of God authority can never instruct, as it were, "from outside", nor can it impose the truth on anyone; and neither should the Christian submit himself to be led and instructed purely passively.[51] Otherwise the Church would find herself entangled in the kind of "lord-servant" relationship that corresponds to a pagan but never the Christian concept of God. "You (Romans) always imagine that God created men to rule over them and to assert his rights as sovereign. You see God as a kind of potentate, and then you pass yourselves off as being delegated by him to implement his power and reign. Thus you stand the gospel on its head."[52] From a Christian point of view, authority can only be an "incumbent duty". "One can relinquish a right but not the performance of a duty." He bitterly denounces the new Inquisition: formerly you tried to maintain the "integrity of dogma" by burnings at the stake. Now that you cannot make the state your executioner, "you withdraw into proud self-sufficiency and boast that you have only to wait for the others to come to you." The alienation of the function of authority from the Mystical Body of Christ allows the latter to fall apart dialectically into "authoritarianism and the lust for power", on the one hand, and "servility" on the other[53]—and such servility is just as much the expression of "ambitious groveling" as of "base anxiety over one's comfort".[54] People dispense themselves from responsibility by obediently shifting it to the one who gives orders; yet in the background there are still pangs of conscience, interior distress and unease.[55] Laberthonnière correctly diagnoses the spiritual affinity of this system with pragmatism and positivism.[56] He is aware that healing can only come from the

[50] Ibid., 122.
[51] Ibid., 79.
[52] Ibid., 146.
[53] Ibid., 76, 139.
[54] Ibid., 115.
[55] Ibid., 117, 136.
[56] Ibid., 156; cf. his *Positivisme et Catholicisme* (Paris: Bloud, 1911).

depth of the *communio*. The period in which he lived was character-ized by a close alliance of neo-Thomism and Church leadership; he finds the common link in the antipersonalism of both and sees the spark of "infallibility" leap across from the Magisterium to theology, which, with regard to the period of Matiussi, was certainly not a misrepresentation. Since the statements of the Creed are infallible, the "qualified formulations of theologians" deduced from them are also to be regarded as infallible. These theologians "call themselves doctors, like the ancient teachers of the law who created unchangeable doc-trines out of their propositions, canonizing authority and, in turn, themselves and not tolerating any other reasoning than their own."[57]

Against this variety of "Romanism", Laberthonnière calls, not exactly for "revolt", but for "resistance".[58] He demands a reform in the spirit of the Church *communio,* such that both commanding and obeying would take place in a spirit of commitment and responsibil-ity to Christ. "Obeying has the same dignity as commanding; the existence of both is justified only if they lead to free brotherly union of minds and souls in love and truth in the bosom of the heavenly Father."[59] Only in this context can one speak of "law" in the Christian sense,[60] because in Christianity everything flows from the personal God and the divinely created personality of individual human beings.[61] So what we have, ultimately—avoiding the overused word "service"—is mutual *help.* This applies to authority which, in the spirit of Paul,

[57] Ibid., 135.

[58] Ibid., 78.

[59] Ibid., 80. To learn how the antimodernistic Roman police functioned one should see the recently deciphered documents of the "Sapinière": Émile Poulat, *Intégrisme et Catholicisme intégral, un réseau secret international anti-moderniste, "La Sapinière",* 1909–1921 *(Paris and Tournai: Casterman, 1969).*

[60] Lucien Laberthonnière, "Le Vraie Sense de la loi", in *Sicut Ministrator* (Paris: Vrin, 1947), 78–95.

[61] Lucien Laberthonnière, *Esquisse d'une philosophie personnaliste* (Paris: Vrin, 1942), 143ff, 288ff., 380ff., 648ff. Summary, 695ff.

should bear in mind that in mankind and in the Church there are no *maiores* and *minores,* but, at most, "elder brothers who should not glory in knowing more than their less advanced brothers but rather *help* them so that they too may come of age".[62] But this also applies in a special way to the Christian who has not been given authority, and this is Laberthonnière's gravest concern, which will not let him rest: "How should people like us act, so that, spiritually deepened by the acceptance of authority, we can contribute to the spiritual deepening of authority itself?"[63]

This last question of the controversial Abbé is still with the Church: the question of mutuality, of *communio.* Among the fresh starts brought by Vatican II, opening the way to this *communio* was certainly the most fruitful for the Church. Therefore the most foolish thing today would be to force Church leadership to act in a preconciliar way, for which, in any case, it has no inclination. The theologians who had to put up with many difficulties in the past can well do without the habitual griping of those today who cry over sufferings they themselves did not undergo. It is a fact that, before the Council, thirty-eight eminent theologians united in chorus to produce their *Critique of the Church,*[64] but what is the point of repeating this kind of exercise *ad nauseam,* and often with an arrogance that reveals the same weaknesses of which Rome is accused? The infallibility of theologians often seems to be a more stubborn sickness than the defined infallibility of the papacy—and the latter is applied with incomparably greater discretion.

In the future, all members of the Catholic *communio* will have to accept their place under the supreme jurisdiction of Christ, the Lord of the Church, who wished to conclude the last Gospel with these

---

[62] Laberthonnière, *La Notion de l'authorité,* 135.

[63] Ibid., 140.

[64] Hane Jürgen Schultz, ed., *Kritik an der Kirche* (Stuttgart: Kreuzverlag, and Olten: Walter-Verlag, 1958).

final words to Peter: "What is that to you?"—i.e., the precise relationship of ecclesiastical jurisdiction to a Church understood as love and *communio.* It is even more appropriate for simple Christians (and the theologian is one too) to take to heart this final statement and, with Peter, to respond to the call: "Follow me!"

We should be grateful to be living at a time when the understanding of ecclesial unity has both deepened and broadened, so that the greatest imaginable plurality within the christological unity is not merely tolerated but actually striven for. Why not gratefully enjoy this gift of real freedom *in the Lord,* rather than splintering it into a purely sociological and abstract freedom? Why, after centuries of hard struggle to depoliticize the Church, should we jeopardize the achievement by putting together a confused amalgam of theology and politics?

3. *The Citadel of Freedom*

After what we have just said, it seems rather paradoxical to speak of *Rome* as the citadel of the freedom of the spirit of Christ (2 Cor 3:17), of the "glorious liberty of the children of God" (Rom 8:21), of "the freedom of the Christian". Was it not the whole Church of the faithful whose awareness of the freedom of her "prophetic office" had to free Rome from her captivity to a fear that in turn made her impose fear on others? But why would the Christian people, together with those theologians whose thought springs from the profound depths of faith, want to rescue Rome at all costs? The answer is that they recognize in her the final guarantor of Christian freedom in the face of the powers of this world. We have already noted this: the freedom for which the Church contended prior to Constantine, led her, after the agreement between Church and Empire, into an unrelenting struggle—often conducted by the pope on his own—for the freedom of the whole Church from being swallowed up by the secular power. The tragic events in the period between Gregory VII and Boniface

VIII were a continuation of this struggle within the framework of the medieval world view. On the one hand, the pope's Avignon exile detached the papacy from the Empire, and on the other hand, it challenged the Christian conscience to restore the papacy's independent dignity (conciliarism). And the later battles, from the Reformation through Gallicanism to Napoleon, were all fought—against Christian confessions and Catholic princes—for the freedom of the Church, and in the last analysis this was guaranteed only if Rome had freedom to make decisions. The definition of Vatican I was the sword thrust that freed the Catholic Church from the stranglehold of Laocoon's serpent, which had held her for centuries. And though the struggles continue externally, internally the principle is clear not only at a level prior to reflection—as it has always been since the first centuries—but also in conscious and hence unruffled reflection.

It is a question of both external and internal freedom. Externally there must be resistance to every attempt by secular powers, be they political, spiritual or ideological, to ensnare the People of God and use it for particular ends. The Church reserves the right to examine all such proposals freely and to decide according to her own discretion. The same applies internally, within the Church, though less attention is paid to it. There is nothing triumphal about the freedom of Christ in the pilgrim Church. Rather, it is the freedom of a faith which is willing to risk giving itself. Just as Christ, in the form of a servant, challenged men to decide to follow him and would rather let them go than overwhelm them by displays of power, so the visible Church, represented by sinners, must also accept the role of servant and present herself as the guardian of freedom; for the Church asserts herself only in order to liberate people; she defines only to confront them with the *mysterium;* she does not compel them by magic but takes the risk of exercising her office, trusting in the free assent of believers. Chesterton illustrates this in a paradoxical, joyous way: "The outer ring of Christianity is a rigid guard of ethical abnegations and professional priests; but inside that inhuman guard you will find the old human life dancing like children and drinking wine like men; for Christianity is the only frame for pagan freedom. But in the modern philosophy the case is opposite; it is its outer ring that is obviously artistic and emancipated; its despair is within."[65]

Soloviev (about whom we shall say more later) expressed this more carefully: the Petrine Church leadership "must be divine in its content to impress itself so strongly on the religious conscience of all informed and well-meaning persons; and it must be human and imperfect in its historical manifestation to permit a moral opposition and make room for doubt, struggle, temptation and all that constitutes the merit of free and truly human virtue."[66]

Here we are concerned primarily with the first aspect. One could trace this through the entire course of Church history and show that Vatican I did not merely give an explanation of principles but a summary of history when it stated: "The episcopal power is emphasized, affirmed and defended by the supreme shepherd."[67] Avitus formulated it concisely in the beginning of the seventh century: "When the Roman pontiff is challenged, not only a single bishop but the whole episcopate is called in question."[68] However, we shall limit ourselves to a few more modern testimonies, which have all the more force since they were given by men of free, enquiring minds who, in searching for a guarantee of ecclesial freedom, were led by compelling logic to Rome, and at a time (around Vatican I) when there was little talk of freedom within the Church, collegiality or dialogue and much more about papal infallibility. These men were converts who, after long intellectual struggles, reached Rome and

[65] G. K. Chesterton, *Orthodoxy* (Garden City, New York: Image Books, 1959), 157.

[66] Vladimir Soloviev, *La Russie et l'Église universelle* [Russia and the universal Church] (Paris: Nouvelle Librairie Parisienne, 1889).

[67] Denzinger-Schönmetzer, 3061; also the examples in Henri de Lubac, *Les Églises particulières*, 122.

[68] Avitus of Vienne, Ep. 31, (Migne, PL 59:248–49), quoted from de Lubac, *Les Églises particulières*, 123.

found they could at last breathe, having found the principle of freedom.

To highlight these men, we shall begin by way of a prelude by recalling the testimony of one who, in the zeal of his later polemics against the definition of 1871 (the significance of which he misunderstood), forgot his earlier insights, namely, *Ignaz Döllinger.* While in the second part of his book *Kirche und Kirchen, Papsttum und Kirchenstaat* (1861) he found fault with much in the government of the pontifical state, in the first part he formulated a magnificent apology for the fact that the freedom of the Church is guaranteed solely by the papacy. The basic thought is simple and is followed through in every historical detail: of her very nature, the Christian Church requires a papacy; the latter's "proper function" is to "represent and defend the rights of all the constituent churches against the power of the state and of princes and to make sure that the Church is not essentially altered, weakened or undermined by involvement with the state." The individual church cannot do this on her own, and that is why the "intervention of the supreme Church authority is indispensable". "It must sustain and support [the particular church] which otherwise would succumb under the pressure of the complex means of compulsion and persuasion that are available to the modern state."[69] Whereas, in the midst of the chaos of the mass migration of peoples, the popes "by the force of public opinion" were obliged to become arbitrators "at the pinnacle of the European commonwealth, proclaiming and protecting the Christian rights of these peoples, settling international disputes . . . and bringing about peace among the warring states", the popes have retreated, in the modern age, "more and more within the boundaries of purely ecclesiastical issues". Here, however, "the Papal See is presently as powerful and as strong, as confident and as free in the exercise of authority as it ever was."[70] At the same time, there has

[69] Ibid., 35–37.
[70] Ibid., 33–35.

never been talk of "total power". "All these representations and accusations are untrue and unjust. The papal power is . . . the most circumscribed that can be imagined", because the Church has long since been in possession of clear legislation, as de Maistre has shown. On the other hand (according to Bossuet), the pope can do anything that is necessary within the divine order. Döllinger correctly points to the medieval teaching that "not only any bishop but the pope himself can be deposed if he falls into heresy, and, if he persists, he must be judged just like anyone else",[71] in the same way that a king may lose his crown if he ceases to be a Christian king. This changed when the Reformation turned its back on the papacy; the Reformed believers were exposed to a despotism as never before,[72] as Döllinger undertakes to demonstrate in minute detail with regard to all non-Catholic churches and countries, including Greece, Russia and England. Nationalization of the churches and then the flight into the "invisible church"[73] are "unavoidable consequences of having renounced, entirely deliberately, the opposite principle, that of catholicity, of the Universal Church."[74] The Döllinger who here speaks so passionately eventually had to bear excommunication, but, consistent with the views he expresses here, he refused to join the new Christian-Catholic Church which was independent of Rome.

John Henry Newman moved from the Anglican Church and toward Rome with slow, carefully considered steps. In his early days, reading Newton, he had regarded the pope as the Antichrist. His change of heart was largely influenced by his theological reservations about "establishment", i.e., the subordination of the Church to the secular supremacy of the king.[75] Newman's religious soul sought a true encoun-

[71] Ibid., 51, text in Congar, *Ministères et communion ecclésiale,* 72ff.

[72] Ibid., 55.

[73] Ibid., 13.

[74] Ibid., 17.

[75] For what follows, see especially the first part of Norbert Schiffers, *Die Einheit der Kirche nach J. H. Newman. Die historische Ausgangsbasis, etc.* (Düsseldorf: Patmos-Verlag, 1956), 39–158.

ter with the absolute God, the Creator, Redeemer and Judge, and with his living authority, an authority in which Christ becomes unavoidably real and is mediated, without distortion, by a christiform Church. Turning away from insipid contemporary liberalism, he and his friends sought clarity in the Caroline divines, the "golden-age" theologians, primarily Hooker,[76] Sanderson and Laud. Initially, Hooker created a completely pragmatic *via media,* deriving both the secular authority of the king and the spiritual authority of the Church from the same nature of God. Here the coronation of the monarch supplied the earthly link: his enthronement signified secular juridical power, his anointing expressed the king's ecclesiastical juridical power.[77] William Laud developed these ideas further: the king can decree laws that are necessary for peace and order in the Church, but decisions concerning matters of faith are in the hands of the bishops. According to Sanderson, the jurisdiction of the bishops with regard to the *forum internum* comes from God; with regard to the *forum externum,* it comes from the king, who is "the sole source of all authority in the realm of external jurisdiction, be it spiritual or secular." Even according to Hooker, the bishop's spiritual authority comes to him in virtue of apostolic succession, which can be traced back, even after the Reformation, to the English mission under Gregory I. In this balancing act on the part of Caroline theology, the young Oxford Movement came down on the side of Gregory VII: for Keble and Froude held that the king received his jurisdiction in ecclesial matters from the Church through his consecration by the bishop. For Newman, however, it is not the Middle Ages but the age prior to Constantine that is normative; a Church that was free from the state, precisely because she was persecuted by it. Newman's patristic studies rein-

[76] Also on the subject, Louis Bouyer, *L'Église de Dieu,* 136; on the Caroline theologians: Georges Tavard, *The Quest for Catholicity: A Study in Anglicanism* (New York: Herder, 1964), chap. 3.

[77] The context in Schiffers, *Die Einheit der Kirche,* 50f.

271

forced his view that state influence on the Church was the fundamentally baneful feature of Church history. Looking back on the period of the Oxford Movement (1850),[78] he formulated his mature insight as follows:

> For even in the ante-Nicene period, the heretic Patriarch of Antioch (Paul of Samosata) was protected by the local sovereign against the Catholics, and was dispossessed by the authority and influence with the Imperial Government of the See of Rome. And since that time, again and again would the civil power, humanly speaking, have taken captive and corrupted each portion of Christendom in turn, but for its union with the rest, and the noble championship of the Supreme Pontiff. Our ears ring with the oft-told tale, how the temporal sovereign persecuted, or attempted, or gained, the local Episcopate, and how the many or the few faithful fell back on Rome. So it was with the Arians in the East and St. Athanasius; so with the Byzantine Empress and St. Chrysostom; so with the Vandal Hunneric and the Africans; so with the 130 Monophysite Bishops at Ephesus and St. Flavian; so was it in the instance of the 500 Bishops, who, by the influence of Basilicus, signed a declaration against the Tome of St. Leo; so in the instance of the Henoticon of Zeno; and so in the controversies both of the Monothelites and the Iconoclasts. Nay, in some of those few instances which are brought in controversy, as derogatory to the constancy of the Roman See, the vacillation, whatever it was, was owing to what, as I have shown, is ordinarily avoided, — the immediate and direct pressure of the temporal power. As, among a hundred Martyr and Confessor Popes, St. Peter and St. Marcellinus for an hour or a day denied their Lord, so if Liberius and Vigilius gave a momentary scandal to the cause of orthodoxy, it was when they were no longer in their proper place, as the keystone of a great system, and as the correlative of a thousand ministering authorities, but mere individuals, torn from their see and prostrated before Caesar.

[78] Newman, *Certain Difficulties,* 2d ed. (1894), 184–86.

In later and modern times we see the same truth irresistibly brought out; not only, for instance, in St. Thomas's history, but in St. Anselm's, nay, in the whole course of English ecclesiastical affairs, from the Conquest to the sixteenth century, and, not with least significancy, in the primacy of Cranmer. Moreover, we see it in the tendency of the Gallicanism of Louis XIV., and the Josephism of Austria. Such, too, is the lesson taught us in the recent policy of the Czar towards the United Greeks, and in the present bearing of the English Government towards the Church of Ireland. In all these instances, it is a struggle between the Holy See and some local, perhaps distant, Government, the liberty and orthodoxy of its faithful people being the matter in dispute; and while the temporal power is on the spot, and eager, and cogent, and persuasive, and dangerous, the strength of the assailed party lies in its fidelity to the rest of Christendom and to the Holy See.

Well, this is intelligible; we see why it should be so, and we see it in historical fact; but how is it possible, and where are the instances in proof, that a Church can cast off Catholic intercommunion without falling under the power of the State? Could an isolated Church do now, what, humanly speaking, it could not have done in the twelfth century, though a Saint was its champion? . . . Truly is it then called a Branch Church; for as a branch cannot live of itself, therefore, as soon as it is lopped off from the Body of Christ, it is straightway grafted of sheer necessity upon the civil constitution. . . .

In 1841 Newman, who was still an Anglican, felt compelled to protest against the establishment of an Anglo-Prussian diocese in Jerusalem, both because it was a political act of the state and because it linked together two churches that had no communion with each other.

The "branch theory" mentioned in the text was the first attempt to find a way out: a Church, integral and self-subsistent on the basis of her adherence to the unity of faith of an (as yet) undivided Christendom. This was what Newman was always looking for: a living presence of God in a Church vitally animated by faith, whose "prophetic office" was led by an episcopal office, and where the latter's definitions were simply the necessary formulations of the whole *mysterium* of faith, to minister to the continuance of that faith. It was a time unaquainted with the proliferation of "innovations" such as were added later by the Latin Church and jettisoned by the Reformation. The unity central for Newman was the *communio* itself. The Oxford Movement's idea of this did not greatly differ from the *sobornost* of the slavophiles (under the leadership of Chomyakov); it was here that Newman located the "infallibility" of the Church that already fascinated him.[79] Here he also found a living spiritual tradition in the interpretation of Scripture through liturgy, prayer, theology and conciliar decisions. Surely one should accept this living stem—on which the Eastern, Roman and Anglican Churches were all grafted—as the living canon of Christ's Church and take one's directions from it? Newman was soon forced to recognize that this theological "classicism" was in fact a romanticism, far removed from reality, because it contained an internal contradiction: how could an authority which was once present in a living tradition (and without which no church can have an orthodox faith) cease to be a living reality and be discoverable only in a remote historical period? To his horror, Newman found that Eutyches, who made a similar appeal to a past tradition in a normative era, was found to be a heretic by the Council of Chalcedon, where the formula of Ephesus was changed in order to preserve orthodoxy, and this with the unequivocal leadership of the Roman See. Unity of faith was preserved by the action of a concrete center, endowed with authority. Moreover, that unity of love, *sobornost,* was very limited in the classical period; was it not already "romantic" in Cyprian? And did it not break up completely in the Arian confusion? To illustrate its continuity with the early Church one might point to holiness within the Anglican Church; but the same would apply to the Roman

[79] John Henry Cardinal Newman, *The Prophetical Office of the Church Viewed Relatively to Romanism and Popular Protestantism* (London: J. G. & F. Rivington, 1837), 112; *Apologia pro vita sua* (London: Longmans, Green, and Co., 116.

Church. Consequently one could only try to clear up misunderstandings between the two Churches. (Now Newman had in mind to write against "the Protestant idea of the Antichrist" which regarded the pope as the Antichrist.)[80]

His whole problem was how to reconcile the two aspects of an authority that is both divine and contemporary in the Church: it had to be unchangeable yet timely, mysterious and unfathomable yet presenting a clear challenge. Both aspects were present in the first councils of the Church. There was no rigid, classicist literalness, and even the Apostles' Creed could accept clarifying alterations. (And did not the letters of the Apostles constitute a supplementary interpretation of the Christ's original words?) All was living *pneuma,* a matrix that could bring forth concrete and contemporary life-forms; everything was alive, no mere skeleton but live flesh on a living structure.[81] Ultimately, "development" is necessary, even in the supernatural organism of the Church, in order to maintain her living identity. This is the point reached in the *Essay on the Development of Christian Doctrine* (1845). However, the exercise of episcopacy by itself could not guarantee universal unity, as *Tract* 90 (1841) had already stated.[82] Consequently, "we know no other means to safeguard the *sacramentum unitatis* of the Church than by a center of unity." In the same year (1845), Newman became a Catholic in order to gain contact with that center.

It is characteristic of Newman's path that, after his conversion, the papacy was by no means in the center of his interest. His reserve

---

[80] *Correspondence of John Henry Newman with John Keble and Others,* 1839–1845, ed. at the Birmingham Oratory (London: Longmans, Green and Co., 1917), 50f; and *Essays Critical and Historical,* vol. 2 (London: B. M. Pickering, 1877); James Henthorn Todd, *Discourses on the Prophecies Relating to the Antichrist* (Dublin: n.p., 1840).

[81] Also the instructive study of Jean Stern, "La Controverse de Newman avec l'abbé Jager et la théorie de développement", in *Veröffentlichungen des internat. Card. Newman Kuratoriums,* 6th series (Nuremberg, 1964); 123–42.

[82] Discussed in *The Via Media* (1888), 259–348.

concerning the definition of infallibility is well known.[83] But it should be noted that he wanted to see the function of pronouncing infallible statements and definitions by the successor of Peter limited to a minimum. He emphasized that the Magisterium was no more free from sin than the "prophetical office" of the entire body of the Church; each has to correct the other. Tensions are part and parcel of the Church, including those between authority and theology (which is regarded as an exponent of the "prophetical office"), since everyone in the Church is subject to the effects of original sin.[84] Continuing the theme of these tensions in the Church, Newman writes (in the last *Rambler* article of 1859) his famous challenge to the laity actively to take hold of their mission in faith. As for the tensions Newman experienced all too frequently during his Catholic period—a book has been written about his "martyrdom"[85]—they were for him simply proof that he had finally reached the realm of *freedom*. What interested him now was not the structure of the Church but how to live in her in freedom: he himself is free to embrace the saints, to make the personal act of faith (*Grammar of Assent,* 1870), to cultivate prayer and meditation in the midst of all Church activities. The focus is not Peter, the individual, but the realm of freedom, of which Peter (a single individual, yet indispensable in the constellation of Christ) is the guardian.

From the other "branch", the Eastern Church, *Vladimir Soloviev*

[83] For a short time he seems to defer his acceptance of the dogma "until the definition is consistently received by the whole body of the faithful" (*Certain Difficulties,* 2:303); but he withdrew the thought quickly: "I do not receive it [the new dogma] on the word of the Council, but on the Pope's self-assertion" (ibid., 304). Schiffers, *Die Einheit der Kirche,* 238.

[84] The famous preface to the third edition of *The Via Media* (1877) refers to this.

[85] Denys Gorce, *Le Martyre de Newman* (Paris: Bonne Presse, 1946).

came to Rome.[86] He was a completely different person from Newman. Aware of already possessing the entire catholicity of the faith of the Creed and of bringing with him to the Latin Church the rich treasure of Eastern wisdom and speculative trinitarian sophiology,[87] he had a triumphal way of showing his Orthodox brothers the plain necessity of a concrete Church center in Rome and of mercilessly unveiling the sins, delusions and cowardice of the Eastern Church. Yet he loved the Church of his origin no less than Newman did his own; both were noble hearts, but Newman spoke more softly.

Soloviev's starting point and motive for leaving were precisely the same as those of the Englishman. Church unity in the entire East, and particularly in the slavophile theological ideology, is in fact a dream, contradicted by harsh reality. Inseparable from this—as both cause and effect—is the Church's lack of freedom under the yoke of Byzantium and Moscow. Like the Tractarians, Soloviev demanded a concept of the Church where the once-for-all foundation, Jesus Christ and faith in him, is a living reality, the realization of his love, where it is to be found as the kingdom of God growing in history, a kingdom for us, a kingdom through us, a kingdom in us.[88] It is to the "kingdom for us" that the structured Church belongs: hierarchy, Creed, sacraments; this is the basis for and the path toward Christian justice in the world. The slavophiles, who characterized the Church as the "conscious, free agreement of individuals" and the "free will and inner synthesis of unity and freedom in love",[89] confuse the goal for which they strive—which they take for granted—with the path along which such an

---

[86] See *Herrlichkeit,* vol. 2, "Fächer der Stile", pt. 2 (Einsiedeln: Johannesverlag, 1969): 647–716. We are concerned here only with vol. 3 of the German edition of the collected writings (see above, note 66). On Soloviev's genuine conversion, cf. Heinrich Falk, "Wladimir Solowjews Stellung zur katholischen Kirche", in *Stimmen der Zeit* (Freiburg im Breisgau, 1949): 421–35.

[87] He describes this contribution in book 3 of *Russland und die universale Kirche.*

[88] Ibid., 151–52.

[89] Ibid., 212.

ideal must be approached. "The difference between idle daydreams and the divine ideal of unity consists in this: that the latter has a real basis (the *dos moi pou sto* of social mechanics), whence victory is gradually won over all the powers of discord."[90] Freedom is the goal, but the Church on earth, "because she is subject to the conditions of finite existence", cannot be "absolutely free" and has to have within herself a "basis" for the possibility of rising from slavery to freedom.[91] And the name of this principle is, without a doubt, Peter. For he alone is able to free the Church from worldly entrapments.

What Newman summarized briefly, without mentioning the horrors and violations that lay behind every one of his examples, Soloviev described in stark detail: the continuous, humiliating repression of the Church's freedom by the Greek and Russian princes. Anyone who will not have Peter as leader automatically becomes prey to the secular powers and to nationalism,[92] and hence to division and discord in the Church. Long quotations from the clearsighted but impotent Aksakov dispense Soloviev from having to present his own critique of the Russian and Greek Churches: "Our Church appears, as far as her administration is concerned, like a kind of vast chancery office that applies all the methods of German bureaucracy, with its endemic mendacity, to the pastoral office set over the flock of Christ."[93] "A Church that is a subdivision of the state, i.e., of a 'kingdom of this world', is compelled to share the fate of all worldly kingdoms."[94] Even if the faith of the people remains universal and Catholic—and according to Soloviev this is substantially so; little attention is paid to

[90] Ibid., 275.

[91] Ibid., 214.

[92] "Die russische Idee", ibid., 54ff: ". . . c'est que des chaines séculaires tiennent le corps de notre Église attaché à un cadavre immonde, qui l'étouffe en se décomposant" [". . . it is as if secular chains would bind the body of our Church to an impure cadaver which suffocates her by its decomposition"].

[93] Ibid., 56.

[94] Ibid., 62.

theological distinctions intended to justify the schism post facto—a state church is not able effectively to lead the people to supranational catholicity. "People are afraid of the truth, because the truth is catholic, i.e., universal; at all costs they want their own particular religion, a Russian faith, an Imperial Church."[95] They "are unwilling to sacrifice our national egoism" to the true God.[96] Even Aksakov, who saw the essence of the Church in the bond of love between hearts, finally had to admit: "The spirit of truth, the spirit of love, the spirit of life, the spirit of freedom: this healing breath is what is missing in the Russian Church."[97] And since the solidarity between the Eastern Churches "is not expressed by any living acts, their 'unity in faith' is only an abstract formula that produces nothing and has no binding power."[98] It remains a "fiction" where "there are only isolated national churches".[99] In the East, anyone who sought for a basis of unity in anything or anyone but the emperor necessarily became a martyr: Chrysostom, Flavian, Maximus the Confessor, Theodore the Studite, the Patriarch Ignatius—all who turned for support to the Roman See.

Why does the Roman See embody the principle of freedom? Because Peter (Mt 16:16–18) made a free, unconditional confession of faith in Christ, reproducing spiritually what Mary accomplished physically in her unrestricted consent. Let us attend to the whole text:

An authentic union rests on the reciprocal acts of those who unite. The action of absolute truth, manifested in the God-man (the perfect man) must be met, on the part of imperfect man, by an act of irrevocable consent that joins us to the divine principle. The incarnate God does not want us to accept his truth in a passive and servile manner. He wants to be acknowledged by man's free act. But this

[95] Ibid., 66.
[96] Ibid., 68.
[97] Ibid., 227.
[98] Ibid., 228.
[99] Ibid., 230.

free act must also be performed in the truth: it must be infallible. Therefore it is essential to establish for fallen mankind an indestructible base on which the uplifting action of God can directly build, a point where human self-determination and divine truth coincide in a synthetic act that is entirely human in form but must be divinely infallible in essence. To be effective, the act of divine omnipotence in begetting the physical and individual humanity of Christ only needed the thoroughly passive and receptive consent of the *female* nature in the person of the immaculate Virgin; but to build the social or collective humanity of Christ, his universal Body (the Church) required both less and more than this. Less, because the humanity of the Church did not need to be represented by an absolutely pure and immaculate person, since it was not a case here of creating a substantial and individual relationship or a hypostatic and perfect union of the two natures, but only of creating a concrete and ethical bond. [Yet the bond envisaged is] humanly speaking more specific and more comprehensive. It is more *specific,* because this new bond in spirit and in truth called for a *male* will that comes to meet revelation and a male intelligence to impart a definite form to the truth accepted. It is more *comprehensive* because this new bond, in creating the basis for a collective unity, cannot be satisfied with a personal relationship: it must achieve permanence as a lasting social function.[100]

It was the freedom of Peter's personal confession of the total (supranational) truth of the God-man[101] that made him the rock that serves as a bridge between the real rock, Christ, who upholds all, and the rock of the Church, in which all believers are placed as living stones.[102] He has been set within the *collegium,* the "primitive council of the twelve apostles", but this *collegium* can only find and maintain its unbreakable unity if it remains in union with Peter: "The divine

[100] Ibid., 248–49.
[101] Ibid., 260.
[102] Ibid., 258–59.

Architect . . . establishes the ideal of unanimity by tying it to a real, living authority."[103] Only in this way can Jesus entrust the mystical principles of inner unity, namely, his Eucharist and the trinitarian life it contains, to the transcendent unity of the Church.[104] Only in this Church are real councils possible even to the present day. The Eastern Churches were not able to call a single one after their separation from Rome, and "according to our best theologians this would not even be possible".[105] Only the Roman Church can cry *"contradicitur!"* in the face of a unanimous band of bishops subservient to the emperor, as the deacon Hilarion, the legate of Pope Leo at Ephesus, risked his life to do.[106]

Again we have the same drama as in Newman's case: Soloviev became a convert, not because he was deprived of collegiality, brotherhood or the mystical definitions of the Church—he had these in good measure in the East—but because he needed that keystone on which the whole edifice rests and which, according to Vatican I, is the pope. He needed the pope, who "could formulate the fundamental dogmas of our religion *sine consensu Ecclesiae,* not by collective deliberation, but by virtue of the direct assistance of the heavenly Father . . . *ex sese."* "Only in Peter's confession does the messianic idea free itself from any nationalistic element and adopt a universally valid form. 'You are the Christ, the Son of the living God'."[107] For Soloviev, the conclusive proof of the rightness of this papacy is the reciprocal interrelation of the history of the founding of the Church and Church history as a whole; cause and effect correspond to one another[108]

[103] Ibid., 257.

[104] Ibid., 273–74.

[105] Letter to Strossmayer, ibid., 16.

[106] Ibid., 318.

[107] Ibid., 252–53. Obviously it is immaterial here whether or not the historical Peter had attained this freedom already at the scene in Caesarea Philippi, because Matthew refers definitely to the post-Easter, equally historical Peter.

[108] Ibid., 276–77. A particularly impressive example (chosen from among innumerable others) is given in the renewal of the German church after her total collapse

above and beyond all historical contingencies and accidents, which the Russian knew just as well as Newman did.

For both of them, the papacy is not an end in itself but a means to and a guarantee of freedom. For both, the Church is the embryonic

---

under Napoleon. A few sentences from Franz Schnabel's *Deutsche Geschichte im neunzehnten Jahrhundert* (Freiburg im Breisgau: Herder, 1959) might clarify it: "The bishops of the *ancien régime* died off and their place was taken by new bishops who, from the experience of the past revolutionary decades, learned that neither emperors and princes nor provincial diets could give them safety but only Rome and the ancient laws of the Church against the still powerful omnipotence of police and diplomatic states" (13). "Like the French episcopacy that asserted the 'Gallican freedoms' of the French church in opposition to the pope, so in the eighteenth century also the four German archbishops instigated the erection of a German national church" (22). "For this the bishops appealed to John's Gospel, which states that all apostles received the power to bind and to loose directly from Christ. Hence, they demanded the rights that 'according to divine disposition' rightfully belonged to the episcopacy: the bishop had equal rights with the pope within his diocese, he did not have to carry out all papal directives under all circumstances nor did he have to forward to the pope all appellations under all circumstances." "The 'Gravamina' of the fifteenth century were revived when the archbishops, in the 'Emser Punktation' of 1786, disputed papal collaboration in the assignments of offices and revenues, etc." The chapter of the cathedral and its bishops "lined up on the side of the pope, because they preferred the existing papal leadership to that of metropolitans or of a primate of Germany" (23–24). On his part, Wessenberg backed the cause of the German national church. "He did not deny the divine establishment of the papacy, he only wanted to have, in lieu of a 'curial' canon law, an 'episcopal' one. . . . But the more he needed the help of the state in his struggle against Rome, the more he was forced to make concessions in that direction" (31). In

city of God, asserting itself in the freedom of love. Their eyes are fixed on this as the only goal, but they know that the obligatory and concrete point of reference, Rome, is the condition of such freedom.

---

the general culture of the bourgeoisie the hatred against the servants of Rome was openly voiced. "Soon after 1815 radical nationalism entered the scene, which saw in the Catholic Church a product of the Roman world-empire and saw its universal spirit incompatible with the geographically limited modern state. But this state demanded a high price when, in its own interest, it supported and upheld the traditional, Church-endorsed culture in civilian life. It strove to subordinate the Catholic Church to its own sovereignty, as it successfully did the Protestant church" (32). Napoleon, who humiliated and imprisoned two popes, "in 1811 called a national council to Paris, from which he removed the opponents by force. He did this to make Paris, the capital of his world empire, also the seat of the world Church. He also intended in this association to establish a German 'national church' under the 'primacy' of Dalberg, the highest ranking prince of the Church in the old empire, who offered him his services. Dalberg and Wessenberg participated in the Council of Paris" (33). "That the impoverished Church, stripped of her power, would easily be misused for secular aims was apparent to all participants from the German episcopate. The bishops of modern times needed therefore a much firmer dependence on Rome than there was in the previous centuries" (36). In Vienna, however, Wessenberg developed his plan for a German state church that was opposed by Pius VII's secretary of state, Consalvi. The freedom of the Church had to be ensured from encroachments by the power of the state slowly, through treaties with individual German states.... Schnabel, *Deutsche Geschichte,* vol. 7: *Die katholische Kirche in Deutschland* (Freiburg im Breisgau: Herderbücherei, 1965), 209–10. We could draw the lines further, up to the regime of the Nazis, when Alfred Rosenberg complained that Rome was trying to establish a "nationless world Church", *Der Mythos des 20 Jahrhunderts* (Munich: Hoheneichen-Verlag, 1941), 175–76.

283

III

Living the Miracle

Love as Self-Transcendence

In Part II we discussed the "constellation" that is inseparable from the real historical Jesus; he incorporated this constellation, together with himself, into his Church. We further discussed the particular nature of Peter's office of leadership within the constellation. It became evident in defining this office how difficult it is to keep it in balance within the integral unity of the Church. While this office is definitely not the center, it must be rooted and maintained *in* the center to become the criterion, the concrete point of reference for unity (and without it unity would fall apart), thus leading beyond itself to *the* center, Christ, and liberating people for Christian freedom. In this official role of the "self-effacing", "unworthy servant" who "only does his duty" and expects no thanks for it (Lk 17:9–10), Peter becomes the prototype of all Christian living within the constellation of unity. This *renunciation* which lies at the heart of Catholic office is not primarily an ethical achievement but is intrinsic to its structure. The office-bearer is bound to exercise an office that is not his own; essentially he directs attention to someone else who "leads him where he does not wish to go"; such an office can only be accepted with "grief" (Jn 21:17) about one's own unworthiness. Seen with such objectivity, Peter can become a valid and awe-inspiring model for all selfless acts of faith and love in the Church. This, then, is the wondrous grace that is understood by none yet challenges everyone to respond to it.

1. Self-Transcendence into the Miracle

The Church, as the Body, Bride, fullness of the *mysterium* of Christ, is both "*mysterium* and miracle",[1] not only in her invisibility but also in her visible reality, because the free gift of God's love "poured into men's hearts" (Rom 5:5) unites all in love. Indeed, God's love resulted precisely in the visibility of Jesus' historical gift of himself "as a ransom for many" (Mk 10:45), and it summons the "many" to respond with a grateful and visible love. The Christian's decision to live his life as a grateful response to God's gift of love includes the will to transcend self and become united with God's unsurpassable love in Christ, which is always given to us freely in advance; and this concrete unity is the Eucharist and the Holy Spirit who breathes as he will in it. And to make sure that the Eucharist and the Spirit always have the quality of gift, which no one can acquire and turn into a possession, the concrete shape of the Church is there, both as a guardian and dispenser of the *mysterium* and as a community which antedates each individual. Henri de Lubac has again and again pointed out the mutual inclusiveness of Church and Eucharist (which is as such the fullness of the incarnate Word): "The Eucharist begets the Church, and the Church begets the Eucharist."[2] And exactly *because* the Church-Eucharist is provided and offered to us by God, it is

[1] No one treated this better or more fully than Charles Journet, "L'Église comme mystère et comme miracle" in his as yet not fully explored ecclesiology *L'Église du Verbe incarné* [The Church of the Word incarnate], vol. 2 (Paris: Desclée de Brouwer, 1951): 1193–228. The same theme is more briefly touched on in A. D. Sertillanges, *Le Miracle de l'Église. L'Éternité dans le temps* (Paris: Spes, 1933), to which Ferdinand Ulrich refers again and again, particularly in *Atheismus und Menschwerdung* in the chapters "Die Kirche als personale Gestalt der befreiten Endlichkeit" and "Die Kirche in der atheistischen Todesdialektik von Herr und Knecht und ihre Freiheit als Dank" (Einsiedeln: Johannesverlag, 1966).

[2] Henri de Lubac, *Die Kirche, eine Betrachtung* [The splendor of the Church], 2d ed. (Einsiedeln: Johannesverlag, 1968), 127–42.

288

impossible to appropriate it for oneself alone. One can partake of it only by becoming a participant in giving and receiving. The first aspect, the unity of a love which offers itself, is miraculously beyond our control, but so is the second aspect, the unity of love in the Church which springs from the self-renunciation of those who receive it. This, and this alone, is the true unity of the Church. Any other unity attributed to her—organizational unity, for instance—is only one aspect, however essential it may be to the whole.

This is important because it renders untenable today's popular opposition between "life" and "structure" (or "institution"). Just as Christ's humanity was not merely a "structure" (or, as the Scholastics began to say, the "instrumentality") through which he lived his divinity, so ministerial office in the life of the Church cannot be regarded as a "structure" (or "institution") separate from the creativity of love (or the "charisms"). Both stand or fall together. Protestants may try to make a distinction of this kind, and we cannot blame Friedrich Heiler, who (like many others) saw the "official" side of the Catholic Church as the principal factor in her departure—or at least her isolation—from the original bond of love of "primitive Church autonomy". Using this distinction, his intention was ruthlessly to expose "the vulnerable and somber aspects of the visible Church institutions" so that "the divine interior of the Church may shine forth all the more brightly . . . the *ecclesia spiritualis,* freed from all earthly shackles."[3] Though Y. Congar is naturally less radical, it is more disturbing to hear him make a fundamental distinction between "structure", even "skeleton"[4] (the bones mentioned by Ezekiel, which wait for the coming Spirit), and "life", whereby he reduces the aspect

---

[3] Friedrich Heiler, *Altkirchliche Autonomie und päpstlicher Zentralismus* (Munich: Reinhardt, 1941), chap. 7.

[4] Yves Congar, *Vraie et fausse réforme dans l'Église* (Paris: Cerf, 1950), 96.

of office to a purely "instrumental" function.[5] Such a distinction can be made only at a superficial level. Looking deeper, one can see the living organism, nailed to the hard wood of the so-called institution, as the very proof of divine love; at this point there can be no distinction between the one transfixed and the wood to which he is nailed. That is why Pope Clement saw the revolt of the Corinthians against the "institution" of their day as a revolt against their own living body: "Do we not have one God and one Christ and one Spirit of grace, a Spirit that has poured out upon us? And is there not one calling in Christ? Why do we tear apart and disjoin the members of Christ and revolt against our own body and go to such extremes of madness as to forget that we are mutually dependent members?"[6] The Corinthian protest was already an attempt to manipulate unity as if it were their own achievement, instead of accepting it as a gift from the triune God. Acceptance of unity as a gift does not imply a demeaning passivity, which man would be inclined to replace with his own constructive activity; rather, it demands from man the highest effort of cooperative consent, namely, *doing* precisely what has been *given* him in faith, *performing* what he has *become* (i.e., "Church") in active response to the incarnate Word.

These thoughts lead us back again to Mary and the constellation around Christ within which the Petrine constitutes one element. As such a constitutive element it becomes much more understandable, being embedded with its own particular character in the constellation of the other elements, each of which has to transcend itself to reach a real as well as symbolic unity and so become one of the pillars of the Church's unity. We have already gone into this; yet it might be useful

[5] Yves Congar, *Jalons pour une théologie du laïcat* [Lay people in the Church] (Paris: Cerf, 1953), passim, especially 148ff. In *Ministères et communion ecclésiale* (Paris: Cerf, 1971), Congar rightly maintains that even charisma needs structure.

[6] Clement of Rome, *Epistle to the Corinthians,* 46, 6–7, in *Ancient Christian Writers,* vol. 1 (New York: Newman Press, 1976): 38.

to review the different elements of the constellation and their interaction. We will limit ourselves to four: Mary, the Mother; Peter, who exemplifies office within (and with) the group of the Twelve, of which the two others are also prominent members; John, the link between Mary and Peter; and Paul—added to the Twelve and mentioned explicitly as cofounder of the Roman Church—whose work of concrete realization and theological interpretation was decisive.

Unquestionably, Mary, as Mother, has the precedence that belongs to the all-embracing element. She bore and reared Jesus, and she maintains the same maternal relationship to his work in all its aspects. But she does this self-effacingly, humbly making room for others; she decides nothing, commands nothing, she is a "handmaid", hoping that others will understand her attitude: "Do whatever he tells you" (Jn 2:5). She is womb and earth, from whom the divine seed can draw whatever it needs. In her humble submission she is the fruitfulness of perfect poverty. "But the poverty of the Church does not belong to her herself. She is humble adoration of the Father's glory resplendent on the face of Jesus. She is the pledge of God's surpassing love that has handed itself over totally to her, because she has placed no obstacle (in the form of a self-subsistent holding-on to herself in her own strength) in the way of the divine self-communication which comes by faith." Neither does she use adoration to keep the ever-greater God in his greatness and at arm's length, with that false humility which claims that it cannot find room enough for him; nor does she make herself the abyss that "swallows and consumes this God (who wishes to become man) in his alter ego". She lets the Son be and do as he wills, namely, as a human being from out of her. Thus, as the fruitful "Mother, she remains a virgin maid, since she can possess the gift only if she does not keep it for herself but uses it for the service of many (and she is one of the many), revealing the glory of God and witnessing to Being as Love making itself finite".[7] Nothing can be more open,

[7] Ulrich, *Atheismus,* 66–69.

more all-encompassing, more Catholic, than this. All other modes of enabling are necessarily included in hers.

Peter is the office: untiring activity of the whole person purely for the name and the intentions of the Lord, who needs someone, anyone, through whom his authority—the Father's authority in the Son and the self-effacement of the Son's authority so as to reveal that of the Father—can become concretely manifest. Thus there is a distinctively Petrine effacement of personality in the office. We can discern, as Schiller said,

> the spirit that animated the Roman court and the unshakable firmness of the principles which every pope felt himself compelled to follow, irrespective of any personal consideration. Emperors and kings, enlightened statesmen and hardened warriors were seen, under the pressure of circumstances, to sacrifice rights, betray their principles and yield to necessity. Such things rarely or never happened to a pope.... However different the popes have been in temperament, ideas and ability, their policies have been constant, consistent and unchanging. Their ability, their temperament, their ideas did not seem to enter into their office; one might say that their personalities became dissolved in their station, and passion was extinguished beneath the Triple Crown. Although the chain of succession to the throne was broken by the death of each pope and had to be freshly established with each new pope, and though no throne in the world changed its occupant as frequently and was occupied or vacated amid such turmoil, yet this was the only throne in Christendom that never seemed to change its ruler, for only the popes died: the spirit that animated them was immortal.[8]

Thus, perhaps (and this is Joseph Bernhart's main thesis in his book on the papacy) it is often almost a matter of indifference what a pope says or does not say, what he does or does not do, as long as he occupies

---

[8] Friedrich Schiller, *Universalhistorische Übersicht der merkwürdigen StaatsBegebenheiten zu den Zeiten Kaiser Friedrichs I, Werke,* vol. 7 (Leipzig: Inselverlag, n.d.): 431.

and holds his post, representing the *centrum unitatis* as Christ meant it to be. Even in times of failure, the papacy remained "a power without doing anything itself, simply by being there; it had an effect without even trying. The very idea it represented, its historical entity, was sufficient to make the world venerate anew this symbol of being-in-becoming, this spirit of 'ancient truth' above the turbulent waters of temporal events."[9]

> It was not the gifts and assistance which the Pope [Benedict XV], lauded and despised, distributed to all sides, not the peace settlement of 1917, which was doomed to fail due to German and foreign sabotage, nor the political expertise of the curia, which was able to preserve on Italian soil a bond of the highest shared interests even with the enemies of Italy; rather it was the mere presence of a spirit hovering above the face of the waters which has renewed the idea of the papacy in the depths of the modern consciousness. But in these same depths dwell the ancient powers of contradiction, whose plans, whether written or not, include the assault on the throne of the world, whether sooner or later.[10]

The Rock, which totally assimilates its faceless office-bearer, stands squarely confronting the "gates of hell". The Rock still stands, though each generation declares that the Church is dead. Yet she is still there as if by a miracle, or rather *as* a miracle, not merely as an idea but as an unconquerable reality. That is Peter's way of disappearing.

Peter disappears, having examined the facts of the faith and found them to warrant belief, yielding his place to *John,* who had given him precedence but now enters the tomb: " . . . and he saw and believed" (Jn 20:8). The Beloved Disciple (whose seeing and believing were made possible by Peter's official activity) has, in turn, his own style of vanishing, merging himself and his personal love into Peter (20:15), "remaining" in precisely that form, as a tree, harvested and bare.

[9] Joseph Bernhart, *Der Vatikan als Weltmacht* (Munich: List, 1949), 306.
[10] Ibid., 333.

Other, less worthy colleagues have taken his place (3 Jn 9), but he is "transported" to another place from where he can become the direct voice of the Lord to his Church: "The words of the first and the last, who died and came to life. I know your tribulation and your poverty (but you are rich)" (Rev 2:8–9). Here too the truth of the all-encompassing feminine dimension is revealed to him (Rev 12:1–17), about which Peter and Paul knew but little. The Church is entrusted to him as a feminine reality, as a loving community. The words of his letters, beneath their pedagogical surface, address the Church's inner-most heart, the heart that "knows all things", that is beyond all changeable personal decisions (because it knows that God is greater than our hearts, for he knows everything: 1 Jn 3:20). He speaks of mysteries that seem paradoxical to the uninitiated but which the Church understands in her heart. He is the saint who, because he loves, can do both things: he can manifest the one Lord in his surpassing love, initiating his Church into this love by giving one hand to Mary and the other to Peter, and then, vanishing, he clasps their two hands together. "Between his body and the creation of heaven there is merely a thin partition", says Mechthild of Magdeburg.[11]

Paul, the untimely birth (1 Cor 15:8), the most dynamic apostle, who finds it most difficult to vanish, appears last to "complete what is lacking" (Col 1:24). He too is included in the Marian embrace;[12] he cannot be interpreted as its antithesis under the heading of *simul justus et peccator.* He is also determined by the Petrine factor that, as we have shown, appears nowhere as clearly as in the letters to the Corinthians and in the way these charismatics were governed. (The

[11] Mechtild of Magdeburg, *Das fliessende Licht der Gottheit* [The flowing light of the Godhead], 4, 23, in *Menschen der Kirche,* new series 3 (1955), 205.

[12] His alleged misogynic tendency might be a radical misunderstanding of the text. Cf. A. Feuillet, "Le Signe de puissance sur la tête de la femme, 1 Cor 11:10", in *Nouvelle révue théologique* 95 (November 1973): 945–54.

first papal letter of Clement takes its example and its courage from Paul's letters.) And he is also determined by the Johannine: beyond office and charisma there is this "higher gift" of love (1 Cor 12:31), without which knowledge only inflates and all theology is merely "a noisy gong or a clanging cymbal" (1 Cor 13:1). In the visible Church he is the one who has to master and reconcile everything, even the contradictory (cf. his being both Jew and Gentile at the same time), combining office and the life of discipleship—for he lives according to the evangelical counsels—cultivating profound *gnosis* among those who are perfect and then "perfectly" laying it aside in order to know nothing but the Cross. He has to demonstrate personally all the different ways of being a Christian and thus become a model to be imitated, like an object on display. From whatever point of view one looks at him, he embodies the Catholic unity in the midst of diversity. And now he, so prominent, has to eliminate himself; eliminate himself as a person, not as the *typos* of the community, as the imitator of Christ, to whom people must look to learn what Catholic universality is (1 Cor 11:1). But precisely by making himself into an objective, impersonal model, he is assimilated, in his own way, to Petrine objectivity. There can be no faction of Paul, of Peter, of Christ, because Christ is indivisible, and Paul was not crucified for the community (1 Cor 1:12–13). His having to be a model is the Pauline "eccentricity", the apostle's "foolishness" because of the foolishness of the community, which, in its immaturity, could be misled and therefore needed these otherwise superfluous extrapolations (2 Cor 11–12). Paul's detachment is such that he can bring his personality into play when required.

> He plays upon himself, because he is absolutely an instrument. He knows neither humility nor pride, only necessity. For him, conversion means irrevocable commitment. . . . He has no need to wrestle, he is in possession of a truth that transcends him so vastly that he becomes a mere instrument on which he plays. For it is not only for Christ that he became an instrument but also for himself. He knows

what a Christian is: sinful and mortal; he cannot portray himself as a Christian, only the Master's instrument.[13]

The miracle of God's love poured out upon this world is fourfold. This love, manifested in Jesus Christ and the Spirit he bestows, miraculously creates the vessel to receive him, inspiring the Yes, the faith, the joyous obedience that leads to the freedom of love and requires the limited, egoistic self to be shed. Even this answer, the ability to say Yes to eternal love, is experienced by the believer as the grace of God, and the Church's origin lies in this encounter between grace given and grace received. The same originating principle underlies the four ways in which the Church is embodied and made visible, and it also establishes the plurality of missions which correspond to the divine fullness bestowed and which make it impossible to describe the Church's unity in abstract and exhaustive terms. Because the particular mission proceeds from its origin in God and is targeted on the center of the Church, its particularity does not limit universality. Just as the universal Church is not the essence of the individual churches, able to prescind from their concrete differences,[14] so the various ways of transcending self to become part of the miracle of the Church cannot be reduced to a single approach (though the Marian remains all-embracing), because each in its particular way opens a unique way into catholicity.

2. Faith and Experience

The fourfold way of which we spoke in the preceding section, one of which is the Petrine office (shared by John and Paul, as apostles and archetypes of the bishops), is also the way for all communities and all

---

[13] Adrienne von Speyr, *Lumina und Neue Lumina* (Einsiedeln: Johannesverlag, 1974), 84–85.

[14] Louis Bouyer, *L'Église de Dieu* (Paris: Cerf, 1970), 340–41.

individual Christians in the *Catholica*. We are digressing here from our primary topic of the papacy because of the present situation in the Church today. There is a general unease to the effect that God seems far removed from the secularized world—he even seems to be dead—and that the hominized environment no longer reveals the direct imprint of God, the eternal Creator, as nature does. It speaks only of its temporal creator. Even in the Church the person who thirsts for religious experience only finds the handiwork of men, the structural framework of a cold, sociological institution. Where—the cry is heard everywhere—where can God be experienced? For man needs at least a basic experience if he is to risk the leap of faith. Thus Mary was addressed by the angel before responding with her *fiat;* the Twelve were called and sent out by the Master whom they knew; Paul was overwhelmed and taken possession of by the glorified Christ in Damascus. But whom do we encounter, that he might unequivocally call and send us?

It seems that the most divergent trends in the Church today can be traced to the common denominator of "experience". Celebrating the Eucharist in the small "core community", people gain an insight into how the first Christians, in their house Eucharists, might have experienced the Church, communion in Christ and in the Holy Spirit. The many, highly differentiated Pentecostal movements promise a direct experience of the Church's charismatic nature: people are taken back to the origins, to the Day of Pentecost itself, when all those assembled together felt the Spirit descending on their heads in tongues of fire, followed by the miracle of speaking in tongues and the unforeseen conversion of many. In actively helping to alleviate the misery of their fellow human beings, in aiding their development and in attempting to storm the walls of an unjust economic order (and the reflection of this can be seen within the Catholic Church), people experience at an existential level what it means to give oneself in faith. The practice of oriental meditation—a totally different road—is an attempt to gain entrance into the paradise of the mystics who claim to have experienced God. These are all different ways of trying to achieve the experience of God that has been postulated as a must before one can commit oneself to the Church—or even to faith at all.

It is true: "How are men to call upon him in whom they have not believed? And how are they to believe in him of whom they have never heard? And how are they to hear without a preacher?" (Rom 10:14f). But what does it mean to preach and be preached to? Paul goes on, "And how can men preach unless they are sent?" And "to be sent", as Paul understands it, means to be given Christ's commission, a commission that changes the whole life of the one "sent" into a testimony, making it a "light to the world", "salt of the earth", a "city set on a hill". But where does one meet such a person? Having lost hope of finding him, many turn to the self-help methods of those who seek to meet God outside the *Catholica*. Instead of receiving the experience as a gift, they reach for it, produce it, make it happen. Hence, it is not surprising that those who see only a distorted picture of the *Catholica* as "establishment" will employ the same methods within her in an attempt to reform her, to bring her back to her own truth. There is too little time left: it is impossible simply to forbid such self-defense measures or to seek to set up ecclesiastical laws in their place.

However, the discernment of spirits is not as difficult here as it would seem on first impression. Even those who seek direct religious experience almost always do so in order to escape from their closed, impoverished and secularized selves, which are not ultimately loved or affirmed by anyone. This search for the certainty of love that alone can give meaning to life is in fact a search for the very heart of the miracle of the Church, where God's absolute love has given itself and is also received by human beings. The reality of "Church" always exists first of all as a community, as a concrete assembly of those who have believed in this love and have been open to receive it in baptism, word, Eucharist and brotherly love. But at this point there seems to be a closed circle of faith and experience that cannot be penetrated from the outside. In the early Church, the candidate for baptism had to go through a catechumenate, in the course of which he learned to comprehend and assimilate the articles of faith, so as to receive in baptism proper the "illuminating" faith experience that initiated him simultaneously into the reality of Christian brotherhood and its miraculous premise: being filled with the grace of Christ, the Holy Spirit. This simple timing of events is bound to seem somewhat artificial to us: the catechumen is already growing in the experience of faith, and the baptized person can grow further in experience, but he can never outgrow faith.[15]

Essentially, therefore, there is a simultaneous growth and integration of faith and experience, but in such a way that, while faith becomes experience by being lived, whatever is experienced in the Christian life acquires a faith-quality.

From the Catholic point of view it cannot be otherwise. Experience, psychologically, is always my own, evaluated by me, pertaining to me. Faith, by contrast, goes beyond me in that I have been dispossessed of my self (and this is always a prior objective reality) by the fact of Christ: "None of us lives to himself, and none of us dies to himself" (Rom 14:7), because "one has died for all; therefore all have died" (2 Cor 5:14). This fact is universal, and thus the faith which affirms it expands into universality (in the fundamental model of the Marian *fiat,* in the truth of the first *Our Father* petitions). Consequently it must exceed all reflex experience and be ready to renounce it, to make way for a deeper self-dispossession, an even wider expansion.

---

[15] Compare the ongoing dialectic of faith and experience even in those Fathers most inclined to gnosis (Clement of Alexandria, Origen) and to experience, *peira* (the homilies of Macarius, Diadochus of Photice, Maximus Confessor). Cf. my "Mystérion d'Origène" in *Révue des sciences religieuses* (1936), 513–62; (1937), 38–64, and *Kosmische Liturgie,* 2d ed. (Einsiedeln: Johannesverlag, 1961), as well as *Herrlichkeit* [The Glory of the Lord], vol. 1 (Einsiedeln: Johannesverlag, 1961): 211–410. Also André Léonard's article, "Expérience spirituelle", *Dictionnaire de spiritualité,* vol. 4., pt. 2 (1961), bibliography.

No man is by nature able to measure the miracle of Catholic unity; he must let it overwhelm him. In order to undergo the basic faith experience, he must allow himself to be painfully deprived of his subjective value system. And if he honestly tries to live selfless Christian love, *renouncing* subjective satisfaction, he will have the crucial *experience* of being able to be expanded by faith and become Catholic. He will be schooled in what it means to live daily in Christ's Cross and in the resurrection to come. In this ever-deeper self-emptying he will feel the chains of egoism drop from him and, like Peter, who found the strong prison doors opening of their own accord, he will be able to say, *"nunc scio vere"* (Acts 12:11).

The models of faith experience in the Church that we have described in the foregoing chapter cannot be surpassed. It is quite out of the question to pursue this experience for its own sake or in order to draw conclusions from it for the life of faith. It is not *because* I have experienced certain psychological upheavals in some Pentecostal church that I now decide to live the Christian faith more fully. Insofar as they are psychological, the religious experiences we have described do not in themselves contain the fundamental law of Christ's Cross and cannot therefore communicate it—except by way of misinterpretation. This is why Paul made light of the "wisdom" of the Corinthians, saturated with pentecostal "experiences", and preached to them nothing but the "naked Cross" that should not be "emptied of its power", which to the outsider seems "folly" but to the believer is "the power of God". And when he continues, "I will destroy the wisdom of the wise, and the cleverness of the clever I will thwart", he is not referring to rational theology (in Corinth there were not many "wise according to worldly standards") but rather to pentecostal states (1 Cor 1:17–19). Be it noted that he did not forbid speaking in tongues; but "he who speaks in a tongue edifies himself" (1 Cor 14:4). More generally, the person who is seeking experience is building his own house and not that of the Church. The decisive factor is *agape,* in the sense and in the measure of Christ and *his* Church.

Just as the Church is only truly concrete in the local church or community, she is only really herself through ever more radical self-transcendence into the miracle of the *Catholica,* the breadth and depth of which "the heart of man" has not "conceived". But paradoxically enough, the Catholic *can* and *must* really "experience" something of this "unsurpassable greatness" of the whole Church. The Letter to the Ephesians invites us "to know the love of Christ which surpasses knowledge" (Eph 3:19). We too are called—it is the same expressed in modern terms—to experience the love of Christ and, in him, the love of the triune God that is beyond all experience. This happens quite naturally in a genuinely Christian life; it is superfluous to torment ourselves here with dialectical cross-relations. There is a certain Catholic *spirit* that is given as a gift to those who let go in faith and do not seek intellectually to recapture what they have thus left behind.[16]

3. The Catholic "And"

This refers to those who are determined to hold fast to themselves and their own views, even in a relativized form. They have never learned to fly; they build their church on their own rock and shape their lives according to their own views and principles. Hence, without admitting it, they claim an infallibility that is continually making definitions,

---

[16] In regard to this reflection about "letting go", i.e., the personal security which faith brings, cf. the important work of Paul Hacker, *Das Ich im Glauben bei Martin Luther* (Graz: Styria, 1966). The inevitable result of this is the division of faith and love (of neighbor)—also blamed by Kierkegaard in Luther. It is significant that the Church particularly wished to condemn the principle of "experience" in Modernism: "Finis quem (apologeta modernista) sibi assequendum praestituit, hic est: hominem fidei adhuc expertem eo adducere, ut eam in catholica religione *experientiam* assequatur, quae ex modernistarum scitis *unicum fidei* est firmamentum", Denzinger-Schönmetzer, *Enchiridion Symbolorum,* 3500.

while the pope only defines matters in exceptional cases and for the protection and good of the whole Church. Thus they "know" on the basis of their infallible principles that the pope is either a rigid, old-fashioned traditionalist or secretly a Modernist and perhaps even a freemason.

The dogmatism of those who cannot let go of their own selves is the opposite of the courage of those who opt for the catholicity of truth, focusing their existence on the concrete Christ, the *Christus totus,* as Augustine calls him. They recognize how hopelessly incomplete their intellectual horizon is and acknowledge that it needs supplementing. Each individual is only one member of the Mystical Body, and even if he were the eye, he would need the functioning of the other members in order to be himself. There are Catholics who have described Ephesians' dictum, that the Church is the fullness of Christ and thus the fullness of all truth, as arrogance vis-à-vis other religions and world views. But have they sufficiently reflected on what Church history shows us, namely, that every heresy condemned by the Church is a part claiming to be the whole? We see this even in Irenaeus' struggle with the gnostics, who separated nature from grace, the Old Covenant from the New, the spirit from the body, and ended up with a Jesus who had no Father, who did not redeem the world and thus left them in their despair. Whenever anything had to be defined, it was a case of protecting the whole against the absolute claims of a part; the whole, which can only be believed and adored, against the part which is allegedly understood, comprehended, mastered. Very often this is done in the sincere belief that it is a service rendered to God. The *soli* of the Reformation—*sola fide, sola scriptura, sola gratia, soli Deo gloria*—claim to defend God's omnipotence against intended infringements of his sphere by his creatures. But if one looks closer, they are forbidding God to be anything other than himself (*man,* for instance, if he should so wish), to be anywhere else but in heaven, forbidding him to shape his creature—his *plasma,* Irenaeus says—in such a way that it can really respond to him (by means of the living spirit breathed into it and the divine word entrusted to it). It is as if God would defile himself were he to enter into marital union with the "other"—which in any case comes from him. Karl Barth cannot abide the "Catholic 'And' ": "Wherever it puts forth shoots, it comes from a single root. Anyone who says 'faith and works', 'nature and grace', 'reason and revelation', if he is consistent, must go on to say 'Scripture and tradition'. It . . . is only an indication, *one* indication, of the fact that the majesty of God in his dealings with men has already been relativized."[17] Should not one rather say that this *"And"* is the expression of the creature's acknowledgment of God's sovereignty to be himself even outside of himself?—an acknowledgment that he, the Creator who grants freedom, is also free to be the Redeemer, "through whom, with whom and in whom" we can praise the Father in the Holy Spirit? From time to time the Catholic may indeed need a warning, lest he become lukewarm or presumptuous; but he has enough saints in his Church to inspire him with a genuine sense of God's divinity.

But the saints are never the kind of killjoy spinster aunts who go in for faultfinding and lack all sense of humor. (Nor should the Karl Barth who so loved and understood Mozart be regarded as such.) For humor is a mysterious but unmistakable charism inseparable from Catholic faith, and neither the "progressives" nor the "integralists" seem to possess it—the latter even less than the former. Both of these tend to be faultfinders, malicious satirists, grumblers, carping critics, full of bitter scorn, know-it-alls who think they have the monopoly of infallible judgment; they are self-legitimizing prophets—in short, fanatics. (The word comes from *fanum,* "holy place", i.e., it denotes guardians of the temple threshold, transported into frenzy by the Divinity.) They are ill-humored, as was Jansenism in toto, which spread like a blight, for centuries, over the spiritual life of France. (Perhaps Claudel and Bernanos were the first to be completely free

[17] Karl Barth, *Die kirchliche Dogmatik* [Church Dogmatics], vol. 1, pt. 2, 619–20.

from it.) And naturally they are critics before all else. Having thoroughly criticized the pure, the practical and the judging reason, there is nothing left of reason but criticism itself, the real "thing-in-itself" that grinds up everything that comes between its millstones—all thinking about God, the language in which it is expressed, every form of proclaiming the message (Fichte began his career with an "attempt at a critique of all revelation"), and every recognizable feature of the Church. Of course, "critical Catholicism", in the radical way in which it sees itself, is a contradiction in terms. Whatever is, should not be: or it should be otherwise; "changing the world"—that is the secret password of these humorless hard-liners. They are rigid, while the Catholic is pliable, flexible, yielding, because the latter's firmness is not based on himself and his own opinion but on God, who is the "ever-greater". They are either fanatically "come of age" (the progressives) or fanatically immature (the integralists who clamor for the tangible exercise of papal authority and elevate to the status of dogma things that are not, such as Communion on the tongue and all kinds of apparitions of the Mother of God, etc.). Just as the fanatics who insisted on the *soli* of the Reformation were condemned, by an iron law of the philosophy of history, to bring about the very opposite of what they intended and thus fall prey to the schizophrenia of dialectics, so today the elements on the fringe of Catholicism, progressivism and integralism, are forever metamorphosing into each other, dialectically provoking each other into existence.

True enough, not everyone in the Catholic Church is what he should be: holy. And not all possess the balance that we have indicated by the reference to humor. Somehow it bespeaks a sense of humor when the Catholic Church, which, since the time of the Church Fathers, through High Scholasticism and modern humanism, was always inclined to absorb and integrate the heritage of antiquity and even of all non-Christian religions, responds to the Reformation with the *putti* of the Bavarian Baroque. And decidedly humorous is the way Chesterton, the defender of "nonsense, humility, penny

304

dreadfuls and other despised things", answers the bestial seriousness and despairing optimism of modern world views—which are united in their opposition to Rome—saying that only the Catholic form guarantees the miraculous quality of being, the freedom, the sense of being a child, of adventure, the resilient, energizing paradox of existence:

> A bird is active, because a bird is soft. A stone is helpless, because a stone is hard. A stone must by its own nature go downwards, because hardness is weakness. The bird can of its nature go upwards, because fragility is force. In perfect force there is a kind of frivolity, an airiness that can maintain itself in the air.... Angels can fly because they take themselves lightly. This has always been the instinct of Christendom.... Pride is the downward drag of all things into an easy solemnity. One "settles down" into a sort of selfish seriousness; but one has to rise to a gay self-forgetfulness. A man "falls" into a brown study; he reaches up at a blue sky. Seriousness is not a virtue.... It is really a natural trend or lapse into taking one's self gravely, because it is the easiest thing to do. It is much easier to write a good *Times* leading article than a good joke in *Punch*. For solemnity flows out of men naturally; but laughter is a leap. It is easy to be heavy: hard to be light. Satan fell by the force of gravity.[18]

"Looking down on things [from Zarathustra's mountains] may be a delightful experience, but there is nothing, from a mountain to a cabbage, that is really *seen* when it is seen from a balloon." " ... at the moment when we attempt to appreciate things as they should be appreciated.... We do actually go through a process of mental

---

[18] G. K. Chesterton, *Orthodoxy*, The Collected Works, vol. 1 (San Francisco: Ignatius Press, 1986), 325–26.

asceticism, a castration of the entire being, when we wish to feel the abounding good in all things."[19]

The book on the humor of the saints has yet to be written. Goethe has given us a short excerpt of it in his *Philipp Neri, der humoristische Heilige* (the humorous saint), particularly in the latter's far-from-reverential exchange of notes with Clement VIII. But what merriment do we find as early as Irenaeus, when he pricks the shimmering bubbles of the gnostic world systems! And in Clement of Alexandria, too, when he juggles with these systems like a circus artist. What a boyish spirit of adventure in Bonaventure's "Chart for the soul's journey to God"! What flashes of humor (for which one seeks in vain in the solemn Reformers) in Ignatius Loyola and Teresa of Avila! And, nearer to us in time, what charming mischief in little Thérèse, to say nothing of Claudel's homely laughter (through tears of passion). What a lighthearted *grandezza* in Péguy as he opens his Christian soul to all Jewish and Gentile values, only to lay down all these treasures, smilingly, at the crib (in *Ève*); what a loving forbearance did Madeleine Delbrêl have for the shortcomings of Christians (whom she wished were burning torches). And I take the liberty, with a good conscience, of appropriating for the *Catholica* the humor of C. S. Lewis (whose tales are more beautiful than Brentano's) and Ljeskov, for whom life with all its terrors remained a single paradoxical miracle. Then there is Kierkegaard, who looks wistfully beyond the limits of his melancholy religion toward the Catholic paradise where, in spite of all its seriousness, one may be "a little mischievous", where "all that is childlike recurs in a heightened form, as a mature naiveté, simplicity, wonder, humor".[20]

[19] G. K. Chesterton, "A Defense of Humility", in *The Defendant* (London: R. Brimley Johnson), pp. 101–2.

[20] Søren Kierkegaard, *Die Tagebücher* [The Journals of Søren Kierkegaard], ed. Theodor Haecker, vol. 2 (Munich: n.p., 1922); 88; likewise Erik Peterson, "Kierkegaard und der Protestantismus", in *Marginalien zur Theologie* (Munich: Kösel-Verlag, 1956), 17–18; Erich Przywara, *Das Geheimnis Kierkegaards* (Munich and Berlin: R. Oldenbourg, 1929), 8off., 169ff.

Péguy's final categories (in the *Note Conjointe*) are the *"morale souple"* and the *"morale raide"*: the pliant, flexible attitude to life versus the rigid attitude that we also find among Christians. For him, flexibility has nothing to do with laxity: on the contrary, it places greater demands on man and on his love than any comfortable rigidity.

It would be useful if at this point we could make a survey of the papacy in a world context: papacy and diplomacy, papacy and humanism (from Damasus through Gregory I to Gregory XVI, up to the writings of Paul VI), a papacy that is easygoing in nonessentials but unyielding concerning the slightest deviation, the merest jot (*homoousios* instead of *homoiousios*) that represents the tip of a hidden iceberg on which the bark of the whole Church would smash to pieces. Most of the time all that is needed is the occasional light touch of the helmsman's hand. Even if not all popes have lived up to this ethos that is inherent in their calling—particularly when the office of Peter was overshadowed by state power—one may still say that it belongs to the very concept and the particular ethos of their mission.

The Crucial Test

1. *The Apostolic Foursome*

We have spoken of the theologically relevant human "constellation" of persons around Jesus Christ, and we have described them in their relationship to Christ as "real symbols" of the Church. This was done to present Peter's position, not as the top of the Church's pyramid — where only Jesus Christ stands — but as that of one particular service (albeit a distinguished one) among others. In this description, however, the lines run mainly in a vertical direction, from each individual person to the Head of the Church. In him they meet and take their places relative to each other.

But after the time of Jesus comes the era of the Church, when the disciples no longer have the Lord beside them but, as the ascended Lord, above them and his Spirit within them; this is the time when they must learn to be the Church of Christ together. In the Acts of the Apostles the constellation changes: the women retreat into the interior of the Church — the Lord's first Easter appearance is now said to be that to Peter, not that to Magdalen (1 Cor 15:5). Two verses later we read, "Then he appeared to James" (1 Cor 15:7), the brother of the Lord who will become the bishop of the primitive Jerusalem community and who therefore must be a special witness not only to the living Jesus but to the resurrected Christ. It is James who seems to have taken Peter's place after the latter leaves Jerusalem (Acts 12:17), and it is he who, in the Council of the Apostles, puts forward the decisive motion of reconciliation between Jewish and Gentile Christians (Acts 15:13–21). With his followers, James becomes a challenge to Paul in that, in opposition to this convert, he represents continuity between the Old and New Covenants, tradition, the legitimacy of the letter of the law as against the mere spirit, yet in harmony with the incarnate Spirit. His episcopate, which he holds as a blood relative of Jesus and which will pass after his martyrdom to another of the Lord's blood relatives, Simon (cf. Mk 6:3), is a kind of caliphate that only comes to an end (in favor of Rome's leadership) with the destruction of Jerusalem. James, who mediated in the most difficult dilemma the Church ever faced—the reconciliation between Jews and Gentiles, between the People of God and "those who are not a nation" (Rom 10:19), between those who are "under the law" and those "outside the law" (1 Cor 9:20–21)—was nevertheless a party man. The concessions James made and which were approved by all the apostles did not please "certain men" around him (Gal 2:12). They pressed for the full performance of all the traditional Jewish customs. It is these traditionalist upholders of the letter of the law whom Paul attacks—Paul, who became a Christian by pure grace, without works and merits, and relentlessly broke with his past—with hard and bitter words about these "false apostles" and "deceitful workmen" (2 Cor 11:13), behind whom tower the "superlative apostles" (2 Cor 11:5; 12:11), James, Peter and John, "pillars" (Gal 2:9) to whom Paul feels "not at all inferior". Four, and only four, dominate the field of force of the developing Church: the exigencies and vicissitudes of their mission will determine, once and for all, the Church's shape and vitality.

Let us try to appreciate, albeit in a necessarily simplified form, the cruciform relation and interaction of these four:

Before examining these tensions, however, we have to remember that what we are talking about are missions within the *Catholica*, within the unity of the Body of Christ and within the all-embracing ambit of the motherly, Marian consent, which is tacitly presupposed. Thus the individual missions participate in the whole; and in participating in the whole, they are involved in each other. James will not put forward

James: tradition, law

Peter:
pastoral office

John:
the love which
"abides"

Paul: freedom in the Holy Spirit

any other law but the "perfect law of liberty" (James 1:25), nor will he be any less firm than Paul in opposing contentiousness (James 4:1). Paul cannot proclaim any freedom that does not express itself in the "law of Christ" (Gal 6:2; cf. Rom 8:2). He expects the Gentiles to accept the faith of Abraham and to be acquainted with the Old Testament prototypes (1 Cor 10:11) and exercises a veritably "Petrine" control in the communities, while constantly holding up to them the ideal of Johannine love. As we know, Peter was only permitted to take office on the basis of his (Johannine) love, and the letters attributed to him clearly show a process of osmosis between his understanding of the gospel and that of the other three. John, finally, is also an apostle, and even in later years can sound a "Petrine" note when it is a question of guarding or restoring order in a local church. All their missions are clearly defined, but, as we have seen, they are not hermetically sealed off from each other.

Once again simplifying and abbreviating much of the richness of the various aspects, one can apportion the four aspects of the Church which they represent to the celebrated fourfold senses of Scripture which provided the basic structure for exegesis in the Church for more than a millennium[1]—a structure which even persists (in a shrunken form) in modern (Bultmannian) exegesis:

---

[1] Henri de Lubac, "Sur un vieux distique. La doctrine du 'quadruple sens' (de l'Écriture)", in *Mélanges Cavallera* (Toulouse, 1948); idem, "Sens spirituel", in *Révue des sciences religieuses* (1949), 542–76, developed in *Histoire et Esprit. L'Intélligence de l'Écriture d'après Origène* (Paris: Aubier, 1950), and in *Les Quatre sens de l'Écriture,* 4 vols. (Paris: Aubier, 1959–1964).

The historical sense (historical Jesus)

The tropological sense   ┼   The anagogical sense
(the ethical sense in   (looking toward an
Church discipline)   eternity already present)

The "allegorical," pneumatic sense (the Christ of faith)

Here the complementarity of the missions and of their particular aspects becomes fully evident. The gospel is a single unity, the living reality of Jesus Christ, who genuinely had to live and die so that, as the Risen One, he could bestow the gift of his Spirit and interpret the whole of (Old and New Testament) history in a spiritual manner (Lk 24:25–27, 44–49). As a result of this, the Christian in the Church is set on the path of active discipleship and appropriation of the Lord, reaching forward to the fulfillment which he will bring when he comes again, revealing the veiled meaning of all things as he alone is able to do. But if these elements are inextricably intertwined, they are also distinct from one another; and they *must* be distinguished if the synthesis of their fullness is to be grasped. If they are separated from one another, or if one particular element is made absolute (relativizing the others as mere secondary epiphenomena), the four possible errors of exegesis will inevitably follow, leading deeper into the four possible distortions of Christian *communio* — distortions that can only be overcome in the encompassing Yes and in the constant effort to achieve unity:

The diagram hardly needs explanation. Each pole can claim to be based on an element of the apostolic charism that underlies it. But since this charism has been taken out of the christological and ecclesiological context, it has sunk to the level of the purely anthropological, evaluated according to categories of sociology, psychology and methodology, and has become estranged from its own Christian meaning. From a Christian point of view, therefore, any discussion

Positivism (in exegesis, Church history, theology)

| The Church seen as organization, administration | Gnosticism, pneumaticism, love as "experience" |

Rationalism (the pneuma which plumbs the depths
of God becomes human reason: dogmaticism)

between such deficient, downgraded forms can only be a semblance of dialogue that can accomplish nothing, because the opponents see only masks behind which they hide from each other. But this does not mean that the coherence between the four types no longer exists (though each, in its alienated form, claims supremacy over the other three and thus produces four forms of self-alienation within the Church): it simply means that their mutual interdependence is no longer seen as complementarity within the Church's love but instead as a harmful dependency that must be overcome by force. A purely pneumatic Church would abolish the official structure and take all responsibility for salvation unto herself by reassigning functions. A purely rationalistic Church (of theologians) would upstage official authority and claim to possess the Spirit, using exegesis and Church history for her own purposes, etc. The all-encompassing christo-logical (and Marian) dimension would no longer be able to assert its influence; in practice it would be appropriated by one pole or the other and used and interpreted by it. In such a situation it is logical that any authority but one's own would have to be re-sisted as "oppressive" (an attitude that is at variance with the ele-mentary sociological preconditions for all social order whatsoever, cf. Rom 13). It would do this, moreover, in the name of a no-longer-understood Christian "love" and *"communio"*, secularized into "democracy".

Let us look instead at the play of forces at work in the primitive

Church, with her awareness of her origin in Christ and her dependence upon his Spirit. Here, while the psychological and sociological infrastructure is naturally not denied—after all, it is a question of individual human beings with different positions in a particular society—deliberate attention is only focused on it in connection with what is built upon it, i.e., a society that, as such, is intended to express the self-gift of divine life and ultimately to illustrate the trinitarian exchange of love of that divine life (Jn 13:34–35; 17:23; and in its ideal realization in Acts 4:32; 2:4–12). In this integration, which is achieved by the unifying principle from a higher level, dialogue between those with cardinal missions in the Church (without any sociological safety nets)[2] is not only possible but necessary, since it is a representation, under earthly conditions, of the "dialogue" and exchange of life that takes place within the Godhead.

In fact, however, this dialogue, in which Peter, his office and the authority that goes with it are involved, is conducted by fallible human beings whose personal lives do not match the ideal of their calling. (Mary is the only one in the Church who has been given this prerogative.) Thus the exchange not only includes those elements of tension that are inherent in the pure polyphony and symphony of the heavenly Jerusalem but also the tensions that stem from the inadequacy of the officeholder or from the perplexing nature of historical situations which the individual finds opaque and hence insoluble. Here the play of forces can assume dramatic proportions, and these are justified as long as the participants allow themselves to be guided by the superordinate unity of the Holy Spirit; and whenever the Spirit blows—even where disagreement is necessary—it is always toward unity of divine love and brotherly love.

[2] E.g., the controls which Karl Rahner envisages to monitor ecclesial offices: *Freiheit und Manipulation in Gesellschaft und Kirche* (Munich, Kösel-Verlag, 1970), 53; cf. the subordination of the bishops to courts of arbitration, ibid., 54.

Throughout Church history, and today more explicitly than ever, there has been an evident *contest* within the Church herself, mostly against the Petrine principle, but it could just as well be against pneumaticism or theological rationalism or the claimed dominance of exegesis. This aspect has a legitimate place and form in the New Testament *paraklesis.* (The word means "a call of many kinds: a calling over, calling on, calling up; then a challenge, encitement, stimulus, initiating movement, constraining, conjuring, pleading, but also encouraging, pacifying, comforting".)[3] And if one takes note of the significance of *"con"* in *"contest",* this calling-to-witness simply has to be a community-creating act. The witness called may be God or other members of the Church, but, while attention is directed to one particular member of the Church, that member is not thereby isolated or excluded from the *communio.* In paraklesis the converse is the case. It is always necessary to correct one or other of the poles to re-establish the balance — *ecclesia semper reformanda* — but this is not done by the other three poles coming to a tacit agreement as to how to deal with the unbalanced pole, but rather by encouraging the deviant to take his place once again within the "concert" (which actually means "contest") of the Christian totality. It is on the basis of this already agreed plan of the whole that Paul in Antioch "contests" against Peter's behavior; the very fact that he makes a point of doing so shows in what high regard he holds Peter's position in the whole.

Naturally, Peter too must be continually learning; he must not think that he can carry out his office in isolation (which could easily tempt him to overvalue it). He too must take his bearings by the all-encompassing totality of the Church, which expresses itself con-

[3] Heinrich Schlier, "Die Eigenart der christlichen Mahnung nach dem Apostel Paulus" (1963), in *Besinnung auf das Neue Testament* [Relevance of the New Testament] (Freiburg im Breisgau: Herder, 1964), 34.

cretely in the dynamic interplay of her major missions and in the laws inherent in her structure. This was thoroughly understood even at Vatican I, and it is the context of that consultation and consent which is rooted in ecclesial *koinonia*. (N.B., in the case of definitions, the consent is already implicit in the consultation!) Revelation is entrusted to the whole Church, and all, under the leadership of Peter, are to preserve it, interpret it and produce a living exposition of it. And since the office of Peter is borne by fallible human beings, it needs everyone's watchful but loving cooperation so that the exercise of this office may be characterized by the degree of "in-fallibility" that belongs to it. More precisely, this means that a pope can exercise his office fruitfully for all only if he is *recognized and loved* in a truly ecclesial way, even in the midst of *paraklesis* or dispute. Those who challenge or reject the office of Peter disobey Christ and his gospel and tear apart the unity which Christ has made between "Peter" and "Shepherd", whether they are pneumatics, theologians or exegetical positivists. If they fail to love the office, they automatically drop out of the communion of the Church, whose concrete unity is created by the *Holy* Spirit of love. Thus a person has more right to "contest" issues in the Church, the more he allows the Spirit of holiness to hold sway within him. The saints are our examples in this regard; yet we must remember that the word "saint" ("holy", *heilig*) is an analogical concept here on earth. Catherine protested ("contested") against Avignon; Chrysostom against the encroachments of the "divine Christian Empire"; Peter Damian against the simony and unchastity of the clergy; Ignatius Loyola struggled discreetly but effectively against the excesses of the Inquisition; Darboy knew how to admonish a pope;[4] and often a silent example, such as that of Francis of Assisi (with his great respect for the clergy), was the most effective way of "contesting" the abuse of the Petrine principle. Ignatius once went to confession to a lukewarm priest in order to show him what a true awareness of sin, a true confession was. Such things were motivated by the Holy Spirit; what has to be corrected is always enveloped in love.

In this connection we will mention three aspects: a subjective one: the oft-proclaimed "truthfulness"; an objective one: the ability of the Church, and of the office in particular, to learn; and a final one: how can we tell that the deposit of faith is kept intact within the tension of forces in the Church, notwithstanding the fact that its formulation and understanding are time-bound and subject to change?

1. *"Truthfulness"* (G. Tyrrell, H. Küng), "honesty" (K. Rahner) and "authenticity" (M. Légaut) are widely felt to be missing from the "official Church",[5] which in her apologetics "employs many kinds of artful distinctions and a theological sleight of hand that cannot be called entirely honest." They have also been significantly lacking in her exegesis and theology.[6] The Church is said to live in a "siege

[4] The beatification process of the Archbishop of Paris has been introduced. After the publication of the *Syllabus* he wrote to Pius IX: "Your reprimand, O Vicar of Christ, has power; but your blessing is even more potent. God has elevated you to the Apostolic See between the two halves of this century so that you may give absolution to the one and consecrate the other. May your work reconcile reason with faith, freedom with authority. From the eminence of the threefold dignity of religion, age and misfortune, with which you are adorned, all that you do and all that you say has sufficient scope either to subdue the nations or to gain their confidence. Give them a word from your priestly heart that will absolve the past, encourage the present and open the horizon to the future." The events of Vatican I may be seen, as a whole, as a sign that this *paraklesis* of the Pope was understood and accepted by him.

[5] Hans Küng, *Wahrhaftigkeit: zur Zukunft der Kirche* [Truthfulness: the future of the Church] (Freiburg im Breisgau: Herder, 1968), 9.

[6] Ibid., 40f.

mentality" that "will not yield an inch to the enemy", all the more since she has been established as a "centrally governed citadel, a Church of power", having to "defend herself more and more" against attack.[7] Because of the "know-it-all" attitude[8] with which she issues "her liturgical, dogmatic and legal decisions, precepts, traditions and customs as if they were God's commands", and consequently demands "the blind obedience of fear",[9] and because of her "paternalistic style",[10] she has largely lost the true, biblical sense of truth—"dependability, sincerity, honesty"[11]—and has driven many away, frequently the best,[12] or forced them into opposing a Church that they continued to love.[13] One of the great men of the nineteenth century, a student and friend of Döllinger, *Lord Acton,* founder of the *Rambler* and author of a never-completed "History of Freedom" (of which at least one part was published as the "History of Freedom in Christendom"),[14] took it as his life's work to call for truthfulness from the official Church, and particularly from the Roman Church. First of all, like many others[15] since Hadrian VI and since Vatican II, he demanded that the Church

---

[7] Ibid., 42–43.

[8] Ibid., 50.

[9] Ibid., 55.

[10] Ibid., 13.

[11] Ibid., 59.

[12] Ibid., 73–87. Demonstrated by the example of Charles Davis.

[13] Ibid., 33. The following are enumerated: Leon Bloy (who was angrily opposed to much else), Carl Muth, Georges Bernanos and Charles Péguy (in the case of these two, one must look closely to see what kind of opposition is meant), Reinhold Schneider (who, in the beginning and toward the end, had periods in which he did not know whether he was a Christian or a Buddhist) and Heinrich Böll.

[14] John Emerich Dalberg Acton, *Essays on Freedom and Power* (London: Thames and Hudson, 1956); Döllinger-Acton, *Briefwechsel,* ed. V. Conzemius, 3 vols. (Munich: Beck, 1963–1971); Ulrich Noack, *Katholizität und Geistesfreiheit. Nach den Schriften von John Dalberg-Acton* (Frankfurt am Main: G. Schulte-Bulmke, 1936).

[15] See, for example, Jean Cardinal Daniélou, *Authorité et son contestation dans l'Église* (Geneva: Claude Martingay, 1969), 8, 10.

make an unconditional confession of sins, seeing in that the best possible apologetic. It would only be possible to speak meaningfully once more about ecclesial authority (to which Acton held fast) if all the weaknesses and faults of the Church, and the consequent alienation of modern culture from her, were ruthlessly exposed. Here Acton was thinking primarily of the misuse of the interdict, of the Inquisition and of excommunication (which overtook his teacher and friend, Döllinger, and also threatened him). He refused to attribute the horrors of Church history to the crudeness of the times. These things flourished "on pure Catholic soil — in the foremost centuries of Catholicism's supremacy — not under foreign influence, not . . . among half-civilized peoples." "The surrender of conscience is as much a precondition of arbitrary rule as is revolution. The tendency toward arbitrary rule is inherent in the papal system: it is the *nisus formativus* of the modern papacy. We are dealing with an immoral power".[16] The exaggeration that comes across clearly in Acton's last sentence compromises his otherwise true and praiseworthy starting point; many of his other accusations are also untrue.[17] However right he may be in many points (like Tyrrell and Küng after him), for instance in his indignation at the practice (which went on until very recently) of condemning theologians or putting them on the Index without first giving them a hearing and without even giving reasons, Acton's notion of freedom and truth, underlying everything he says, is highly questionable in that it is not critically substantiated. He applies his notion univocally to the spheres of both Church and state (or science), to the *mysterium* as well as to humanist ethics and scholarship. We cannot counter this by proposing a "double truth" or a "double freedom"; yet there is a difference between the honesty of the scholar

---

[16] Döllinger-Acton, *Briefwechsel* (May 1882), 3:263f.; also quoted by V. Conzemius, "Lord Acton", in *Propheten und Vorläufer. Wegbereiter der neuzeitlichen Katholizismus* (Zurich, Einsiedeln and Cologne: Benziger, 1972), 153–55.

[17] Ibid., 156.

who must take responsibility for his own successes and failures and the honesty of a person who is commissioned to represent and defend a truth (and indeed, a freedom) that he himself can never grasp in its fullness. For here there is an intrinsic dualism between the person and what he represents; and this is again connected with the "eccentric nature of the office", to which we shall return in the final part of this book. It is this dualism—and not the modern papacy's tendency toward immoral power, in Acton's words—that makes it by no means obvious, in certain borderline issues, where the "truer truth" actually lies: whether in the ruthless exposing of one's own weakness and guilt or in covering the guilt of others with the mantle of love. The objection is clear: it is not the guilty who should spread this mantle over himself; rather, this should be done—after he has confessed his guilt—by the one who has forgiven him. But who *is* the guilty party? Is it Rome alone or all of us Catholics? And who will pardon Rome? Perchance we theologians, we who are devotees of "truthfulness", we charismatics, once more willing to put up with the insufferable "Church establishment"[18] and its "hypocrisy"[19]—or perhaps it is God, rather, who needs to pardon us all?

In this century the new *pathos* of Christian honesty began with the youth movement (*Jugendbewegung*); it came to fruition as it became clear that individuals possessed the criterion of truth within themselves in the *experience* of faith. Thus the "living" and "authentic" Christian has become the measure of truth (and this is alleged to be the biblical view): he is in a position to pronounce a verdict on the miserable skeleton of the "institution". (Cf. our remarks on Marcel Légaut at the beginning of the book.) In this connection Jean Daniélou complains of "the cowardice of the many contemporary intellectuals who reject solidarity with any and all exercise of authority, even when this is done in an entirely authentic manner." The *whole* Church,

[18] Küng, *Wahrhaftigkeit,* 20.
[19] Ibid., 46.

he continues, "should ceaselessly challenge (*contest* against) herself in the name of Jesus Christ, because she is not completely faithful to him."[20]

As a sociologist, Wigand Siebel even questions the abandoning of the Index—something that has been taken entirely for granted—as well as what amounts to Rome's discontinuance of trials of theologians. For "the question of what the author really meant is given primary emphasis, while the issue of whether the particular thesis has endangered the propagation of truth and created uneasiness and uncertainty in the faithful is relegated to third place. All the same, under the existing conditions of Church and society, one may regard these changes as reasonable or even indispensable. Yet one does not need to agree with all the related attempts to promote *ad infinitum* the theologians' emancipation from Church authority."[21] Despite assurances of loyalty to authority, Acton's presentation of the univocal nature of truth and freedom hands over the setting of standards for discerning truth—and thus hands over authority—to scholars and theologians.[22]

[20] Ibid., 26–27, note 15.

[21] Wigand Siebel, *Freiheit und Herrschaftsstruktur in der Kirche* (Berlin: Morus, 1971), 78f.

[22] Very significant is Acton's dialectic between an ideal "ultramontanism" (not far removed from that of the fiercely attacked Lamennais) and a real ultramontanism, the "black sheep" for all the sins of the Church. Cf. Noack, *Katholizität und Geistesfreiheit,* 242, 346. Hans Küng foresees a division between "pastoral ministry" and "teaching ministry": "Pastors cannot simply become teachers, and teachers cannot simply become pastors. The theologian in the Church presumes too much if in his teaching service he also wants to take over the leadership of the Church. On the other hand, the shepherd in the Church overreaches also when, besides his pastoral duties, he presumes to decide scientific(!) theological questions in an authoritative manner." *Wahrhaftigkeit,* 180. Hence, not only does the professor inform the pastor—as the present-day pastor is no longer qualified to be responsible for the purity of teaching, unlike the pastor in Paul's time (pastoral epistles; Acts 22:30–23:10)—not only is there genuine collaboration between the Magisterium and theology, which is obviously necessary; instead there is an evenly divided authority. This sounds like an echo of Döllinger's statements regarding the Syllabus: "Of what *we Germans* call science or the scientific approach to a subject, they (in Rome) have no inkling", *Kleinere Schriften* (Stuttgart: Cotta, 1890), 201f.

The true standard is to be found by returning to our ecclesiological schema, where it is a case of "doing the truth in love" (*aletheuein en agapei:* Eph 4:15), not "in knowledge" (*en gnosei*), between all four principles. Love does not limit truth and the doing of it but shapes and defines it: it provides the universal standard. Love provides the standard for revealing and veiling, for accusing and forgiving, for including and excluding. Within this context it is possible to accept the statement that "anger, particularly today, needs to be rehabilitated in the Church".[23] The Church may call to mind the anger of Jesus and, even more explicitly, Paul's anger at the excesses and fanaticism of the people "around James", while not forgetting all that Paul did for James' community in Jerusalem, not only materially but also spiritually. Thus, for the sake of peace and unity, and to avoid a schism in the Church, he yielded on the advice of James to a Jewish Temple custom to show that he was still loyal to the law (Acts 21:24). This was perhaps the prime example of a *sacrificium intellectus* in the whole of Church history, and on this occasion he was arrested by the Jews—as a result of betrayal by Christians, the moderns would say—and handed over to Gentiles. No one who fails to see this action on Paul's part and take it as his example has a right to assume the stance of an angry challenger within the Church. Nor should Peter's reaction be over-looked: in one of the latest documents of the New Testament we hear, as it were, an echo of the Antioch episode: "So also our beloved brother Paul wrote to you according to the wisdom given him, speaking of this as he does in all his letters. There are some things in them hard to understand, which the ignorant and unstable twist to their own destruction, as they do the other Scriptures" (2 Pet 3:15–16). This is a heartfelt sigh of the bishop over a dear brother's gifted writings, which are too deep for the ordinary member of the flock but which Peter supports with his authority, praising their wisdom and conformity with the teaching handed down, of which he is the

[23] Küng, *Wahrhaftigkeit,* 18.

guardian, while also warning the flock against reading them with immature faith or unbalanced judgment. Lovingly he situates Paul's writings within the total context of the "other Scriptures"—all of which are susceptible of being twisted. Such censorship is necessary within the Church's communion of love if Peter is to fulfill his ministry,[24] just as it was necessary for him to overtake the waiting John on the way to the empty tomb, so that, alone, he could "officially" verify the facts. (It would be totally perverse to conclude, from the fact that Peter disappeared from Jerusalem because of persecution [Acts 12:17], leaving James to take over leadership of the community, that Peter's primacy in the gospel was only temporary or only partially recognized—in the communities in which Matthew 16:18 originated.) The serious theological differences between James and Paul which inevitably had to be ironed out (Rom 4:2–3 versus James 2:20–23), and which reveal the conflict between traditional Judaism (insofar as it was legitimate) and a Gentile Christianity basing itself on the most ancient tradition of the Old Testament, only mirror, at a theological level, the whole primitive dilemma between Jewish and Gentile Christianity. Furthermore, this dialectic will characterize the temporal course of Church history until the return of Christ (cf. Rom 11): the Christian—and his theology—can rejoice in his election only with fear and trembling as he reflects on how the branch of Israel was "broken off" (Rom 11:20). He must ask himself again and again whether he can produce the "work" that James demands, so that the faith of Abraham may be brought to perfection in the Church. And how characteristic it is that John stands aside from this ongoing struggle to find balance in the unity of the Church! The love that

[24] In practice, all great heresies or harmful one-sided judgments of the West can be traced back to Paul: the teaching of predestination by the aged Augustine, the consequences of which were devastating; the theses of the Augustinian monk, Luther, those of Calvin, Baius and of Jansenius' *Augustinus* and all its consequences. Paul, least of all, must not be isolated from the foursome of the "pillars".

"abides" does not dispute, does not enter into arguments: the most it does is repeat the one commandment of the Lord and lead people into a deeper understanding of it. At the beginning of the Acts of the Apostles John always appears at Peter's side as if they were inseparable. Then, when the brilliant convert, Paul, comes on the scene, John silently disappears, to set up on the sidelines that "school" of love which is also a school of obedience to the principle of office. Polycarp, Ignatius of Antioch, Irenaeus—with John's followers the Church's great theology begins to unfold. This is the model and the standard for truthfulness within the Church.

2. It follows from all this, precisely if the apostolic era is to remain normative for all ages of the Church, that the Church's unity (with the specific nature of her constitutive missions) both *is* (because these missions are implanted in her) and continually *comes about* (because in every situation they have to be lived in a new way, realized and brought into harmony with each other). *Y. Congar* has put this succinctly: "Catholicity is the Church's *universal capacity for unity,* or, in other words, the dynamic universality of the principles which yield her unity."[25] It is agreed today that this dynamism is only inadequately expressed by the concept of "development"—an expression that became common, after its emergence as the central characteristic of the modern world view, in the dogmatics of the nineteenth and early twentieth century. The concept of development applies to finite and mortal organisms (as individuals or as a chain of consecutive forms of life)

[25] Yves Congar, "Conscience de la catholicité", in *Esquisse du mystère de l'Église* [The mystery of the Church], new ed. (Paris: Cerf, 1953). This thesis comes from the year 1937 (cf. 7) when Congar's first important ecumenical work, *Chrétiens désunis* appeared. One reads there: "Catholicism means universality; universality means assembling in unity (*unus, vertere*). . . . If, in effect, the Church is able to and is destined to spread over the whole world, it is because of the universal capacity of assimilating her constitutive principles. The Church's catholicity . . . is the dynamic universality of her unity." *Chrétiens désunis* [Divided Christians] (Paris: Cerf, 1937), 115–17.

and suggests the un-folding (e-volution) of something that has already been en-folded (in-voluted), the actualization of inherent potentialities, in an essentially irreversible direction. The application of this to the history of Christian doctrine led to the unfortunate impression that it was a case of a progressive discovery, definition and hence mastery of revealed Christian truth. This view, applied consistently, furthermore implied that what was originally merely believed was being transformed into a more and more complete understanding, even if the latter did not replace faith. However, it was an approach that was too much opposed to the Church's faith-consciousness to be entertained for very long.

If we take Congar's formulation and apply it to our earlier diagram of the interplay of forces in the primitive Christian Church, it becomes clear that unforeseen situations may arise in the ongoing interaction of competing principles. No one can have a comprehensive view of all possible combinations a priori, not even in a chess game, otherwise the players' tremendous effort in every new tournament would be superfluous. Yet the role and significance of every principal figure is invariable (like that of each chess-piece), which is a precondition for the game's taking place. And each game is new and unpredictable. And as far as the Church is concerned, we are not dealing with mere arbitrary games played with different combinations but with a deep seriousness and responsibility on the part of the Church in her faith-understanding in every new world situation. Our example falls short in many ways, however. The diagram oversimplifies by showing only the four main tendencies, and in the "game" of the Church it is never a case of winning over an opponent; the outcome is never "checkmate" or "stalemate". All the diagram is intended to do is to show that, despite the set roles of the figures involved, guaranteed by the guidance of the Holy Spirit, the Church's unity in the multiplicity of integrating principles contains unforeseeable possibilities of unification and comprehensibility. Furthermore, these actualizations of potentialities are not irreversible, as with finite organisms; the seeds of eternal

324

life are planted in the Church to unfold unhindered in the dimension of time also. So what I have called "involutions" (*Einfaltungen*)[26]—i.e., the simplification and concentration of elements that are dangerous when isolated from one another, by means of reflection on the given totality—is in no way a one-sided regression to origins but a significant step forward (pro-gression). And on the other hand, the Church cannot grasp at a single glance the whole breadth of her potential development. If it is true that the historical Jesus did not make plans for a Gentile mission (and in that case a text such as Matthew 28:18–20 must have been based on long experience of the Church in the Holy Spirit) and that the apostles turned to the Gentiles only after having "failed" with the Jews and that Paul only gradually became aware of his special mission while Peter had to be convinced of his, against innermost resistance on his part, through the Joppa vision, it still cannot be maintained that Jesus' concept of the kingdom was confined to the internal Jewish horizon. It is obvious that it contained all the potential and capacities necessary for a universal role.

To be more specific: even though the apostles—and we may include all the four mentioned above—only gradually understood, with the help of the Holy Spirit, what was implied by the Church's catholicity, this growing understanding was not a completely new addition to their carefully guarded heritage of faith; it was something that had always been latent within the latter's fullness (which is never completely graspable), but they had simply not been explicitly aware of it. Well may they be astounded when, at Pentecost, the Holy Spirit reveals to them the global dimensions of their mission through the miracle of tongues. But what was then openly brought to light had already been implicit in their unreserved and trusting self-gift to their Lord and Master: it is into *his* truth that the Spirit now leads them (Jn 16:12–25).

[26] Hans Urs von Balthasar, *Auf Wegen christlicher Einigung* (Munich: Kösel-Verlag, 1969).

According to the Acts of the Apostles this learning process also had to be applied to the representative of the pastoral and teaching office in a drastic, thorough and detailed way, significantly before Paul's appearance on the scene (Acts 10:1–11, 18). The mission of the Magisterium had to learn just as much as the other three; humanly speaking, Peter, like the others, was conditioned by the conceptual horizon of late Judaism, as we can see in the disciples' question to their resurrected Lord as to when he would finally establish the kingdom of Israel (Acts 1:6).

Yet, learning in the Church cannot be reduced to the mere addition of knowledge coming from externally discovered truths. Such assimilation does take place, no doubt, on the empirical level, with time-bound people and conditions; it also applies to the acquisition of new perspectives in Holy Scripture, in tradition (which is inexhaustible), as well as in the insights gained from advanced cultures and from the values of foreign, and as yet unassimilated peoples and cultures. On this level, non-Christians, and perhaps even anti-Christians, may call the Church's attention to something she has not fully realized or, in the course of her history, has forgotten. But it is exactly here that another characteristic of the Church emerges, as Ferdinand Ulrich has rightly pointed out: as regards her innermost being (which transcends the empirical), the Church, which is the fullness, the Body and Bride of Christ, cannot learn anything from outside that she does not already know from her intimate communion with Jesus Christ, "in whom are hid all the treasures of wisdom and knowledge" (Col 2:3). Paul does not cease to pray for the communities, asking that they "may be filled with the knowledge of his will in all spiritual wisdom and understanding, to lead a life worthy of the Lord, . . . increasing in the knowledge of God" (Col 1:9–10); like "the word of truth, the gospel . . . in the whole world it is bearing fruit and growing" (Col 1:5–6). They should recognize in the Church's communion ("with all the saints") the four infinite dimensions, "the breadth and length and height and depth" of the love that God offers, in which they already abide, so that they "may be filled with all the fullness of God" (Eph 3:18–19) and in which they are forever "rooted and grounded" (Eph 3:17). In learning to fathom her own depth, the Church does not thereby change her own reality; she only becomes more aware of her true self. Whatever stimulates her from the outside—be it Marxism or orthopraxy or Buddhism with its contemplation—only calls forth something that lies within her, and that is actually better formed and in truer proportion to the whole context. All this applies to the three forms of the Church's infallibility, i.e., that of her general self-consciousness, that of the ordinary Magisterium (through the college of bishops) and that of the special (papal) Magisterium. While these three are steeped in the empirical-historical learning process, they surpass it at an essential point. Furthermore, the three forms of infallibility are designed to complement each other, since Peter is one of the four pillars (that always support the whole People of God) but, because of his special mission and charism, is not simply on the same level as the other three. This fundamentally determines the living relationship between traditionalism and progressivism, which we can sum up in the words of *Erich Przywara:*

Church, in her very special, organic shape, is, so to speak, *the* form of Catholic transcendentality. For she herself is the midpoint between traditionalism and dynamism, neither pure rest nor pure motion, but rest in motion, self-affirmation in self-development. This is the oft-misunderstood statement concerning infallibility, the ultimate expression of which is the pope's infallibility when he speaks *ex cathedra,* that is, exercising his supreme office as pastor and teacher of Christians, defining a doctrine concerning faith or morals, with ultimate authority, to be binding on the whole Church (Vat. sess. IV cap. 4). In this way the Church is sharply distinguished from two forms of traditionalism. First, traditionalism in the narrow sense, holding fast to rigidly defined forms, such as we find in Eastern Orthodoxy (in the liturgy) and in orthodox Lutheranism (in the Bible). For the living Church's ability to make decisions is essentially

327

free from the prejudice of "what has always been". Secondly, it is different from traditionalism in the sense of a philosophical school which accepts new forms only as consequences of already existing ones (the logical-objective tradition) or because they are accepted by majority opinion (tradition in terms of living persons). The living Church's power to make decisions is as independent from evidence presented (but not defined) on behalf of a new decision—for such evidence may be faulty without affecting the infallibility of the decision—as it is independent of any majority opinion, cf. the historical majority in favor of Semi-Arianism! On the other hand, the "ongoing development" is not a dynamism in the sense of a continual breaking of new ground because, according to the teaching of the Church, "revelation . . . has been closed with the apostles" (*Decr. Lamentabili,* prop. 21). It is the living self-unfolding of forms that are in themselves permanent, since this living Church, essentially rest in motion and self-affirmation in self-development, is autonomous.[27]

3. However, this defines merely in a formal way the vitality and "elasticity" inherent in the Catholic principles of unity (Congar). There still remains a final question: in this dialogue between the principles which sustain unity, what must the dialogue partners focus on, so that they may form a right judgment as to the proper shape of unity to be presented, here and now, to the Church and the world— including its material content? We have already seen the various sociological kinds of disintegration and alienation which threaten to gain power in the Church, brought about by her own inertia and by the persuasion exercised by the secular world. Johannine love can degenerate into orthopraxis or a universal humanitarian benevolence that takes its values from a "change in social structures" which would redistribute goods more equitably. The tradition of James can sink to

[27] Hans Urs von Balthasar, "Religionsphilosophie katholischer Theologie", now in *Religionsphilosophische Schriften. Schriften,* vol. 2, 2d ed. (Einsiedeln: Johannesverlag, 1962), 428–30.

the level of that anxiously integralist, reactionary clinging to obsolete forms which Przywara rejects; the Pauline "all things to all men" can become a diplomatic *aggiornamento* to all that is popular and fashionable, which so amused Voltaire. The Petrine distortions have been too often exposed to need further mention here. One decadent element elicits another and either perverts it or pushes it into a sterile antithesis. We have presented elsewhere[28] the criterion of truth that has to be kept in mind concerning the Church's internal play of forces, namely, the *"eschatological center of gravity"* of the gospel of Christ, the highpoint of the grace received by the Church for the salvation of the world, which is only one aspect of dynamic catholicity. Obviously it can be damaged or destroyed in various ways—through the radical assertions of liberal exegesis, for instance, which attack the foundations of Christian faith, the "pro nobis" of God's saving work in Jesus Christ, his atoning death, his Resurrection, etc. In such cases the Magisterium does not find it difficult to draw the line. But there are cases where it is extremely difficult to weigh the reasons for and against, particularly when one tries to keep in mind the "eschatological center of gravity", not only because some current situation did not exist in the period of biblical revelation, which means that conclusions have to be drawn from the spirit of a unique historical past and applied to a very different present, but also because Christ's Church contains a wide spectrum of human possibilities or obstructions, at the same time contributing to and detracting from a perfect human response to the perfect grace of God in Christ. Peter proceeds more slowly to the tomb than John, because as shepherd he leads not only loving saints but also sick members of the flock (and not infrequently mangy sheep), as has been foreseen since ancient times (Ezek 34:16). A decision that is justifiable for those whose love is alive might be

---

[28] Hans Urs von Balthasar and Joseph Ratzinger, "Warum ich noch ein Christ bin", in *Zwei Plädoyers* [Two say why], *Münchener Akademie-Schriften,* vol. 57 (Munich: Kösel-Verlag, 1971).

impractical for the lukewarm or otherwise defective masses; on the other hand, a decision made to suit these latter could seriously endanger the balance of the Church's eschatological response, the ideal of those who love. This is the impasse (where a single solution is expected) such as the Pope encountered when he issued the much-maligned encyclical *Humanae vitae.* He opted for the ideal of the small, loving, devoted company and so unleashed a storm of indignation among the mass of people both inside and outside the Church. He made this option seemingly without regard for the majority of his panel of advisors and without attending to the sociological contraindications. It may be that he deliberately disregarded important factors that should have been taken into account, but this has not been proved. The crucial difficulty in his decision had nothing to do with the question that concerns us here—namely, deciding according to the criteria of eschatology—but lay in the fact, as Hans Küng has rightly pointed out, that by issuing an encyclical (that cannot claim infallibility), the Pope was burdening and binding the consciences of married Catholics in an issue that had serious consequences; this resulted in a crisis for the more recent trend which had endeavored to mask the exercise of authority. While this is, of course, no small matter, we can leave it aside here and concentrate on the actual content itself. It is probably the form rather than the content that needs to be criticized. It might have been sufficient to point to the ideal as a "normative goal" to satisfy the objective, eschatological emphasis of the Christian concept of selfless and self-renouncing love, the personal ideal of the committed, while at the same time both stimulating and reassuring those who were either too unable or too perplexed to follow this course. For who does not see the devastation created in the sexual area by the separation of pleasure from the risk of self-giving, as well as the tremendous weight of sociological arguments on the other side? This example again illustrates the whole meaning of the apostolic "foursome": though empowered and obliged to take the final, personal responsibility alone, the pope is directed to share in a dia-

330

logue with the other three partners of the "foursome" we have described—which only represent a far more complex constellation in the Church.

2. *Roma aeterna?*

The force-field of the christological constellation generated the apostolic missions in the age of the primitive Church. Only at the very end of this period do we encounter something—an extra-biblical factor—that subsequently will become central and inseparable from the Petrine office: a free Roman citizen appeals to the Emperor and is taken to Rome. As a result, Rome becomes the guardian of the graves of Peter and Paul and grows so prominent among the other apostolic sees that she is soon called simply "The Apostolic See". There seems to be an affinity between the claim to universality and concrete unity on the part of the *Catholica* and the similar claim of the Roman *Imperium;* the consequences of this for the history of Europe and the world are beyond assessing. The successor of Peter, the personified center of Catholic unity, resides in Rome, which never saw herself as the (Greek) ideal human state but as a real, worldwide politico-economic entity, organized by a uniform law. Hence the inevitable question as to how closely these two universalisms are related and to what extent Catholicism is necessarily based on the Roman model. More precisely, how far is the papal *plenitudo potestatis* modeled on full imperial authority? And if such a relationship can be established as fundamental to the papacy, does this not provide the strongest reason for an anti-Roman alliance of all non-Catholic Christians? This subject—the idea of Rome in the Western world—is endless in its scope,[29] and it

---

[29] See also Friedrich Klinger, "Rom als Idee", in *Römische Geisteswelt* (Leipzig: Dieterich, 1943); Wilhelm Gernentz, *Laudes Romae* (Diss., Rostock, 1918); Joseph Vogt, *Vom Reichsgedanken der Römer* (Leipzig: Kochler and Amelang, 1942); Walther

concerns us here only in one narrow aspect: can one say that the "Roman" papacy, its ecclesial status and its claim, are intrinsically related to the secular (or if one prefers, "sacral") concept of the Roman Empire?

One might surmise that the idea of a close internal connection between papacy and imperium was entirely abandoned by Catholics after the tragic ideological conflicts of the Middle Ages and is now of only historical and not theological interest.[30] But the facts do not bear this out. Dante portrayed himself led to the threshold of Paradise by Virgil, the actual creator of the ancient world's concept of Rome; Dante's *monarchia* is the most sublime and balanced attempt to relate Empire and Church; in his footsteps Theodore Haecker, author of *Virgil, the Father of the West*,[31] can say with deep conviction: *Imperium sine fine dedi.* This is the *fatum Iovis* (the will of Jove). For we all still live in the *Imperium Romanum*. It has not died. Whether we like or not, whether we are aware of it or not, all of us are still members of this *Imperium Romanum* which, after following false trails of cruelty, freely accepted Christianity; it cannot now give it up without surrendering its own self and its humanism. What Virgil celebrates in poetry is not a mere "idea but reality . . . the thing, the *res*, flesh and

---

Rehm, "Der Untergang Roms im Abendländischen Denken", *Erbe der Alten,* vol. 2 (Leipzig, 1930): 18. General works on the relation of the Church and the Roman Empire: Christopher Dawson, *The Making of Europe* (various editions); Alois Dempf, *Sacrum Imperium* (n.p.: 1926); Wilhelm Kamlah, *Christentum und Geschichtlichkeit* (Stuttgart: W. Kohlhammer, 1951); Edgar Salin, *Civitas Dei* (Tübingen: Mohr, 1926).

[30] There would thus be more interest in a criticism that deromanticizes Western Church history, particularly after the fusion of the concepts of Church and state by Constantine. Cf. Albert Mirgeler, *Kritischer Rückblick auf das abendländische Christentum* [Mutations of Western Christianity] (Freiburg im Breisgau: Herder, 1961; revised, 1969); Rudolf Hernegger, *Macht ohne Auftrag* (Olten: Walter-Verlag, 1963).

[31] Theodor Haecker, *Vergil, Vater des Abendlandes* [Virgil, father of the West] (Leipzig: Hegner, 1935), 99f.

blood". Virgil is plainly the "pagan of the Christian Advent",[32] the most perfect *anima naturaliter christiana* of antiquity,[33] who permits himself to be led by the word, by what is "uttered" (*fatum*), without protesting. Haecker cites "the bold, easily misunderstood" dictum of Sainte-Beuve: *"La venue même du Christ n'a rien qui étonne, quand on a lu Virgile."*[34] One can read similar statements in J. Sellmair's *Humanitas Christiana*,[35] which shows the influence of Haecker, and again in Reinhard Raffalt's controversial lecture, "The End of the Roman principle" [*Das Ende des römischen Prinzips* (1970)].[36] Here he describes the "Advent" quality of Roman *pietas* and *humanitas* — its "harmony with the laws of the cosmos, the state, the family", its "inclusion of the dignity and the weakness of human nature", its understanding of the destinies that cause the rise and fall of nations — which is taken up as potential and refashioned and perfected in Christian reality.

> What Roman thought prefigures, by recognizing the limits of human knowledge, has been completed by the Church through the truth of revelation. The Church responded to the need for harmony with the entire cosmos by presenting the security of the divine command, the crown of which is love. History, as a continuum, stretches out through the Church to become the great plan of salvation drawn up by the Lord of history, who will bring it, through the troubles of temporal existence, to a hidden but glorious end. The presence of history in the here-and-now was heightened by contact in prayer with the souls of the dead, the saints in heaven, and ultimately by the constant presence of the Redeemer under the veil of the sacrament. The *mos maiorum,* the invocation of the custom of the Fathers, found

[32] Ibid., 26.

[33] Ibid., 28.

[34] Ibid., 94.

[35] Joseph Sellmair, "Roms Wiedergeburt aus dem Glauben enthält das Geheimnis des Westens", in *Humanitas Christiana* (1949), 152.

[36] Reinhard Raffalt, *Das Ende des römischen Prinzips, Münchener Akademie-Schriften* 52 (Munich: Kösel-Verlag, 1970).

spiritual expression in the Church through the spiritual pedigree which could be traced back through the bishops, the bearers of plenary Christian authority, to the apostles, and which was valid and certain because of the unbroken succession of episcopal consecration. Such mutual interpenetration of the basic ideas of ancient Rome with corresponding parts of the Christian idea provided a sufficiently firm ground to support the revolutionary new ideas of Christianity. . . . Thus it is the universal striving for agreement, for harmony in accordance with laws, that characterizes the core of the Roman principle. In this, *pietas,* the tradition of integrating religion and law (as understood in antiquity) was fused with the Christian relationship between time and eternity.[37]

It is precisely this humane, preliminary grasp that is being lost today. The concept of cosmic order is replaced by the will to change the world; hence authority, equated with power, is rejected as a premise. Moreover, "too much has happened in the world: we are suspicious of any institution that tries to exercise a right that is *eo ipso* dubious."[38] "The end of the Roman principle is not imminent, it has already arrived."[39] Raffalt sees the pope "leaving Rome and moving to Jerusalem, to build there, at the grave of Christ, a Church of humility, completely different from the one that has become so superhumanly difficult for him to maintain in the Holy See."[40]

These examples should suffice; their weakness is evident. Roman humanism and piety, here heightened and idealistically transfigured, are that *natura* which, according to authentic Catholic thought (that does not separate God the Creator from the Redeemer) is the "precondition" for grace: *gratia supponit naturam.* This truth is best formulated negatively (*non destruit*) and in terms of transformation (*elevat*); even then it cannot encompass what is distinctively Christian,

[37] Ibid., 10–12.
[38] Ibid., 24.
[39] Ibid., 7.
[40] Ibid., 44.

namely the Cross and Resurrection. This principle, being universal, is broader than the reality of Rome. When Rome meets Christianity she becomes historically and factually identified with the latter. All the same, if Greek universalism of thought and speech, and Greek ideas of a cosmic state, were the preconditions that made possible the spread of the gospel from a particular, tiny corner of the world, this ideal state still had to become a tangible reality, as a result of Rome's political realism, if this preaching was to be promoted. Thus Pope Leo I says: "So that the effect of the ineffable divine grace may be spread over the entire world, God in his providence provided the Roman Empire. . . . It was most appropriate for the divine plan to have many states of the world united in one empire, thus making it possible to disseminate quickly the universal message of the gospel to the nations, because all were under the rule of one state."[41] So the Pope thanks providence for "having safely hidden the Christian faith in the fortress of Roman imperialism."

One might add here a few important features that the Roman Empire attributed to itself, which were not without attraction for Christian thinking.[42] First of all, Rome's alleged *aeternitas* that supposedly exempted her from the law of coming into being and passing away.[43]

---

[41] Leo I, *Sermo* 82, 2. Also Origen, *Against Celsus,* 2, 30, in *The Ante-Nicene Fathers,* vol. 4 (New York: Charles Scribner's Sons, 1913): 443–44.

[42] Short, excellent description by Endre von Ivánka, *Rhomäerreich und Gottesvolk* (Freiburg im Breisgau: Alber, 1968), 26–42.

[43] Also C. Koch, "Roma aeterna", in *Paideuma* 3 (1949); "Roma aeterna", in *Gymnasium* 59 (1952); H. U. Instinsky, "Kaiser und Ewigkeit", *Hermes* 77 (1942): 313ff. While Polybius—following Plato's cyclic theory of the state and Aristotle's typically Greek dramatic scheme (beginning, middle, end)—foresaw the end of the Roman imperium, the Romans (Virgil, Ovid), despite their realistic awareness of history and the criticism of political and moral conditions, develop the wishful idea of an eternal Rome, whose "guardian spirit" would guide it through all dangers to good fortune, as Plutarch describes in his youthful work *De fortuna romanorum.* Even in the midst of ruin during the decay, Claudian, Rutilius and Namatian tried to maintain this. The contradiction between the generally accepted antiquity of the

This led Tertullian to see in her the *katechon,* the one who holds the Antichrist at bay, so that he can come only after the collapse of the Roman Empire at the end of historical time.[44] Then there is the unique coincidence of virtue (*virtus*) and fortune (*fortuna*), which is related to that other one where established order and guaranteed peace coincide in time (in the *pax Augustana*) with the birth of the Messiah, which brought peace from heaven to earth. The Roman Empire manifests a further unique connection, namely, between a masculine law that liberates people from compulsion and unfreedom and that "maternal" aspect which causes Horace to speak of the Imperial City as *Domina,* an originally oriental title given to the great mother divinities.[45] Later, in his famous verses,[46] Claudian praises Rome as mother, the only conqueror who maternally takes conquered peoples to her bosom,

---

world and the notion of eternity was reconciled by Ammianus Marcellinus and Florus by the idea of a "new saeculum" that, during the reign of certain emperors, would break into the aging world with a kind of rejuvenating eternity. For the Roman idea of rejuvenation, cf. Percy E. Schramm, *Kaiser, Rom und Renovatio,* 2d ed. (Darmstadt: W. Gentner, 1957); Johannes A. Straub, *Regeneratio Imperii* (Darmstadt: Wissenschaftliche Buchgesellschaft, 1972). The contradictory forms in which the Roman idea continues to survive are clearly described by Michael Seidlmayer, "Rom und Romgedanke im Mittelalter", in *Saeculum* 7 (1956): 395–412.

[44] Tertullian, *Apology* 33, in *The Ante-Nicene Fathers,* vol. 3 (New York: Charles Scribner's Sons, 1918): 42–43.

[45] Hildebrecht Hommel, "Domina Roma", in *Die Antike* 18 (1942): 127–58, shows that the address first used by Horace (*Odes* 4, 14, 43f.), which swiftly became generally adopted, had been commonly used in the East and was connected with cults of the mother-goddesses, and was also known in Italy; a "mater Roma" seems to have been at least presumed by Virgil, *Aeneid* 6, 781ff. Livy calls the fatherland "mother" (5, 54, 2). The goddess of the City of Rome was depicted on coins, following Alexandrian models, as a helmeted female head. Numerous texts which address Rome as "Domina" (*rerum*) can be found in Guilelmus [Wilhelm] Gernentz, *Laudes Romae* (Diss. Rostock, 1918), 125ff. The titles *regina, mater, genetrix* (*hominum et deorum*) were also used, ibid., 126ff.

[46] Claudian, "Haec est, gremium victos quae sola recepit/Matris, non dominae ritu, civesque vocavit/quos domuit" (*De Consulatu Stilichonis* 3, 150ff.).

welcoming the vanquished as citizens. How many latent tensions there are in this Rome that served as a mirror to the emerging *Catholica,* reflecting the dynamic forces at work in her! And what a temptation it proved later, after the obvious dangers had been overcome—in the period beginning with Gregory VII—for the Church to see herself, model herself more and more exactly along Roman lines, and even to see herself as the authentic continuation of the Roman Empire![47]

Eusebius' theology of empire has already succumbed to this temptation. Not only does he understand the unity of the Empire, like Pope Leo, as a means for spreading the gospel, but—according to Endre von Ivánka's careful analysis—his earnest speculations[48] put forward a synthesis of world-historical proportions between two realities: on the one hand, a (pagan) religion that had always existed (this was also the view of Clement of Alexandria)—so that the ancestors before Abraham "might be described as Christians in fact if not in name"[49]— which had now been given concrete, worldwide political form in the Roman Empire of Constantine; and on the other, the religion that grew up among the Jewish People of God, which had reached its perfection with the appearance of Christ. This synthesis did not mean the secularization of Christianity but a universalization of the religion of Christ that, in Palestine, was only potentially catholic, but was made practicable and actual by the dispersion of God's peculiar people, the Jews, throughout the whole Roman world. This new interpretation by Eusebius of the Pauline synthesis between Jew and Gentile (which is also that of the entire New Testament) was decisive

---

[47] This is conveyed in strictly organized form by Sägmüller, "Die Idee der Kirche als Imperium Romanum im kanonischen Recht", in *Theologische Quartalschrift* (1898), 50–80.

[48] Not in his eulogies of Constantine, but in the introduction to his *Ecclesiastical History.*

[49] Eusebius, *Ecclesiastical History,* 1:4, 6.

for the justification of the imperial-Church theology of Eastern Rome, leading ultimately to the "Third Rome", Moscow, as Hugo Rahner has shown in an enlightening address.[50] But did the first Rome accept this "Constantinian" theology? And if not, why not?

In the encounter between the Petrine Church and the Roman Empire there are three factors that contradict the simplistic Eusebian synthesis.

1. First of all, spiritual/intellectual resistance to Rome[51] existed among her subject peoples, particularly in the East and most strongly among the Jewish people, long before the rise of Christianity. Christianity took over and continued the resistance during the persecutions, as it recognized in Rome that "Babylon" which was portrayed in such gigantic proportions in John's Revelation and of which Peter wrote in his first letter: "She who is at Babylon, who is likewise chosen, sends you greetings; and so does my son Mark" (1 Pet 5:13). This is the more remarkable as neither Jesus nor his disciples were inimical to the state; rather, they advised obedience to the government and prayer for it. The general criticism of Rome was directed against her inordinate desire for power and possessions.[52] Augustine repeated these reproaches

[50] Hugo Rahner, "Vom ersten zum dritten Rom", inaugural address as Rector of the University of Innsbruck (1949), in *Abendland, Reden und Aufsätze* (Freiburg im Breisgau: Herder, 1966), 253–69.

[51] Harald Fuchs, *Der geistige Widerstand gegen Rom in der antiken Welt* (Berlin: Walter de Gruyter, 1938).

[52] From among the many examples given by Fuchs, see first of all the two lectures of Carneades in Rome (2–4), the story of Antisthenes (5f.) and the Book of Daniel and the Sybilline books (7f.). The new discoveries of Qumran, of which Fuchs was unaware, could have made an important contribution (cf. the edition of the texts by Johannes Maier, vol. 2, 1960, under the entry "Romans"), as well as the bitter pages of Sallust that were the model and source of Augustine's criticism of Rome. See also the first epodes of Horace, which recommend emigration from Rome (9f.); the plans of Caesar and of Antonius to move the capital elsewhere, which Constantine eventually accomplished (12f.); see also the attacks of Dionysius of Halicarnassus and other Greeks, who were "striving outright for the kingdom of

against the pagans in his *Civitas Dei,* but not without making careful distinctions. Christians did not give the state an unconditional Yes— just as Jesus could not condone the politicized Jewish theocracy, they cannot accept the sacralized divine Roman Empire— but neither did they give a total No. It is significant that Hippolytus comments in *Rome* on the Book of Daniel, interpreting the "fourth beast" as the Romans.[53] Tertullian strongly opposed the falsehood of making a priest of the emperor, and even more strongly his "divinization". Justin applied to the emperor the Lord's words: "Render to Caesar. . . . " Origen undertakes the difficult task of explaining that even the perse-cuting state's power has been granted by God and is good, and only its misuse is evil.[54] He sees the laws of the state as natural law, presupposed by divine law. Beginning with Clement of Rome, all Christians pray for the state. Some (like Aristides of Athens and Justin) are convinced that God preserves the world and the state because of these prayers. Others (Origen, the *Letter to Diognetus*)[55] see Christians as the salt of the

---

the East" and forcefully exposed "to what critical degree bitterness spread in the cultured world because of the unspiritual and devastating role of Roman despotism" (15). The reproaches of foreigners against Rome in Pompeius Trogus' *World History* also mentioned greed and bloodthirst; Tacitus' *Agricola* (17) speaks of "Thieving world conquerors whose urge for destruction, finding no more land, searches the depths of the ocean, greedy where the enemy is rich, for the sake of glory when he is poor. . . . Robbing, murdering, stealing, is falsely called by them 'dominion'; and when they have produced a wasteland, they call it 'peace' " (17). Lucian's compari-son between Athens and Rome is unfavorable to the latter (18); the Romans of Silver Age latinity—from Lucan and Seneca to Tacitus—are altogether critical of the actual regime (Ivánka, *Rhomäerreich,* 16ff.). So were the Christians also, though Fuchs gives a somewhat distorted image of them (particularly of Augustine, 23).

[53] Hippolytus, *Commentarium in Daniel,* in *Griechisch-Christliche Schriftsteller,* ed. G. Nathanael Bonwetsch, vol. 1, 1 (Berlin: Akademie-Verlag, 1897): 206–8; see also 162–69.

[54] Origen, *Commentarium in Romanos,* 9, 26–30.

[55] Origen, *Against Celsus,* 8, 74, in *The Ante-Nicene Fathers,* vol. 4 (New York: Charles Scribner's Sons, 1913): 668.

state, the soul of the world. On the whole this shows—in the midst of the period of persecution—an astonishingly nonfanatical sense of superiority.

2. The second fact is important for the connection between the papacy and Rome. The "Donation of Constantine", a fake fabricated in the ninth century (and not in Rome), was used by the Church for the first time as a political argument in the eleventh century. The Roman community never justified its precedence in terms of Rome being the capital city of the Empire but in terms of her being the seat of Peter's successor and possessing the graves of the two chief apostles. Of course, the latter by itself does not give a juridical entitlement but merely supports the former. In his decisive claim to succession, Pope Leo I (following the thought of Augustine) interpreted Peter's faith in a highly spiritual manner: it is not the man but his faith that has the durability of the rock,[56] "and as what Peter believed of Christ abides, what Christ has instituted in the person of Peter also abides."[57] And if a successor has to exercise his authority "more extensively and more powerfully" (*plenius et potentius*) than Peter did, it is because more duties burden him; this increase is not by investiture from, or in competition with, the imperial power but follows solely from the apostolic mission itself.[58] Leo attributed all the authority he possessed to Peter: "Let us rejoice in our leader and give thanks to Christ for giving him such great authority and making him 'first' in the whole Church."[59] By understanding Peter and his manner of using authority as the concrete, *real-symbolic* model of all episcopal office, Leo, already in the direction of Vatican I, surpassed Cyprian's idea that Peter's precedence was temporary: "To all shepherds in the Church, Peter is presented as the model. Thus, his particular authority is ever present;

[56] Leo I, *Sermo* 4, 3; 51, 1; 62, 2; 83, 3.
[57] *Sermo* 3, 2.
[58] *Sermo* 3, 3.
[59] *Sermo* 4, 4.

any judgment made has to conform to his equity (*aequitas*): there is neither great severity nor excessive mildness. Nothing is bound or loosed except what the blessed Peter himself would have bound or loosed."[60] And the Pope rejoices that his task is "not so much to preside from his see as to serve it".[61]

We have already shown how Pope Leo thanked Providence for having "hidden" the Christian faith in the "fortress of the Roman Empire". Yet in reality this protective fortress was not the Empire but the papacy, which is *ipsa apostolicae petrae arx*.[62] Rather, Rome was "more firmly founded" by the two most prominent apostles, her true fathers ··' shepherds, "than by those who erected your walls and by the one .io gave you his name but defiled you by fratricide."[63] And precisely because ancient Rome was so securely held in demonic chains, it was the prince of the apostles who "had to be destined for the citadel of the Roman Empire"; it is from the center of all errors that the truth of Christ should shine forth.[64] Leo praised the emperors of his time and was grateful for t · assistance, "but Rome is no longer indebted to them for her fa In Leo's view, henceforth Rome's prestige is purely Christian."[65] ie might speak of continuity, but only in that Rome's first founding was replaced by a second founding. This is far removed from Eusebius' synthesis. Once the Christian edifice stands, the framework can be removed, even though later, after the fall of the Empire, when necessity forced the popes to take over secular ·ninistration, certain elements of this framework proved to be se.

᠊. But the real crisis of ancient R o. .e, her final demythologization

[60] *Sermo* 4, 8; cf. the unity of collegiality and primacy in *Sermo* 5, 2.

[61] *Sermo* 5, 5.

[62] *Sermo* 3, 4.

[63] *Sermo* 82, 1. The motif recurs frequently.

[64] *Sermo* 82, 3.

[65] Pierre Batiffol, *Le Siège apostolique* (Paris: V. Lecoffre, 1924), 359–451, 432.

and secularization, was brought about by Augustine's *City of God*[66] some twenty or thirty years before Leo took office. This felled a mightier "oak of Odin" than that which Boniface tackled. Here the myth of Rome was destroyed to its roots in all its phases: her founding (through fratricide),[67] her ascendance (through insatiable greed for power and fame),[68] her peace, *pax Romana* (paid for by inhuman wars[69] for which Augustine does not seem to have any theological justifi-

[66] The most balanced interpretation regarding the question that concerns us is by Georg Maier, "Augustin und das antike Rom", in *Tübinger Beiträge zur Altertumswissenchaft* 39 (Stuttgart: Kohlhammer, 1955). This also includes earlier literary references. The final judgement, after all the detailed individual opinions, is too crude if it is applied to the entire phenomenon of Augustine, though it might apply to the "later" Augustine (212). It is fully justifiable to reject the attempt by fascism to "Romanize" Augustine (cf. the references in footnote 10, p. 14). The final judgment is: "*Romanitas* appears to be the most important historical form of political religiosity, as the complete apostasy from God", and therefore "he [Augustine] refuses all conciliatory views of history that attempt to unite *Romanitas* and Christianity" (208). "*The City of God* is an answer to the pagan philosophers' faith in Rome as well as to that of Christians. The one who believes in Rome and identifies its fall with the end of the world takes a stand against God" (78).

[67] The city's foundation on fratricide was seen already by Horace as foreboding (Epode 7, 17ff.). This motive is taken up by Tertullian, Cyprian, Minucius Felix and Lactantius (see Maier, 103, 172). But it reaches the full power of its symbolism first in Augustine, because he elevates it explicitly as "primum exemplum et ut Graeci appellant, archetypos" (*City of God*, 15, 5) of "the way in which the city of man is divided against itself" (ibid.). Subsequently, Augustine brutally demythologizes the whole of heroic antiquity.

[68] On the relationship of *libido dominandi* and *cupido gloriae,* see Maier, 107–8, 126.

[69] The fact of the Augustan peace is not denied: "verum est. Sed hoc quam multis et quam grandibus bellis, quanta strage hominum, quanta effusione sanguinis comparatum est!" (*City of God,* 19, 7).

cation).[70] This "hewing down" to the roots, about which Raffalt complains, is not something happening today: it was the work of the Bishop of Hippo. Augustine could make use of all the admonitory self-criticism by Rome's most able writers (first of all, Sallust);[71] but his most decisive stroke against the political superpower—a power conglomerate with purely materialistic motives, which seemed to him much like an organized band of robbers[72]—is a deep theological antithesis, contrasting two extremes: selfless love (*caritas*) and self-seeking greed (*cupiditas*). These define the two *civitates:* the *Civitas Dei,* on pilgrimage through world history though having its home in heaven, and the *Civitas terrena,* alienated from God by worldly self-sufficiency. Augustine accepts with equanimity the destruction of *Roma aeterna* by Alaric in 410: why should what is perishable and sinful from her very origin not pass away?[73]

One cannot find a positive theology of Rome in Augustine, and

[70] "This simple passing over of the famous synchronism" between the Augustan peace and the birth of Christ is itself full of meaning" (Maier, 181). It declares the "fundamental profaneness" of Rome, by which Augustine frees Christianity from political ties to a disintegrating world. He does something similar to Jeremiah, who destroyed the Jews' superstitious faith in the Temple: the Christians clung to the apostles' graves in Rome, which "nevertheless was set on fire" (*Sermo* 296, 6).

[71] Besides Sallust, whose dark descriptions are made even darker, Livy, Cicero, Varro and occasionally Virgil are also referred to.

[72] Augustine, *City of God,* 4, 5. The statement is made about Assyria but is obviously applied to Rome.

[73] Augustine gave four sermons in the year 410/411 about the Fall of Rome, in which he calmed the feelings of his audiences; *De Urbis excidio* (Migne, PL 40:714–24), and *Sermones* 81, 105, 296. In these he takes a stand against the alleged "eternity" of Rome's status. Since man is created perishable, so are his works. "And if the state does not fall now, it too will have its ending" (*Sermo* 81, 9). Augustine speaks of transitoriness but does not announce an imminent end of the world. The claim of Rome to eternity is a blasphemy; it claims not to be subject to being a creature. Already earlier apologists took a stand against this, cf. Martin Dibelius, "Rom und die Christen im ersten Jahrhundert", *Sitzungsberichte Heidelberg* (1941–1942), 2.

therefore there is no connection between his speculation about the relationship of the papacy, to which he is loyally devoted, and the Roman Empire.[74] His only concern is to uproot Rome's human self-glorification, until the honor (*gloria*) is returned to God to whom it rightly belongs.[75] At the same time he recognizes, within limits, some positive values in pagan Rome. It is not true that he sees the pagan virtues, as such, merely as splendid vices; they are insufficient only because they remain below the level of *caritas*. On their own level, they can be a challenge and a model for Christians.[76] But in the Christian sense only what bears the sign of love, Christian love, is positive, and this could be—as Augustine's "mirror for princes"[77] points out—a ruler who serves the Christian *Civitas Dei,* such as Theodosius (5:26). But Christianity, being all-encompassing, has sufficient resources

[74] Concerning Augustine's attitude toward the papacy, cf. Pierre Batiffol, *Le Catholicisme de saint Augustin,* 2 vols., 2d ed. (Paris: J. Gabalda, 1920). Although Augustine does not deal with the papacy in *The City of God,* it is obvious that for him the segment of God's kingdom on earthly pilgrimage is the Catholic Church, a paradoxical *civitas permixta* (of good and evil, true and nominal Christians), with a visible and sacramental structure. On the pope: letter 43, 7 in *The Fathers of the Church,* vol. 12 (Washington, D.C.: Catholic University of America Press, 1951): 182; letter 176, ibid., vol. 30 (1955): 91–94.

[75] Augustine, *City of God,* 5, 14, with reference to Jn 5:44.

[76] Some ancient Romans are praised for their virtues, for example, Regulus or Scipio Nasica. They are "nobilissima exempla", but they remain within the bracket that bears the negative sign of seeking fame or power; they are "non quidem jam sancti, sed minus turpes" (ibid., 5, 13). Their goodness is rewarded by God in earthly time and serves as an example also for Christians (ibid., 5, 13–50). Cf. the letter (138) to Marcellinus, in which the imperium as a whole is given as an illustration to Christians to make them recognize that purely immanent goals cannot satisfy man.

[77] In the letter to Macedonius the ideal picture of a Christian civil servant is outlined (Letter 155, 7–9). The mirror of princes (*City of God,* 5, 24), with its "cataloging of the virtues of Christian princes", remains conventional and pale in comparison, for example, with the "compact realism" of Eusebius (Maier, "Augustin und das antike Rom", 137).

to originate its own humanism.[78] "The persecution period's apocalyptic enmity toward Rome, which ceaselessly contrasts the great harlot Babylon with the city of the saints, manifests itself for the last time with Augustine."[79] He contrasts the peace of Augustus with a completely different peace, the heavenly peace of heart given by Christ (book 19). Nor should it be forgotten that Augustine's thinking was Platonic, which always sees two things together: the earthly is merely a shadow or resemblance [*Schein*] of the unearthly ideal, but at the same time it is also a real, perhaps necessary manifestation [*Er-Scheinung*] leading gradually, by the ladder of appearances [*Erscheinungen*] to truth and justice. The crude dualism can always be moderated by a monism in which—even for the Platonic Christian—nature and supernature are not distinctly separated.[80] Certainly, monism dominates the theology of the Eastern Empire (with the Christian emperor as a manifestation of God at the head of the world), while the theology of the *Civitas Dei* contains a dualism that will have an ongoing effect throughout all the "platonizing monisms" of the Roman-Germanic Middle Ages. At the birth of the "Holy Roman Empire of the German Nation" stands the *radical "anti-Roman attitude" of Augustine.*

We have placed this discussion under the main heading of "The Crucial Test" because it leads us for the last time directly to a tragic,

[78] Thus even in early outlines of Christian formation (*De Doctrina Christiana*), Augustine's cool distancing from the (primarily rhetorical) education of the ancient world contrasts with the vacillations of Jerome between yielding to its charms and opting for asceticism.

[79] Augustine does not believe in the possibility of changing men—except through the life of faith—nor, consequently, in historical progress in a secular sense; the principles that shape history, the two *civitates,* stand permanently opposed. "Nos sumus tempora; quales sumus, talia sunt tempora" (*Sermo* 80, 8).

[80] See particularly Étienne Gilson, *Introduction à l'étude de s. Augustin* [Introduction to the study of Saint Augustine] (Paris: Librairie Philosophique, J. Vrin, 1929), 299ff.

345

seemingly insoluble situation of the papacy, inherent from its origin in antiquity to the onset of modern times, and throws a harsh light on this period in connection with what has been said about the eccentric nature of the papal office. Considering the very practical consequences that Gregory VII and all his successors up to Boniface VIII have drawn concerning state power, one can rightly speak of "political Augustinianism".[81] When the representative of the *Civitas terrena* is a Christian (like Theodosius, or later, Charlemagne, the Ottonians and the Hohenstaufens), he can be invested with this sacred duty only by the one to whom Christ entrusted responsibility for the *Civitas Dei* during its earthly pilgrimage. Gregory VII, who not only placed the rebellious Emperor Henry IV under interdict but deposed him (after Henry attempted to depose *him* in 1076),[82] saw in this final, long-postponed means of freeing the Church from the grip of the state as well as from the evils that grew out of this, simony and licentiousness. He was aware that, according to Augustine, he should seek only the glory of God, but it was equally important that he should remain faithful to the tradition of the papacy.[83] Did not Gelasius, when he distinguished between the two highest powers governing the world, "the holy authority of the popes and the imperial authority", immediately add: "Of these two, the burden of the popes is heavier, because they have to give an account even for the kings of men before the divine court of justice" (DS 347). Gregory the Great felt this kind of responsibility toward the Merovingian rulers, whom he bid "to let all our instructions be carried out for God's and St. Peter's sake".[84] For Isidore of Seville, the prince becomes the worldly arm of the Church,

[81] Henri-Xavier Arquillière, *L'Augustinisme politique. Essai sur la formation des théories politiques au moyen-âge,* 2d ed. (Paris: Vrin, 1955).

[82] In Worms he had twenty-four bishops sign a decree of deposition of "the false monk, Hildebrand".

[83] "Nil novi facientes, nil adinventione nostra statuentes", Gregory VII, *Registrum* 4, 22 (Migne, PL 148:283–645).

[84] *Registrum* 6, 5.

346

who "through the threat of discipline achieves what the priests cannot accomplish by preaching. . . . The princes of the world should know that God will hold them accountable for the Church, whose defense he has entrusted to them."[85] The emperor's coronation signifies the consecration of worldly power for the service of the kingdom of God made manifest in the Church. Gregory VII, in his letter to Hermann of Metz, clearly lays down that the highest duty of the king is a spiritual one, "and if it is no small effort for the ordinary Christian to save one soul, his own, how great a burden is placed on the prince by his responsibility for thousands of souls!"[86] Kings consecrated by the Church should therefore take on the office, "not for the sake of fleeting glory, but for the good of the souls of many. . . . They should always place the honor of God before their own."[87] From such a point of view—held by Augustine as well as by papal tradition—there was no longer a need for the "Donation of Constantine". Innocent IV referred merely to the "two swords" given by Jesus Christ (the Priest-King according to the order of Melchizedek) to Peter, who lends the secular sword to the prince.[88]

It was inevitable that Roman law—preserved by Eastern Rome and reshaped in a Christian fashion—should be utilized to support this claim based on Augustine's anti-Romanism; but because it was in reality Roman law, it could just as well be turned against this claim. Augustine's total secularization of old Rome led necessarily to a sacralization of secular law by the highest authorities of the visible *Civitas Dei.* Where this law became aware of its (Augustinian!) secularity, it developed into an anti-Roman protest that was simply the echo of Augustine's protest, which was justifiable at his time and in his

[85] Isidore of Seville, *Sententiae* 3, 51.

[86] *Registrum* 8, 21.

[87] Ibid.

[88] Arquillière calls the papal bull *"Aeger cui levia"* of 1245 "the most absolute expression of pontifical theocracy in the Middle Ages", *L'Augustinisme politique,* 35, note.

circumstances. This was the "crucial test" of the Middle Ages; it is no longer ours. Peter was seen as the absolute focus of the world, through which, as through the narrow neck of an hourglass, the kingdom of God gradually becomes manifest in the nether sphere of the world; his "eccentric nature" was made absolute: the whole fullness of secular law was seen to proceed from Pauline "justification" and *"dikaiosuné"*, and the pope was held to be ultimately responsible for its implementation.

The disintegration of the Holy Roman Empire into secular nations, and consequently the disintegration of sacred law into particular national laws—as well as, beginning with Thomas Aquinas, the growing differentation (but not separation) of nature and grace—have gradually transformed all the papacy's direct claims to the realm of the state into indirect claims (above all in the ecclesiology of St. Robert Bellarmine). As a result, Peter's successor was once more situated in that "foursome" where, without forfeiting anything of his mission, he could adopt more Christian forms of responsibility and, consequently, more christianly motivated forms of humiliation than in the unprecedented "extrapolation" of his office in the post-Augustinian era. "Every society, every culture has only a limited number of ideas at its disposal for understanding and dealing with current events. One cannot demand that the popes, who are supposed to be the guardians of the pledge of eternity, should be several centuries ahead of their time in matters of human culture."[89]

Augustine's struggle with Rome has established one thing for good: the awareness that Christian Rome is not bound by internal necessity to Imperial Rome. As Petrarch said at the time of the pope's captivity in Avignon: "The pope may be in any place; where he is, is Rome."

From then on one cannot speak of theocracy in the "First Rome" in

[89] Ibid., 48.

the sense in which the "Second Rome" understood this term, or as this understanding has become secularized in the transition to the "Third Rome". What was "sacred law" in the Second Rome, has become, in the Third, "sacred", i.e., world-transforming economics. Second Rome foundered as a world power, but new crucial tests face us: the choice is between a papacy in the Church that understands the nature and limits of the *Civitas terrena* and a new, secular infallibility that claims to transform the miraculous grace of the *Civitas Dei* into manipulative economic miracles which will change human beings and the world. Moreover, it is passé and pointless for Christians to attempt to weaken First Rome by shooting at her over their shoulders; such sniping always misses its mark, even when it is aimed at a real but long past form of the papacy.

3. "Where You Do Not Wish to Go"

When he was installed in office by the risen Lord, Peter received no other promise than his death on a cross: "When you were young, you girded yourself and walked where you would; but when you are old, you will stretch out your hands, and another will gird you and carry you where you do not wish to go" (Jn 21:18). Peter may not have understood this to mean his crucifixion; rather, he may have thought it referred to the conduct of his office and its implications, which assumed an ever-increasing predominance over his private life and spontaneous decisions, making him the "prisoner of the Vatican" and placing on him a superhuman burden: *sollicitudo omnium ecclesiarum* (2 Cor 11:28). He might have accepted this office, giving a Yes merely to the fate to be expected of any man burdened with public duties, had there not been a mysterious something "more", as the Evangelist (in retrospect) expressly mentions: "This he said to show by what death he was to glorify God. And after this he said to him, 'Follow me!'" (Jn 21:19). The command to follow evidently refers to both things:

349

the following of Christ in the office of the Good Shepherd, and its consequences, namely, giving his life for his sheep (Jn 10:15). The latter, if it is a true following and bears Christ's imprint, is not an accidental grace appended to the former; rather it is deeply inherent in the nature of discipleship, whether or not a pope actually dies on a cross. If the exercise of the office is characterized as "functional", then death on a cross—in whatever apparent form—is an essential part of this function. It is not an additional private work of supererogation that may be either rendered or omitted.

Here too, as so often, the apostle Paul's self-analysis provides the best illustration. Just as Simon, without having been asked or consulted, was bowled over by being given the title "Peter", "Rock" (Jn 1:42), and then had gradually to learn how to be of service in this office; so also Saul, in Damascus, was overpowered and propelled into his ministry. Before he saw or understood anything, he was blinded by the sovereignty of the Lord and, though blind, was commanded: "Rise and enter the city, and you will be told what you are to do." And Ananias, who "happened" to be the one to meet Saul, was told: "I will show him how much he must suffer for the sake of my name" (Acts 9:6, 16). Thus from the outset they are summoned for service and for the suffering that this entails. We do not have to present Paul's whole theology of the "suffering Christ".[90] It is sufficient to state that it is the apostles who, in view of their office and calling, are consigned to be "last of all, like men sentenced to death; because we have become a spectacle to the world, to angels and to men" (1 Cor 4:9). Paul here repeats Jesus' words about the "last place" that a person should take voluntarily, particularly if he is prominent in the Church, having been called to any office (Lk 14:10; 22:26; 9:46–48). But in Paul

[90] Bibliography in E. Güttgemans, *Der leidende Apostel und sein Herr. Studien zur paulinischen Christologie* (Göttingen: n.p., 1966). This is also an objective description of recent discussions, which are noteworthy even if one cannot always agree with the author's point of view.

350

the words are sharpened by the bitter experience that it was the community's fear of the cross and obliviousness of grace that compelled the apostle to take this "last" place. They felt already "satisfied", already "rich", without having "received"; they assumed that they possessed what they should have sought to obtain, not just once but persistently, from the office which was there to serve them. Thus they rendered it superfluous. "We are fools for Christ's sake, but you are wise in Christ. We are weak, but you are strong. You are held in honor, but we in disrepute" (1 Cor 4:10). Jesus shed tears over his people and his city because they refused to accept his service (Lk 19:41), and he was nailed to the Cross (the place of his last, decisive service) by the Jerusalem who murders the prophets; likewise, Paul was pushed to one side by a "sated" community, being thrown into the gutter like a criminal: "We have become, and are now, as the refuse of the world, the offscouring of all things" (*peripsēma:* literally, the scum that forms when washing with soap). "I do not write this to make you ashamed but to admonish you as my beloved children. For though you have countless guides in Christ, you do not have many fathers. For I became your father in Christ Jesus through the gospel" (1 Cor 4:13-15). These are like two sides of the same thing: the ignominious "last place" to which the Church consigns the apostles and the latters' fatherhood to her. Obviously, the question arises whether this is right or normal. The answer is suggested by Paul's modulation of his tone (in 2 Corinthians, for example, Paul's tone expresses half of his theology!) from a bitter, deliberately provocative sarcasm—that is part of his *paraclēsis*—to a quiet but in no way resigned statement that *this is how it is:* in the saving plan of God, who delivered his Son on the Cross, this destiny is appropriate: "God has consigned us apostles to the last place. . . . " The apostle's office was given concrete form as a result of a shocking scandal. Paul, however, was not indignant on his own behalf—because he was treated like "filth"—but solely for the community that acted this way, because it obviously understood nothing at all. He would not have fulfilled his office had he not confronted the community with what they were doing. He would not have given right service had he practiced the personal virtue of silent acceptance, because his life was not his own: it was entirely devoted to service. The way he was treated was the way the office was treated; and the charismatic Corinthians had to be made aware of how they were treating the office established by Christ. They had, therefore, to receive sufficient proof that office and officeholder (no matter how much the latter annoyed them) simply could not be separated. They could not be allowed to feign respect for the office while they criticized the officeholder ("mild when present and only bold when he is absent", 2 Cor 10:11). Nowhere is the eccentric nature of the office described more clearly and in finer detail than in the last chapters of 2 Corinthians. Paul is provoked by the eccentric behavior of the community: "For I fear that perhaps *I* may come and find you *not* what I wish, and that *you* may find me *not* what you wish. . . . Examine yourselves to see whether you are holding to your faith. Test yourselves. Do you not realize that Jesus Christ is *in you?* — unless indeed you fail to meet the test!" Paul prays that this shall not happen: "But . . . not that *we* may appear to have met the test, but that *you* may do what is right, though we may have seemed to have failed" (2 Cor 12:20; 13:5, 7). In this instance the "eccentric nature" of the office—which is compelled to appear as pure law (wielding the "rod")—can be blamed on the immaturity of the community. But Paul goes a step further. He is willing to take the "eccentric" last place—of failure, of shame, of the cross—if by that means he can avert the failure of the community. These are the "birthpangs" he suffers for the community "until Christ be formed in you" (Gal 4:19).

This analysis of the apostolic office as a whole includes the special role of the Petrine office. The anti-Pauline attitude of the Corinthians, and certainly also of the Galatians (under Jerusalem influence), does not differ basically from the anti-Petrine attitude of any and all the communities under the jurisdiction of Peter and his successors (DS

3064). It has fundamentally the same theological locus, importance and character. And if an anti-Pauline and an anti-Johannine attitude (3 Jn 9) is displayed toward the office of the bishops and toward the priesthood loyal to them, and if the apostles must listen to "haughty words" from "grumblers" when the "scoffers" cause "divisions" in their dioceses because they are "devoid of the Spirit" (Jude 16–19), then all this grumbling and mocking will be poured in concentrated form on the successor of Peter. *Because Peter has an "impossible" task:* he has to embody, in the world and in continuity of form, something that, on the Cross, smashed all forms and entered into a superform that cannot be imitated. In the fragile earthen vessels of word and concept he is obligated to guard the authenticity of that tremendous content that transcends all thought and understanding. He is to bind and loose on earth—and hence establish a law that is intelligible and defensible on earth—things that, in heaven, are bound and loosed by a law known only to God. Surely it is obvious that he will err again and again at this intersection of time and eternity? Either he will betray the eternal for the sake of the temporal by trying to imprison it (putting eternal truth in "infallible statements"!), or he will betray the temporal by clinging to illusory formulas that seem to be eternal, thus missing the ongoing reality of his own time. People mock him; his mission should rather elicit laughter or weeping.

This means that *the structure of the office instituted by Christ in the Church is modeled, as such, on the Cross, independently of the officeholder.* In discipleship of Jesus it is unavoidable, particularly for sinners who take offense at him, to come into collision with the "Rock"; but since what they strike against is a living man, he feels the blow. He feels it, as it were, undefended, while those who "kick against the goad" also find it "hard" (as the Lord said to Paul: Acts 9:4; 22:7–8; 26:14–18), though initially they may think it amusing. The office of the shepherd proves to be essentially eccentric in that, while it is anchored in the center, it must incline toward the periphery for two reasons: because the sinners and the weak cannot be led to pasture without the shepherd's staff, and because an ordinary, fallible human, a sinner, holds the office that in its highest function must manifest itself as adequate (infallible). This is the structure as it was established, and it is futile to hope that by "changing the structure" the situation of the Church would be bettered. The pope can strive to discharge his office as humbly and as competently as possible—but Paul too was competent and yet had to take the "last" place. The dioceses and communities may take pains to prove worthy and not provoke the office to its "eccentric" limits, but there will always be something that needs straightening or putting right.

If in its eccentric nature the office has the shape of the Cross, then the officeholder's way of following Christ is also determined by the office itself. The irreversible duality between the office and the man who holds it, between the dignity of the office and the unworthiness of the officeholder ("Depart from me . . . ": "Henceforth you will be catching men"; Lk 5:8, 10) is bridged by the office itself. It has become evident that even long periods of poor administration could not reduce the Christian people's respect for the office; the period of conciliarism expressed a deep concern for the office, and the polemics against the way it was exercised rarely suggested abolishing the office but rather reforming it. However, there is a deeper meaning precisely in the personal attacks on the officeholder. Whether or not the attackers know or intend it, their action causes the Cross inherent in the office to become manifest: *fulget crucis mysterium.* Paul knew this well. Concentrated attacks on the office at present, rekindling the ancient anti-Roman sentiment, have succeeded in singling it out— primarily the Petrine office, and secondarily the episcopal and priestly offices—as "a spectacle" to attract all eyes, placing it, as it were, "in the pillory" (*theatron* in 1 Cor 4:9; *theatrizesthai* in Heb 10:33) where no one could miss it. This very intentional humiliation of the office, its defamation, and even the blanketing of it by complete silence, brings it into the limelight: not the officeholder but the office that he holds and that holds him: the humanly unbearable burden, the Cross. Being mocked for the unworthiness of its bearer, the office glorifies itself. Whether or not the humiliated office-bearer humbles himself before the world may play a role, though not an important one, even if he renounces the *sedia* and the *tiara* and other such external accessories, which actually do not belong to him, but solely to the office that he personifies.[91]

Raffalt is right to distinguish the personal humility of the pope from the humiliations consequent on his office. To accept these wholeheartedly is not the same as having an inclination toward making personal acts of humility. Paul did not need to make such acts: he was completely one with the office which was humiliated in him.

Undoubtedly the ever-renewed humiliation of the office also contributes to its purification and clarification. But we repeat: it is *God* who puts the officeholders in the "last" place; it is not they themselves who voluntarily take it, nor does the community have any mandate to put them there. The fact that there is an office in the community is certainly a cross for the community too: an authority that is more than human, indeed even supernatural and therefore claiming to

---

[91] "An important controversial question is whether badges of honor, titles, and bishops' palaces were superfluous or harmful signs of wealth. . . . This wealth does not belong to any individual and cannot be disposed of by him as he pleases. Neither can the wealth of the Church, such as sacred music and the feasts of saints, be disposed of arbitrarily. The elimination of all this wealth would not lead the Church to evangelical poverty, as proven by the iconoclasm of past centuries, but to a decline of reverence and devotion." Siebel (*Freiheit und Herrschaftsstruktur*, 70) responds to the present trends without insisting that "in all circumstances" the "insignia of dominion must be retained"; rather, any change should be made only "to strengthen the dimension of representation". Palaces may be relinquished if "under the given circumstances and times they are merely seen as expressions of wealth . . . representing a particular economic class." But giving up such distinctions purely as an act of renunciation would be a sign that the person in leadership "has ceased to be convinced of his mandate to govern (and of the greatness of his calling). By doing so he permits himself to be used as an agent of a new iconoclasm" (ibid., 71–72).

speak for God, constantly reminding men with their thirst for autonomy that they also have to be crucified to the world (Gal 6:14). Moreover, the office urges the whole community to go outside the holy city to the place of ignominy, where Jesus suffered, where the *offal* of the sacrificed animals was burned (Heb 13:11–13). All Christendom is the "offscourings". Hence the drive, in turn, to crucify the one who disturbs the peace: this reciprocal action and reaction will go on as long as the world exists. It will continue to rein the Church in when she blindly tries to flee from the Cross into activism, world-transformation or anything else—fortunately for her, otherwise she would get lost in all kinds of alibis and abstractions. How could the Eucharist be celebrated in the Church as a *memoriale passionis Domini* without the office, which makes the Cross present in a visible and tangible manner? It would remain merely a sentimental calling-to-mind.

*

The figure of Peter is an impossibility, made possible only by the will of the One who created him. A fisherman from Galilee is planted at the center of the Empire, inherits it by being killed by it—but he is not killed as his Lord was, whom he betrayed. He is crucified upside down, with his feet uppermost, to make amends for his betrayal. It is too sublime: it is positively grotesque.

> Like Sancho Panza and Don Quixote, Simon Peter and Christ form a constellation. Simon Peter stood by the Lord without any psychological complications. Anyone who has observed a good sheep dog at work with the shepherd will have noticed how the dog eagerly waits for a sign from the shepherd and is positively distressed until it gets the command. Peter was like that: without the Lord, he immediately became unsure, indecisive, blundering. There is the closeness of the one who—as it is written—rested on the Lord's breast. Then there is the closeness of the intellectual that also implies a certain

356

distance. Peter's closeness to the Lord differs from that of John or Paul. It is the closeness of someone who is most exposed to violent shocks, the closeness of the believer who nevertheless, deep down at the core, retains a peace, the peace of a child. Actually Simon Peter could be called a child in a deeper sense than John: he remained a child throughout his life, until his death. Hence his rashness. Peter was rash, too rash, like boys are, rash even in the presence of the eternal dimension, in the presence of the peace of those who are clothed with eternity. Peter resembles a schoolboy who cannot wait for his teacher to ask him a question. Yet he is not what his classmates would call "pushy". It is simply that everything in him is bubbling over. It is always the individual, as such, who is a slave of sin. Peter is not an individual; he is the people, the heart of the people, a legend that towers to the heavens and makes him Number One there — or at least the first person to be encountered in heaven, the keeper of the gate. Down here, however, he was as insecure as a child learning to walk. Is he not like such a child as he walks toward the Lord on the surface of the sea? And in the same way he does not want the Lord to wash his feet: "No, no! Who am I that this should be done to me?!" But then he wants the Lord to wash him all over, his whole body. When the Lord is taken prisoner, the disciples stay behind . . . , but Peter follows at a distance. He manages to get as far as the courtyard. And there it happens. How wonderful, how full of innocence is this world where the Number One proves to be over-hasty! In antiquity, man had no idea of how deeply an individual could be torn open by God. He could not conceive of such an intervention by the One God but rather saw man and God bound together by fate. From this followed a lofty tone in the relationship between the human and the Divine (that excluded all possibility of a divine incarnation), a high ethical level, heroism, fame, and so forth.

Not so the men of the Bible, because the living God bursts in on them — he who "both raises up kings and brings them down — so that, like sacrificial animals, they are profoundly torn open by God, and at the same time this wound is their sin, the sin of the believer. There is only this one sin, *the* sin of the believer, just as there is only one

357

sonship, the sonship of the believer. There is no other greatness on earth and in heaven."[92]

[92] Rudolf Kassner, "Simon Petrus", in *Neue Schweizer Rundschau*, new series 15 (1947-1948): 717-27. The article was omitted from the Kassner bibliography, *Gedenkbuch zum 80. Geburtstag* (Zurich: Rentsch, n.d.). We have not indicated the omissions from the text. We could have ended with a passage by Reinhold Schneider, who understood, perhaps even more profoundly than Kassner, the "impossible possibility" of the Petrine office: his Innocent III has a much harder time than Francis, his Celestine V deserts into holiness and thus leaves his place to the "monster"—as Schneider depicts him—Boniface VIII. Only his sketch of Gregory is peaceful, even though it was Gregory who embodied the grief, in the face of the ruins of Rome, of the man who finds action lacking in vision and vision lacking in action. Reinhold Schneider's thought is profound, but at the decisive point he confuses tragedy with the Cross. The concept of the "child" is missing; it is this that Kassner, a born Catholic (who later became a "gnostic"), perceived intuitively. As far as Peter is a "child" in the midst of the "impossibility" of his assignment, being torn apart by "having to be form" where no form is possible, he becomes the mirror image of the eternal Child of the Father.